ZEN ASE

# Plenty of Guppies

*and Other Dating Misadventures*

*Lust, Loss, and Lessons of Love*

*—— From 101 Dates ——*

*A Memoir told in Poetry and Prose*

*Plenty of Guppies*



ISBN: 979-8-9853597-4-9

Icon illustrations:

Icon by Fasil on freeicons.io: Fish icon

Icon by icon king1 on freeicons.io: Pen icon

Icon by shivani on freeicons.io: light bulb icon

Editor: Million Dollar Pen, Ink.

Cover designer: GetCovers

Interior Designer: abdul_moeez(fiverr)

Printed in the United States of America

Published by Million Dollar Pen, Ink.

Email: *editor@mdpink.com*

Follow Author Zen Ase on social media:

*https://www.facebook.com/authorzenase*

I believe that no experience is a waste. Mine either taught me what I desire or what I should deny my time and energy. Life is a school that gives us the test and, ultimately, the lesson. Here are the lessons I learned on my seven-year journey. Hopefully, these experiences will enrich your life. They certainly enhanced mine.

Each lesson is fully described at the end of every chapter. I previewed the list here for curious readers or those who want to reference it later.

Happy reading.

# Contents

The scenarios in this book reflect the author's recollection of events. Most names (and a few identifying characteristics) have been changed to protect the privacy of those depicted. Dialogue has been re-created from memory and journals.

# Plenty of Guppies Timeline

Lessons 1-5

Lessons 6-26

Marriage 1<br>1994-10/2000

Marriage 2<br>8/2003<br>7/16/2014

JJ<br>8/2/2014<br>-2/2015

Gatzby<br>3/2015-<br>7/2015<br>7/16/2016<br>-12/2016

The Muse<br>8/2015-<br>7/14/<br>2016

Harlee<br>1-2017<br>-7/26<br>/2017

Gatzby<br>8/28-<br>12/16/2017<br>1/1/2019-<br>6/2019<br>2020/2021<br>on & off

Ace<br>12/2/<br>2017-<br>3/2018

The Young Lion<br>7/2018-<br>11/2018

Des<br>9/2019-<br>10/2019

The Poet<br>1/2020-<br>4/2020

RJ<br>7/2020<br>- now

DATES 1-34

Dates 35-70

Dates 71- 101

# CHAPTER 1

# Attitude

I belong to a classification of women some men don't believe exists: single by choice and content.

Many men fancy themselves as fairy godfathers sent to warn women to wed, settle (down), and commit before the clock strikes old age, and we're left in the cinders with only birds and cats as company.

Once upon a time, their warnings might have stuck, but that was years ago, before my odyssey.

I started out like most young women; a virgin saving myself and fearful of sex. It was like seeing a roller coaster I'd always wanted to ride, but I couldn't honestly picture myself mounting. Pregnancy and STDs posed enough of a threat to keep me on the kiddie rides, safe, secure, and thrill-less.

Marriage came and went. It was a long haul. Start 8/13/03. End 7/16/14. Save for my children, unfulfilling. It was not at all like people said it would be. Divorce, for me, signaled a new beginning.

Enter the first online profile.

I posted a picture wondering if any man would even notice me and got 100 inboxes in three days. The ugly duckling was a swan, it seemed. And I was ready. After being attention and sex-starved for years, this was a chance to see how the so-called "single and ready to mingle" half lived.

I lined up 16 meet and greets in as many days and in waltzed JJ.

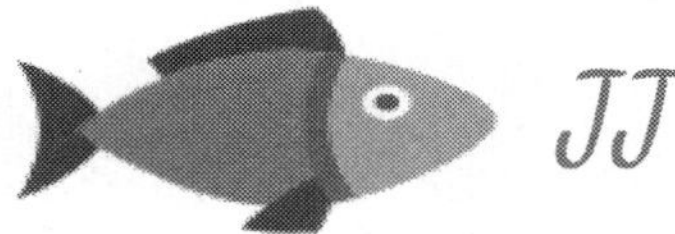

## JJ

Dad bod, but with the smooth, practiced air of a man who knew how to mac. He was just what I wanted, needed, craved; a good listener, patient, and willing to give me as much sex as I could handle. And after nine years of dealing with someone with impotence, I could handle A LOT. He was wine and flowers and soft jazz romantic. Taught me I was multi-orgasmic- something I didn't know- even though I had been married twice and was 43 years old. He was FUN, carefree, and asked for nothing. I was spoiled.

I didn't have to cook, clean, wash, put up with BS. I didn't get grilled, ignored, neglected, or have to beg for attention. He was perfect except for one thing, he didn't want to commit. He was burned, wary, and happy being a bachelor- for life.

I'd never met a man like this. I'd never been a woman like this. I loved both.

We had a fabulous six months and two weekends. No regrets. My favorite Gemini ever.

I have to admit, I'm eager, my story wriggling like a puppy in a dog shelter, ready to jump into your lap. Nothing is that simple. So I should go back a little.

## Pre-date Prep:

The online profile had been my divorce gift to myself. The first, no the second thing, I did after walking toward the bright lights of downtown outside the Houston courthouse.

The first was the purchase of a smartphone I couldn't work; my first foray away from the flip phone I'd had for years. The constant Blackberry updates drove me mad, but it was a step forward, a necessity for step two, the online profile.

A few months earlier, I'd lunched with a colleague, hoisted myself into a massive monster of a truck, and sat back for a quick ride across the freeway to Subway. On the way, he'd shifted gears, unexpectedly brushing my thigh. I flinched. He apologized, startled by my reaction, and frowned harshly as if to say, did she think I was hitting on her? Then I saw his expression change as it slowly dawned on both of us.

I'd reacted that severely because I hadn't been touched by a man in so long that it startled me.

My face reddened as the Prince lyric,<br>
"Darling, I know it's been a long time<br>
Since you've been satisfied",<br>
playing on the radio,echoed in my mind:<br>
I can tell by the look in your eyes<br>
You need it real bad (real bad)<br>
You need it so bad, so bad," it continued.<br>
The universe had jokes, jokes at my expense.

My coworker cautioned softly, “Don’t let any other man see you react like that. They might take advantage.”

We never spoke of it again and moved the conversation along. I was married. Husband in my home, in my bed, yet had not been touched in eight months.

That was the day I called my lawyer to check on my divorce status and started researching dating sites.

By the end of that fateful day at Subway, I had my pictures ready to post, a profile ready to upload to the website. I was determined to never flinch from a casual brush against my knee again.

I’d filed in January and thought the divorce would be done by Spring Break. No such luck, but I posted my profile anyway. I began shedding my past by listing myself as separated and looking for casual dating. It took a few months to sort through the hundreds of messages that came in. I was looking for only four things- chemistry, intelligence, good communication, and someone separated or single. By June 14th, when I walked out a free woman, I’d narrowed the field to 16 men, repeatedly conversed with each, and arranged dates, one after the other.

(Yes, I was impatient. Horny. Lonely.)

Like dominoes, I was looking for all to topple but one, the man who would become my new boo.

I genuinely hoped I’d enjoy meeting and conversing with each and everyone, but I wanted one and only one to stand out.

And had I met Mr. Met My Four Standards on date one, I was perfectly willing to cancel the other fifteen dates. But somehow, even though I’d been out of the dating pool for almost 11 years, that seemed highly unlikely. Still, I don’t think you’ll believe the 15 dates I had. I’m going to describe them. Brace yourselves.

Sometimes I wonder if JJ was really that suave or just so "normal" compared to the funhouse freaks I encountered.

It started out so auspicious, the first three phone conversations decadent. Compliments thick and sweet, a caramel mocha of words topped with whipped cream, and a chocolate drizzle. After years in a silent house, perfunctory salutations, and family meetings that replaced small talk, the pet names, being noticed, and the active listening while mirroring what I said with understanding was a heady brew. Because of the thick sweet, and beguiling conversations, I was somewhat infatuated with the first three guys before I met any of them.

## Date One: Lance AKA Dough and Jowels

The first was Lance, who gifted me with a pic so tastefully erotic it inspired this poem.

### Lance

*He carries the perfect name, ready and waiting like a spear.*
*Chiseled like his namesake,*
*Strong of mind and sure*
*Manly and decisive*
*Precise and finely tuned*
*Crafted like gilt armor*

*Resisting him is doomed.*
*From bronzed arms to cut abs to places never seen,*
*From carved pecs to strapped shoulders*
*Nary a hair is seen, and even if the underbelly is downy reddish brown*
*The goddesses will squeal and swoon when Adonis drops his towel.*
*Seeing Lance arouses fire enough to build a thirst*
*And touching him must make the fires. . .*
*so much worse*
*Apollo will kick himself, and Hercules will scowl*
*'cause no one in Olympus's court looks so good in just a towel*
*Filled with swag and confidence, his demeanor should be*
*Quite a specimen of man, this Lance turned out to be*

We met at Papasitos on the patio. I walked up, sun in my eyes, and sat, eyes adjusting. The sun glared off his bald head. My eyes slid down his frame, recalling the picture, my poem. My creative juices flowed again. He earned the first nickname I ever gifted a date-Dough and Jowls. Wrinkled, oh so much sexier on film. I drank a glass of water and chatted for a few minutes, then I excused myself.

One down, 15 to go.

I know you have so many questions. How did I feel? I was catfished. Mind you, I didn't know the term catfish at the time, and it actually didn't occur to me until right now that I was bamboozled. At that moment, I was stupefied. A myriad of thoughts twinkled in my head. I'd always been told that white men liked thin women, and I stood there: plus size, busty, athletically built, Queen Latifahesque, not a dainty bone in sight. Yet, my inbox was filled with 70% white men. I was unprepared.

Then my mind flittered to arguments, pleading, even me crying which I almost never did. I'd asked my former husband, Drew, for two things nine years before: Take me out once a month and get checked by a doctor to find out what's causing the ED." He refused both for nine years, although I circled back to the questions like a metro bus on a route. Every few months, I'd ask again, hoping that he'd listen and see there was no reason for me to stay if there was no hope. I hoped our relationship, our connection, our vows, our family was more vital and important than his ego and his denial. They were not.

So I was actually surprised, stunned, a little angry even, that a stranger got dressed, drove, and sat waiting in the restaurant, ready to offer me anything on the menu for a moment of my time. I blinked several times, taking in this newness. I was not invisible. A man, not the one I'd expected or wrote the poem to, but a living, breathing, flesh and blood testosterone pumping man was smiling at me, flirting with me, asking me questions. I wanted to dissect him under a microscope. What made him different than the cold fish who could walk into our house and head to our bedroom without a word?

I followed the conversation in a daze, every now and then responding to questions about my divorce; "my husband," the "ex" still somewhere, intangible, not practiced on my lips.

Lance was sympathetic, had a similar story. He was the first I had told, feeling embarrassed, that I was a reject who couldn't make my husband- the man who had sworn to always love, honor, and protect me- desire me. Confidence non-existent. I was shook by his protestations that I was "gorgeous," "sexy," "very desirable."

Cognitive dissonance was fully in place. If all that was true, why was I divorced… twice?

It's crazy when you get exactly what you want, but not from the person you wanted it from. You just stare at it, turning the jewel over and over in your hand, unsure of how to wear it or even if it really belongs to you. Unworthiness, the parting gift of my husband, Self- doubt a close second, and Insecurity loomed third.

All three negative voices were talking so loudly I could barely hear Lance cutting each down. After all, he was a warrior, but I was still occupied territory, mentally and emotionally. He was unable to liberate me because, at the end of the day, there was nothing physically I found attractive about him.

## Day/ Date Two: Leatherhandz

He was a wordsmith who had my head swimming, imagination brimming. Visions of us making love filled my head before we met. It seemed inevitable, likely, and then the farthest thing from possible when I saw him, all arms and legs, gangly, like a grown man teenager who hadn't grown into his growth spurt.

He smiled at me broadly while I reciprocated shyly as I mentally promised myself to never spend months talking to someone before meeting him. For the second time, I adjusted my expectations down to basement level. He hugged me. We stood awkwardly in line at Starbucks, waiting to order, and he leaned over to whisper that he couldn't wait to hold me as he masturbated. At first, I was so distracted by the feeling of his leathery palm the words did not penetrate. Then I was confused. This was how he opened? This was his "ultimate orgasm"? I searched for a reply, came up empty, and just said, "This was a mistake," and walked out.

Two numbers purged from my phone; I tried to shake the melancholy. How could I feel dirty after a five-minute interaction? I flashed back to our conversations, confused. Leatherhandz seemed to understand me so well, **then**. What had changed?

I missed the early days of my marriage. I walked around in it cocooned, comforted, consoled from every difficulty in the world. Everything easy, natural, love like a warm blanket pulled over my shoulders that fit like a second skin.

I stripped my clothes off, jumped into a tub of water so scalding it hurt at first. I scrubbed, exfoliated, loofahed my body, disgusted; disgust layered like a dust that I hoped I could rinse off if I attacked it hard enough. I took pleasure in the suds draining, the day/date draining into the sewers with all the other filth.

## Day/ Date Three: The Penitent (Pen)

I was nervous about this one, not because we were going someplace fancy or expensive. But, because out of the sixteen dates I'd planned, this was the man that I'd spent ample time getting to know. And the other two investments had turned out so badly.

This was going to be my first meet and greet, a drive-through date, a pit stop in our day where we looked each other over and gave our assessment. KFC was the place. Six was the time. He drove up in a white van, and momentarily I thought of what that color and that vehicle had meant to kids growing up in the '70s and '80s.

We both got out of our vehicles. The moment suddenly felt like a sappy chick flick. His eyes glowed. He was tall, beautiful hands, long eyelashes, hair short and curly, a button nose and a perfectly formed mouth, a grown-up caramel Gerber baby. He thought I was beautiful. My body reacted instinctively, breath quickened, pulse raced, loins throbbed, hands eager to touch. It was akin to the proverbial "a woman knows within five minutes if she will sleep with a man" moment.

It only took 30 seconds.

The way he looked at me only made me want him more, making it hard to concentrate on the words he spoke. He touched my arm, hands soft but firm. Instantly I imagined his fingers in mine, in my hair, on the small of my back pulling me close, then lifting my chin for a kiss. And then the mood changed, his eyes darkening, looking away. He hadn't expected to feel so attracted, so drawn, so intense. He'd just gotten divorced; this felt like cheating. I gasped and pulled my hand away. His guilt loomed strong and heavy. The hope I'd felt rising in my heart, the joy, the excitement of possibility squashed in an instant like a candle's flame between two fingers. Every time he looked at me, I felt the stir, the almost desire to be there, to wait, to invest the months or years till he was ready. Yet, I knew that there was no guarantee. I had just finalized my divorce, after waiting nine years for my husband to be ready, to take me out once a month, and finally admit to a professional that he needed treatment for his impotence.

When that day finally came- that is, when my husband sat before a doctor asking for help- I'd filed for divorce six weeks prior, and it was too late. My heart had been broken too long to offer second chances.

Now I sat across from another man who was not ready, a PENITENT. Three dates, three mirrors. The first, showing me my insecurity, unworthiness, and self-doubt. The second, unearthing my fear that my ex-husband not valuing our marriage over his ego meant somehow that I was of little value. The third, making me wonder if something was wrong with me, dating this soon, not waiting, and NOT feeling guilty. The lack of shame transformed into a sudden source of shame.

I lined up these dates to find the man who would brush my knee, my body, my breasts, my lips intentionally; who would replace eight months of isolation with companionship and sex; who would replace nine years of impotence with something solid and reliable. However, all I was meeting was...me. Different sides, different shades, different issues.

When I walked back to my car this time, it was more challenging. I didn't want to. I wished I could erase this meeting and turn back the clock to the flirty conversations that got us here; his deep voice, his wit, his intelligence. After being married to a man who was the opposite of an intellectual, who couldn't form an opinion that wasn't the first broadcast over talk radio, I was floored by the Penitent's eloquent brilliance. I didn't know the word sapiosexual then. I just knew I could listen to Pen for hours, days, weeks, months, maybe even years, and never get bored. Part of me wanted to keep seeing him, talking to him just for that. But the other, more substantial part, the greedy part that wanted to seduce him just to see his eyes locked on me again, to replace guilt and shame with pleasure, was barely restrained. It didn't care that he needed time, space, healing. It wanted him: all, bare, mine.

I was better than that. Pen deserved better than that.

I kept walking.

Three dates. Three strikes. And although I had thirteen more lined up, this track record was not good for my already shot confidence. I came from a line of married women, long marriages, not good ones. And suddenly, I was wondering, not for the first time, if it was my fate to meet men who wanted me whom I did not want. And men I wanted who also wanted me, but not enough for it to make a difference.

I guess I should mention the elephant in the room. So many dates. And this was just the beginning.

There's this prevailing belief about serial daters, which suggests they are just looking for a free meal, uninterested in the men, and just using them (like notches on a belt).

If you noticed, I had three dates/meet and greets, and so far, not one dime was spent on me. I'm not typical; I was never a dater. I went on one date, prom, in high school. I married two homebodies who took me out probably a half dozen times in the six year (first marriage) 11 year (second marriage) we were together. Most of those outings were family functions.

So this was not about free meals, or me being bored, or me bragging to "my girls." It was me climbing step by step out of the valley of isolation and becoming re-acclimated to men, dating, sex, and love. I saw it as my path to redemption.

## Day/ Date Four: Mr. Literacy

I thought I screened out the married men, both in the categories I picked on my profile and in my pre-date questions. However, as I sat sipping peach herbal tea at a local coffee shop, across from this dark mocha being with short dreads, a stocky body, and a personality halfway between a jock and a geek, I learned he was indeed married and was only on this date because his wife wouldn't "do it doggy style." He also wanted to convince me to do it without condoms, or he'd lose his erection. The bluntness once again startled and confused me. He could say this to my face but not on the phone and save us the meeting? That made no sense.

So I asked him why he hadn't told me this earlier.

He said he thought I might be swayed by our vibe and his appearance, two advantages he couldn't use on the phone. Neither mattered to me.

I felt sorry for his wife but also annoyed. It seems this was a couple who should not have married; probably one of those couples who assumed sex would come naturally and didn't discuss sexual compatibility, so now he was searching online. He was very likely to find what he was looking for, given his vibe and appearance, and he knew it. I imagined his wife knew nothing, and I felt annoyed that she let such an easy thing a woman could do, get between them. It was like my ex refusing to admit to a doctor he had E.D. even though I'd offered to pay costs with my flexible spending card. I'd made appointments (which he kept) and talked about the high blood pressure he'd hid from me for two years and got his HBP meds changed three times. But he wouldn't open his mouth to speak about E.D., and she wouldn't open hers to lick, suck or swallow.

I felt like a candid camera victim swept into a different version of that movie. You know, the one where a man is about to divorce because his wife doesn't give head. Regrettably, my fourth date was just as short as the first three. Mr. Literacy was just another man I'd never speak to again.

By now, I was keeping a log on my computer and telling my best friend, a guy I'd met through Black People Meet but never met in person, all the deets. And I'd picked up a habit. Each guy had a nickname, Dough and Jowls, The Penitent, Leatherhands, and Mr. Literacy. He'd been so engrossed in a book when I first walked in that I almost left because I didn't think my date was present. Had I not called and heard his phone ring, I would have left.

Everyone in these online dating sites had these weird monikers that I couldn't remember, and who knew if the name they were giving me was even real? So, it just seemed a natural outgrowth of this unnatural way of meeting. New guy, new nickname.

## Day/ Date Five: The Scanner

The Scanner picked a fabulous sports bar that served craft beers, hundreds of them, not that I was a drinker. I just didn't know there was even such variety. Ambiance prevailed, but he was so nervous I almost excused myself. He scanned the crowd like a convict on the lam. Another married man, wow, two in a row. He was married to a foreigner who'd paid for marriage to him to get her green card. Now he needed loving. He only stopped scanning after two beers, then it turned out- surprise, surprise- he had a personality after all. But I didn't have an appetite or a thirst. I hadn't made it home before he was hitting me up on the app, asking me to be nice and give him a great review so that he had a better chance at meeting someone compatible. I hadn't even explored the app enough to know that there were reviews. So I replied asking how to find them and went and looked up all my upcoming prospects. Most had no reviews, but a few had intriguing ones. People evaluating other people on a dating app. Who'd a thunk it? One star = dead fish, two = interesting, three = a good time, four = a blast, five = a keeper, and a space for comments, some of which rated stamina, size, and performance.

Well alrighty- then.

I was not leaving a review. He was somewhere between dead fish and interesting. And interesting only because I never thought I'd meet a modern version of a mail-order husband. Ironically I ran into him a few months later at a thrift shop, standing in line, looking awkward, scanning. I guess that was his perpetual air sans alcohol. He didn't notice me, and I kept it moving.

## Day/ Date Six: Riko Suave

Another bar, my first alcoholic drink, and a Hispanic lawyer with the sexiest accent I'd ever heard who touched my hand the entire time we talked. Another married man. No excuses. He wanted variety. Now I was feeling antsy. Did something in my profile, pic, and demeanor hint I was mistress material? Again I balked, but he walked me to my car, even though I declined the offer. He kissed me unexpectedly. His taste lingered on my lips, seductive, a promise so intoxicating I almost forgot he was taken. He'd slid up to me and had me in his arms in one second so smoothly I didn't even have time to protest. Smelling woodsy, he pulled me in just right; forceful, possessive, like a man who knew what he wanted, what I wanted and had every intention of fulfilling my every desire. The pleasure that ran through me instantly parted my lips closed my eyes, and his lips and tongue were there, a part of mine. Joined, dancing, intertwined as I softened further and melded to him head to toe. Had our clothes been off, we'd have been making love. So close, so joined my head spun. My eyes flew open, staring into his, an amber brown under dark eyebrows, passionate eyes, sinful lips. I could feel his erection. I lingered there a moment. Unable to remember the last time I had felt any of this. Wondering had my husband ever taken possession of my body like this. I didn't think so. Everything in me wanted to surrender. The word yes in my mind, the softness of my body, the question in my eyes. I shook my head, swatting away the question- could I do this- forcefully, and he pulled back, opening my door, watching me sit, and closed the door with a pat. Good with words, better with his body, I knew he would have been a good lover. But I had enough guilt from the kiss. The words of The Penitent replayed in my head. Though I'll admit, for a minute, I thought," I'm not married; he is." I took no vows. He did. But that was rationalization, pure and simple.

I drove away.

Although I wanted to look at his reviews, I didn't. I didn't need to. It wouldn't have been good too. Although I knew he was a cheater, I was jealous of his wife for a minute. All that in a few minutes, and she lived with that at her disposal. He was the second sexpot in as many days. Gorgeous, fit, sensual, flirtatious and . . . unfaithful. I decided before I sat down and engaged with any other dates, I was asking again- are you married. I texted the eleven men left, stating in no uncertain terms, I was not a mistress. Your vibe and looks won't sway me. You can't seduce me, so don't waste your time. Then I went to brush and gargle Riko Suave away.

## Day/ Date Seven: Grizzly Adamz

Lunch brought me Grizzly Adamz, the risk-taker who bungee jumped and raced motorcycles, who entered Pappadeaux's, and encouraged me to order whatever I wanted. Once the food arrived and we'd begun eating, he proceeded to complain about his wife, who took his money, was perpetually learning a new skill, taking new classes ( spending his money to do so), and then not getting any job related to her new certifications. But she did give him a whole box of condoms before his last business trip with the advice- have fun- and she did swing with him and a couple from Craig's List.

I'd forgotten to ask whether he was married before I sat down. I probably assumed the text would have deterred him had he been. I sat my fork down and asked, "Why did you ask me out? I told you on the app, and in our phone conversations, I was not interested in married men."

He replied, "I was interested in meeting you anyway. Who wouldn't want to entertain a beautiful, intelligent woman?"

My ex-husbands. They didn't want to take me out or "entertain" me.

I don't need any reward but your company Grizzly had said, your smile, your warm demeanor, your banter. I shrugged. He wanted that… he got that. We were already there. I was already eating, drinking, being fascinated by his lifestyle, this couple. People really lived like this- swingers, open marriages, had rules and all. His tale was too crazy to be made up.

I considered this my walk on the wild side. Tomorrow I would be back on the straight and narrow.

## Day/ Date Eight-Ten: Mobie Dick, Morriz Dayzed, and Preacher Boy I'll cover together.

I met each at Denny's, and we talked in the vestibule and never made it to the table. Mobie showed me a dick pic of his giant penis, hoping I would follow him to a hotel. That was not on my agenda. Dayzed was more androgynous than any man I had ever met, and I wasn't sure he was into women, so I excused myself. Preacher Boy talked about the ministry, then asked for pictures of me to jack off to. After that last one, it took a pep talk from my best friend San Antonio to keep me from canceling all the remaining dates. San told me I'd invested time, and I had no alternative. He said they couldn't all be that bad, and I should just go through with my plan and re-evaluate if I hadn't met someone after date 16. I agreed. (Yes, I met my best friend on a dating site. But we'll get to that later.")

## Day/ Date Eleven – Thirteen: Prime Time News, Mr. Nice Guy, and Reggae Mon

Prime Time News, Mr. Nice Guy, and Reggae Mon were drinks and boredom so profound I regretted leaving my house and wished I had set up the "emergency call" fifteen minutes in to rescue me. But although I hadn't set up that call, JJ did call me each of these three nights, replacing boredom with interest in him, anticipation for our date, and hope that he would finally be - the one.

## Day/ Date Fourteen and Fifteen:

These two dates were the first to end in insults. The Incredibly Hulky Lecher arrived at Applebee's thirty minutes late and told me he almost stood me up and asked why I picked a restaurant on the feeder of the freeway with construction in the area. Well, I didn't know about the construction, and GPS helped me navigate it perfectly. Well, he hadn't been able to use his GPS because his phone was almost dead, and he was out of data, and he didn't have a phone charger. And he stared at me as if all that was my fault. He sat down complaining the restaurant smelled, it was empty, and there weren't many drink options on the menu, and of course, they wouldn't have his brand of alcohol. He was **OBNOXIOUS**. But he was all smiles when our waitress arrived, a college student, a new transplant from out of state, studying something ( I forgot what). Every time she came over, he asked her new questions. More questions than he asked me. He looked at every woman who entered the restaurant or left her table, up and down. Still, he was most enamored with our twenty-something server, a black version of Calista Flockhart.

She, so thin.

I, so voluptuous.

If she was his type, I most definitely was not. Or, was anything in a skirt his type? Hmmm.

When it came time for dessert, which was included in the package we had ordered (appetizer, meal, dessert), he commented about the calorie count and alluded to what I had already eaten, and I was done. I thanked him for dinner, walked out, and was about to enter my car when he came rushing out - incensed.

"Why are you in such a hurry?" he bellowed.

"I already told you good night; you didn't have to come out here. It was obvious you were more interested in every woman in the restaurant, especially our waitress."

"Huh? She's young enough to be my daughter."

"And? You spent more time getting to know her than you did me. She and I were both extremely uncomfortable. You didn't even seem to notice. I hinted you were grilling her, and you simply shrugged it off and kept going."

"Don't change the subject. You're trying to get home to Bob." By this time, he was in arms reach of me, having walked as he talked.

"Bob?"

"Yes, your battery-operated boyfriend. Got a full-blooded man right here, but you're rushing home to Bob."

I saw red and almost hit him. I'm not a violent person, but that statement pissed me off. From beginning to end, he'd been an absolute jerk. He was a personal trainer; one would have thought he'd know more about women and how to treat them since he probably had several as clients. He was also a "motivational speaker." I didn't see how that was possible.

The Lorax met me at a Chinese restaurant. A self-described workaholic, he had only one other passion, the environment. He spent the entire date complaining. He lamented how backward Texas was, the poor zoning, dearth of conservation, lack of effort to plant trees, and constant construction of new buildings. I listened, but I must not have appeared moved because the more he talked, the more passionate he became. Finally, he lumped me in with the other city dwellers who didn't realize we were stealing our kids' and grandkids' futures for consumerism. He paid, threw a few disgusted looks my way, and left.

## Day/ Date Sixteen: JJ

I was antsy all day. We were meeting at my favorite restaurant, but at the last minute, his schedule changed, and he couldn't meet me till an hour and a half later. 9:45. The restaurant closed at 10. Well, this would be a short date if it went poorly, and if it went well, we could go somewhere else and continue it. We'd talked so much beforehand, I was almost worried he or I would have nothing to say. I got there early, sat at the bar, and had a glass of wine, trying not to think about the last 15 days/dates.

He walked in, sat next to me, and smiled. Relaxed. Unhurried. As if we had all night. We talked, and suddenly he was too far away. I scooted over. We were shoulder to shoulder, laughing, talking, holding hands. The perfect date. And then I looked at the time. 10:15. We both knew that the restaurant was closed. We were far from done. He asked where I wanted to go as he pulled me into his arms and offered his place.

I accepted. It was close. 10 minutes. I was nervous, excited, a little afraid. He was ex-military and had this way of making me feel womanly and safe just in his presence. I had a feeling driving down the freeway that my life would never be the same.

I arrived, and we sat in his living room, and he talked for an hour about himself, his family, his divorces. He wanted me to get to know him and decide if I wanted to see him again. I relaxed. He didn't expect anything to happen, didn't expect anything from me.

We kissed, cuddled, and when I expected him to say, "It's getting late, you should go." I took his hand and led him back to what I assumed was his bedroom.

I was right.

I loved his apartment. Big. Mostly empty, but a fully stocked bar, massive entertainment center, a set of Samurai swords, a huge wrap-around couch, and lots of books. I pictured adding a few womanly touches here and there.

I lay in his bed, clothed; he was too. And we kissed, slowly; he let me take the lead, sliding his hand under my shirt, cupping my breast, removing my shirt, his, our shoes, socks, pants, everything slow and deliberate. And when he was fully undressed, I cupped him, wrapped my hand around his shaft, and held it. I'd forgotten what a penis felt like, looked like, erect. He lay there and let me hold him for what seemed like an eternity. It was one of the most precious gifts I'd ever received. I had made him erect. Something I hadn't been able to accomplish with my husband in years. And when he entered me, he paused, waiting for my ok to continue. I felt like a virgin again. Everything felt new. This man I barely knew made love to me. And then held me, and we slept.

The following day, we showered. I brushed my teeth with a brand new toothbrush he had in the guest bathroom, and we made love again, talked about the future, what I wanted, what he wanted, where those met. I saw him 3 times a week most weeks, spent the weekend most weekends, ate food he cooked for me, and cooked for him once, even brought work I needed to finish to his place. We went to restaurants, movies, shopping, and we talked. Sometimes I cried. I had so many questions about my marriage, my life, and he answered in generalities, trying to put himself in my exes' shoes, telling me often he could not. He invested in me in ways a man never had, taught me my own body, and made me feel my sex drive was something to celebrate, not a problem that needed to be managed. Had I been more healed, less damaged, I would have fallen in love. But love was far from my mind. I was starved for sex and attention, and he loved giving me both, and I loved giving them right back. He told me he would be transferred somewhere else, but before he left, he wanted to set a bar, to teach me how I should be treated and make me so used to it that I would never settle for less. He did. I haven't. When I drove to his place that first night, I knew I would never be the same.

I was right.

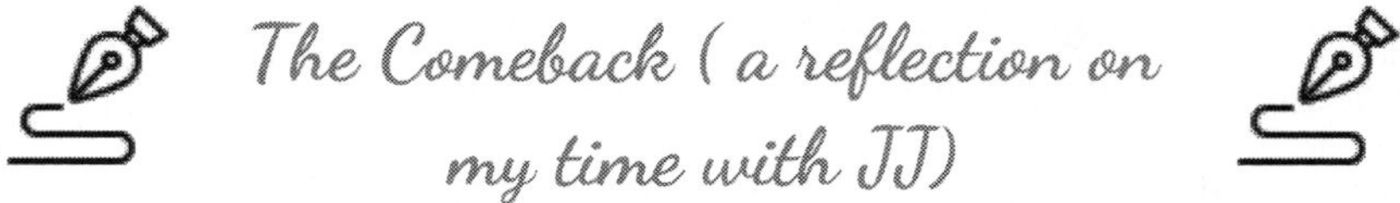

## The Comeback (a reflection on my time with JJ)

*You don't know who you are till your heart's been broke*
*And you try to put it back.*
*First time it's shock,*
*Second pain,*
*Third, you don't bounce back.*
*Anything more you begin to doubt*
*Wonder what love's all about.*
*You battle bitter, insecure.*
*You lash out quicker than before*
*You're not as stable, not as sure*
*Cause underneath a strong veneer*
*A well of teardrops molder.*

*But it is nice to find release,*
*To find a soul that offers peace,*
*To meet someone who gives you rest,*
*For this, I count myself as blessed.*

*Today my steps were somewhat lighter*
*My future seems a little brighter*
*My cracks don't seem as deep and dark,*
*When someone cushions my battered heart.*

I already described JJ physically, but if you want to know more, flip the dictionary open to "holding space." His illustration will be there. He was holding space for me before the term ever went viral. Being physically, mentally, and emotionally present for me, totally focused on me supportively, non-judgmentally as I felt my feelings was one of the greatest gifts he gave me. The other was the knowledge that I was multi-orgasmic.

Before JJ, sex was over when I came. I was always the last to come; sometimes, I didn't climax at all. But very early in our fromance (friends + romance), he stopped me from getting up from the bed after my initial shuddery release, "What are you doing?"

"Getting a washcloth."

"Are you done?"

I smiled. "Did you not just feel that?"

"Not did you cum. Are you done?"

I cocked my head.

"Are you tired?"

I shook my head.

"Sore"

I shook again.

He made love to me all over again. More deeply, more thoroughly, more intently. On a mission. I matched him, wanting to take him higher. And then it happened.

A wave, rush, lift, roar, a million electric sensations, pulsating, throbbing. My toes curled; eyes rolled back; body arched. The orgasm possessed me. Muscles I didn't even know I had, clinched, unfurled.

And when it began to die down, he thrust again, and it rose, crescendoing louder, faster, harder. And when that began to ebb, he started stroking slowly, intently, methodically till my entire body became a thrumming string with him its masterful conductor.

When I could speak, I looked at him. My eyes were full of questions, "What did you do to me?"

He shrugged. "You're multi-orgasmic. You didn't know?"

I shook my head. What else didn't I know?

It's hard to explain how unselfish JJ was. I often asked him why he took such good care of me. We weren't married or committed. He said because he could because I needed it, and I deserved it, and it made him feel needed, wanted, and gave him purpose. He said I was easy to please, and he loved making me smile. He brought me flowers. Would have wine and dinner ready when I came over, took me out, and when he got the final word that he was leaving, urged me to set up 16 dates again, hoping lightning would strike twice and I'd meet his replacement before he left. He didn't want me to be alone.

I once asked him what he got from seeing me. He gave me so much. It didn't seem like an equal exchange. He stared back. Tsked.

"You really don't know your value. What do I get from seeing you? Damn, girl. Peace. Respect. You listen and accept what I say. You don't put words in my mouth or tell me what I 'meant to say or what I 'really mean.'" He said, air quoting. "You give me space. And you don't expect anything." He shook his head as if this was the most incredible thing in the world. "You appreciate everything. On Father's Day, you brought me a gift. We'd been dating one month. You weren't my girl, and you brought me a gift. You've brought me food. You give a lot. You're just so used to doing it that you don't even notice what you're doing. You're the ideal woman. . . and you value silence. You'll let me watch the game, listen to my music, read. And you'll just enjoy my presence. I don't have to say anything. What do I get from you? I can just be. Just motherfucking be. You don't know what a great gift that is. I've had dozens of relationships and two marriages, and not once could I just be."

I squeezed his hand and took it in. This compliment. This validation. This expression of my unique contribution. "Thank you."

He kissed my hand. "No, thank you."

JJ's married now, three months. We haven't talked in almost five years, but we met up twice right after he moved away. I see him on Facebook from time to time.

As a teen in church, I heard the rose metaphor. Basically, I (and all girls) were roses. If we were passed around and handled by men, each man took a petal. Consequently, when our husband came, we would have nothing to offer him: no beauty, no wholeness, no worth. The only way to retain our value was to abstain from sex. Then, we could give ourselves purely and wholly/holy to marriage.

No one thought what would happen to a woman raised to think that way once she is married. What if her husband cheats? Her whole rose wasn't enough to keep him home. What if he's abusive? Her untouched rose wasn't enough to tame his tongue or stop his fists. What if she gets divorced?

She's now without petals, having given all she had- her beauty, worth, and chastity- to her former mate. Making girls roses also reinforces the outdated patriarchal idea that women have a short shelf life. Old Maid, anyone? Who wants a wilted rose? Every day, every wrinkle, every stretch mark, every scar is another petal gone.

JJ taught me I was no rose. I was the whole damn bush- able to give a flower and still grow, able to weather storms, able to sink my roots in good soil, able to defend myself with my thorns. Did you know, rose bushes symbolize courage, and rose petals are edible- both tasty and nutritious?

JJ rekindled my desire to be savored like fine wine. I learned that having sex with him was not giving away a petal I could never regain, one I would regret losing because that meant losing my worth. Our intimacy helped me bloom with restored confidence.

**Lesson 1:**

Stop being a rose. Be the whole damn bush.

# CHAPTER 2

# Boldness

In 2015 a term was trending. It was everywhere, and nowhere in particular like that famous tipping point idea where monkeys on one side of an island learned to use a tool. Suddenly monkeys on the other side of the island, who had never seen the tool or the other group, started using it. The zeitgeist had changed. There was something in the ether.

The idea of the damsel in distress was out of vogue.

This was new to me.

I was raised on fairy tales and romance, always a woman waiting for Prince Charming. Rapunzel stuck in the tower. Sleeping Beauty in a coma. Ariel, who gave up her natural body and her voice, talk about symbolism, for a man.

I'd spent nine years in distress, a damsel, swooning, trudging in the ashes, confident my prince of a husband would rescue me, our marriage, our sex life, our love. His quest was just to the doctor. His dragon just an unknown ailment. And I was his lady love, the one he'd vowed to love and honor till death do us part. How could this tale go wrong? All my training said he would slay the dragon and return with the Holy Grail.

Damsels in distress were always rescued. Always.

But this was reality, not fantasy. Turns out I had to be my own hero.

Slay the dragon of life on my own, again. And enter the dating pool on a quest.

After 16 dates, I had my Holy Grail, and it was so worth it. I had rescued myself. Gone on my crusade through bogs, briars, and the Valley of Filth, and arrived at Prince Charming's castle. I no longer needed the dating app. It was time to stop receiving inboxes, a slew of emails, and enjoy my plunder.

But before I deleted my profile, something unexpected happened.

I was just about to push the button and got a message. I almost ignored it, but something said to check it out. CM, San Antonio, about 8 years older than me, online now and wanting to talk NOW. I'd never had a live conversation in the app, and I declined. He countered, stating I know it's late. I know your profile says you only want someone local, but you intrigue me. Give me 5 minutes. If I bore you and don't make you laugh, hang up. Here's my actual phone number, call me anonymously.

I was intrigued. I called. We laughed and talked for five hours. And talked every day for two years straight. And then we met. But that's a story for another chapter, another year.

I'd grown to love my castle. I adored Prince JJ, but all things come to an end. He was leaving, getting transferred, and he, still a prince who put me first, suggested finding a replacement.

Part of me was annoyed by the suggestion, maybe even a little hurt. Part of me was hoping the transfer would fall through, that he would be needed in Houston longer. Most of me could not picture replicating anything like this with anyone- ever. I had been alive for 45 years and had never experienced this type of dating.

But eventually, somewhat half-heartedly, I gave in.

This time around was different, 2015, divorced 6 months now, used to regular and AMAZING sex. I was nothing like the damsel in distress who had posted a profile pic and expected no one to respond.

I was glad I had deleted the old profile. I was different. New. Improved. Much more comfortable in my skin. Unapologetic about my sensuality. Bolder. Blunter. Braver.

I shed the last dating site and started over.

Before I go any further, let's discuss dating site profiles.

I probably don't have to tell you this, but I am NOT a picture taker. I avoid them if at all possible. I knew I'd have to have some when I created a profile. My phone was crap. I hadn't yet traded it in, and I noticed on a mall trip with my sons buying prom gear that there was a photo kiosk. Voila. Two pictures. Two pictures I didn't want to take in the first place. Two pictures while I was still going through my divorce (can you see the resignation on my face?) Two pictures when I think it had been six years since I'd been on a date because my husband wouldn't take me out. Two pictures when I hadn't been touched for about eight months and was absolutely terrified of putting up a profile that got no response.

Looking at my chest in these pics, I have no idea how I thought that I'd get no response. I also have no idea why I thought I was extremely overweight. Looking at these pics and thinking back to my self-image, I realized I had low self-esteem.

But six months later, I was in a different place, mentally, emotionally, physically.

Those profile pics, that profile description did not fit who I had become. Besides, that app seemed haunted by the conversations that went nowhere, the disrespectful virtual catcalls, the obscene suggestions that I'd deleted, that still came to mind whenever that app's icon flashed on my screen.

Deleting the profile and building a new one on a different site was like cleansing my palate. Coincidentally, around this time, I found out that JJ himself was a palate cleanser according to urban slang. He was my fling that cleared the debris of my divorce, preparing me for my next serious relationship.

I don't remember what pics I used for my new profile. But I do remember doing an internet search on how to write a fab dating profile. Before, I'd expected no responses. I was ready for a slew of attention this time. I wanted my profile to narrow the stream to a small trickle. Here are the guppies this new profile snagged.

Mr. Metrosexual- All was going well at Denny's till he asked to see my hands and replied, "You have nice nails, but my girl will hook you up, boo. Exfoliate you, do your cuticles." I expected a snap and a head flourish, and even though those were not forthcoming, I saw Metro as someone I might take on a spa day. Still, I would never be attracted to a minute more.

Mr. Cleen, who looked like the proverbial cartoon just black, and The Musky Mentalist both had body odor so strong it almost made my eyes smart, and I made an excuse and left.

Sugar Daddy, was offering just that- funds for sex and attention, a married man who hadn't had sex with his wife in years. They even had separate bedrooms. He stayed just so she wouldn't get half.

The Bassist- gorgeous, sexy, took me back to Riko Suave in my head, but he was not married, just attached to his third baby mama, mother to two of his six kids. He was on tour and gave me a walkthrough of the tour bus, the venue, and an autographed album.

## Day/ Date Twenty-Two and Twenty-Three:

Vinzent Price took me to an Irish pub with stairs I thought I might kill myself climbing in heels. It was dark, dingy, and grimy. I think they had this place in mind when the phrase "greasy spoon" was coined. I didn't want to eat, drink or even touch anything. Then he began talking about death. I tried to change the subject, but he wasn't having it. He had the most charming English accent, but all I could think about was asking if he could do the Vincent Price laugh. I refrained, but after meeting this guy, I went into super scrub mode that night for the second time.

The Beautician spent our whole date describing his nine kids who needed a mother because theirs had passed. Coincidentally, he showed up in the people you might know on Facebook a year later, and he was, in fact, married by then, having found his replacement bride.

## Day/ Date Twenty-Four through Twenty-Six:

Rappers 1, 2, 3, there was nothing to describe. No personality. No conversation. No interest on my part. I wondered if men memorized the lines they used online and in the initial conversations. Were there some scripts they were reading from? How could these guys seem like candidates one minute (online/ on the phone) but deserve a 1- dead fish rating in person?

## Day/ Date Twenty-Seven and Twenty-Eight:

The following two were nice dates, kind of.

CLH_sat at the bar. He complained the place was hard to find, and I instantly flashed back to the Lecher. He was distracted between the bartender and the baseball game on the screen. I suggested sitting in a booth, but nope, he was fine where he was. We ate in near silence, and as he walked me to my car, he gave me the Church Lady Hug, arms barely touching me, butt stuck way out. Awkward. Weird.

The second was nondescript, nothing to report, until the end of the date when he gave me THE WORST KISS EVER. In all of about ten seconds, he alternated between trying to stab me with his tongue, swallow my tongue, bite my lips and tongue and nuzzle me. Then he asked if I was as turned on as he was ( HUH? NO!) and if I wanted to get a hotel. When I said absolutely not. He said why. And I explained that nothing had stimulated me, and we didn't even know each other. He asked, not even the kiss? I said, especially not the kiss. And he stomped off, saying he'd never gotten any complaints before. Yep, I thought, they probably had no idea what to say to what had just happened to them. They were stunned into silence.

## Day/ Date Twenty-Nine and Thirty:

These two dates almost didn't happen.

***S.I.A.*** The first was because our schedules kept clashing (I should have taken it as a sign). He took me to breakfast, and I could swear I was in a Dr. Seuss book. "Do women like good men?" he asked. Then, he answered himself. They will not date them in the rain (bad times). They always want these men to change. They will not date them with no car. They will not date those who live far. They will not date them if they smoke. They will not date them if they toke. They will not date them if they drink. And will not tell them if they stink. They will not date them; tell them scram. They will not date them (SAM I AM, I tuned out all the rest of his complaints and nicknamed him on the spot).

That was the whole date, a one-hour litany of reasons good men are ignored. He asked me for a second date when he was done, and I was speechless. He said I was a good listener, lol.

F.T's date almost didn't happen because he kept gushing about how beautiful I was, how much he wanted to meet me, and how he imagined what he would do to (and with) me. He made me so uncomfortable I told him to stop or I wouldn't show up.

I walked into Papasitos. It was lunchtime. Everyone in business attire grouped three or more. My date wasn't here. The only man sitting alone had to be 75. My date was 45, a year older than me. I was turning to leave when he waved me over. I walked over, wondering why, and he said, "Thank you for coming."

I said, "Sorry, I think you have me confused with someone else; I'm waiting for someone."

He said, "me."

I said no, someone my age.

He said, "I like younger women. You wouldn't have come had I told you my age.'

I looked at his jowls and the age spots on his hands and said, you're right, and you shouldn't have lied. His nickname was Father Time.

## Day/ Date Thirty-One and Thirty-Two:

The Creep I met him at Boudreaux's, a place I'd heard raved about. The food was terrible. The company worse. He critiqued and criticized everyone: the wait staff, the customers, and people in the parking lot. I couldn't wait to leave.

Mr. Nine Months Later- So when I was doing my winnowing in February 2014, there was one guy who had almost made it into the first sixteen, but he suddenly stopped replying to my calls and texts. Then he re-appeared, eager to meet; a meet and greet at Popeye's was arranged. He arrived. As did I. He was in socks and sandals, knee-length shorts, and a wife-beater, underarm hair long and protruding from the pits. He was a mess, and he told me he thought I was more petite. I wasn't his type. Thank God, saved me the trouble of telling him something similar.

Sixteen dates, no replacement. I took a break and enjoyed my last month with JJ, with no further interruptions.

Sixteen was not my magic number this time. I was more than a little surprised since this go-around I'd actually shelled out what felt like a pricy $35 membership only to learn this sea held the same guppies.

I also learned lesson two- I would never again play the victim with no voice, the sleeping beauty too comatose to seize life by the horns, or the passive princess who didn't think to cut her own hair and make a rope of it to climb out of her isolation. I had stayed in my marriage for my sons, but they were now men, and I was not going to ever just stay with a man hoping he would change.

I was more resourceful than that.

Around this time, I came across a name I had never heard before- Lilith. First, I'd heard it when I ran across some footage of Lilith Fair. I was intrigued by the name, even more by the myths. To sum them up (and provide my own little spin):

The Bible contains two stories of creation- one where man and woman were created the same day as equals, the second where man is created first, given dominion over everything and a job- naming everything. Then woman is created from his side (not his rib, mistranslation). So in Jewish mysticism or Kabbalah, the first creation was Adam's first wife. She embraced her equality, refused to have sex missionary style (aka submissively), learned the real name of God, spoke His name blasphemously, and instantly lost her human form. She became a seducing spirit. In some myths, Lilith is the serpent who tempts Eve into seducing Adam with a fruit.

Thus Genesis shows two different women. Lilith, who feels equal to a man- her husband. Lilith, who has all-powerful intuition and a voice so potent, she changes her fate forever.

And then, there is Eve. Eve was a follower. Her husband blamed her for enticing him to eat the fruit from the "tree of knowledge. She was punished by God and was made to desire her husband and birth children in pain. She is why man earns a living arduously. She only received a name after giving birth. Thus, Eve had no identity outside of motherhood and marriage, no name before Adam named her, just as he did all the other animals under his dominion. The only words she spoke were apologetic. She apologized for wanting knowledge, for wanting more, for wanting equality.

What a contrast!

Lilith has been vilified for thousands of years. In fact, it is only recently that she has been portrayed in a positive light. She just happens to be the woman in touch with her sexuality, boundaries, and intuition. She is so prescient she is even privy to God's secrets. Lilith also just happens to be the one more knowledgeable than her husband.

But Eve doesn't fare much better. Like Pandora, she is the scapegoat for original sin. Eve is the second archetypal "reason" women should be distrusted, controlled, and not allowed to make decisions. She is the "reason" that women should be barefoot, pregnant, and ignorant. In fact, some men and even ministers thought painful childbirth (God's punishment on women for the fall) should not be eased, so they railed against epidurals.

And interestingly enough, although Genesis acknowledges Eve's motherhood, it is Adam who "gives birth" to humanity by providing the source for Eve's very existence- his "rib". Therefore, a woman is subservient even in childbirth; bearing children for the man who gave her her name and her very existence as a continuation of his lineage.

And what a horrible picture of marriage this paints- for women. And God ( as depicted in these stories) seems to have failed miserably at matchmaking. The first marriage results in divorce, the second in eternal consequences.

The Garden of Eden is a place of perfection because a woman's voice and intuition have no foothold there. A bold, sexually aware woman, Lilith, is transformed into a seductress, a succubus- sucking the life from men, a demon. And the more submissive woman with no name, no identity except what is given by her husband speaks up once and pays for it for the rest of her life. Her female progeny pays for it too.

Well, I guess it's good that I don't live in the Garden of Eden, because I decided lesson 2 was:

**Lesson 2: (Boldness)**

Be bold enough to want to know, to want to grow, and to slay your own dragons. No more patient, passive damsels in distress.

# CHAPTER 3

# *Caution*

Nature abhors a void. So, when JJ moved, life filled the time with everything that had faded to the background.

"Honey, do projects" my ex-husband had never gotten done, adjusting to living on my single paycheck, and of course, my 21-year-old twins picked this moment to start acting out because, although they'd predicted the divorce six years ago and thought they were ready, they weren't.

I wasn't.

I didn't think there would be anything to grieve. Shit, I'd been grieving nine years. I had even gone to therapy trying to adjust to my loveless, sexless marriage.

The first time I'd gotten divorced, there had been therapy and a divorce support group at a local church for months.

After my divorce from Drew, there was therapy and JJ. And JJ was gone. And in his absence, I felt, once more…

## Invisible

*Sadness dwells in the spaces between*
*desire and possibility.*
*The absence of a goal's reality*
*Like a cold blanket enveloping me.*

*Sadness lives in the wonder-*
*What might have been.*
*The questions of why X didn't happen.*
*The doubt of whether you were better off*

*Then.*

*So visible. Yet so obscure.*
*Surrounded. But alone for sure.*

*Belonging to no one. Anymore.*

*Invisible.*

*I had so many, many, many*

## Doubts

*A date, a kiss, a word, a text*
*Will this latest try at love grant success?*
*Will the chemistry fizzle, or will it grow?*
*Trustworthy enough to let my feelings show?*

*Why's it seem like love was easier at 15, 25, or 32?*
*Why hit 40 and suddenly in love I have no clue?*
*Does his past life matter?*
*Will his words be harsh?*
*Has he really changed? Can wildness just depart?*
*How long to wait before sexual intercourse begins?*
*How important is our ability to be friends?*
*Is the inner warning sacred or just fear from the past?*
*Will I make the same mistakes I made with my last?*
*Have I healed? Am I ready to love fully again?*
*Or should I simply try exchanging benefits with a friend?*
*So many questions swirling*
*Answers, they are few*
*So how does a 40-year-old woman know what to do?*
*Is he a good man, kind and sure, trustworthy and fair?*
*Or is he just pretending, acting like he cares?*
*Is he here to take advantage, a wolf in disguise?*
*Is that deceit or honesty shining from his eyes?*
*I wish I knew the answers.*
*I wish I knew the score*
*All I truly know is love needs an open door.*
*But what lies on the other side is never certain, never sure.*

Therapy dredges up the past. You sift through old memories and see how much you healed or if the healing process started at all. My first marriage sometimes became the topic of conversation. I was naive, gullible, so book smart, yet very clueless about men. I'd chosen the path less traveled, abstinence till marriage, and that had meant one real boyfriend in high school, two in college, and very little knowledge of what to look for in men. Then my list was Christian, church-going, and " a good man." I don't believe "good" matters much anymore, but that's a conversation for a further chapter. Husband 1 was charming, church-going. I had him say the sinner's prayer myself and took him to church, and he was the only man I'd met in my teens and twenties that seemed to understand me. The only one who didn't use words to describe me like " intimidating."

Once he had my guards down, it wasn't long before I fell.

## Blue Water, Green Tree

*She carries him like a mother carries her child,*
*But he's her husband.*
*Trusts him like the sands that slip through her fingers*
*at the beach,*
*Loves him like an Oak loves water.*

*Born on the Mississippi, she's known water,*
*water as deep and dark as Mississippi Mud,*
*or as clear as Bahama breezes,*
*water as cold as a hail storm,*
*and hard as a steel door,*
*water that closed around like death,*
*as she waits to exhale.*

*He is her water; she is his tree.*
*He runs, plays, visiting the beaches.*

*She stands toweringly waiting.*

*He rages,*
*rips houses apart,*
*but just rolls around her roots,*
*snagging only clumps of clay.*

*He gurgles bubbled melodies*
*to her whistle in the wind.*

*He compliments her, supplies her, feeds her.*
*Happily incompatible,*
*they feed each other,*
*Separate,*
*but joined by life.*
*Moody like the moon,*
*his tide waxes and wanes,*
*waxes and wanes.*

*She stands-rings centuries around her stature,*
*holds the wealth of a million generations of*
*mother-lover sense*
*in her outstretched arms.*

*Her leaves fall into his ripples,*
*a million tears of change.*

We'd had a tumultuous almost six years. I lost myself then and in my second marriage. The first time, trying to become whatever would not set my husband off. The second time, trying to make myself believe that I could find total fulfillment from the titles of wife and mother sans conversation, sex, touching, dates, affection. Both times, I emerged a shell of myself. I gained tons of weight, began hiding my body under layer after layer, and sought obscurity so no man would notice me.

Being noticed meant problems in both marriages. During the first, accusations that I was flirting, cheating, and the host of slurs that go with women who do both. Throughout the second, notice created a different problem, the longing for all that was missing at home that I could not possibly indulge in with a man I wasn't married to. My sons already had one cheater in their biological father. If I cheated, they would think no one in the world was faithful.

In 2015, post-divorce, I started shedding all that negative programming. My goal? To feel comfortable in my skin, my space; to reclaim the right to have whatever attention came my way. JJ had given me the gift of embracing my sexuality, something both husbands had used against me.

To the first, I was Jezebel. To the second, Eve spoiling our garden of Eden because I wanted the fruit that I should have seen as forbidden because my second husband, Drew, declared our sex life over unilaterally. Being woman, wife, mother- I should have listened and had no say.

I'd silenced my sex drive with food, by keeping busy at work, with duties at home, and sometimes with exercise and journaling, fasting, and prayer. Sexual toys and oral sex had long ago stopped being pleasurable, so much so that by the end of my second marriage, I preferred toilet cleaning to either.

JJ had celebrated, enjoyed, and encouraged my sex drive. And after starving then gorging, it was fully, ravenously alive now.

## My Alter-ego's Ultimatum

*It's been a couple months, and she's hungry.*
*My alter ego is about to pounce like a zombie.*
*Can't control her, keep her caged for your safety.*
*But she hides behind my eyes like a banshee*
*Never was one who could wait quiet, patiently,*
*Always had a predator I had to sate*
*I never let it go this long. I got sloppy.*
*No, not really, just met nobody.*
*He has to be someone special, Alpha male-ish*
*Intelligent, articulate, and slightly fearless.*
*Zena is a force of nature, almost peerless*
*Only a hero can make her growls demurish.*
*She's not fun. She's demanding, overzealous*
*She's amoral, way beyond coquettish.*
*She's unemotional; it's true*
*Craves passion; he who gives it can subdue.*
*But she's unforgiving to those with no skill*
*Zen has tact. Zena has nil.*
*She is my burden since I was a teen*
*Stayed in relationships to keep her unseen*
*Slightly harder to do now with pickings so rare*

*So I train really hard and work hours that scare*
*To keep her too tired to even appear,*
*But she woke me up last night just to say hello,*
*And she's whispering to me as I push her low,*
*"You choose, or I choose. It will get done.*
*This is your last warning before I come.*

The poem seems a little dramatic, but it's how I felt. Writing intensely was one way to purge some of the feelings. Talking also helped.

The month before JJ left. San Antonio and I got close. We talked every day. If I saw JJ that day, it was a quick chat during my drive to or from JJ's place. If not, we talked longer. We shared commonalities, our upbringing, our fathers' passing, problematic relationships with family, a sexless marriage, a recent divorce. We were mirror images- male/female.

When JJ left, I talked to him too. In fact, I considered the whole long-distance thing, and we set up one rendezvous precisely a month after his move, and he stood me up.

No call. No text. No show.

I was devastated.

I hoped our reunion would help me get through a tough anniversary, the second anniversary of my father's passing. Now that week loomed, and I had just been stood up.

I went to work that following Friday, feeling on edge. Someone said good morning to me, and I burst into tears. My boss sent me home. I called JJ. at 7 a.m. He answered and told me he was sorry. Things would get better, and I just needed to pull myself together. I'd hoped for more than a two-minute conversation. The call felt shallow and curt. I tried to make excuses for the brevity: It was early. He might have been preparing for work.

All of them seemed so flimsy.

I called San Antonio, and he talked and listened and consoled and said he had to get ready for work and would call on his break. I went home, cried myself to sleep, talked to my sister, and drank. I wasn't a drinker, but it seemed like it might help.

Then San Antonio called and asked a strange thing, "Was I hungry? Had I eaten?"

No, I hadn't.

And he said to come to Chili's on 1960 by 45 North right now. There was something waiting for me, for me to call when I arrived. I hung up, put on my shoes, and drove, thinking he had bought me a meal. How sweet. I arrived. I called. He stepped out of a car. I stepped out of my car. We embraced. He kissed my cheek.

I was stunned. Confused. "I thought you were at work."

"I was. I took the weekend off, packed a bag, rented a hotel suite across the street. I needed to see you were okay."

"What?" I knew I hadn't misheard him because he was standing right in front of me, but the one word was my attempt to give voice to the depthless surprise inside of me.

"Spend the weekend with me. Let me take you out, take your mind off things, feed you." He slid his arm around my shoulders. "Let me take care of you."

Now, maybe there are women out there that have had this happen before. I never had. Who was this man that dropped everything for a voice on the phone, a woman he had never met? Yes, we had our daily heart to hearts, but he drove 3 hours to feed me. Booked a hotel to make sure I was ok.

We ate.

## Date Thirty-Three:

I went back to his hotel. He filled the hot tub with bubbles, and we soaked and talked and drank wine and made love all night and the following day. And he fed me: breakfast, lunch, dinner, and hours of conversation.

It was my first baecation. Then he returned to San Antonio, and we kept talking every day for the next two years. We still check on each other now about three times a year. He's in California. He did my first logo when I became a performer. And he badgered me to write this book for six years.

Before I wrote what follows, I thought about it for about two hours. How do I explain GATZBY? I don't fully understand our interaction myself, but maybe in writing this, I will. We will. Let's see.

I started on a new site. Lots of hits. Lots of messages sent and received. And then I saw him, his profile pic, flawless, gorgeous, Smooth skin, Long eyelashes. Perfect eyebrows, nose, and cheekbones. Decadent lips and teeth. Bald head and beard.

I… just ….stared.

I don't know if I read his profile. I mean, I always read the profiles beforehand, so I should have, as a matter of course, general principle. But he was otherworldly beautiful. Broad shoulders. Pecs. A big guy, no doubt. Even though all I could see was his pecs and one picture. Most guys had several. Both should have been red flags. Neither was.

I inboxed him. He replied. We exchanged numbers. Talked. I wanted to meet. He put me off. So long, three weeks, I almost walked. In chapters one and two, I already explained why I wanted to meet quickly. I'd already been catfished and disappointed so many times. I don't know if I gave him an ultimatum or just started to distance myself, but finally, we met.

## Date Thirty-Four:

Mexican food. A new restaurant. Fifteen minutes from my house. I got there first, sat, waited nervously. All the booths were taken, I sat at the table, not my preference. Booths cocoon and provide more privacy, more coziness, it seemed to me.

Then I saw him walking to the door.

He was much bigger than I expected. So big. I was glad I was at a table. So big, I wondered about the chair's sturdiness. He sat. I was uncomfortable. Felt conspicuous. And then he smiled.

In person, he was still gorgeous. And his smile? In the words of F. Scott. Fitzgerald, "He had one of those rare smiles with a quality of eternal reassurance in it, that you may come across four or five times in life. It faced, or seemed to face, the whole external world for an instant and then concentrated on you with an irresistible prejudice in your favor."[1]

Hypnotized for a moment, I shook off the effect of his pearly whites, smiled back, tried to gain my equilibrium, but I'll confess, I'd lost it, and with him, I never found it again.

He had me.

He was the most charming man I'd ever met. Made me laugh harder, talk more freely, share more, relax deeper than anyone ever had. First date? Posh. We had to have known each other millennia. Eons. Since time began.

His eyes. His lips. And that smile…

Fitzgerald would have said, "It understood you just as you wanted to be understood, believed in you as you would like to believe in yourself, and assured you that it had precisely the impression of you that, at your best, you had hoped to convey."[2]

As I replay that date in my mind's eye, we engaged like a couple in love, a once in a lifetime love, a star crossed, come what may, devil may care, love.

We closed down the restaurant. Looked up, and no one else was there. It had been packed, and then it was us - two alone. We walked to the parking lot and talked by his vehicle for another thirty minutes at least. And then he hugged me. I pulled back jokingly and said, "No kiss?"

Why did I do that? I should never have done that. My intuition should have warned me.

---

1 The Great Gatsby by F. Scott Fitzgerald

2 The Great Gatsby by F. Scott Fitzgerald

For a moment, his eyes turned mischievous. I'd slid his hands from my waist to where my back began to curve. My brows rose at the look in his eyes. We kissed.

## Supreme

*Sitting in my empty bed*
*Thinking of a kiss that stole my soul*
*Branded me, bonded me, never let me go.*
*The eyes were oh so gentle,*
*Cloaked in passions true*
*The hands, they were a roaming,*
*As hands are wont to do.*
*The touch was firm and sensual.*
*An intimate delight.*
*Man, I truly have never been the same since that night.*
*Lovemaking is a marvel.*
*I've been blessed- I know that's true.*
*But that kiss was otherworldly.*
*How'd you do what you do?*
*It's been years, still, I remember*
*Like it happened yesterday.*
*And when I lie alone at night, my mind begins to play.*
*My soul forever altered, after your lips touched mine*
*My knees get weak; my body melts; my limbs all but unwind.*
*You should've warned me first*
*Though I would not have believed the tale.*
*A kiss, who knew, could alter the marrow of my cells.*

*I shake my head in awe of other things you've done.*
*You may not have been first, but you indeed are number one.*

I think I always thought " weak in the knees" was a metaphor. Now I knew it was literal. One kiss. Then another and a third. And when we parted. I grabbed his chest. Not sensually. For balance.

I was dizzy.

I was floating.

I was not the same woman who had met him for dinner so many hours ago.

I wanted to make love to him, but I was terrified to. I walked away, glancing back all the way.

The next day, we talked. He asked what I was doing, and I said, "Getting ready for a date," He paused. I could feel the hurt on the line.

There was so much I wanted to say, "It was already planned. I'm not looking for a relationship. I'm running away, trying to convince myself that you did not just make me yours last night - with a smile and three kisses."

But I just said, " It was already planned, and you and I didn't plan a second date, and I just got divorced. I'm not looking for a relationship right now. You knew this."

I heard the confusion in his pause like he was saying, "Did she not feel what I felt last night? Does it not matter to her?"

Yes, I felt it. And I was terrified to let it matter.

This dating was supposed to be fun. An adventure. Confidence building. Casual.

I was supposed to get back to feeling normal.

He made me feel anything but normal.

And the idea of a man, any man, having that much control of my mind, my body, my emotions was absolutely unacceptable.

I would not be that woman, needy for his time, attention, affection, lost without it, ever again. I was going to be different. Stronger. Less vulnerable. Unable to be hurt.

It was just a first date, after all. He shouldn't be so attached. I wasn't.

I was.

I absolutely was.

He should not have put all that (whatever that was) on me. It might not have been a Gatzby party, but that date was too much.

He asked too much.

He was Gatzby with an impossible dream. A dream I could have fulfilled had he met me pre-marriage, but he was a trucker, always on the road. He was a momma's boy, living in her house. He did not have his own vehicle and had borrowed his sister's for the date; getting her car from her was why he had been slightly late.

Not to mention, I had already married two men who earned three times less than I did, then left me in charge of the finances, and who had me feeling so masculine because I was the breadwinner, the decision-maker, the responsible one.

And then there was his size. I had just divorced a man who was thinner but hid high blood pressure from me for two years, and six weeks after our divorce, made the grand gesture of going to the doctor (something I'd pleaded for nine years). He'd been diagnosed with diabetes and nerve damage from it, possibly permanent.

I was not going to enter a relationship. Especially not with a morbidly obese man who lived with his mom and had no car.

I did not get divorced to end up there, regardless of his kiss and his smile.

That was final.

I was also confused. How did we even get to the date?

I always asked, "Are you an employed nonsmoker with your own car and place?"

In fact, I had that question saved in my phone's clipboard, so I could simply copy and paste it. I used it EVERY TIME. Without fail. The first step on qualifying who should stay on my list of possibles and who should move to the reject pile. I eliminated the man if the answer was no to any of those questions. We did not talk, did not meet, did not kiss.

Did he lie? Did he not answer? I could have sworn he said yes to all four.

Now I was suspicious and angry. This was all his fault. We should have never met.

I'd told him I was newly divorced. Just casually dating. And he wanted a relationship? I mean, not the day after he met me, of course. But the expectation flowing from him during the conversations we were having was as strong as the chemistry was the night before.

I'd paid for my freedom in cold hard cash- the divorce, giving my ex-husband the funds to relocate (he did pay me back). I had sacrificed to be this single woman, and he wanted me to give it up so soon, in less time than it had taken for me to get divorced? The arrogance, the presumptive audacity. Only a man could think like this. That he arrives, showers you with attention, and your whole life should stop, upend itself, and include him.

Did he ignore everything I said? I was in therapy. Still trying to regroup. I had told him all this. I told him in unequivocal terms, "I can't be with you. I won't be with you."

This hurt, this guilt was his fault. I was trying to take my life back, and he wanted me to compromise, for what? For a smile, a kiss, great conversation, a feeling I had never felt before, an overwhelming rightness in our chemistry, an attraction so undeniable I hurt… hearing his hurt, confused breath on the line.

The following weeks are a blur, but somehow we ended up at my house. On my sofa. Where for the first time in my life, I sat on a man's lap and felt his stomach, not his penis. He kissed me. I wanted him. I took him to my bedroom. The bedroom no man had been in except my husband for 11 years.

He sat on my new bed. The old one had too many bad memories. He sat there reassuring me that his weight would not be an issue. I didn't believe him. I wanted it to be. I wanted a final definite reason, an incontrovertible incompatibility. Stronger than him having no house, no car. Stronger than the nagging question of how we even got here when he did not meet my standards. Stronger than the knowledge that Gatzby's dream was I would grow to want him as my man, that I would heal given enough time, and he would be the one I would choose.

And if I did that, if he was right, then I deserved whatever came my way. I deserved once again to carry more than my share in a relationship, a marriage. I deserved to be disappointed that we were not equally stable and successful, equally yoked. I deserved to long for him to have a place I could come to and never know when that might happen, to be his chauffeur or have to wait on him to get access to a car, or Uber, or Lyft. I deserved to feel like I was dating in my teens again with no control, his mom having more say than I was comfortable with about our ability to see each other. I deserved for him to become an invalid and me to assume the role of nursemaid, something my mom hadn't had to do for my dad till her seventies. I deserved whatever misfortune came my way.

It would have totally been my fault if I had ended up in any of those scenarios. I could have chosen better.

I didn't think that the opposite scenarios could also be true. He could be a provider and later get us a new place. He could buy a car. And he could remain healthy forever.

I had never considered myself a pessimist, but in my head, there was only a set of worst-case scenarios, and sex was right there on my list of expected disasters.

Although body count was super important to me back then, I was willing to increase it by one- him- to kill two birds with one stone:

To finally sleep with this man I had craved since our first kiss and

In doing so, get him and this damn chemistry out of my system.

A sexual disaster would solve everything. I did not predict the reason: no erection, an inability for us, both plus size, to fit together, or just awkward, unsatisfying sex.

I was ready.

How wrong I was.

# The Rain Master

*It's raining outside, can you hear It?*
*Bass and boom and pitter-patter.*
*Crash and clap, rain droplets spatter.*
*And I spin in circles like a top.*
*Grab my hand and make it stop.*
*Pull me close, let my tips linger*
*Dance across me with your finger.*
*Bite my lip, caress my breast.*
*Grind your groin, make my thoughts rest.*
*I want to sink into your splendor.*
*Lick you like a Butterfinger.*
*Purge me of my cares and woes*
*Satisfy me till I doze*
*If only for a little while*
*Replace frowns with erotic smiles*
*You look so delicious; I just stare*
*Imagine your skin luscious, bare*
*Your hands caress and stroke and knead*
*And as we merge, I beg; I plead*
*Don't stop. Don't stop.*
*Oh damn, so good.*
*Soak me like the sodden wood.*
*Outside my door, my windowpane*
*Beat into submission my rabid brain.*
*So all it thinks is you, just you.*
*No other thought but you, just you.*

I fucked up. Really. Fucked up. Colossally. This man should have never had access to my body. I'd had good sex, great sex, mind-blowing sex. I'd been with JJ for six months. But when I was on top, riding myself into oblivion, he cooed, "Slow down. This isn't a race. You don't have to rush to get yours. I'm not selfish." He grabbed my hips, moving me slower than I'd ever moved, half the pace, maybe 1/4 the pace. "We've got all night. I want to savor you."

He met my thrusts with his own. We took each other to the limit. Then beyond, Exotic thrills our heartbeat's song. The marathon. His sighs and moans. His lap became my favorite throne. Positions countless. We made up shit. I was creating poetry in my head: when I could think.

I learned what transcendental meditation was that day. I left my body, saw the first amoeba slide from the primordial ooze, grow legs and take to Earth. I saw planets form. I shot through the Milky Way, rounded Pluto, and came back, reborn, reincarnated into the woman who matched his every thrust, contorted into positions Houdini would have admired. I was transfixed, transformed.

Fucked. Up.

We looked at each other afterward. Saying nothing. Marveling. Stunned.

If I thought we had problems before, they had just begun.

We made dates. He stood me up.

I raved.

He craved me, but the emotions were too intense, and so he'd agree to see me and decide at the last minute, he couldn't do it. That was his excuse.

But every time he called, I said yes. No matter how many times he stood me up. And truthfully, I don't know if he stood me up a lot because I was floored that he had done it even once and remained in my life. No other man had.

But his pull was like a black hole, inescapable, no matter how many times his behavior made me feel rejected, unworthy of even a call, a 5-second text.

He was cruel. I was too, lying in his arms, the lovemaking each time wilder, better, wetter. Each time transformative. And I still told him we couldn't be together. That he wasn't what I wanted. I'd been wrong about the sex, but I wasn't wrong about this.

I had settled in both my marriages.

The first time for a man who hadn't finished college and had no money at all.

The second time for a man who never started college and had no money at all.

Back then, I'd believed a "good woman" was willing to support, build with and nurture the potential of her man. Although I still did believe that to some degree, I expected much more than I had in my twenties or thirties.

Gatzby had a degree, no place of his own, no vehicle, and family/friends/church that gave him abundant excuses to stand me up. There was always a fire to put out somewhere, a cat in a tree to save, and he was the only fireman on Earth.

WE. COULD. NOT. BE. TOGETHER.

EVER.

We could date. Then, when this intensity wore off, we would move on. It was an enjoyable and practical arrangement.

Later he would refer to this as me "making the rules." To me, I was just extending what we had already been doing, dating, into a holding pattern. I didn't want it to progress to a relationship. It was no different from a freelancer who decided to remain in that role rather than become a salaried worker. To me, it was the best of both worlds, freedom, and intimacy.

I didn't think my words; my thinking was like nails in his heart. He wanted to grow, to settle down, to plant roots.

I was unwilling to break the promise I made to myself. I swore that any root planting I did would be with a man who was more stable, more responsible, more available than my exes had been. I promised myself I would choose better. That was the whole reason I got divorced, to stop the pain, and do better. It was an absolute must.

In my mind, committing to Gatzby meant once again choosing a build a man over another adult. I was done with committing to adult-sized boy men. I wanted a fully grown man, and I did not see that in him.

He said that was because I was blind.

I couldn't explain then that The Rose Doctrine was at play here too. If the goal is marriage to save your precious petals, the gardener doesn't matter so much. What matters is he chose the flower to adorn his home. For the first time, I was saying to a man that choosing me was not enough for me to choose him back. His commitment was not the prize I was after. His worthiness mattered more to me.

Taking commitment off the table as the main card a man could play was an incredible feeling to me. Now he, or any man for that matter, would have to actually stand on his own merits.

Could he stand, or would he fall?

Gatzby called this way of thinking me being a "control freak." But I wasn't trying to control any man. I had just decided that men and their relationship titles were no longer going to control me.

It didn't matter to me that he would ask, what if I got that established man, and he treated me like shit? Or was unfaithful? Or stingy? Or neglectful? Or horrible in bed? What if the man I wanted lost it all?

I'd answer, "I've been treated like shit by the boy men who weren't stable or successful, so at least it would be a step up." My standards of him treating me BETTER, him being emotionally and mentally mature, would weed out boy men who acted like that anyway. I was also convinced that my ideal man, unlike both my former husbands, would be resilient, able to get anything he lost back.

I didn't have an answer for the sex.

Gatzby was the first man who had wanted commitment after my divorce, and there was something satisfying and healing in saying, if only in my head, "I don't want it. I don't need it. I'm PERFECTLY FINE without it." I don't think I had ever thought or felt that way before. In 2015, I would have agreed with every woman who said she WANTED a man; she didn't need him. Now, I don't feel that way- I both want and need a man, but that is a conversation for another day.

I remembered I'd also had another reason to turn him down. We were incompatible. "We argue. I never argue with anyone, but I do with you. We can't get along."

"That's only because you frustrate me because I want you and can't have you. You just won't believe that I am self-sufficient. That

I'm with my mom to help her, not the other way around. You won't believe I'm totally healthy, that I'm responsible."

"It's been a year, and you have no car, still. You've stood me up more times than I can count. Why would I ever think you're responsible? Because you claim it? Not good enough."

All he heard was that he was not good enough.

But in one area, he was not only good enough, he was too good.

*I've never been drunk on wine or booze,*
*you are my drug sublime.*
*I've developed a tolerance,*
*Need more and more,*
*Your essence sates my mind.*
*Your kisses are ambrosia.*
*Your touch? It's heavenly.*
*I've lost count of orgasms and positions*
*when you're loving me.*
*I'm good, I know, can drive you wild.*
*You, too are oh so rare.*
*Impeccable.*
*So edible.*
*Strong, sensual delight.*
*You bend me, twist me, pretzel, spank me,*
*Drown in my delights.*
*I throb.*

*I shake.*
*I shiver more.*
*I give it all right back.*
*You moan, you growl, you flip me over and*
*Take me from the back.*
*I kiss you like you're fine as wine from head to toe;*
*You groan.*
*Pleasing you is like a drug*
*It gets me in the zone.*
*And once I'm there, the whole world stops.*
*Becomes centered in you.*
*Nothing exists when we make love.*
*Just pleasure and us two.*

**Lesson 3:**

Now I can say to you, , beware the maintenance man may be laying crack pipe.

CHAPTER 4

# Delve

My escape came from Facebook.

A comment on a post in a group called OG 35. Brilliance. Eloquence. Insight. Wisdom. Maturity. I clicked on the profile pic, and I was floored for the second time in my life. The man in that picture had walked out of my dreams into flesh- the perfect face, the perfect body, absolute perfection. I inboxed him. Left my number. He replied with his. I saw his text an hour later, called, and we spent 5 hours on the phone.

## Date Thirty-Five:

The Muse_and I sat at a lunch meeting the next day, then watched a movie. I didn't ask my four questions. I didn't even remember they existed.

The sun was bright in the sky, high noon, as we walked towards each other on the sidewalk outside a downtown movie theater. He was still perfect, bronze, muscled calves like works of art.

We stood before each other and kissed before we even said hello. My hand slid into his, and we walked into the mall, grabbed some Chipotle, and sat. I felt lucky to be there with him. Just sitting next to him felt like winning the lottery. The food was horrible. I barely ate a bite. The movie was a blur. I just felt his hand in mine and was happy.

We went to his place, a crammed with too much shotgun house on a too narrow street passed down to him from deceased parents. I hated it. His window unit kept his room cool. The rest of the house, including the bathroom, was stifling. The most unromantic date I'd ever been on.

The best date I'd ever been on.

I didn't go home till 10. We talked and cuddled and kissed all day. It was the kind of conversations you didn't even know you wanted to have, didn't even know you could have: raw, real, revealing. It was a nakedness I didn't know I'd longed for, didn't know I needed. But once I felt it, I was hooked. I wanted to know everything, to share everything, to experience everything with this man. This man who felt like my best friend, my soul mate, my fantasy all rolled into one- in all of two days.

People always ask on social media, "Do you believe in love at first sight?" Before that day, that walk down the sidewalk, that glimpse of his profile pic, I would have said no. Now, I only have one answer, yes.

I've experienced it. I nicknamed him "The Muse."

Gatzby did not come to mind once.

When I left The Muse's, I called Gatzby. I told him what had happened- briefly, the experience feeling too magical to divulge details. One Facebook post. One DM. One number exchange. One date. A decision I would stop seeing Gatzby and see The Muse.

It was 2016. Gatzby had been in my life a year : May 2015- May 2016. I walked away believing The Muse was the man I had waited all my life for. The man of my dreams. Mr. Right. HIM.

I didn't think about Gatzby, his shock, surprise, abandonment, how he must have felt betrayed, led on, lied to. If I HAD thought about it, I would have thought I TOLD him we could never be together (all the time), he HAD to expect me to leave.

In fact, if I had thought deeper, I'd have thought that he and I had been set free. The spell over us was finally broken. He could find someone who accepted his size, living situation and life on the road, and I could have a man with no reason to stand me up, no conflicted feelings about wanting me.

The Muse was our escape clause.

By the second time The Muse and I saw each other, we were in a relationship. We talked every day. I was on summer break from school. He called me any spare moment as he drove the company vehicle, his only vehicle. Once again, a man who had not met my standards- he had no car. And the Houston heat I experienced in his home? I didn't understand how he could live there. You couldn't cook or even use the restroom without sweating buckets. That first week, I thought I'd made a mistake. He saw something that needed to be fixed and couldn't/wouldn't do it. He reminded me of my ex-husband who had been in denial about his impotence.

Then I came over, and The Muse had bought a whole house air conditioner. I was floored. Stunned. He wasn't an excuse maker. He was a doer.

We spent each weekend together, working out, me helping him work on his house. Going on day trips. Exploring new restaurants, tourist locations. Having been married to two homebodies, I'd never been anywhere. Now, I was everywhere. He bought me "just because" gifts. I was in LOVE, LOVE.

He was out of my league. So sexy. So suave. So worldly. His previous career as a photographer left him with a portfolio of thousands of photos, some of celebrities. He'd attended places and events I'd only seen on tv. He was glamorous, debonair, brilliant, thoughtful, and the third worst lover I'd ever had.

I was so in love that I cried about it when I was alone and ignored it when we were together. Fate seemed cruel. It gave me the best lover I'd ever had in the body of a man I couldn't commit to, and the man that I fell in love with at first sight had no rhythm, no stroke, no stamina, no skills… at all. I tried to teach him, coach him. It was pointless. For the second time in my life, I accepted that I would have basically a sexless relationship.

But this time *was* different. If that was the 20% I had to sacrifice, the 80% made the compromise seem like a fair bargain. I had never felt so alive, so me. I only needed to mention I wanted something, and I had it.

The part of me that I had buried, the writer- she was peeking out from the dungeon. As a child, I'd vented on paper. That was safer in my dad's authoritarian household. My journals had been my sanctuary. My first husband had read them- all. Mocking me. Misinterpreting what I wrote. I'd poured my virginal lust on pages instead of acting on it. But he didn't believe that. He believed I'd slept with every man I fantasized about, that what was only imagination and fantasy was step by step reality. I threw away my journals, my poetry. They felt sullied and beyond repair.

And when I remarried, I still found it hard to find that place of complete transparency where my words flowed onto the page.

The Muse was intrigued by me being a published poet. Though I couldn't show him my publishing credits. I'd written in the two years between marriages, but not once till my second divorce.

Once my first husband felt I was spending too much time reading, so I came home from work one day, and he had taken all my books and set them outside on the patio where the rain had drenched them from 6 AM to 3 PM. I did not have a single book left intact, and the copies of my three publications were there. Sodden clumps of pulp like a handful of mud in my fingers.

Dating The Muse, I started to write again

I finished this whole book and tried to come back to elaborate on that sentence. But I can't. I do not have the words to describe what coming back to writing was like after 11 years away from it. I don't have the words to explain what feeling safe was like (as a writer, a thinker) after spending 16 years of my life NOT doing one thing that makes me who I am.

So I simply state it again. Dating The Muse, I started to write again

On February 19, 2016, I wrote, "He started calling me, "his Zen." That's the third time in my life I've been called that, in college, at work, and now in my relationship. I wanna perform as Zen. *Zen*, I like the name. Unflappable. Unperturbed. Immovable. Unfazed by applause or rejection. Centered. Complete."

I signed up for an open mic as Zen. We went. They applauded my good-naturedly. "She's a virgin," the host had said, "And we love virgins, 'cuz virgins are always.."

"TIGHT," the audience answered.

I smiled, then read my poem- "Blue Water, Green Tree." I'm an English teacher, an expressive reader, dramatic even, but I'd never experienced this.

The silent bated breath. The eyes. The nods. The smiles. The feeling was electric. The compliments unexpected. The Muse captured it on film and then drove me to his home raving, more excited than any man, any person had been about anything I had ever done in life. I watched him, my cheerleader, feeling so proud of me. I felt proud of myself. I felt with him at my side, I could do anything. I had a binder of rejection letters from college and the two years between my marriages. A binderful to get three acceptances. I wanted to earn his pride again. To justify his faith once more. I started submitting. And got accepted. Again, Again. Again. 10 times in ten months. I'd been accepted 3 times in 45 years. He was my muse. I began working on a book. He designed some chapter illustrations.

Then he became inspired. He wanted to make more money. How could he do it? What could he do? We brainstormed, came up with cyber security. He needed a computer for the class. I gave him my son's barely used one. He was on his way.

I wanted him to get a car also. Being a chauffeur had begun to wear on me, I found him one, cheap, reliable. He bought it. By the time he sprung on me that we were "incompatible," I'd helped him complete a class that tripled his pay and inspired him to get an air conditioner and find a car.

Now I was the one shocked, surprised, abandoned, feeling betrayed, led on, lied to. We'd exchanged keys to cars and houses. Talked about marriage. I'd even accepted our abysmal sex life. If that was the price for this synergy where both of us were making money, living our dreams, if that was what it took to be one half of this power couple, I would pay that pound of flesh.

I'd passed my biggest test a month before, Gatzby had called out of the blue. His name and number were still saved on my phone, and I had accepted the call. We had talked, a poignant conversation walking down memory lane. I remembered our passion, and wanted it badly, needed it badly, sex-starved for the second time in my life. But I had told him not to call me again and deleted his name and number. I had chosen my bed, and I was going to lie in it.

And regardless of the dismal sex, I'd been happy to luxuriate in this bed. This sanctuary made me feel safe to be fully, vulnerably, ME. The writer, the thinker, the creative, the artist- this side of me that I had never shown anyone. Not even myself, in its full glory. She was here. She was thriving. He was why.

## Axis

*Who knew when I met you that you would shift my orbit,*

*My rotation would stop, envelop you, then resume with you at the center.*

*My foundation.*

*My inspiration.*

*And that I would be magnetized, energized, galvanized by your presence, your thought, your word.*

*Every moment emblazoned on my psyche.*

*Your essence key*

*To my proliferation.*

*I sit here reaching for you*

*But you're not here*

*No answers*

*No respite*

*No recourse.*

*My axis is gone*

So I couldn't believe the last week of my relationship with The Muse. I'd met him before Mother's Day in the year after his mother and father died. Separately but consecutively, one of his parents followed the other into the afterlife like a modern-day Romeo and Juliet.

He was grieving, lost.

Some days- holidays, special days, he was so depressed, it was scary. I got him through Mother's Day, Father's Day, their birthdays, their anniversary, Thanksgiving, Christmas, Memorial Day, Valentine.

And when my grandmother began to die, he broke our pattern of spending Sunday together and took me home, crying, and left me there, crying … alone.

I was the one shocked, surprised, abandoned, feeling betrayed, and used. I'd never needed him emotionally before.

And when I did, he wasn't there.

And as far as our "incompatibility," it was only sexual, and I was the one suffering. He called himself, "sexually reserved," said he put his sex drive "on pause" after his divorce, and couldn't really seem to restart it. So I was the one horny, unsatisfied, and he was probably mortified, but I had stopped trying to have much sex at all.

He disappeared three days, this man I had talked to every day for ten months, and then told me we were incompatible, and our relationship was over. And then disappeared for six days. Wouldn't return my calls or texts. He blocked me from his social media. He still had my keys. I still had his stuff at my house. I packed it up, and on the seventh day, Sunday, drove to his house just as the sun was rising. He was coming out of his house, wouldn't let me in. We exchanged keys, and that was that. Except for a slight flicker of pain on his face, not another word.

*In your desert, I planned to be the hidden spring*
*that you could sip from.*
*A cactus leaf, with nectar to quench your parched throat.*

*In your storm, I vowed to be the eye. The calm. The center.*
*The lighthouse keeping you on track, away from the reefs and breakers.*

*In your turmoil, I sought to be the cool washcloth,*
*the hand on the shoulder.*
*I sought to be the rainbow after the flood.*

*I was all this.*

*I expected all this.*

*I got a canteen, an umbrella, and a cold shoulder in return.*

*Six days and nights of silence as I trudged bare footed through a wasteland.*

*A turmoil of questions sand stormed my path.*

*In my raging sea, you left me to drown.*

> My editor said the format of this poem was different from all the others; she's right. It begins with my expectations- three stanzas, three promises, three goals, and what I felt would be my reciprocation. Then the separation. The isolation. The lines can't follow each other, single file, because each was a separate realization, an epiphany on its own, a separate betrayal and devastation.
>
> My poetry will not be consistent. It was not written for this book, or for an audience. It was written to release the ache within, and its form will vary with the intent and the content.

The last Sunday we spent together, we'd gone to church. Ironically, I was the one who had started us going. He hadn't been in years. I was craving spirituality, looking for something deeper, and religion had been where I'd gone before. But like the sex I had with

The Muse, the services were empty, barren, only a few flickers of connection so faint as to almost seem like mirages.

During the service, the pastor had mentioned fornication, which was totally off topic from the gist of the entire sermon. It was a non sequitur that I almost all but ignored.

After church, The Muse took me out to eat at my favorite place that he'd introduced me to, and asked me, "What'd you think of the sermon?"

I shrugged, "It was ok."

"Hypothetically, what would you think about us becoming abstinent. Like the pastor said."

I smirked, a half -hearted laugh erupted, soft, angry, and bitter, "If I'd wanted to be abstinent, I would have stayed married."

I was silent. Seething. Sex had been the thing that had turned my marriage from loving and perfect to distant and cold. At its end, I spent each night lying next to a man who didn't touch me for 8 months, didn't speak to me unless it was about the kids or the bills, didn't even look at me. The man who had unilaterally decided then announced our sex life was over, and I needed to adjust. The man who had told me I was selfish because I wanted him to get examined by a doctor when he was clearly uncomfortable talking about this problem he wouldn't even name.

Me.

The Muse had just asked *me* if I would *voluntarily* choose abstinence. How could he even form those words? Over lunch? In public? In casual conversation? As if the lack of a sex life hadn't changed my entire life.

If I could have just done without it, we wouldn't even be sitting there eating Cajun pasta and breadsticks.

I would be happily married and abstinent.

He didn't know me at all.

Yet he was offended I didn't want to hear his reasoning.

I couldn't hear his reasoning and still respect him.

I knew sitting there, our relationship was over. But I hadn't accepted it. I couldn't accept that I had made the same mistake again.

When my ex-husband Drew became impotent, I learned where sex stood on his list of priorities. It was an option, dessert, not the main course. Totally skippable.

I hadn't known that, dating pre-marriage, even for the first two years. I had not known till he couldn't perform, and it was suddenly stripped from the menu of services offered in my husband's establishment. And I was told I could accept it, or I could find another provider, just as long as I was discreet and respectful of our home.

Now my boyfriend had stopped speaking to me for three days because I "laughed at him when he was being serious," and because I "didn't listen to his reasoning" on abstinence.

I couldn't listen. He had just shoved an icepick into the deepest wound in my heart without even batting an eye.

I had thought I could have love and sex and compatibility and inspiration, all in one place, with this man, in our relationship. And now, I realized I hadn't ever asked what role sex would play in our relationship. How important it was to him. If it was a priority. I had assumed it was. I was wrong.

Nevertheless, I had no regrets regarding this time spent with The Muse. I'd learned I could love again. Believe again. Trust again. And I had ten publishing credits. In fact, the day that The Muse broke up with me, my poem "Monopoly of Marriage: debuted in Jonah magazine. I was, once again, not the woman who had begun this relationship. I was transformed.

Transformation is an amazing thing. It's a major topic of this book, and I think it's about time we deal with another significant topic - social constructs and philosophies, or mindsets.

I used to be a very religious person; though, I would not have called myself that. I can best explain my mindset shift through a parable. Let's say there are two people- seeker one and seeker two. Both start out on a dimly lit path and move towards the light, which seems bright, warm, and welcoming. When seeker one reaches the light, she builds a fortress to house that light, and it lights her whole house, her whole life. She becomes devoted to that light and would fight to protect that light from anyone or thing that might extinguish it. Seeker one is no longer a seeker but has become a devotee, a devotee of the light of religion.

Seeker two, likewise finds the light, but in exploring the light, learns how to turn it off, and when it is turned off, seeker two sees another light. Seeker two then realizes there are many lights, and each one illuminates different landscapes, provides different experiences. Each one leads to more enlightenment. Seeker two knows that in pursuing the other lights, she will have to walk away from the current light and go into partial darkness, semi confusion, and maybe even frustration. But seeker two is a philosopher, a lover (philo) of wisdom (soph). Security is not the goal, exploration is. And the idea that one's life can be spent going from light to light, from landscape to deeper, higher, better landscape, is thrilling and intoxicating and worth the effort and the search.

For the first several decades of my life I was the devotee. In the last seven years, I became a full-fledged seeker.

That also meant that those lights led me to see that the foundations I had built my life on, like The Rose Doctrine, were not laws and were not even morality. They were social constructs. Social constructs designed to keep me within the four walls devoted to one light, restricted to very limiting measures of my worth.

A law is scientific. No one has to tell you what goes up comes down. You knew that before you ever learned the word gravity. Likewise, your conscience can guide you on morality- what brings you peace, what causes you inner turmoil.

Social constructs are those ideas that have been accepted and pushed on others by members of society. For example, when I was growing up, the streetlights coming on meant I should be home. That's not a law. That's not morality. But ask someone 20 and younger what streetlights meant in their household, and you might be met with a blank stare. Mores and norms have changed. So as you go through this book, you will see me come to grips with and often discard as harmful, repressive, and false social constructs I was raised with.

For example, virginity is a fact. Losing virginity equaling the loss of value is a social construct. If a girl is riding a horse and gets jolted violently, breaking her hymen, she does not fall to the ground and get up uglier. She may have no idea that she no longer has a symbol of something prized in many societies.

I hope as you read this book, you begin to delve.

**Lesson 4:**

Delve: Discuss what role sex will play in your relationship before committing. Dig, excavate, uncover what social constructs you've accepted as laws or as morality that aren't at all.

# CHAPTER 5

# Explore

Before I get into my reaction to the break-up, I want to pause here for a minute and address what may be the elephant in the room. Two years, four sexual partners. Some people are reading this book and haven't even noticed that. Others have been keeping count. The dreaded "body count."

First, we'll address that. Then I'll bring up a closely related topic, the "Hoe Phase," before we delve back into the story.

Mores are changing. Many girls may no longer be raised on The Rose Doctrine, and maybe where you live, body counts are a non-issue. I was raised to think they were a big issue. I expected to have one lover for life- the first man I was engaged to, then two- my first husband, and when three came around, it really bothered me. Four was my second husband, and part of the reason I stayed so long was NOT wanting to increase that number.

Some people might say, "Every woman has a whore/hoe phase." I don't believe that. But I'd never presume to speak for every woman. I'll just say, I found it ludicrous at 50 that I was worried about some critic out there, some future boyfriend/husband/date scoffing at my number. Who gave him the right to decide how many partners I should have? It seemed to echo the birth control debate. Insurances would often cover Viagra but not birth control for women. I guess in their minds, the consequence of having sex was motherhood. If women weren't trying to procreate, we shouldn't be having sex.

In my mind, I'd gotten *more* discriminating about my sexual partners, not less. From 18-43, I had gone on 6 first dates with different men. All six dates later turned into relationships. Four of those relationships became sexual. Two of them became marriages.

So that was 4 out of 6, or in other words, a man dating me then had a 70% chance of sex. Although I only recorded 101 dates in this book, there were 147 and 8 lovers total, including the 4 from chapters 1-4. That means a man had a 5% chance of sex with me from the time I was 43 till now. I'd hardly call that a hoe phase. Twelve is a nice round number, above the average seven lifetime partners (I read somewhere). So the idea of a "Hoe Phase" seems farfetched to me, again according to whom on what grading scale?

Some people think knowing the "body count" tells them something about a person. I wonder what that something is. Does it tell you a person is frigid or promiscuous? What number equals which? Does it tell you he or she can or can't be faithful? How?

I believe that I was born in interesting times when a woman like me could write a book like this to talk about my life and the society that shaped the people I met. I see my journey as representative of other women's; those who shed The Rose Doctrine, the obsession with being chosen by a man as commitment worthy, the bondage of constantly worrying about her body count or what she did/said/wore that could get her called a hoe. We are women, biologically mature adult females, and we are ladies, classy and respectable, and it's not your judgments that make either so.

After the break-up, I spent a day stunned, heartbroken (I actually don't think I'd fully gotten over the loss till writing this book, an unexpected catharsis).

Then I thought of Gatzby.

I was horny.

I'd been horny so long that it had become like an ache, like an old war wound I felt with every motion.

I'd deleted Gatzby's number.

I tried to see if it was in the cloud somewhere, nope.

I went back to my ATT statement ten months before and found the three most frequently dialed numbers. #1, nope, #2, no dice, #3, Gatzby.

I was embarrassed, apologetic, rambling incoherently, explaining what happened. He was sympathetic. He wanted to see me. Needed to call me back. I hung up. Then I felt confused. I was wet. Why?

Shit. I forgot what it felt like to be aroused.

THAT was stunning. I had been in LOVE, **LOVE**, but sometime, long ago, I had stopped feeling aroused. I let that realization sink in.

Then, I waited all night for a call that never came.

I called him back the next day. Why didn't you call?

"I did," he said.

"I didn't get a call."

"Did you block me?"

I checked. Yep, I did. He had called. Like seven times.

He said, "I'm on my way."

He came, walked through the door, and enveloped me. We didn't speak, just stripped and fell into each other.

I was not gentle. I clawed up his back. He did not mind.

He was not gentle. He left palm prints on my ass, pulled my hair so hard I winced. I did not mind.

We made love till we could no longer move.

He said, "You're never leaving me again. You're mine."

I said nothing. I didn't trust what I would say.

To him, us making love meant I had never loved The Muse. That wasn't true. I hurt deeper from his loss than either of my two divorces.

## Synopsis, to all the you's I've loved.

*I can erase you from my Tango, erase you from my phone,*
*erase you from my timeline, but the memories aren't gone.*

*I can wash away your fragrance, drop off all you owned,*
*But a piece of me is altered, a part of me seems gone.*

*I picture me at 20, like an uncut diamond.   Prime.*
*Full of life. Full of love. leaving sheltered life behind.*

*Naive and full of promise, with no ceiling overhead.*
*My first boyfriend's lies trash my name, reputation dead.*

*On to 22, sex is all brand new*
*But insecurities bloom fully*
*When critique is all you do,*
*And suddenly forever*
*evaporates like morning dew.*

*24 brings marriage, babies, bills*
*The bliss of young love turned to chills,*
*Rejection, infidelity, selfishness galore*
*Was l the only one signed up to love, honor, adore?*
*Two things I couldn't picture happened right before my face.*
*Security and commitment usurped by hatred and disgrace.*

*31, disgusted… all men do is seem to lie.*
*I make a list of 10 traits I wish HE would live by*
*And when I couldn't hold much longer, you came like summer rain.*
*For a moment, you seemed to wipe away all my pain.*
*But you were a runner, when challenges arose*
*Leaving me alone glaring problems nose to nose.*
*Hardest things I've ever done, I had to face afraid*
*You left me feeling worthless, broken, and betrayed*

*43 And starting over,*
*a half a lifetime gone,*
*I hit the internet for frivolity and fun*
*Didn't know it was a whirlpool that could suck up all my time,*
*Didn't know I'd wade through fuckboys like slidin down soul train's line.*

*46, and older, wiser, stronger, more secure*
*But unsure how many new starts I can endure.*

*I can erase you from my Tango,*
*But a song still brings you near.*
*I can erase you from my timeline*
*That doesn't stop the fears,*
*Of lost time, lost money, new scars*

*I guess somewhere inside me, like a pack of nesting dolls*
*Is the love, trust, hope, and certainty that exists behind my walls*

The next six months were frustrating. Gatzby took standing me up to a whole new level. He felt justified. I had left him for a whole other relationship. I told him his feelings were illogical. We were never together.

He said, "Then why does it bother you I stand you up?"

I'd say, "It's disrespectful to stand anyone up."

Then came the fence.

After a local thunderstorm, my fence was never the same. The homeowner's association was hounding me. I had homeowner's insurance and a $1000 deductible. I couldn't afford the deductible. Gatzby said he could fix it. I told him it really needed to be done.

I'd gotten two estimates. The cheapest was $700. He told me he could do it for $200. We went to Home Depot, bought the materials. They sat for a month. I got fined $25 from my HOA. I hounded him more. They sat for another two months. Two more fines. $75 total. I stopped speaking to him. Texted him to lose my number,

San Antonio was ecstatic. He HATED Gatzby, said Gatzby treated me like shit, that all his excuses were bullshit.

During these three months, Gatzby and I barely communicated, much less saw each other. Later he would say that he was having health issues. He hadn't wanted to see me because I already had this complex about his size and what that meant for his health, and he didn't want his health concerns to add fuel to the fire.

At the time, so many things went through my mind. When I came back after The Muse, Gatzby claimed he'd moved out, got a car, and that his mom got sick again, and he moved back, and he crashed his car. That I "missed" the proof that he was self-sufficient and financially stable.

That was convenient.

With his more frequent absences, our distance, I thought he might be married.

Anyway, he said he wanted me to believe in the possibility of us, that we could have more than just sex, and I gave him the fence.

And he worked on it one day, replaced three boards, and never tended to it again.

I hated him. I felt embarrassed talking to the HOA, embarrassed giving the news that he'd done nothing to my sister and San Antonio.

I started dating again while I tried to find a contractor I could afford.

## Date Thirty-Six:

King Kong_had the biggest dick, according to a picture he showed, that I'd ever seen. Too big to attempt, in fact. Well, him showing me that picture backfired.

## Date Thirty- Seven:

Prinz was a longshoreman covered in tattoos and muscles, but he gave off so many mixed signals our whole date that a string of questions from the song "Controversy" was playing in my head.

## Date Thirty- Eight:

Don Juan Daffy Duck- I was actually having a really good time with him, although he smiled really hard and big like elementary school kids who haven't gotten used to their teeth yet. We started making out in my car after a movie. He totally ruined the mood by trying to talk sexy but sounding more like a cartoon character. I stopped kissing and wanted to say, "Do it again. Do it again." but was afraid I would laugh. I've never found cartoon characters sexy, so that was the end of romance for us.

## Date Thirty- Nine:

Game Boy spent our whole date on the phone, checking on the online game that he'd left to meet me.

## Date Forty:

Nazcar- showed me all his Nascar pictures and rushed our date to make sure he was back home for the opening ceremonies.

## Date Forty-One:

One Minute Nate was sexy, very desirable, and we met at Tutti Fruity for frozen yogurt. He got excited over our first kiss. Too excited. Stain on pants excited. I didn't know men in their 40's still did that.

For the first five or so months after The Muse, I wrote very little. But followers on Tango kept asking, so eventually, I started posting poems again. And one day, there was a DM that stood out. I had posted something pretty metaphysical and didn't really expect anyone to read it or respond. He did both, understanding the totality of the poem on such a level that I almost wondered if I had somehow plagiarized his brain. We exchanged numbers and, for a week or two, talked. Conversations I had never had before. Metaphysics, crystals, meditation, astral projection, and more. Once, I would have never even let these be mentioned to me. It was unorthodox, heresy, satanic, I'd once been told.

But those same people who warned me against sage burning, tarot, palm reading, and horoscopes had gone silent in the face of real evils like the sexual abuse I'd experienced as a child and the domestic violence I faced as an adult. Their judgment seemed suspect to me now.

I thought about meeting Mystique, but two things stopped me. One, he was celibate till he met the woman he planned to marry. You already know how I felt about that. Two, he wouldn't go out with me unless I deleted my profiles and saw only him.

Now, I was no stranger to exclusivity, and I had given it to JJ for six months and Gatzby for even longer, although neither had ever asked. It was organic. Something I wanted to do because my needs were met, and I had what I wanted at the time and did not need to look any further. But a man demanding it even before a first date screamed entitlement to me. I heard his arguments- Mystique didn't want to compete. He wanted to know I was truly invested, focused; not distracted by other men. He wanted to build trust and couldn't see spending money on a woman who was still "looking" at and for other men. To me, these all said insecure, controlling, and premature. To me, it harkened back to the days of yore when Old Maids wrung their hands hoping for a male glance and felt oh so honored when male interest came their way and did anything to keep it.

His stimulating conversation was not proof of relational compatibility. In fact, after The Muse, I didn't plan on committing to someone unless we were sexually compatible, and he was celibate. I was NOT committing to a man who might leave me high and dry, double entendre intended, literally.

I declined. He hung up, and I expected I would never hear from him again.

But he had me thinking, researching, exploring, and I wrote this:

*In the beginning was the Word, and the Word was God.*
*And that Word told Adam and Eve that they could eat from all the trees of the garden*

*but*
*The tree of knowledge.*
*You are knowledge infinite.*
*I see it, recognize it, crave it like Eve did the power to become as God,*
*having access to all that is hidden*

*That desire destroyed a perfect Eden,*

*Whether it is Pandora or Eve, the story is the same, search for*
*forbidden knowledge*
*and be cursed, bring suffering and shame to all*
*You embrace all ways of knowledge as coming from one Source.*
*I see one way as Truth, and all others as deception.*
*You believe all knowledge is divine.*
*I believe that just as a child may be too young to learn certain truths,*
*mankind as a species is immature to handle the unknowable.*

*For you darkness, the unknown, is something to be embraced,*
*something you claim*
*as your identity.*
*I am a child of the light, having come out of darkness.*

*You seek knowledge.*
*I seek Love.*

*If Eve had chosen love over knowledge,*
*mankind would have ruled over the Earth*
*in its perfection.*
*But she chose knowledge and fell.*
*Although I have not found my Adam yet, I choose to love him.*

*In another life, I might have sat under a cassava tree feeding you figs and nectar,*
*fanning your face after you preached to our tribe,*

*In this one, I chose my path.*

*You are darkness, the unknowable, the hidden, the occult.*
*I choose to walk in the light.*

Reading that poem now, I have mixed feelings, as you probably noticed in Chapter Two when I mentioned my feelings on Eve. Once, I too blamed her for seeking knowledge, now I applaud her. Once I saw her search as a betrayal of her love for God and her man. Now I feel that she should never have been asked to choose between self-actualization and spirituality or love.

Back then, I saw light and dark as separate, opposite. Now, they are a continuum, one arising from the other, one incomplete without the other.

The biggest light in my life then was my sons. Brilliant. Talented. Handsome. I'd put them in college during the summers while in high school. They'd attended the exclusive Wunsche High School that was covered in 60 minutes. A school that required an interview, recommendations, a contract, and excellent grades to be accepted. A school with a waiting list.

They were lights. And sometimes, they were headlights heading straight my way, about to crash into everything I'd tried to build for myself, for them.

I missed having a dad in the house, but not enough to get back with Drew.

## Date Forty-Two:

And then I got a Facebook dm that gave a compliment, a number and asked me on a date I called the number, was impressed with the guy and accepted. Harlee Davidson_and I met at Texas Roadhouse. Leather jacket, cool, laid back, his style drew me in and made me smile.

### The Click

*I wonder if it's only me,*
*I hate partial compatibility.*
*The man who's cute but bores to tears.*
*The fun dude lacking suitable years.*
*The one who's stable with no time.*
*The one who lingers on my mind.*
*But may be too scarred to love again.*
*The one who just wants a "friend,"*
*The mama's boy, the baby maker,*
*The heart broken still pining for his ex, chaser.*
*The one without a thought to share*
*Who looks so cool and debonair.*
*The jealous one, possessive, scary.*
*The one who wants a living Barbie.*

*I hate to say it.*

*Men hate it too.*

*When will a "real man" come through?*

*It matters if you can talk and think.*

*It matters how you dress and eat.*

*They matter, your priorities.*

*a job's not all I want or need.*

*Stability, and intellect*

*Articulate with some respect.*

*Masculine and supportive.*

*Sensual and erotic.*

*No milk toast man will do for me,*

*No feminine wiles I need to see.*

*Shallowness is unappealing.*

*Have something to you worth revealing.*

*Don't make excuses for your faults.*

*Don't point the finger; pay the cost.*

*I'm constantly working on me,*

*I'd like that in my mate to be.*

*Goals, plans, a little discipline,*

*No victim mentality at hand.*

*What once was called - a man's man.*

*Can handle his woman*

*Hangs with the guys too*

*Is balanced about what he needs to do.*

*Has got an edge, an alpha bold.*

*Knows what to do without being told.*

*The man who causes that inward sigh.*

*The anticipatory twinkle in his eye.*

*How I miss you, how I crave you,*

*how I hope to see,*

*You one day standing next to me.*

*A square peg a round hole will not fit.*

*Show up. I wait for our satisfying CLICK.*

The chemistry was intense, electric, heady. The food was great. The conversation steady. I was having fun, and then I remembered the fence.

"What's wrong?" he asked.

"Just something I need to fix. I'll figure it out."

"Maybe I can help."

I told him the story. The storm. The letter from HOA. Gatzby. 3 months. 3 fines. Now the HOA was threatening court.

"I can fix it."

I laughed.

"No, really, I can fix it. This week. I'll need some help; can you get one of your sons?"

"Yeah."

He came over, looked at the pile in the garage, the $200 haul Gatzby said I needed, shook his head, and we bought a whole new set of items. My 22-year-old son helped him. I cooked lunch, dinner, brought them beers and sodas. In one day, it was done. And beautiful. And he and my son had bonded to boot.

The next six months were incredible. Month one, we became committed, after a long conversation in which I asked, was he sure, was he ready. I didn't want to introduce him to my friends, family, kids as my man, and then we break up.

He was ready. He was sure, with a capital S.

I committed. We cooked together, spent weekends together, did chores together, hung out, and had sex. Sex was a problem. His performance. My drive. Once again. Every time I committed; it was an issue. But with JJ and Gatzby, the men I had no title with, sex had never been an issue.

I was so tired of it. Although I wrote the poem below for The Muse, parts of it still fit Harlee. My second try at a relationship after my divorce, and we felt like star-crossed lovers.

*A voluptuous woman in your bed,*
*for most that shit goes to the head.*
*But him, he felt outmatched and drowned.*
*Instead of up, his dick fell down.*
*And that shit sucks; it blows; it stinks.*
*A gorgeous man with sexy winks*
*whose skills in bed are so unsure,*
*you wonder if he's tried before.*
*The fucker can't undress a doll, can't stroke, can't hang, can't fuck at all.*
*You've tried to teach him; that's for sure,*

*But even a pro fails an amateur.*
*Where to begin with his reserve?*
*He blushes just to see your curves.*
*You tame yourself. It's not enough.*
*His bruised ego isn't tough.*
*You're quiet, patient, damn near sleep,*
*But to him, your sex drive is steep.*
*No matter you're in neutral, pause.*
*He lacks the skill to slick your draws.*
*Intimidated, he breaks down.*
*Throws in the towel, forfeits the round.*
*You're matchless, and he knows he's beat.*
*He runs, a rabbit, for the street.*
*You watch him, shattered, having given*
*All the passion from you driven.*
*You sacrificed your soul for love*
*Because his heart fit like a glove.*
*A man he wasn't, a boy instead*
*Who couldn't handle a tigress in bed*
*Such a waste, such loss of time*
*But for a moment, a love sublime*
*Had fired your heart, had filled your head*
*It crashed and burned when bodies met bed.*

My poetry absorbed the brunt of my sexual frustration. I was happy with everything else. And I had my family back. My kids, grown men now but still needing guidance, had a man around they felt comfortable with. I felt maternal and settled and so at peace. Holidays were holidays again. Presents. Food. Family. Extended family. I felt a wholeness I had not felt since the divorce.

I could do this for the rest of my life.

We were even planning our first vacation. Vegas. I'd never been. I was so excited. Summer was coming. We were going.

May 3, 2017- I wrote this in my journal. I titled it Peace. I rarely title my journals, but this one had that one word description, "It is pouring down right now. This time last year and all the years before, I would have hated hearing the rain drops. Rain made me long for physical connection, and it seemed like I was frequently alone when it happened. But this year is different. I'm so much more at peace. Able to embrace solitude, even when it rains. I have more faith in the future, and it has a lot to do with the man in my life. He has weathered many storms, and they've made him calm and decisive, and grounded. He has rubbed off on me. I'm learning to relax in areas where I was a little impatient. And I'm grateful for that lesson."

Then Harlee told me he was filing for bankruptcy. Huh?

He'd just bought a motorcycle four months before and told me to plan a vacation three weeks before. Now he was in over his head, meeting with a lawyer.

Why did he even bring up a vacation? I felt like I couldn't trust his judgment. That peace I had felt suffused with, from his words, his "decisiveness" was ripped away.

I had been happy, content, at peace, and he led me on, made me imagine new adventures and horizons we'd explore. Then abruptly announced that was all a pipe dream.

That was our first fight. And afterward, he was moody. I wrote in my journal that night:

> "Today I saw a man post a question about why women were moody. He was given the answer- hormones. True, but I gave a different response. People are moody.
>
> Men have been moody for centuries, and women have been by and large socialized to cater to men's moods- to not appear too smart, too forward, too provocative, too accomplished, too assertive, too anything. The whole world has revolved around men's moods. We even have sayings like "boys will be boys" to explain away men giving in to their "moods". But now, women are refusing to water themselves down, and for some men, this change is a problem.
>
> The scene from "Coming to America" comes to mind, the woman trained to like whatever the king liked, exaggeration for sure, but a partially accurate depiction of male- female relationships for centuries.
>
> So, deal with it. People have moods. Some are more even tempered than others. But women are no longer socialized (except in the workplace) to hide their emotions for fear of displeasing men.
>
> Also, you, as a man, have a tremendous influence on our moods. Romantic words, kind gestures, compliments, sex, being helpful go a long way with most women. A man with the right skill set learns his woman and knows what to do with each mood.
>
> Women have learned to deal with men's moods for centuries; it's your turn."

I wasn't having his moods, and I wanted an apology. I'd asked him not to even bring up things- like vacations- that were wishful thinking and have me thinking they were something we were going to do. I'd had that done before. I hated it. He apologized. Things went back to normal.

He told me that he didn't "have time for a relationship" a few weeks later. His job had doubled his hours from 8 to 16, and while that would solve his money problems, it meant there was "no time for us."

What? 16 hours? People work that all the time and make relationships work, I said.

Well, he didn't see how he could.

I was dumbfounded.

"I just asked you about being sure, being ready. I didn't want to introduce you to my family and friends if you weren't sure." My mind flitted back to a comment my brother-in-law had made about part of his excitement for the upcoming holidays being centered around who I would bring to dinner. This ironic jab seemed unfounded since I'd only ever brought one person since my divorce, The Muse. Still it stung and made me embarrassed. I'd thought Harlee would be my plus one at all the future family gatherings, but I guess I was wrong.

I remembered when my brother-in-law's comment was made I laughed, picturing the memes about what aunt are you. There was an aunt always with a new boyfriend. Never thought I'd be her when I hadn't even shown up with boyfriend #two yet.

"I know. I'm sorry. I didn't see this coming," Harlee stated, interrupting my thoughts.

"Huh… I thought you were making the decision that whatever came, we would work it out; we would work through it, figure it out. You mean you were telling me you were committing to me only if nothing changed in your life if nothing got challenging?"

I was disgusted. People throw around the word commitment and want to save sex for "relationships" for a title that's supposed to provide security and safety, and longevity.

I'd had more commitment from Gatzby, who kept calling and texting and coming over even when he knew I was still dating and had heard me say probably 50 times since he met me that we couldn't be together. I'd even gone off and had another relationship, and he'd responded when we reconnected, " You're never leaving me again. You're mine."

I had said nothing to Gatzby's comment, had dropped him again after a DM, a first date, a chance at a "committed relationship" with a man with his own vehicle (two of them), his own house, a job that had him home every night.

I pictured a stable home life and family, and I got ALL for six months until his work schedule changed. I found out our plans, our declarations, our "love," our future, all erased by a schedule that could be changed back just as quickly and arbitrarily as it was altered at first.

It felt like deja vu.

My ex-husband, years before, had acted as if going to the doctor and taking me on a date once a month was an impossible task.

Now Harlee saw it impossible to make time for me with a 16 hour a day schedule. He still had days off. But they wouldn't be for me, for us. They were only for him. Alone.

I knew men who had stuck by their wives, their girlfriends, through infidelity, through terminal diagnoses, through mental illness. In both cases, other couples would have easily made this work. Other men would have barely even registered these as challenges.

I felt really disposable.

As much as these men espoused my value, and even though my ex-husband Drew finally did go to the doctor and then spent the entire time I was with JJ, Gatzby, and Harlee trying to convince me to take him back- begging, pleading, apologizing, I still felt…

When I was a little girl, I saw daddy's girls and marveled. So secure. So pampered. So adored.

My father was different. He'd married my mom knowing he was a rebound, a fling, just because she was pregnant,

I might be his, and he'd seen my grandfather beat my mother with his fists when Pappai found out my mother was with child.

It was my father's duty to raise me, not his joy.

And a few times in my life, he let me know this.

I mostly tried to stay invisible, out of the way, and ask for nothing. I wasn't owed anything. He provided all my needs, except the need to feel wanted, loved, appreciated, connected. That came once in a while, like Christmas or my birthday, an unexpected present dropped off unannounced. In fact, I never fully got it till I was grown when my dad apologized and began trying to make up for the wounds he caused.

What was automatic for other children, for other women, seemed to be a tall order for men to give me.

I worked so hard at getting it- that love, acceptance, recognition- security- that feeling that this was my place and nothing or no one could take it from me.

I tried to be the perfect daughter, girlfriend, wife. Let me cater to you.

My actions, attitude, demeanor, appearance, ME, alterable, malleable, like putty in their hands. I was fitted to their mold, trying my best to be perfect for them- the ones I committed to.

Then all that sacrifice, catering, pampering, compromise was no longer good enough. Me asking for next to nothing was still asking for too much.

I was suddenly too visible, My demand for their time, bodies- an inconvenience.

And this time, I felt near my breaking point.

## The Breaking Point

*Sometimes I wonder if it's out there,*

*The point of no return.*

*Especially after reading Facebook posts*

*Damn, some of us been burned,*

*And scarred and changed*

*And warped so badly*

*That it's plain to see*

*The bitterness and suspicion broadcasted so broadly.*

*When I divorced, I feared this most,*

*Not singleness but spite*

*Not loneliness*

*Not emptiness*

*But losing all delight*

*All hope, all faith in men per se*

*Instead seeing just dogs,*

*Users, abusers, pieces of crap,*

*Feral worthless cogs.*

*I've dodged those landmines four years now,*

*But still I've come so close*

*To losing all respect for those with opposite chromosomes.*

*You seemed so special, different all*

*With promises so new*

*But it's all lies six months in.*

*What's a girl to do?*

*Breaking up seems pointless.*

*To do what? Restart the cycle again?*

*Cheating seems so cliche*

*Should we go back to friends?*

*Can't change my orientation though it crossed my mind to try.*

*Just wanna strike out, punish you*

*for now my endless sky is fragmented and shrunken,*

*A broken picture in a frame*

*Because love, commitment, promises*

*Seem like just some kinda game.*

## The Dearest Bill

*I loved a man with a heart so true.*
*Silly me, thought he was you.*
*But I forgot how deep dreams flow.*
*They change the tides*
*Illusions show.*
*They make hell, heaven.*
*Lies are kissed.*
*Signs of betrayal,*
*All but missed.*
*The mind is blind*
*Once love arrives.*
*Bound, gagged*
*Deaf to reason's cries.*
*That's why betrayal's so severe.*
*A sudden drop from heights so sheer*
*Mirages twinge on its facade*
*Heat dancing, an oasis' mirage.*
*A beautiful lie.*
*A well-played part.*
*All it cost was my whole heart*

**Lesson 5:**

So on July 26, 2017, I learned lesson 5A- A title does not equal commitment and lesson 5B- Define commitment.

A month later, Hurricane Harvey hit Houston. The flood took his Harley, a lawnmower I gave him, and the house he'd said he needed time to work on. It took his car too, and he had no way to get to work. And he lost the job that he was working so many hours on. He got evicted. He reached out to me and told me all this. And I said, If we were together, you'd have a place to stay… with me.

He said, I know, and cried.

The flood brought something else. Gatzby.

CHAPTER 6

# Focus

On July 26. 2017, I got dumped for the second time in my life. In high school, in college, I'd had three nonsexual relationships. I'd ended each. I'd been married twice and had one boyfriend between those two nuptials. I'd ended those three. Then The Muse dumped me, and now Harlee.

I didn't handle this second rejection well. How the hell did I go from being the dumper to the dumpee? Gatzby said I was a control freak, and though I'll deny that absolutely and totally, 7/26-8/16/2017 might be the only evidence that might support his description of me.

In fact, I'll call this month my T.I. period, Temporary Insanity.

First, I told Harlee, he wasn't breaking up with me. I wouldn't accept it. Then I tried to figure out solutions that I proposed one after one, none of them viable. After a week, I admitted defeat. I let him go.

The next week is a blur. The third week, I called Gatzby.

I was bitter. Angry. Disappointed. Disgusted. With Harlee. With Gatzby. With men.

I'd gone 6.5 months without good sex, and I was out $75 for the fence Gatzby had promised to fix and never did. I suddenly wanted my money and my pipe.

In my head, both seemed like reasonable asks. I actually felt I was owed both- payment for the inconvenience. It feels strange typing this. But that was how I felt, and I felt utterly justified. And this… is why emotional decisions may be poor decisions.

Maybe I was the one dreaming the impossible dream.

And it was probably not the first time I was making a totally emotional decision. When I met my first husband on my first job out of college in 1994, I had told him we had nothing in common, that we'd never be together. I was attracted to his body, his personality, his intellect, not his face, his background, or his lifestyle. We were opposites.

But I didn't know the power of love. Of feeling loved. I'd never had a man look at me, compliment me, seduce me the way he had. I'd never felt accepted unconditionally, pursued relentlessly, idolized. He put me on a pedestal, and I liked being there. It was the first time in my life I felt princess status, daddy's little girl.

Contrary to popular opinion, it isn't only the women who grow up with no father who desire that unconditional love daddies are supposed to offer. But I didn't know that then.

Anyway, he went around work telling everyone I was his wife.

He'd never spoken to me.

I confronted him, asked why. He said, "You are; you just don't know it yet. You're everything I want in a woman." He rambled off my qualities. He was right about me being all those things. I was impressed. He was observant.

He asked me out. I declined. I thought he was presumptuous, out of line.

He backed off, but not for long.

He would ask. I'd decline. But he kept shining at work. I saw how other women wanted him. But he declined them. He wanted me. I'd never had a man after me who was a "commodity." The idea was enticing. The next time he asked, I would say yes, I decided.

The next day he drove up in the car I wanted, an Audi, black, leather, rims, tint. Sexy AF. That was my car. My absolute dream car. Why was he driving it? He ushered me into it and asked me out again. I said yes. We went out that day after work and had a blast.

After one of our first dates, he'd said, "I know men find you intimidating. You're brilliant, ambitious, accomplished, driven," he nodded appreciatively. "I see inside. Behind those walls, you're just a little girl who wants to be loved."

He was right. So right, I was stunned. I'd never seen myself that way, but when he said it, the rightness of it hit me to the core. So deep, I was never the same again. So deep, I felt that someone understood me for the first time in my life. Someone saw me.

I hadn't even been trying to be seen, but I was, and it felt more incredible than any feeling I'd ever had.

And at that moment, my emotions took over, and I was his. I loved being loved, and I felt loyal to him for loving me.

The fact that we were opposites who had barely met and came from two different backgrounds with two different lifestyles vanished, inconsequential. Love could conquer all.

Temporary Insanity.

When I picked up the phone to call Gatzby, I wasn't angry or bitter or even determined to get back my $75; I was curious. Would he even take my call? We hadn't spoken in 6.5 months. I didn't even remember the last thing I said to him. I'm sure it was something like I depended on you. You failed me. Lose my number.

He did answer. I was surprised.

I fell back into my old pattern with him. Flirtatious banter. Small talk. Gauging his interest. I asked how he'd been. Good. Better than good. He'd reconnected with an ex and was getting married.

"What the fuck? Married? It's been six and a half months. How the hell are you getting married?"

"What are you mad for? You dumped me," he said. 'And aren't you in a relationship?"

"No, I'm not. And who gave you permission to get married."

"Permission? I'm a grown-ass man. What the hell?"

"I don't care how grown you are. You weren't a grown-ass man when you were standing me up, making me wait on a fence you never fixed, costing me $75. Where was the grown-ass man then? Grown-ass men take care of their fucking business. They are men of their word. They aren't liars who break promises to the women depending on them. They don't establish expectations and then fail to follow through. Bitch ass niggas do that."

I actually did not know where these words were coming from. They weren't planned. I'd only cussed two other men out in my life, both on the day I decided to divorce them. Why was I cursing at Gatzby? Why was I livid? What was this really about?

"I don't know who you think you're talking to, and I don't know why you're mad. You got your fence. You got your man. One better than me. So why would I wait around on you, especially after it's the second time you dumped me?"

"We were never together. I can't dump you," I interrupted.

"Well, if we were never together, why the hell are you mad I'm getting married? You didn't want me. Did you actually think no one else did?"

I didn't have answers for any of that. I think I just hung up, or he did. Regardless the call was over. We were over. And he was getting married.

Marriage. He could have it. I'd wish her good luck. They deserved whatever it brought. I hated the word. It was a cage. A prison. One I'd been released from, and most days, I could never see going back to.

Tying the knot. Yes, tied in knots was accurate. The old ball and chain, yes, that was accurate too. I belong to that classification of women that men don't think exists, a woman from a two-parent household who grew up seeing long-lasting marriages. My parents, grandparents, uncles, aunts, cousins- everyone, was married. Not one divorce till I was in 8th grade, and even she re-married and stayed married.

I knew marriage. That was one reason I told both my ex-husbands we came from different backgrounds. They were raised by single mothers. I was raised by both my parents, especially my father, whose word in his house was law.

I knew marriage. I would have never posted that famous question on Facebook- "Why did our grandparents' marriages last and ours don't?" I know how to be our grandmothers. I know why their marriages lasted.

Simple answer - fear. And lots of it.

I felt it walking down the aisle, so strong, much stronger than love.

I was going to be a wife, a mother. It was my job to keep the family strong. If I didn't, it was my fault (fear). People would think I was the problem (fear). I couldn't keep a man (fear), keep a home (fear), keep my children in line (fear). I would have failed as a woman (fear).

Besides the petals of my chastity, this was the real rose that mattered. Stay married at all costs. Compromise. Placate. Please him. Submit.

Those were a wife's duties. God said so. So did society, especially the black community.

The idea that someone's representative can last only three months is false. For me and some of our grandmothers, the representative lasted the whole marriage. Fear extended its lifespan - a lightning bolt of energy to this Frankenstein monster cobbled together from 1/4 image, 1/4 what will people say/reputation, 1/4 you need help providing, 1/4 children need their father/ broken homes are breeding grounds for criminals.

Trained to fear.

Trained that no decent woman is a single mother. Those women that end up like that are broken, selfish, slutty, worthless.

More than anything my husband could do to me, I didn't want to be one of those women, a statistic.

Marriage was a cage.

I don't mean that I didn't love it some days, weeks, months, years.

I did.

It was a wonderful, plush, cushy, stimulating, comfortable .... cage.

So nice, you didn't see the bars till you ran into them one day and wondered what they were. And at first, they didn't bother you. You had so much freedom, so many blessings, and opportunities as long as you stayed in your place.

Ironically, I thought when I left home and got married, I'd experience greater freedom. My husband saw me, knew me, better than my parents, better than I knew myself. What big eyes you have, the better to see you with, my dear. What big ears you have, the better to hear you with, my dear. What big teeth you have, the better to gobble and spit out the parts of you I don't like, so far away you'll never be able to find them, my dear.

I was good at being married. If I had to divide myself into parts, in marriage one, it would have been 1/4 spirituality, 1/4 intellect, 1/4 sexuality, and 1/4 personality. The first three were allowed, the last was forbidden. Marriage two though not physically abusive in any way, only permitted 1/4 spirituality.

Can you even imagine how incredible it was with JJ to express 100% of me? Indescribable. Intoxicating. I was too in love with the freedom to ever fall in love with him.

And then The Muse unearthed another portion that I didn't even realize was a crucial part of me, the artist- creative expression. I was no longer 100% but 125%. Bigger. Better. Expanding. Growing. A whirling dervish. A Tasmanian devil. A nexus. A nebula. I just had to nix my sexuality, and I did. It was less than I'd given up in my marriages. Totally doable.

Gatzby, let me have it all. 125%. He could "handle me," another phrase men hate. They don't want to admit that they, as a group - of course there are exceptions- encourage, inspire and even require that women censor themselves.

## The Tightrope

*Be too forward; You're a slut.*
*Too demure, and you're a prude.*
*Cover up, and you're a tease.*
*Reveal- you're oh so rude*
*Too sexy one day.*
*Too shy the next*
*Can't think too much, Just butt cheeks flex*
*Mouth open wide, and you're a bitch*
*Mouth closed, you put men to a test.*
*It's exhausting, This fine line*
*Of less No more, More, No less*
*A button open, a button closed*
*Don't smile too big or else....*
*Don't laugh too loud.*
*Don't look too long.*
*Sit patiently on the shelf*

*So tiring to play these games*
*Could men grow up and choose?*
*Because ultimately with all these jumps to conclusions*
*Both genders lose.*

I thought about how angry I'd been with Gatzby and wrote this:

*There's some people that hurt us, and we let it slide.*
*We tell them. We move on. We swallow our pride.*
*Femineity dictating we need to be -*
*Understanding and gentle and NOT demanding.*
*But one day he repeats: we come bearing claws.*
*Spouting legion offenses, his mistakes and flaws.*
*Pissed to the nth, no holds barred*
*Sex that once pacified,*
*Is no longer received,*
*Explanations submitted, rejected with ease.*
*And we realize surprised,*
*Cut him off at the knees.*
*We forgave nothing,*
*But held in reprieve*
*We expected recompense for every game played,*

*And to feel all was worth it at the end of our days.*
*So he walked around thinking he had a blank slate*
*While accumulating late fees in our layaway.*

I may have subconsciously felt Gatzby owed me late fees and more, but in one way, he didn't owe me a thing. I'd never walked a tightrope with him. Nor had I done so with JJ, another man I was not "committed" to. I was myself with them. I wasn't sure I knew how to be myself in a relationship. When Gatzby first brought up the word relationship, I'd said, "I'm done with cages, boxes. I don't want one." For two years, I'd meant that. Wholeheartedly. Absolutely.

Then I met The Muse, and I was back in a cage again, deleting, suppressing, restricting the side of me he didn't like. I replicated the same thing with Harlee, but unlike all my relationships before, it wasn't enough. They dumped me. But I had learned my patterns.

Commitment, to me, was connected to compromising my full expression of myself. Maybe there were relationships, marriages out there that didn't follow this pattern. I'd never seen one. Maybe I needed a new pattern, a new way of connecting, one I had no idea of how to even begin creating. With commitment came fear of losing that attachment. For some, that led to jealousy and suspicion. For me, it led to catering and compromising. How do I commit without fear? Without compromising? How do I commit and include all of me? Do I wait for the man who likes it all, but I thought I had him four times, and it never was the case. I was always TOO MUCH.

Hence JJ and Gatzby. Safe spaces. Cocoons. Open fields to explore. Not a cage in sight.

Now, Gatzby was getting married. I don't know if I believed it. Supposedly she lived with him in his apartment. This was the second time he'd miraculously moved out while I was occupied elsewhere. I almost wanted to text and ask for pictures of the girl, the place. Oh, he also had another car. Let's get a pic of that too.

Well, whether he was lying or telling the truth was pretty inconsequential. I was sad. Sad over Harlee. Sad over Gatzby.

I was alone.

Single single.

I laughed.

There were men out there who would "take me seriously" now. I didn't have anyone I was "talking to." No ex. No boo. No fwb.

I was perfect.

Unspoiled by outside male influence.

Well, it was time to create another profile, I guess. One day soon. One day when I had words to say to make men flock. Not today. Not for a while.

Now I would hibernate. Cogitate. Meditate. Masturbate? Naw, not really my thing.

Use my gym membership.

And write.

And call San Antonio.

**<u>Lesson 6:</u>**

Focus: Learn your healthy and unhealthy relationship patterns.

# CHAPTER 7

# Guidance

Writing this chapter is like going back to a nightmare that you don't want to relive. Hurricane Harvey. I'd grown up shuttled between Baton Rouge and Houston, spending August-May-the school year in the H, summer in the BR. Floods, hurricanes, tropical storms, depressions, seen them, no big deal.

Not Harvey.

Harvey was unlike anything before it or since.

We were warned. And people took precautions. Four days of rain were coming. Torrential. Hail too. Lightning. Thunder.

I'd been through storms, always with my parents or married.

Now I was single.

I was pretty secure. My mom kept checking that we had all the supplies we needed. I had all the standard ones. We were well stocked.

Then the day the first band of rain came, the news stations told us to get more supplies.

Unlike previous storms, this one was going to sit on us. We shouldn't expect to move freely for a week. 4 days of rain. 7 days of flooded streets. Impassable.

This was new.

Mother Nature was beneficent. We were supposed to have six hours with no rain. Get your supplies.

I woke up at 8. We took my car, my son's car. Me and my son in my car. My other son and his girlfriend are in a second car. We headed to Kroger's.

The parking lot was packed. Took a while, but we found two spaces. We got in, and every register had a line from the front of the store to the back. No baskets. We picked up empty cardboard boxes and went looking.

The shelves were empty. We found a few items. Bought them. Came home.

I was shook. There was no bread, no chips, no fruit, no milk, water. The list went on.

The rains came. The streets flooded. It was then that I realized for the first time where I was situated. My house was situated in a neighborhood with a bayou in front, on either side and one directly behind my street. I lived in Bayou City, surrounded by four bayous.

I did have flood insurance, but that was not comforting.

We watched the rain. It rained for four days- straight, unceasing. The street outside my house was a river. The water was calf-deep.

The street behind mine? The water was chest deep, just above the belly button. The bayous had crested and overflowed.

It was hard to sleep with the rain. I feared I would wake up to go to the restroom and step out of my bed into water.

The house began to feel like a prison. The electricity was on and off constantly.

I had never been so scared of a storm in my life.

The phone was always ringing. People checking on each other.

On day five, that ring was Gatzby.

“Are you okay? Do you need anything? I’m coming to check on my mom. I’ll stop by.”

“We’re okay. No. Okay, I’d love to see you.”

The fight we had? The cursing? It was all forgotten. His engagement? Canceled. His relationship? Over. My questions, none.

We were back. But this time was different. He’d called. Then showed up when I was vulnerable, scared, overwhelmed. And he’d helped. Mentally. Emotionally. Physically. Neither of my ex-husbands had called. Nor had JJ, The Muse, or Harlee. Harlee called the next month to tell me all the things that had happened to him because of the storm.

But only Gatzby checked on me before the waters fully receded. Only Gatzby said the storm showed him two things. The two people he was worried about were his mom and me. That he’d never gotten over me. That he didn’t think he’d ever get over me. And that he thought I was so angry to hear he was engaged because I loved him.

Did I have another explanation?

Temporary insanity hadn’t occurred to me then. And I don’t think I’d heard Sommore’s Dickmatized yet, so no, I didn’t have another explanation. I replied, we can’t be explained. I’ve stopped trying.

When he came over a few days later, he channeled his own version of Jagged Edge's lyrics for "Let's get married." We can't leave each other alone. We always come back to each other. "We ain't getting no younger. We might as well" be together.

I was glad he was sitting on my couch, in the flesh, next to me, in arms reach. That was amazing. But also nonsensical.

I'd committed to men, gave them my all, and they bounced.

And I'd never committed to him, and he was here.

Did I not know how to pick men? Had my quest to keep my rose intact left me naive and easily manipulated, thirsty for attention?

And I had no idea how to proceed. We hadn't dated then committed. We had been on three dates in two years, had lots of sex, and I had rejected his offers of commitment.

He knew me. Totally. Every thought. Every fear. Every desire. Everything. There was no holding back, no compromising.

And I had no idea WHAT he wanted, except me.

For this relationship he was asking me to commit to, I had no road map. Absolutely no fucking clue.

I agreed. In Aug 2017, after two years of asking me to commit, Gatzby finally got my yes.

*I woke up looking for a poem, for you, me, us.*
*Surely I've written, one, a dozen, a million.*
*I found none.*

*Just sheets slightly stained from your essence,*
*my essence, interwoven juices.*
*Smelling sweet like peach and almond, like cocoa butter and sage,*
*like cologne and whimsy.*

*I woke up typing words on my phone*
*For surely, I've captured every minute of our journey in rhymes.*
*The rhythms of our souls beat so strong, like African drums.*
*I doze and wake, you're here. More tireless than I've ever seen you.*
*Having bested me again. I lay spent.*
*Curled after being unfurled and penetrated.*
*After moaning your name in languages not yet invented.*

*You are you. So much. Yet not enough.*
*So much more. Yet insufficient.*
*Chemistry complex like a circuit breaker.*
*Your energy courses through me,*
*Lighting me, igniting me. Irresistible.*
*Your kisses, magical. Your touch, impeccable.*
*Lovemaking, impressive, the 8th wonder of my world.*

*I woke up looking for words written on some day of eloquence,*
*Capturing your elegance, Your presence. Your essence.*

*You are mine forever. Yet not.*
*You cannot leave me yet. We cannot be*

*What is that? Fate? Destiny? Star crossed lovers?*

*No matter- In the sheets, you're mine.*

*Open soul, open heart. Raw. Untamed.*
*And I do not question the stars that aligned to bring me you,*
*At least not while I'm entwined..*

*I unwind and bask amid your perfection.*
*Directionless we are,*
*but what does that matter when we exist outside of time and space,*
*Wrapped in each other's embrace*

*A twilight zone to taste eternity. How many lifetimes have I loved thee?*
*It seems ancient. Like my soul knew your breath.*
*Like the first time we met was the millionth..*
*Like knowing after today, everything will change. Rearrange.*

*This poem like our love has no center, no compass. Just an ebb and flow.*
*Just a let go. Just an inner knowing*
*That in some things, one has no control. DESTINY.*

It'd be so romantic to tell you that I was ecstatic for months, years. Overjoyed. Pleased as punch.

Day one, I wrote this and read it to him.

## Gatzby

*I wrote a list of 28 qualities I need,*
*And you had all but 3, a 91 indeed.*
*An A in any grade book, a stellar score no less,*
*But I kept bypassing you and landing in a mess.*
*I wasted time and hurt us both, and now it's plain to see,*
*The problem was I was just too damn greedy.*
*You gave me some. I wanted more.*
*You gave more, I wanted less.*
*Again I tied myself in knots,*
*And put you to the test.*
*Now I see more clearly,*
*My fears I've laid aside,*
*I want to praise the man I love in whom I feel such pride.*
*Intelligent and reasonable*
*No tokes will dank his smell*
*Employed and available*
*Articulate as well*
*Faithful and loyal*
*Hardworking it's true*
*And unlike some others, able to read my cues.*
*Intuitive, in other words, and passionate in sex*
*When it comes to lovemaking, he's better than the rest*
*A sensual kisser, techniques so divine*
*That even when you make me mad, I still find you sublime,*
*Romantic and attentive,*
*Listens and speaks his mind,*

*A more intelligent man is certainly hard to find,*
*Spiritual and familial, helpful to a fault,*
*And the chemistry between us never seems to halt*
*Hygenic and masculine, no girly-man for me,*
*Just a man who's been patient and deserves to see*
*that I see the good in him,*
*Fully and completely*

I was all in. Posted my status change on Facebook. In a relationship. I was excited. I posted his pic behind my cover photo. That evening he told me to take it down. It was too soon. He was a private person. It wasn't anyone's business.

I complied, stunned, hurt, confused. I did it with a sinking feeling in my chest.

None of his "take it down" reasoning made sense to me, not really. I know people on Facebook say they don't post their status and all that. I'd just never run into someone, in person, who really felt that way.

And too soon? I'd posted both Harlee and The Muse immediately, And I'd known them a fraction of the time I'd known Gatzby. I began to look for changes to distinguish our new status, and I asked the question. When would I see his place- once again? Supposedly, he once again had an apartment. He said soon.

Three months I waited. Then we planned to go out, as a couple, a concert at the Woodlands lake at 7, dinner before- 5:30. He was picking me up.

It'd been years since I asked for a date since he went AWOL often. Besides, he said that was me asking for "girlfriend benefits" when we weren't together.

But this time, I was his. He didn't have to worry about developing feelings for me, didn't have to hold back. I had earned the "girlfriend benefits." All his reasons/excuses should be settled/squashed. I was excited. But there was a little trepidation. First, he had a horrible track record with showing up for dates. Second, he was coming to me after doing errands with his mom and his pastor.

He told me he had planned his day, and allotted plenty of time to get done with them. He even said he had established boundaries with them and let them know he was in a relationship, and they could no longer take up all his free time.

I exhaled and got ready.

- 5:30 passed. Then 6 PM. I called, No answer.
- 6:30. I texted. No response.
- I was stumped. He couldn't have forgotten. Something had to have happened. I was worried.
- I left frantic messages on messenger.
- I checked his Facebook, asked where he was on his Facebook timeline. He blocked me.
- 8:30 - I posted on his Tango. He blocked me.

We were done.

I'd given him what he wanted. No matter how much I believed, he was not the one. And I still got the same disrespect and lack of common courtesy.

He didn't love me. He couldn't. That was all a lie. And he probably still lived with his mom or someone. I wouldn't know. I still had never seen "his place."

I learned lesson seven, follow your first mind. I believed he was wrong for me. He was- regardless of his claims and evidence. Going along with his reasoning had given me an oil change relationship- three months. And really, nothing had changed between us. We talked more. We made much more of an effort to stay in touch. I cooked for him. That was all.

I still hadn't seen his place, met his family and friends, and we didn't even go on one date as a couple. It was the most pointless" relationship" I'd ever had, further solidifying my position that titles mean nothing.

I'd had a deeper connection with JJ, who I spent weekends with, who once gave me money, who cooked for me and let me sleep over. I even had clothes at his place.

Relationship with Gatzby? What relationship?

When I woke up the following day, there was still no call, no text. I reflected. In college, I'd been stood up once, and I'd experienced it another time after my divorce. Gatzby had stood me up more times than all the other men I'd dated put together.

This reminded me why-

- I don't trust time as a predictor of whether you know someone. People surprise us all the time.
- I don't believe "friends first" helps at all. Being friends does not guarantee compatible world views, priorities, or levels of effort. In fact, in my case, it led me to make excuses for behavior I would not have tolerated from someone I'd just met and started dating.

I picked up my phone and texted.

"Good morning. I realized 4 things reflecting on last night.

1. This situation will never change.
2. I believe being stood up is disrespect and that only death or unconsciousness prevents notification of a no-show. You believe contact is ideal but only if convenient.
3. I believe apologies require regret and change. You believe a statement of what happened is enough.
4. I also believed giving second chances would eventually be rewarded. I now realize it just invites the same behavior to continue.

Good luck. Goodbye."

**Lesson 7:**

Guidance: Follow Your First Mind

# CHAPTER 8

# Heartiness

Writing this reflection on the last seven years may be shocking to some, tame to others. There are probably women and men who have never had sex outside of a committed relationship. I was once one of those.

I already mentioned growing up under the ROSE doctrine. I'd accepted it without question; certain purity would lead to marital bliss. After being engaged, I'd succeeded in waiting till my senior year of college to have sex.

I said yes to the man kneeling before me on the rooftop of a beautiful building downtown, the skyline of Houston providing the perfect backdrop. He'd said, "Marry me. I believe in family, our family. I'll do whatever it takes to take care of you, of our kids. I'll make something of myself." I pictured till death do us part. I never guessed that in the next six years, I'd file police reports, gain a protective order, and this kneeling man would be in jail, charged with a felony related to his abusive behavior.

The ROSE doctrine gave no guidance besides picking a "good" Christian man who valued my chastity. Back then, I didn't know then that the chauvinism and patriarchy that supports the idea of women as fragile flowers only valuable when untouched would also want them subservient, obedient, unquestioningly silent. It would want them harnessed to whatever square of land allotted: choiceless, voiceless.

Divorce, the first and the second, not only meant a change of title but a reclaiming of my power, my sexuality, my freedom, exploring for the first time at 43, what many explored in their 20's, sexual expression, flirtatious freedom from repression.

I married and soon became a mother of twins. Parenthood was the focus, as it should have been. Still, now that my kids were grown and leaving the nest, I was free to go on my own quest of self-discovery, set my own parameters for fulfillment, and ultimately, my own standards for romantic success.

I'd been given one barometer- marriage. I'd done that, twice. Put my all into it, twice. Poured my faith, money, time, energy, prayers, service- lay my body, brain, and soul on the altar as a sacrifice to "I do." But he/they didn't. They asked me to marry, made the promise to love, honor, cherish, and didn't.

The first time I blamed myself. Aren't women trained to do that? It did not matter that his rap sheet was 12 pages long. I had chosen wrong. I had missed red flags. I needed to choose better.

So I read books, went to church, attended divorce recovery counseling and support groups. I worked on myself. Exclusively. For 1.5 years. And at the end, I had a list on my wall of 10 character traits.

"Write the vision and make it plain."

Qualities like maturity, self-control, great communication skills, respect, openness, great work ethic, responsibility, and more. But not one word about passion, intimacy, affection.

Like many women, I took those for granted. Sexual compatibility was a given. If I just did my part, the physical would work itself out. The ROSE doctrine promised that.

In 2003, I knew nothing about the five love languages. But after my second divorce in 2014 and MORE therapy, I learned Drew's language was acts of service, and mine, physical touch.

His acts of service were appreciated but did not make me feel loved. And my need for physical touch seemed like a spoiled girl's longing for unnecessary luxuries to him.

I'd done as I was told. Waited. Almost till marriage. Married. Had kids. Been a good wife and mother. But looking back, it seemed that I had been trained to live by a different set of rules and standards than my husband. I remembered vividly the argument that led to my first divorce, the very first time I'd cussed anyone out.

"I can't believe you have the audacity to say that you are a great husband!" I hurled these words at my mate as I sat on the sofa.

It was amazing that five years of marriage and three years of conflict had come down to this statement. He had no clue what it took to be a good husband and would never change regardless of how much I said or how much time passed. Suddenly the choice was clear.

"I'm a great husband," he had said, "I just need to keep a job, control my temper and my language."

Wow! How low his standards were. I wouldn't dare say I was a great wife because the house was not immaculate. There were dishes covered in soapy water and bottles in the sink; the twins' toys lay sprawled across the tan carpet decorated with sprinkles of graham cracker crumbs. Hamburger Helper served our meals, and I was not the same size or shape he married.

How could we define "great" so differently? If he was a great husband, then we must have a great marriage, and that description of us could keep my side in stitches for weeks.

After he made that statement, I'd lost my temper for the first time in my life, and I went off on him for two hours, Two full hours. listing every way that he was NOT a great husband. I didn't care about his reaction, and I think he was too stunned to even react. His docile, silent wife, who always walked on eggshells trying to keep him happy, was cussing him out, telling him his failures in vivid detail.

Great.

Marriage was supposed to be great. Love, sublime. Commitment, the goal.

Although marriage and parenthood definitely gave me a sense of purpose and joy, these last seven years of being single are where I found my greatest happiness, my thirst for life, and personal growth.

JJ, Gatzby, Harlee, The Muse, San Antonio, and a few others you'll meet were pivotal in that process. 147 dates, 8 lovers and over 300 poems, 2 articles, 3 books, 60 shows, 4 workshops, 60 podcast episodes, 3 businesses, and a multitude of products I designed filled my life during this time. My imagination was bursting as if somehow leaving behind the traditions, roles, religion, and repression of my youth led to a nexus of unending content. Prior to my second divorce, I'd had 3 publications and nothing else.

Not even an inkling to create anything else.

My married life was a rut, a circle of same shit different day.

Now, no two days were alike. No two dates were alike. No two dalliances were alike. All was new. And in the new, all seemed possible.

I'd taken providing satisfaction into my own hands. Once I'd been the flower waiting to be plucked. Now I was the florist.

After Gatzby stood me up that day, I was single once again.

I was writing poetry regularly, and I added something new to combat the increased stress at work, performing at open mics.

I was writing **a lot**. In a really good place mentally, emotionally. Content.

One day I went out to Happy Hour at a Mexican Cafe. A guy sat next to me. We started chatting. About nothing. Everything. Life. And then some black couple commercial caught his eye, and he said, "I've never had that."

"What?"

"Support from a black woman. Acceptance. Respect. Encouragement."

I waited for the punch line. There wasn't one.

"You're serious? Never?"

He shook his head.

"I'm sorry," I said. "That really sucks. On behalf of black women everywhere, I apologize. Everybody deserves those things in a relationship. If your partner isn't willing to give them, why are they even in a relationship to begin with?"

We went our separate ways, but the conversation bothered me.

I'd met JJ on one site. San Antonio on another, and Gatzby on a third. I'd gotten invited to Tango by one of my dates and never left. It wasn't a dating app, just a Facebook-esque site with video chatting capabilities. I'd started posting my poetry there. That night I posted this poem:

*God made you and broke the mold.*
*Who else is so fearless and bold?*
*In dreads and beards*
*And glasses too.*
*The universe whorls like your do.*
*Your smile so bright, a thousand sons*
*Bow before your silver tongue.*
*You rap, you rhyme, language is new.*
*Shakespeare stands in awe OF YOU.*
*You walk, and women stop and stare.*
*Gray sweatpants make the panties bear*
*The secret garden held within.*
*You know the power of your grin.*
*Your voice, a bass, beats like a drum.*
*Your muscles ripple in the sun.*
*Nothing on earth compares to you.*
*You are divine spark given hue.*
*You breathe, and the whole world suspends.*
*You dance, and the whole world joins in.*

*You are wisdom with your grays and gnarls.*
*You're candor with your beats and bars*
*You're business savvy, hustle too.*
*They planted you- like seeds you grew.*
*You're massive, but you're still a man*
*I can hold you in my loving hands.*
*I can knead your shoulders,*
*Bring you wine*
*Love you down if you are mine.*
*You are a pleasure head to toe*
*Richer than Midas' purest gold*
*Just wanted you to know I miss*
*The grandeur of your warmest kiss*
*Your hands so rough yet gentle too*
*Did I say how much I adore you?*
*In all your shades and all your hues*
*from lightest tan to blackest blue*
*You enrich my every day.*
*I love to hear the words you say.*
*You've pissed me off a time or two*
*But there's magic in all you do.*
*I love you not ashamed to shout*
*You're beautiful without a doubt.*

I went to bed and awoke to dozens of friend requests, shares, comments, and some phone numbers.

For a minute, I thought I'd somehow slid into someone else's account. Guys were responding to a poem? They read it? I responded to the comments, and yes, they had read the poem, talked at length about what they liked. Thanked me for it. It was weird, unexpected.

I had fans. They went back and read all my other poems. And three of them asked me out. I looked at their pages, very handsome guys, local, looked at their comments, intelligent.

I wasn't on a dating site, hadn't posted a profile, wasn't even really advertising that I was single or available, and a poem (or some poems) had brought me prospective dates.

I didn't even know if I wanted to date. I still felt a little like I was trying to purge Gatzby from my system. I still felt absolutely no closure on that debacle that happened when I gave him what he wanted and still got the same result.

"When people show you who they are, believe them the first time," Maya Angelou said. But after two-plus years of knowing him, I still didn't feel I knew who he was. He was so utterly contradictory.

For about a month, I got to know three of these "fans." I called them my three musketeers. We talked on the phone. That was all. That was more than enough for me. I didn't really want anything else.

Then the Christmas season arrived. In a day, I'd be off for two weeks. I was looking forward to it. Maybe I'd go on a date with one of the three musketeers. I had also reactivated my POF profile the night before because I'd be off for two weeks, but maybe I wouldn't even look at it. I might actually click with one of the musketeers.

Either way, the respite from work was what I was longing for.

My phone rang at 1 AM; groggily, I answered, "Hello."

"Ms. J, you need to come to the Exxon on 1960. Your son's been in an accident in your car."

"My car's outside."

"No, it's up here on 1960."

I pulled on a robe and walked outside my house to an empty driveway. An hour before, I had told my son he couldn't use my car. It was too late. He'd lost his license. He didn't need to go get pancakes from Denny's. There was food in the kitchen.

My car was gone. My son was not in the house. And my neighbor said he'd been in a wreck, but he was okay.

I called an Uber. Once I saw he was okay, I wasn't. The car that I was going to pay off in three more payments was totaled. He was lucky to be alive. He'd fallen asleep at the wheel, narrowly missed a gas pump, and hit a small palm tree.

While I was so grateful that he was uninjured (except for a sprained ankle), I knew I would be digging myself out of this ditch-literally and figuratively-for years to come. First, dealing with the insurance company (I did have full coverage, but he wasn't a covered driver), getting another car, and starting over from scratch to pay it off. I had no savings. Depending on what, if anything, I got from the insurance, I'd have to rob Peter to pay Paul to scrape up a down payment. And how was my credit? Decent. Not stellar. Not to mention my car insurance payments would skyrocket for years.

No more relaxing Christmas holiday for me. I'd be lucky if two weeks was long enough to sort this mess out. I pulled what I could from the rubble of the car and went home. When my son arrived after being thoroughly interviewed by the officers, I told him that he had betrayed my trust. I didn't know how to sleep in a house with someone who might again take off in my vehicle in the middle of the night, and I didn't feel I should have to lock my bedroom door or sleep with my keys under my pillow. I told him, "You can't stay here anymore. Call your dad, your other relatives, your friends. You need to find somewhere else to live."

He was 22. A grown man. He'd made a grown man's decision and needed to accept the consequences.

Right on schedule, my phone rang. It was evening. My three musketeers were checking on me. I didn't want to talk at all. But eventually, each drug the story out of me. I was stunned, hurt, scared, overwhelmed. They wanted to make it better. Buy me a drink. Had I eaten?

I didn't want to eat or drink. And I didn't for about three days. I just made calls and tried to fix the mess. And then finally I went out, day four.

## Date Forty-Three:

N'awlins- Like me, he was from Louisiana. This country boy was sweet, direct, manly, mannish, and very concerned. He made me laugh when I wanted to cry. Took me out two days in a row until he became so aggressive sexually, I never saw him again.

I'd been calling, surfing the internet, and physically walking into car dealerships. The insurance company had paid off my car (They covered my son), and I had $1000 total, a few hundred left from the payoff, $800 I scrambled to put together, to find something drivable.

I felt stuck. I felt humble. I would have been on the bus if any bus lines were near me. I'd forgotten what it was like to be without a car; for one setback to knock out years of progress. It was humiliating, terrifying and made me feel more vulnerable than any one event in my life ever had.

Enter Bread. Bread was probably the sweetest guy I ever met. I loved talking to him, even more than San Antonio, and that should tell you everything. There was only one problem, well, two. Bread, hated bread- my favorite food, and was abstinent, not partaking in my favorite stress relief.

## Date Forty-Four:

Even though I had once been abstinent, I didn't understand Bread.

"I really want to date you, but you should know I'm abstinent," he'd said.

“You’re kidding, right!” I replied, alternating between feeling grateful that it was too early in our interaction for me to have had any fantasies about him and being pissed that he had, in one sentence, rendered this date pointless. I was at a point when I had enough male friends (remote and long-distance, true, but with years of contact with me). I was only dating to find Mr. Right or Mr. Right for the Foreseeable Future. Both those titles came with a sexual requirement.

“Woah, that question sounded awfully intense. That pisses you off?” He asked.

“Of course it does. I mean, it’s your body and all, and I’m not upset because I expected us to have sex. But you’re wasting your virility. For nine years, I was married to an impotent man. He couldn’t get and keep erections. And you are wasting this time that you can get them being abstinent. 50 % of men over 40 have erectile dysfunction, low testosterone, or premature ejaculation. But you’re perfectly healthy and just putting yourself on ice. For what?”

“I’ve had plenty of sex. I’m tired of it meaning so little. You can’t understand that?”

I nodded. I could.

“I know the risks,” he said. “I’m taking care of myself, healthy diet, exercise. I’ll be fine, and if not, it’s still worth it.”

“That’s what I hear.” I pursed my lips and shrugged.

“You do?”

“I see so many Facebook posts on abstinence that it’s mind-boggling. Why the fascination? Before joining singles’ groups, it was not a topic I’d even thought about since I left college. Adults have sex, just like they do a million other adult things.

Reading these posts, I wonder:

1. Are some men so insecure sexually that they want a woman to have forgotten what sex feels like and be happy with anything?
2. Do some men believe a woman can only be "tight" if she abstains?
3. Why do some people seem to act as if abstinence is the only measure of virtue?.
4. Why will some hang their faith on this issue as if every other transgression that impacts mind, body, and soul evaporates if one is abstinent?
5. Why do some people act as if they lose the ability to evaluate the person once sex is involved? ( I mean Gatzby had asked me if I was ready before we had sex the first time, and I really wasn't ready for the intensity of our chemistry's effect on me, but it didn't take away my ability to see his flaws. They still showed quite clearly, I thought)
6. Some people will have great sex lives till they die. Others will hit middle age and have all types of sexual issues. Abstinence is banking on something that will never come for some women/men- marriage or a serious, committed relationship. Abstinence also has been known to increase the likelihood of sexual problems in the marriage. Two people with repressed drives coming together expecting fulfillment, who have no idea what the other likes and whether they can provide it, is a recipe for disaster. They also have no idea if their unleashed sex drives will be compatible or if they've wasted their prime sexual years on abstinence. But this abstinence scenario seems to be touted as the solution for everything.

It's very interesting. Like watching people who claim to eat only raw food try to convert omnivores. Well, this omnivore knows how to diet, fast, and enjoy a damn good meal when one I really want is being served." I realized I was pontificating and fell silent.

He smiled. "That's a trigger for you."

"Yeah, one day I'll think about those nine years and shrug. That day is not today. You know I really like you."

He nodded and looked sheepish, "I think this is gonna be the first time a woman has told me she doesn't want to see me again on date one. It usually takes longer."

I looked away. It hurt a little. Meeting someone I really liked who had a dealbreaker. Even worse than that, a dealbreaker that pissed me off. There was no way on this planet I would ever date him. But by the end of the date, I was glad we met. Even though he sent his plate back because it arrived tarnished by a slice of garlic bread, we still had a great time.

Of all the men I met, he's the one I still miss sometimes. The conversations were legendary. But we couldn't be friends, or in other words, I wouldn't let us remain in contact because I wanted to seduce him.

Ace hit his stride in week two. I was full-on depressed. I'd gotten more doors slammed in my face at car dealerships than I even believed was possible. I needed a particular payment, had a low down payment, and wasn't trying to pay an arm and a leg for a vehicle. No one wanted to work with me. Ace was sort of a poet, a rapper, so beautiful women looked twice, a two-time felon, making money by being a medical guinea pig, a test subject for drug trials. He paid his bills on the gig economy, hotshot driver, handyman, you name it, he did it. Industrious. Trying to build his life back up after a stint inside. He was philosophical, fiery, poetic, and utterly magnetic. And young. 32 to my 48.

## Date Forty-Five:

Ace and I met at Subway, and I had to be the worst company on the planet, at first. Angry, bitter, depressed, quiet, you name it, I was probably it. I hadn't even wanted to meet him. He called, asked where I was. I told him Subway, not thinking it meant anything. And he used the find your friend's radar on the app to find which one I was at. Had I been in my right mind, I probably would have freaked. But I wasn't. I was totally in my emotions. And this beautiful man walked in. I didn't even realize it was him at first because I didn't really believe the picture he'd posted online was him. It didn't do him justice.

At all.

I had no make-up on, shorts, a t-shirt, tennis shoes, a cap. He acted like I was Ms. America. Raved about my poetry. Made me forget that once he jetted off to his next delivery, I was walking home.

He made me laugh, and before I walked home, I stopped, took out my phone, and captured my latest fantasy.

### Fire and Ice

*He said, "How can I destress you?"*
*I smile say, here's what you can do.*

*Start right here. Hands on my ass.*
*Clothes disappear.*
*Now I relax.*
*Take your time, so sensually,*
*Dip once, twice, thrice, inside of me.*
*Then stop and linger, meditate.*
*Traveling fingertips cross my face.*
*Kiss me deeply, then resume.*
*Pull me close, thrust hard,*
*My thoughts consume.*
*Take both hands and palm my chest,*
*Knead softly the nipples of each breast.*
*Kiss my neck, moan, grunt, crave more,*
*Flip me over. now explore.*

*Face down, ass up,*
*Rhythm resume.*
*My nails dig into pillow plumes,*
*I bite my lip, look back and smile,*
*Throw it back, show you my style.*

*I flip over. Now I ride.*
*Slick thighs, slide, grind, slide.*
*I'm having fun. Sex is a game.*
*A bite, a slap, I call your name.*

*We've tried three positions, time for 4,*
*Reverse cowgirl, or scissor, want more.*
*I'm nonchalant with sex half rate,*
*But great sex?*
*I will fill my plate.*

*Come back for seconds, maybe thirds,*
*Till sore and satisfied, I purr.*

*You asked what you can do for me.*
*I answered, Now let's wait and see.*

*Will it get done?*
*I'd like to know.*
*I hope the question wasn't rhetorical.*
*Because I need an answer real.*
*Pure pleasure I can feel.*

*I'm craving fire.*
*So warm and nice.*
*Don't give me unsatisfying ice*

*It's cold outside. I need your heat.*
*Warm flames would make me feel complete.*

*Now I have a question back?*
*Are you fire, or are you an ice pack?*

He was definitely fire and fun.

Once, while I was still car shopping and he was without a vehicle because he had no pending deliveries, he walked two miles just to see me. He introduced me to "The Wire," which we binge-watched from the beginning over the next three months. Two miles of walking just to watch tv with me. Netflix and Chill before there was even such a thing.

He made one of the most stressful times of my life bearable; a time I look back on with the fondest memories. And when he asked me to be his woman, I declined.

"You're here, but your family is in San Antonio- your ex, your kids." I said in explanation.

"She doesn't want me," he replied.

" I actually don't believe that. From everything you've told me, she sounds hurt and doubtful you've changed, not done with you."

"I don't want to put myself out there and get rejected."

"Bull shit, you just did it with me. You're not destroyed because I said no. All she can do is say no. But at least you will know for sure, and if she says yes, you've got your family back."

These discussions had begun on New Year's Eve, when he wanted to start his new year, 2018, with me. A woman who accepted, supported, encouraged the new him. But I didn't know the old him. I just knew the gorgeous, brilliant intellectual who'd made bad choices, had two felonies, and was rebuilding his life. The romantic, sweet, generous lover who doted on me. But he was a father. And he wasn't as active in his kids' lives as I would have liked him to be, and that was not cool with me. My kids were not gonna be replacements for the ones he was not raising, so I encouraged and motivated him to go back to his ex and his kids.

I actually thought that might have been the reason we met, and when they reunited, and he left my life for good. I was glad. It felt right.

It was Spring. Love was in the air. And I was alone again. Ace had gotten me hooked on Netflix. I was done with "The Wire," and I ran across a new to me series on cable, "She's Gotta Have It." I had never watched the movie, but I liked the series. Nola Darling was refreshing. A heroine unlike any I'd seen before. Unapologetically herself. Her sexual freedom was mind-blowing.

I thought back over the first day of each of the last four years: 2015 JJ, 2016 The Muse, 2017 Harlee, 2018 Ace, and before that, the first lover after my divorce, JJ. Five men in five years. Nothing compared to Nola Darling. Maybe a week for her. But she did not live in the world I lived in. The world with The Rose Doctrine.

I flashed back to college, orientation, freshman year. I had been a shy high school student, an introvert. Now I was away from home. I wanted to be outgoing - popular. I remembered smiling big and introducing myself to any and everyone. And suddenly, there was a rumor about me.

Me- the virgin. Though they didn't know that. I wasn't exactly publicizing it.

What was the rumor?

I was too friendly. I smiled too big. I must be easy.

Since when did a smile and an introduction translate to promiscuity? Apparently, in East Texas at an HBCU.

Nola Darling never got called easy or fast or promiscuous or told to "know her worth" in any episode I ever saw.

At 24, engaged, I had sex for the first time. What was it like to live in a world where a woman dressed as she wanted, smiled, was friendly and even sexual, and that was considered okay? I'd never seen that world.

When I was a virgin, I was accused of holding out, being a cock tease solely to try to manipulate and control men. But then later, when I *was* sexually active, men who weren't sleeping with me, who wanted to date me, were angered that I was single and not abstinent.

They wanted to know how long it had been since I had had sex, who with, was he still around. They claimed my being sexual was solely to try to manipulate and control men.

Huh?

Damned if I do. Damned if I don't.

So early in this dating period, I decided I could not, would not choose to have or not have sex based on some man's, often some stranger's assessment of what I should do.

I was not going to fall into the quicksand of ever-changing rules- you need to be married, in a committed relationship, dating. It couldn't be a first date, but you couldn't have a 90-day rule either. If you were sexually active, dating, "talking," that meant exclusivity.

I declined it all.

My body. My choice. He, they, could think what they wanted and spout off their pronouncements. I had the final say.

I'd followed The Rose Doctrine almost to the letter, and it hadn't paid off. So now, I was a lawgiver when it came to my body.

Now my body count was up by five, with no engagement in sight.

But I wasn't looking for a ring, a marriage certificate, or a new last name now. Marriage was still appealing. Maybe the third time's the charm, the ideal final destination. But now the lesson seemed to be-

**Lesson 8:**

Enjoy the journey. Eat the fruit. Drink the wine. Carpe Diem.

# CHAPTER 9

# Imagine

I belong to that group men don't think exists, single and satisfied. I'm mentioning that because there might be someone reading this, and seeing that JJ, The Muse, and Ace are all happily married now while I'm still single, who thinks my relationship status bothers me. Someone may think that I interpret that turn of events as me being *unwifeable*, not chosen, left behind.

But I never saw it that way. I had been married twice, proposed to four times. Both my ex-husbands had tried to get me back for years. And I viewed turning Ace down as a feather in my cap because I was a major reason a black family was now intact. Those were and are all wins. I felt privileged that I had met three men, each broken in his own way, and I had been as much a part of their healing journey as they were a part of mine. And this is where I will divulge one of my strongest beliefs.

**Relationships are where human beings grow.**

It is in that fulcrum that iron sharpens iron, that you see your mirror image, that you see the best and worst of yourself. And you change and grow.

So, contrary to popular beliefs, or the slew of memes on Facebook, Instagram, and everywhere else in the known universe, **a relationship that does not end in marriage is not wasted time, wasted energy, or a wasted investment.** That is such a limited view.

I spent 17 years of my life married. I spent the last 6 years single. Guess where I grew the most. Guess where I published four books, started three businesses, was interviewed dozens of times, started a podcast that ranks in the top 10% globally. Guess when I got two national and two local teaching awards, a Congressional award, and had the best sex of my life. Hint- not during either marriage.

And the men that entered (and left and sometimes returned to) my life were pivotal to every one of those accomplishments. They supported me, encouraged me, pushed me, cheered for me, more than either of my husbands ever had. In fact, in my first marriage, when I tried to share just a minuscule view of the goals I had, my ex said, "Why can't you ever be satisfied? Why do you always want more? You just don't know how to be content."

We had one car, a two-bedroom apartment, crappy credit, no savings, and together brought in less than $35,000, and he wanted me to be content?

But I had attained that coveted status- married, wife, marriage material.

Now, I don't even converse with men who think like that.

Although I love marriage and think it leads to some amazing power couples, it can also be its own dead end, more often than people want to admit.

It was now 2018. I was **single, single** once again, and reflecting. Feeling grateful, I penned this tribute to Ace.

## Impress Me

*I love when I go about my day,*
*And someone takes my breath away.*
*He makes me smile and blush a bit,*
*Surprises me with style and wit*
*A flirt, a comment, I admit*
*Intelligence, sexy voice, that shit*
*That makes my mind aflutter imagining,*
*Us face to face, and mingling.*
*His hand in mine.*
*His kiss. My lips.*
*My knees swoon, desire hits.*
*An hour seems a minute long,*
*My mind rehearses smooth love songs.*
*I smile, demure and coquettish,*
*I tease a little, anticipatory relish.*
*His face replaces other sights,*
*Jumping to mind, my heart in flight.*
*Infatuated? Intrigued? Or less,*
*Emotions swell and ebb, no rest.*

*He can talk about anything, it seems*
*Eloquence of course my waking dream.*
*Can seduce a little, not too much,*
*Knows how to move forward, back,*
*One touch,*
*Says a mouthful,*
*Then those eyes,*
*Volumes speak,*
*My glance replies.*
*All is uncertain, that is true,*
*But he came correct,*
*And ... that... is.... new.*
*Been years since someone approached right,*
*Not too much, just make me bite,*
*Put your bait out, back off then*
*State your intentions,*
*I take them in,*
*Tell me a little about yourself,*
*Then ask me out*
*And prep yourself.*
*On time, smelling good, a rose in hand,*
*Okay, I say, THIS IS A MAN.*
*Suggest a drink, I order, we dine.*
*Go to a park and walk and find,*
*So much in common, chemistry.*

*I like the way you look at me.*
*I like the way you hold my hand.*
*I know you want to be my man.*
*I forgot completely what this was like,*
*To be pursued, feels strange and frightening,*
*To know where I stand, no guess involved,*
*Seems others lost this as relations evolved.*
*You're reaching a buried part of me,*
*I locked away for security,*
*You unlocked the door and tossed the key,*
*And she looks out, tentatively.*
*And takes a step,*
*Feels like a fall,*
*You steady her, help her stand tall.*
*She doesn't know what to do at all.*
*Out of practice, heart in stall.*
*Feels like learning to drive a stick,*
*Gears crunching in my head,*
*They stick.*
*I ask for patience, you comply,*
*I smile, breathe deeply, gasp a sigh.*
*You impress me.*
*That's no lie.*
*Thank you*

As I look at my life somewhat objectively, I know that my choices may seem strange. That poem, penned for a two-time felon, may rankle a few feathers, or it might be appreciated. Men seem so contradictory (and they call women that). They want us to build with them, give them a chance, see them as more than wallets, realize they are human and make mistakes, but when we do, we are often judged for giving the "wrong men" a chance. But Ace was no Jody, living with mom, ambitionless. He was a man who had rebuilt his life, seen his errors, and actually changed… for good. I was proud of him and felt grateful to have had him in my life.

Since age 18, I'd been in relationships.

- ✓ Two abstinent ones in college. 3 years each.
- ✓ Then marriage 6 years.
- ✓ Then a year-long relationship.
- ✓ Then married for 11 years.
- ✓ 6 months with JJ (FWB).
- ✓ 10 months with The Muse.
- ✓ 6 months with Harlee.
- ✓ Then 3 months with Ace (FWB).
- ✓ And of course, Gatzby (FWB).

I had never been alone for more than six months. Not ever. Having a relationship, being in a relationship, was normal to me. They took different forms, but I was always in one. I had been in so many that being "single" never scared me. Being alone was not something I ever considered as a possibility.

It was like being hungry when you have a fridge or a pantry full of food. You're only hungry because you haven't made a plate…yet.

In this metaphor, the fridge and pantry are the men I remembered on dating apps, the ones who had inboxed me, that I hadn't met or gotten to know.

Spending the next nine months single was very interesting because it was a conscious choice, to avoid even the possibility of meeting "Mr. Right." I went on dates… eventually. You'll hear about them. But for the first time in my life, I didn't like what I remembered in the fridge, what was shelved on the pantry- at all. I actually was willing to starve rather than eat. And that was new….

At first, fearing there was fungus growing in the dating pantry and fridge was funny, then disturbing, then for a moment, I got scared.

But just for a moment. It was like seven days. I fretted, cried, let the inner voice spout doom and gloom. At first, I avoided the negative predictions, but then I let them go wild. I let my imagination paint a dire picture of me dying alone, single forever.

No dates. No sex. No love.

And then I realized I could survive all of that. A little sad, disappointed, but not regretful of a single choice. Intact.

I wouldn't go back to a single ex because of that fear.

I literally heard the lyrics of Gloria Gaynor playing in my head, "At first I was afraid. I was petrified. Kept thinking I could never live without you by my side. But then I spent so many nights thinking how [love] did me wrong. And I grew strong. And I learned how to get along."

After that, there was a calm and clarity I had never experienced before.

## Introspection

*Turning away from noise to calm,*
*Finding pleasure in solitude*
*Peace my haven.*
*Silence my balm - like a warm cocoon.*

*I need nothing.*
*But maybe a pillow; a blanket*

*or a well-worn book.*
*A sunrise, sunset, a lakeside stroll,*

*a song without a hook*

*And something beautiful to look at or taste.*
*Lounge softly in the grass,*

*make pictures of the clouds*
*Or draw or write or even laugh.*

*Leaving the world behind, Sublime.*
*Divine.*
*Unwind.*
*Escape the Grind.*
*And find me time.*

I liked being alone. Although I really had no idea how to do it. I was now an empty nester, but I still cooked like I had a family to feed. (Stopping that was amazing, liberating.)

I couldn't get used to sleeping in my bed alone. I still slept on one side and filled the other side with seven pillows, plus I had a boyfriend pillow wrapped around me. I was learning to adjust to being by myself.

And…

I'd never felt so liberated. So comfortable in my own skin. So me. For the first time not compromising or adapting to anyone's wants and needs.

Plus…for the first time in my life, I wasn't scared of being smart.

I'd heard that I was "deep," "intimidating," "used too many big words" so many times that I hesitated at times before I spoke. I dumbed myself down. I watered down my conversation. Especially when I was dating. With JJ and Harlee, with my FWBs, I didn't have to, but meeting new men, yes, I did. Now, I asked…

## What's the Matter with Being Clever?

*I grew up reading tales of woe*
*From philosopher savants of long ago*
*Who promised pure catastrophe if curious I chose to be.*

*See here Pandora and there Eve.*
*Spread knowledge like a fire thief*
*be punished for eternity*

*Don't brag on beauty*
*Snakes you'll find entwined in locks that make men blind.*

*Don't boast on skill or end up trapped*
*spinning a web to catch a gnat.*

*Don't think that you can change your fate*
*Make Cassandra's hearers hesitate,*
*Too clever you may seal the fate of*
*Children too impulsive to wait.*
*And when they soar too near the sun*
*Your work, like wax, will melt and run.*
*And all your warnings, be undone.*

*So cleverness is not a shield*
*A banner on the battlefield,*

*It is a target*
*On one's back.*
*For those with brilliance get attacked*
*Reduced to labor, killed, transformed*
*But that's how revolutions form*

*Because if they alight ONE mind*
*They achieve success divine*

But now, I had a new love, well, two of them: the page and the stage.

Singleness was my new muse.

I was writing new things- essays, and they were getting published.

I had never seen myself as an essayist. I was a poet. That was it.

Apparently not.

And then I started performing. Stress made me do it. I couldn't work out enough to purge the stress, and I wasn't having sex, but the stage was a rush.

The energy, addictive. The interaction, sensual, seductive, a give and take, just like lovemaking, better than lovemaking sometimes.

I had a phone full of artistic contacts. I had a calendar full of open mics. I had an itinerary full of calls for submission. My life was full.

To bursting.

Not a man in sight. And none were desired.

Every date required rehashing my history: why I was single, what I was looking for, who I was, what I liked to do for fun. By this time, I had already said all that 45 times, from 2014-2018.

The idea of starting all over again was mind-numbing.

Performing was mind stimulating.

I definitely had made my choice.

I knew from past experience that it generally took nine dates to find a guy I wanted to see. And that just seemed like a tall order. A Herculean task.

Why was I single?

I didn't even want to begin the process. Text, call, meet, repeat.

Nope. Not now. Maybe not ever. I loved men. I mean everything about them.

Their look, smell, taste, touch, energy.

I loved men.

I was just tired.

And performing was my Red Bull.

But let's not get it wrong. I was never and will never be a woman that says,' I don't need a man!"

I may not need my own individual man, one committed to me romantically. Still, I need male energy in my life.

I can feel myself getting hard, brittle, rough around the edges without it. Sharpening like a stone.

The Rose Doctrine doesn't account for the fact that male energy stimulates femininity, at least in me.

I'm softest when I interact with men, even platonically.

My nurturer is called forth.

Just like when I gave birth, my nipples spouted twin fountains whenever my infants cried.

Something warm, wholesome, and generous unfurls inside of me in the presence of male energy.

As Terry Mcmillan so aptly put it, I held my breath without male energy, waiting to exhale.

And then he/they entered- a text, a call, a message, a flirt from someone I knew, who knew me, saw me, heard me, valued me.

And then it happened. Breath released. Body relaxed. The exhale.

The flow of mother's milk.

The clink, clink clink, of a dozen locks opening in unison as I unwound, relaxed, unclenched.

And all it took sometimes was a phone call.

So...

I never would say...

I don't need a man.

I called San Antonio, by this time, I had another buddy in Indianapolis, one in Louisiana, and one in New Jersey. I called the last three my NEW three musketeers.

I could talk and get that bass in my ear. Flirt a little, talk about my day.

For now, that was good enough.

More than enough.

No man. Not even the prospect of Mr. Right being somewhere out there was enough to make me want to text, call, meet, repeat in person.

Not even a little bit.

And the bonus now? The four men I conversed with were my intellectual harem. They stimulated my brain, my creativity, my possibilities. They were entrepreneurs, every one.

Black. Successful. And the last thing they found intimidating or too deep was a talented woman exploring her intellectual gifts.

If the song in my heart was a piano concerto, they were tuning my piano to pitch-perfect status. I could hear my voice stronger than ever before. I was single, single. But I felt invincible.

And curious. I'd reopened my POF account but never checked it because of the car accident when my son totaled my car. I logged on and looked in my inbox. Full. Okay, let's start at the beginning. My first hit was a minister (he announced this in the greeting he sent me). Lol #1. And when I told him we weren't compatible based on that and everything else in his profile, he responded, "What could be more compatible than having Christ?"

Uh, a million things lol# 2

I have nothing against Christians. I was one for 35 years of my life, but it shocks men to learn that it is not a feather in their cap in my eyes. I'm neutral. Nothing gained. Nothing lost. I think for some men, this is more disturbing to them than anything else I could say about myself. Shrug. It is what it is. I like dating men who consider themselves spiritual, who believe in God and pray versus those who claim Christianity or Islam. Why? Because they're stronger. They don't make excuses like God's not done with me yet to cover their own failings. They don't think prayer and patience will solve everything. They're so much more confident, assertive, proactive, and rational. Faith seems like a crutch, not a strengthener for too many men. It's okay that I don't have a job, a car, that I still live with mom or never finished school because I love God, and he's gonna work everything out for my good, they say. All I've gotta do is have faith. And they think any woman who doesn't understand that must not really be a good Christian Proverbs 31 woman.

Well, I guess I'm not that type of woman.

I checked inbox two- illiterate. "Lovely profile you in here."

Why don't dating sites have a simple test? Type two complete sentences that make sense. If you can't pass it, you can't join.

I logged off. This was why I had stopped dealing with dating sites last time. They made my blood pressure rise.

I had joined a few Facebook singles' groups, though. They were funny, often filled with jaded, bitter men and women. People I didn't want to be like.

So much blame floating around. So much staunch views that there was only one way, their way, to date, to interact with the opposite sex, to live. I'd spent most of my life in those boxes, following rigid doctrines that sought to control a world that can't be controlled.

I was done believing there was some magic guide, some rule book, handbook, ten commandments of dating that would guarantee success. Life was about living. Getting up every day and embracing the uncertainty with relish, anticipation, and gusto.

So many seemed driven by fear.

I recognized that intimately. I had feared my sex drive once, feared I'd be one of those women, fallen, impure, no rose petals left. I'd feared rejection, judgment, ridicule, being used, taken for granted, overlooked.

My fear never gained me one thing. Running from all that led me right to situations that caused all the above. **What you resist, persists. What you focus on, you attract.**

Now I focused on love, laughter, joy, peace, the page, the stage, and all that was coming in abundance. I remembered playing volleyball for six years, my coach saying, look where you want the ball to go, then serve.

I was looking. I was serving. I was taking control of the direction of my life. My focus. No longer fixating on what I lacked, a relationship, a partner, but falling in love with what I had: time, choice, freedom. Me.

Creative. Intellectual. Growing. Changing. Me.

I had me. Beholden to no one. Kowtowing to nothing. Deciding on goals and smashing them. Choosing a path and dancing down it to the beat of the drum in my soul. And that music, which once was silent, was now loud enough to drown out every other voice.

I remembered scandalizing a male member of one of these Facebook groups by responding to a post asking what group members slept in with one word- nothing.

He was flustered, sputtering long paragraphs on why that was improper. I smiled. The image of me, bare skin next to 1000 thread count Egyptian cotton, lotioned, smelling good, entwined in soft sheets or freely walking around my bedroom, air bathing, air conditioning caressing my body. Luxurious. Sensual. All this proved too much for a man who felt more comfortable with Little House on the Prairie nightgowns buttoned right under the chin, long sleeves even in summer, and hemlines almost touching the ground.

Why was so much energy spent by men trying to keep women tame, controlled, and covered, even in the privacy of our own homes where no one could see us? Why was so much energy spent telling us that we "thought too much," wanted too much, were too much?

It was mind-boggling.

And for the first time, insulting.

Looking back to The Muse and Harlee and my two marriages suddenly felt like looking back at a stranger. Who was that girl? That woman? She wasn't me.

Not anymore.

My social media reflected that. I had gone from one page on Facebook with 600 friends to two pages with thousands. I also opened an Instagram account. More people knew me by my stage name than my real name.

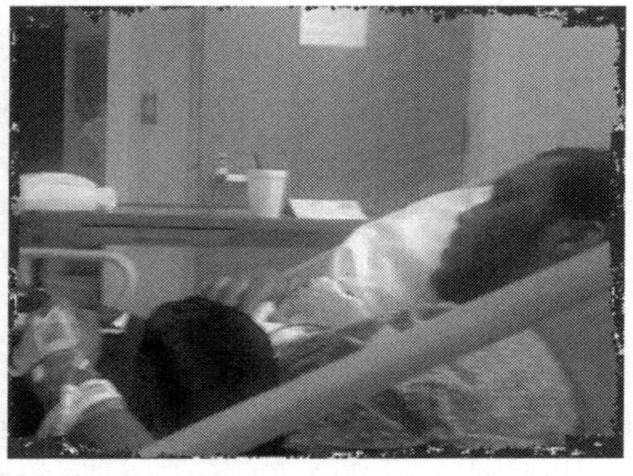

I was interested in seeing what this new me would do, where she would go, and where the less traveled road would lead.

First, it led me to my sons. The twins had both left home at my request. Both were back. It was nice having them under my roof again. I knew they were cared for, safe. No matter how old your kids get, you feel that way as a parent.

Our road led to a pretty dark place in April of that year. An emergency room, emergency surgery, days of my son hovering between life and death. He'd been shot.

My ex-husbands came to the hospital, and my sister, my other son, my son's girlfriend, and my grandson. I didn't leave for five days.

I don't know what it's like to lose a family member to a senseless shooting. I do know what it's like to come close.

To know that, had the bullet that hit my son been in a different place, he could have died or been paralyzed.

To know that had he made it to the hospital fifteen minutes later, he would've bled out.

To know that he could have lived his life with a colostomy bag, unable to walk. Instead, thanks to God, he is healing. His son has a father.

It's been three years and six months, and every day is a little better. But back then, every day was a struggle. My son had a long, painful physical recovery and an even longer, more painful mental and emotional recovery. I think he still has PTSD, though I did get him some counseling. My other son needed counseling as well. As for me, I had four counselors. I went to one, once a week but had the others in my phone, so I always had one available.

The memories of that time are few. My mind didn't seem to want to focus and store what was happening.

One night, I had the craziest dream ever. All I did was cry all the unshed tears inside- wants, needs, what coulda, shoulda, mighta been, loves lost, lives wasted, money spent to ease the pain, every stupid decision, every cruel turn of events, every disappointment.

Like a damn breaking, unstoppable, I cried for three hours in that dream.

I can probably count on both hands the times I've cried in reality, name incidents off like bullet points on a grocery list. Still, these tears that never stained my pillow felt endless, like circling the Milky Way, rounding the Big Dipper, and stopping off at Pluto. Like they'd become my life's work, and nothing would ever be done till they were spent.

I don't think I'd ever felt so alone as when I was awakened, hastily, summoned before daylight from three hours of sleep/mourning to help my son. And I pulled on my robe, dry faced and went to work. Because that's what women do, what mothers do so often. We bear our griefs alone, in silence, releasing them only in prayer, in meditation because our work must go on.

It wasn't what almost happened that was so bad, the near-death. It was the after-effects. My son was a black man in America. He had struggled having no dad after the divorce. He'd looked for a father figure in the wrong places, gotten attached to my second husband, and then went back to trying to define his manhood with the wrong crowd after the divorce. He felt betrayed. Alone. And in so much pain. Bones had shattered inside. He had to walk with a walker for two months, a cane for another month. And when the pain meds weren't working fast enough, he was a different person. An angry, bitter, threatening, scary person.

Those three months, he bounced around. Partly because when he was on drugs, he wasn't himself. There was no talking to him, high. No calming him down, no controlling him.

I thought I'd lost him. That his brother and I had lost him. But month four brought a change.

It was almost like a switch flipped, and life went back to normal.

To someone who didn't experience it, I can't explain it.

But after 90 plus days, he was sane, safe, stable, and back home with me.

But we were all scarred. I didn't know how much till years later, but we'll get to that in an upcoming chapter.

I went through this period alone, mostly. I had a couple of talks with Gatzby, chats with San Antonio and my intellectual harem, and a new friend.

## Date Forty-Six:

Mo- We'd met on Facebook. In some groups. I'd posted about missing my muse. And he responded. He knew exactly what I was talking about.

I'm a writer and a poet. San Antonio is a professional musician. Mo was also a writer. We discussed how we see connection with the opposite sex differently from many others. Creative types are generally at their best when they are inspired. And so he and I have acquaintances, very few friends, and at our most creative, we have a muse, that person who inspires us, and their conversation and presence keep us sparked. We are whole and complete without that person, but we struggle creatively. We are also intensely passionate and sexual. So in dating, we may sift through quantity to get to quality because finding that muse is an undeniable, unignorable motivation. In my search for a muse, much time has been wasted. But the alternative is much worse. Artists create beauty, but they also generally experience the world more deeply. Thus they struggle with depression, addictive tendencies, being workaholics etc. Searching and finally finding a muse may be time-consuming. Still, compared to the alternatives, it often seems like the healthiest way to deal with the world we live in.

He was the closest thing I'd had to a Muse since 2016.

He was the first friend I called from the hospital. I was freaking out. I couldn't calm down. I was totally losing my shit. And I called him. And he talked to me. For hours. Just talking. Calming me. Listening. Praying, sending positive energy.

I got off the phone, at peace.

Once, he said I'd love to see you, but I'm scheduled all over the country for the next six months.

I replied, "Your words have power. Ask the universe to make it so, and watch the world bend to your will."

At the end of the month, he was the one at my door who changed the locks on my house because I didn't want my son to get in without me being there. It wasn't a date per se. We didn't go anywhere. We sat on my sofa, drank wine, and talked after the lock change. And no, we didn't have sex.

We just held each other. And he listened to me talk.

For those four months, I was in a different headspace,

Looking back on it now, it's hard to describe how I was this grieving thing one day, and the next, I was back to normal.

And when I first started writing this chapter, I had no explanation. But now I do.

See, as I write to you, I stop and read my journals. So far, I've read the first two of nine. Those covered years 1998-2000. I figured I should start with the oldest journal, who knew what I might uncover that might be pertinent to explain this journey. And Voila, I found an explanation.

There were three pages of records that I didn't remember writing or even happening. A catalog of abuse after my divorce was filed against my first husband. And then in the following pages, nothing related to that. I'd turned the page. Literally. It was almost as if all those things never took place.

So my abusive marriage had trained me to just move on when the crisis was over, to just go back to "normal." But at least this time, I was getting counseling during that whole four months.

But after four months, I stopped.

And after four months being single, single, I had to deal with …

## The Hunger

*Nails on chalkboard*
*Nerves on edge.*
*Breathing shallow.*
*Tense and stressed.*
*I know the problem.*
*It's clear to see.*
*Know the solution.*
*That can't be.*
*Being single has its perks,*
*but sex is rarely in the works.*
*Those with great skills are jerks instead.*
*Those with great hearts suck in bed.*
*Can't call the former, seems demeaning.*
*Can't call the latter, self-defeating.*
*Just long for love AND sex, it's true.*
*Wasting my time, got much to do,*
*But treading water, can't think too well.*
*Sometimes rambling on as well.*
*My mind is clearer when I'm seated.*

*I function better. Activated.*
*Hate the current options seen..*
*Need one worth something. Nice and clean.*
*Take a deep breath. Maybe work out.*
*Try to remember what life's about.*
*But when I'm hungry. Ravenous. More.*
*It's hard to act normal. Emotions pour.*
*Long overdue. My patience short.*
*My tolerance level on abort.*
*Maybe tomorrow will be a better day.*
*But not unless my minx can play.*

## G.E.L.

*That's it. I'm done.*
*I must admit.*
*Tried seven dating sites.*
*Not one worth shit.*
*And at the risk of being politically incorrect,*
*Or earning the ire of the "Know Your Worth" sect,*
*I think I'm ready to just admit.*
*I think I'm done looking for HIM.*
*I'll take a GEL that fits.*

*What's a GEL?*
*I do declare,*

*A Good Enough Lover, and maybe a spare.*
*Who am I joking?*
*The first is hard enough to find.*

*I'm not talking fantasies of love sublime.*
*Of toes curled in bliss, eyes rolled back in my head.*
*No, just someone with a clue what to do in bed.*
*A little stamina would be nice.*
*Semi-hardness once or twice.*
*Some mental stimulation is needed true,*
*And a few passionate kisses/caresses will do.*

*Seems a very easy list to fill.*
*Shrugs. Well, it seemed that way for real.*
*I used to consider myself a savant.*
*Sensual, skilled, just elegant.*
*But singleness has had its toll,*
*I think I'm jaded, heart and soul.*

*Lose interest in conversations record speed.*
*Keep my hormones on ice till my knees get weak.*
*Don't know what to say/text or confess.*
*Sometimes I'm just fantasizing him undressed.*
*But I've had enough lemons to be somewhat stressed.*
*When the day of reckoning comes, no less.*

*I've stopped expecting much.*
*That seems wise.*
*But still, it would be a welcome surprise*
*To find a GEL between my thighs.*

Even though I was horny and feeling beyond ready for casual sex, it's one thing thinking it. A whole other thing to actually do it. And whenever I would venture onto Tango or dating apps, the men reaching out to me made me turn right back around.

First, it was this new word I saw all over the place. Drama. Men didn't want a woman who had drama in her life. Well, what the hell did that mean?

I was probably the least dramatic person I knew. I was nicknamed Zen, for Christ's sake. Unflappable. Stoic even.

But I had two kids in their twenties, finding themselves, and finding car wrecks ( like the one that totaled my car), tickets from speeding and no insurance, on and off relationships with their girlfriends, and most recently a whole near-death experience, and a close call with drug dependency. Was that drama? Or just life?

Did that not matter because my kids were grown?

How the fuck should I know.

It just made my head hurt.

And then there were the dick pics. I constantly got them in my DM on Facebook, and so much on Tango, I deleted the app. There was something about being deluged with them almost daily that made me leery of the judgment of all men. Why send a stranger a nude pic? What is that supposed to mean? Don't these men understand that sending a pic of their dicks was like sending a pic of an oven. Does it work? Do you know how to use it? Let me just say that both my ex-husband and The Muse could have sent beautiful dick pics, as could Harlee, though none of them was the type. They might have been sued for false advertisement had they been. So they were the first thing that came to mind when I saw any dick pic.

Length, girth, color- all great, functionality and/or skill to implement, totally lacking- was what I pretty much assumed.

Thirdly, being on my own, away from the church, had finally allowed the questions that I always had to take center stage. And that also made me question dating.

My first husband had informed me that I had been the problem in our relationship around this time. I hadn't stayed in my place. I hadn't understood that as a man, he couldn't cheat. That cheating was a new concept. Hadn't Solomon had 300 wives and 600 concubines? Hadn't almost every patriarch had more than one wife? Yes, Old Testament vs. New Testament. Well, he wasn't a deacon or a pastor; therefore, he didn't have to have one wife. His logic seemed crazy, but I actually couldn't dispute it, not from the Bible. A holy book that seemed to have two sets of rules, one for men, one for women. That was a problem.

Then, there was my second husband and The Muse. Both men felt sex was an activity of the flesh, even in marriage; an activity born of lust that needed to be monitored, controlled, and treated, if not as a sin, as a gateway to it.

That was also a belief kind of hard to dispute. There was the Song of Solomon and certain Psalms that glorified married love. Still, it was interesting to find out when I researched that several church leaders never wanted that book, those Psalms, as part of the Bible. They wanted them relegated to the dung heap like the many other books that had not made the cut.

The history of the church and the Bible was also the most sordid tale ever told; mass murder, burning of "heretical texts," ex-communication, the Spanish Inquisition, and devices of torture.

Looking for God, I seemed to find the devil at every juncture. Alive and well and in the church and its leadership.

So I never went back to the church except for weddings, christenings, funerals. And there had been a lot of those. Some I had not attended since they were out of state.

2013 my dad, and my second husband's mother and father (my in-laws) had passed. In 2017, my grandparents passed, and my first husband's parents (my first in-laws). Seven deaths in four years. My kids suffered. I suffered. We grieved. We pushed through.

At funerals, ministers and mourners extol how your loved one is not that body, not in the grave, but in a better place. We all acknowledge that WE are not bodies but souls, spirits, consciousness. Then the following Sunday rolls around, and suddenly not only are you your body- and at war with it, but God is personified, male, white, with all the human characteristics- judgment, jealousy, and the need for you to fear HIM.

The more death I experienced, the more those ideas rang false.

I am - consciousness. God is the ultimate consciousness, not a white-haired replica of Zeus.

The more research I did, the more I realized the echoes of mythology in the Bible and the depictions of God and Christ. And I did A LOT of research. I had started in high school when I read the Bible all the way through seven times. In college, I'd enrolled in seminary. I really don't recommend doing that if you want to silence questions about God and religion. After a year, I had triple the questions and half the faith in traditional Christianity.

I'd spent 1994 to 2017 reading the history of religion, the Bible, the church. And by 2018, I'd exhausted whole sections of college libraries. There was nothing left to research.

If I wanted to experience the wind or sun or moon, I wouldn't go inside a building and look at images of them, hear a person talk about them, read about them. I would go outside and experience them.

Prayer, meditation, nature became my churches. Quiet, intimate, one on one.

And when I looked at dating profiles now, I didn't want to see "good Christian man," "God-fearing." So that narrowed my focus to "spiritual," "non-religious," "New Age," or many other labels I no longer remember. Any man who expected me to be church-going would be sorely disappointed. I was no longer that girl.

I was now the performer. Regularly.

So now It's time to introduce Baba.

Baba Fana, a drummer, but much more. Old enough to be my father. And not a romantic interest at all. I don't know where to put him in my book because I'm not sure when we met, but this was the year that I finally accepted his invitation to come to his class at The Shrine of the Black Madonna, Conversations in African Culture and History.

Whether he had invited me for months or years, I couldn't tell you. We performed together a lot. Unplanned. Open mics are that way. Running into people and taking the stage together often happened with poets and musicians. He was the only one who ever took the casual encounter and followed up with calls and texts.

I'd never been to a shrine and still had enough Christianity in me to find the idea sacrilegious at first. But finally, I went, and I never left.

I drove into the parking lot. Got out of my car and stopped mid-step. As a performer, I know energy. It swells in the crowd. It dies off and is revived. It energizes the performers and the audience. It is a living, breathing thing.

I had never felt energy in a parking lot. Delicious. Pure. Like stepping into a crystal waterfall but not getting wet, cleansing, refreshing, renewing, invigorating. What was this place?

The energy got stronger as I walked across this massive parking lot, divided in two by a median. There was a handicapped ramp to the left of the steps entering the building, although I knew it was for wheelchairs. I had a distinct impression that anyone who rolled up that ramp might stand up and walk.

I opened the front door almost hesitantly. There were two tables in the vestibule on either side. One was covered with business cards, community newspapers, and flyers; the other was empty. An ad for the Buy Black Market 1st and 3rd Saturdays was plastered on the inner door.

I opened the second door and walked into an expansive room. A counter with African books in a glass case was to my right. To my left, African sculptures, masks, tapestries covered every inch of the walls. Several classrooms, doors closed, could be seen across the room in a slightly sunken area that one had to descend three steps to get to.

Every person I'd ever lost felt like they were here. The energy of a thousand ancestors.

I'd never been in a mosque before, and this was not one. But I suddenly understood how a room could be filled with hundreds of people kneeling on prayer rugs doing obeisance. Their prayers one unified voice to the Almighty.

I hadn't known I was homesick for this place of connection, for the presence of those I had lost, but when I walked in this shrine-that was the right word for it, I realized. It suddenly felt like I had never lost a loved one. Not my father, grandparents, or in-laws; those seven people felt there, loving, lifting, encouraging me. I wanted to drop there and offer thanksgiving, lift my hands, lift my eyes and kneel to the splendor of my culture and those who had come before me carrying it in their heads, hearts, hands. Their souls and voices were the hum in the air, an almost audible welcome home.

Tears welled in my eyes, and no one had said a word to me. Someone walked up and ushered me into Baba's class. I walked into classroom four. It was a library with half the room empty. The front had a map of Africa, more sculptures, and tapestries. A drum sat in the center of a circle, a small table next to it with a bowl of water and a small empty woven basket, an offering receptacle.

He smiled at me, gestured to an empty chair. Our eyes met briefly. Pausing, I registered he knew what I felt. I knew then that he'd known when he invited me that I would feel just that. Class began.

There is not enough space to explain this class. That would be a whole book in itself. Suffice it to say this, close your eyes, picture yourself in Africa on a plain. A griot sits crossed-legged in a long robe, his back resting on a cassava tree. Like all his students, you are sitting on the ground before him. His voice rises and falls, explaining the origins of the universe, your people, your place in the world, your duties to the Creator, your tribe, the larger world. He explains the world outside your tribe, the toxic attitudes you will face, and how to overcome them.

There are no questions in your mind. As soon as they are formed, those are the next answers that pour from his mouth.

Every word spoken feels not like language but like sustenance: chunks of mango, slivers of banana, a handful of almonds, barley cakes with honey, and the crispest, sweetest apple juice you've ever tasted to wash it all down. You eat, nourished. You drink, hydrated.

You rise at the end, hug him and your classmates, give or don't give an offering, and feel re-born.

That was class.

I never knew that I'd wondered what it might have been like if Wakanda were real, if the colonizers had never invaded, if there were a piece of African culture left pristine, untouched. But in the Shrine, in that classroom especially, it was our own Wakanda.

I was there every chance I had. I tried to explain the experience to others, but I don't think I ever did it justice until now.

2018, writing, performing, The Shrine, The Class, were the pillars of my new life.

So when I went back to dating sites, the contrast was even starker than it had been previously, and the ability to walk away quickly was even more pronounced.

Before, I'd had my four questions as sifters, but now I was much more attuned to energy. How did I feel when I encountered his voice, his presence? What was his energy like? How did we vibe?

I woke up and went to bed, listening to affirmations. I journaled about my hopes and dreams like I had when I first got married. I was beginning to walk, think, live and breathe positivity.

In my personal life, I had never been happier.

At work, I had never been more stressed.

So I protected my personal life and energy with a tiger-like ferocity. No man would take this place of peace from me that had taken my whole life to achieve.

Earlier in this chapter, I had explained how I had me- mentally, emotionally, what the Shrine and the Class gave me was me- culturally and spiritually. There was no doctrine. No religion. No name for this belief system. There was the Creator, the tribe, and me.

There was no war between my flesh and spirit for the first time in my life, no conflict between my head and heart. I was following the path of Maat, balance. I was living based on principles, divine laws.

Spirituality is the recognition that things we cannot see are as essential and life-altering as the things we can see. For me, it includes the acceptance of universal truths. These ideas have been believed for millennia and are often verified by science. Like, but not limited to…

1. There is a source. There is order in the universe.
2. We are eternal (energy is neither created nor destroyed).
3. We are energy, and that energy can attract and repel things, situations, and people.
4. Emotions and thoughts, and words can both harm and heal.
5. Balance, rest, and stillness are essential in life, as are actions.
6. You should treat others as you want to be treated.
7. Actions have consequences.
8. The mind has the power to change reality.

9. Worry, fear, and stress should be replaced with peace, expectancy, and detachment.
10. Know thyself. Be true to thyself.
11. Both solitude and community are important

## Symmetry

*I am made in the image of the goddess, the universe, the source.*

*Good and evil,*

*Light and dark,*

*Cold and hot,*

*Yin and yang.*

*Balance.*

*And it feels good to embrace the dichotomy.*

*It feels ... right.*

*More right than 30 years of Abrahamic faith,*

*Hating my flesh,*

*Crucifying my desires,*

*Finally, I understand-*

*Faiths that cause believers to be at war with themselves*

*Cannot*

*Cause them to live in peace with others.*

Some called this The Conscious Community. I couldn't tell you if I was a part of that or not. I rubbed shoulders with them, but I had one teacher, Baba.

Who had taught them? What did they believe?

I didn't know. It wasn't important.

Unlike Christianity, there was no need to proselytize and make every other faith wrong. There was the Creator. We were the children of the Creator. We were all here to bring beauty, harmony, and communion within and without. That simple. That inclusive.

Universal truths, like those below, were available to all.

1. Everything begins with thoughts. Thoughts become things. Changing thoughts and attitudes can alter one's lifestyle and future. (The law of mentalism)
2. The law of correspondence. Spiritual, mental, and physical reality are connected. The outer reality reflects the inner reality.
3. The law of Polarity. Life is balanced. Good and evil. Yin and yang. Hot and cold. Up and down. In between the poles, I exist. I can focus on either the good or the evil. What I focus on is strengthened.
4. The law of vibration. All is energy. Emotion, matter, and thought are all energy. Energy cannot be destroyed; it can only be transformed.
5. The law of rhythm. Life moves in cycles. What goes up must come down. Peaks and valleys. Life is like a pendulum swinging. When it reaches the farthest arc, it moves in the opposite direction. Wisdom is about knowing when you're high, enjoy it, and plan for the low, and when you're low, to remember it won't last forever and plan for the high.

6. The law of sowing and reaping or the law of cause and effect. What is sown will be reaped; every effect has a cause. Everything happens according to universal laws.
7. The law of process- results are rarely instantaneous. Most things have a gestation or incubation period. If you want the results, you must sacrifice and be consistent during the process. There are only two reasons for failure: you quit or die.

But the strange thing about change is the world didn't change with me. There were still the same dating sites, with the same people, asking the same questions, and eventually, HALT led me back there.

I went to a Weight Watchers meeting once, and the facilitator said HALT. We generally made poor choices and found it challenging to stick to an eating plan if we got too HUNGRY, ANGRY, LONELY, or TIRED. I was notorious for HL and T.

Those eventually led me back to the dating trail. My H was a certain Hunger. I wrote about it about six pages ago. It seemed there was not enough spirituality in the world to silence it. Then there was the L, and the T. Weight Watchers warned that any one of these was enough to start and fuel a binge; two or more could derail one's progress altogether. I'd had three alive and active for months. I sat in that Weight Watcher's meeting, not thinking about food any longer, but about men, my track record, and how it seemed an eternity since Ace had left.

Let the dates begin.

**Lesson 9:**

Imagine: Turn up your heart's radio. Blast your inner stereo loud.

# CHAPTER 10

I was looking for my next Ace or JJ, or even more miraculously, Mr. Right.

It was 2018. I'd been divorced four years and had four amazing lovers. And the two not-so-good ones made up for that disappointment by being amazing men who deeply enhanced my life. As I reminisced, I wrote this poem in homage to the lovemaking that I had experienced that was now just the stuff of my wet dreams.

*Can I drive you wild…before we intertwine?*

*Can I make you moan? Call my name?*

*Lose your mind?*

*Maybe add in a massage? Give some head, 69?*

*And when you penetrate; hold it there for a sec.*
*Hear me gasp, kiss me deep,*
*let your dick stroke my clit.*
*Slow stroke me like a violin,*
*Play my body like the sax.*
*Feel me wrap my legs around the middle of your back.*
*Our tempos mesh, I grind on you.*
*You slap my ass, resume.*
*Flip you over it's my turn. Reverse cowgirl ensues.*
*You bite your lip and match my thrusts.*
*I take my time. I lick. I suck,*
*Head thrown back, I savor grind. I revel in your feel.*
*Cumming isn't next. Let's see what else reveals.*
*Maybe take me from the side.*
*Or doggy style might do.*
*I want every muscle worked as I release stress through you.*
*I've lost count of positions.*
*The clock is outta mind.*
*With your stamina and mine, we capture the divine.*
*"Oh God! Oh God! Oh God." So good how could we quit?*
*Want to savor every second you slide between my lips.*
*So sensual. So mesmerized. Problems cease to exist.*
*We're in a fuckcation, off on a sensual trip.*
*You may pull my hair or choke me.*
*I might scratch or bite, it's true.*

*We both can be wildcats unleashed, but we can be gentle too.*
*I ride on waves of pleasure. My body humming like a song.*
*And we just keep going as the hours tick along.*
*I'm insatiable. You're ravenous. But eventually, we're filled.*
*Another marathon is ending.*
*We feel sated and fulfilled.*
*Our legs weak, we must lie still*
*till we have to rise and clean.*
*3 hours? Uh huh. More like 13.*

Back to the dating apps I went, and the first one out the gate was…

## Date Forty-Seven:

6 foot 6- The tallest guy I ever dated, handsome, intelligent, articulate, sexy, a good kisser. I discovered he was a good cook on our second date when he invited me over and made dinner. Then he proceeded to turn on The Real Housewives of somewhere. I hated shows like that and had told him so. With cable, DVDs, regular tv, and, I don't know, actual live company in your apartment, I couldn't believe he picked reality tv of the lowest sort. I left.

## Date Forty-Eight:

Slingblade- When we talked on the phone, the conversation was fine, but in person, he repeated himself and made um hmmm sounds just like on the movie "Slingblade." At first, I thought he was joking and asked why he was doing that; he proceeded to respond, "Doing what?" It was hard to ignore and harder not to laugh. I succeeded in subduing my chuckles but felt no chemistry to pursue another date.

Now that you're 100 something pages into this book, and I'm on date 47, some men may be complaining that these guys I stopped seeing seem like "good guys." Every few weeks, some guy on Facebook complains about how he's been put in the friend zone, or women only want thugs. Here are my thoughts on that. A grown man needs some tools besides the one he was born with between his legs- conversation, his touch, his eyes, and his kiss, to begin with. If he doesn't give the appearance of having those four, most women will friend zone him or dismiss him altogether.

**<u>Tool 1: The Conversation</u>** is where date #48 lost me.

Can you hold a conversation on more than one topic? (Sex questions don't count.) Are you a good listener? Does she feel valued because you ask about her, not her height, her bra size, her choice of underwear? Does the interaction leave her feeling comfortable or dirty? Conversation rules the nation.

## Date Forty-Nine:

The Heavy- I really liked this guy. He was tall, stocky solid, but felt cuddly when I hugged him. We had a blast on our date. Then he pawed me. I wasn't ready. His hands, like two skin-covered sledgehammers, reached for me, groped, jerked. My face fell. He pulled back. Pulling his hands into himself as if he were Edward Scissorhands, and he had just nicked me.

"I know," he said. "You don't want me to touch you."

"I did. I REALLY did. Was fantasizing about it, in fact. Can you be gentler?"

"No. I can't. It's been a problem for years. It's always a problem. Some men have clammy hands. I have these paws. And they just aren't gentle. At all."

We talked about other things. And talked for weeks after. But he never again touched me, and I was sad. He lacked **Tool 2: Touch.**

A man should be able to stir and maintain desire by knowing how to caress, knead, massage, stroke, and maneuver a woman's body. He should be able to show his ability to touch her from the first date, brushing her hand, putting his hand behind her, and ushering her to the table, kissing her hand, giving her a hug, holding her hand. He should pay attention to her body language, touch her like she's precious but not fragile. Touch her like just the act itself of running his fingers across her skin is a privilege. And she should do the same for him. That touch alone should be like silk and satin; like the man or woman is writing their names on every inch. No expanse should be neglected, overlooked, or unexplored. The touch itself should be erotic, seductive, purposeful, and unhurried. The kiss and the touch together ... ah, the sweetest bliss.

## Date Fifty:

The Nose Knows impressed me. Nice dresser, smelled great, great manners, sophisticated, worldly, accomplished. But every time my eyes would linger on him, and he should have returned the eye contact, he didn't. I'd catch him stealing glances at me. He flirted. He was very consistent in pursuing me. But the lack of eye contact made me feel he was self-conscious about his appearance or just hiding something. It destroyed the whole vibe.

Some may say, "He was just not that into you." Possible. Though he pursued me enough to get the date and was footing the bill, but of course, he could have had ulterior motives. So maybe that's true.

Beauty is in the eye of the beholder. I'm a woman, and we are often our own worst critics. As a pre-teen, I cringed when peers nicknamed me Dolly Parton 2. I wanted to be willowy, not robust, dainty, not curvaceous. And when athleticism ruled my days, my thigh muscles bulged as I strutted. Leg pressing a whole stack leaves its mark. When I was a size 8, 14- pounder who worked out 2-4 hours a day as a college athlete and had 15% body fat which my trainer told me could cause me to stop having periods, I still thought my 25-inch waist should be smaller.

Having kids had put several extra pounds on my frame, but since it gave me double D breasts, wider hips, and a rounder backside, I was actually getting much more attention than when I looked like a female body builder.

I've told you I had no confidence in 2014. I felt unattractive. I'd been even heavier during my marriage. I'd hired a nutritionist the year I got divorced and worked really hard to change my eating habits.

But four years into my single life, I was finally embracing the skin I was in. It was okay that I was voluptuous. After twins and heartbreak, pounds gained and lost, I think I'm finally at peace, done apologizing for my full lips, my thick waist, my 38 DDs. Size 18 sounds nice and right and round. Size 8 was fabulous, and sizes 12,

14, 16, I enjoyed. But I revel in my hips and dips. The swell of my cleavage. My voluptuous body matches my mind, my mouth, my sex drive. Take me or leave me. Those that can handle me 100-proof deserve me, and those that can't weren't for me to begin with.

I am zaftig, buxom with a zest for life and love. Primal, regal, unrestrained. I am desire personified.

So when a man dates me, to me, it means he accepts and is attracted to me- BBW, full-figured, thick, or even fat if that is what he sees. Acceptance is empowering. It gives serenity, and it also gives me the right to want him to look at me and use…

**Tool 3: His Eyes.** The eyes have it. They're the window to the soul. If your eyes don't show your desire, then you're a fucking liar. Don't waste my time. Looking at a woman as you pleasure her should be a thrill; a turn-on; should heighten the mood and intensify the arousal. The lights should be dim, not off. You should wanna see the results of your handiwork because you should KNOW before you step into the room what the result will be. Total satisfaction. Seduction. Intense orgasmic pleasure beyond words. If you don't wanna see that, hmmm. I guess you don't have the tools to make it happen. The same goes for the woman. If she's not looking at you, she's probably thinking about someone else. Ratchet.

## Date Fifty-One:

The Braggart- He took me to my favorite restaurant and seduced me with his words. I sat across from him- wet, needy, ready for the date to end and the lovemaking to begin. In my head, we were half undressed. He walked me to my car where he proceeded to give me the second worst kiss ever.

**Tool 4: His Kiss.** The kiss at the end of a first date can be a deal-breaker for me. It's like a movie trailer; it sets the mood and whets the appetite for the main event. The man who pulls me to him and slowly, sensually captures my tongue and caresses my lips paints an image of seduction and finesse to come, total mastery in the art of lovemaking. He knows he wants me, and he makes me feel his desire down to the depths of my soul. That kiss can leave me breathless, coming back for seconds or thirds or an all-nighter. The quick peck - automatic friend zone. The hesitant - I don't know what the fuck I'm doing kisser, just annoys. The I don't do that PDA stuff non-kisser is too boring and strait-laced to handle me.

I mentioned early on one thing that drew me to my previous lovers was that they could handle me. I didn't have a bad attitude or childish behavior. I didn't throw temper tantrums. I just had a high sex drive, high enough that it was problematic for my second husband, The Muse, and Harlee. So having a man that could handle it was one of my top priorities, and kissing was one sign of that, not a flawless sign, but one that didn't require too much intimacy.

Before I continue with date #52, let me say as human beings, we love categories. Fruit or vegetable. Liquid or solid. Pure or sinful. Christian or heathen. H20 can appear as liquid, solid, or gas. But nature and life are not usually that simple. So if it bothers you that the last chapter was high vibrational and spiritual, and this one is sensual, I guess I should say that I had long left the dogma that stated there should be a division. That I couldn't have both. Or all.

In this book, you might see spirituality alongside politics and sensuality and black consciousness and environmentalism and intellectualism. Realize that these beliefs are all me. No boxes, fluidity.

Dates Fifty-Two to Fifty-Seven all lacked **Tool 5: Balance.**

## Date Fifty-Two:

Musclehead Barbie was gorgeous, truly beautiful, and you know how much I like handsome men. He should have been a shoo-in, but he droned on about sports incessantly. I don't think he took a breath the whole hour. He certainly didn't eat. Although I played volleyball and basketball and had no problem watching a game with a man I was dating, talking about sports on a date was something I had never done and never want to do again.

## Date Fifty-Three:

Airport was a pilot. You would think he would have the most amazing stories, be personable, charming. Nope. He just complained and complained and complained. I didn't know one person could have that many gripes. It was truly mind-boggling. I began to wonder if there was anything on Earth that didn't annoy him.

## Date Fifty-Four:

Tiny Toons blathered on about, you guessed it, cartoons, anime, Manga, Comicon, superheroes.

## Date Fifty-Five:

The Interruptor; Well, the name says it all. He interrupted me so much that I stopped talking altogether.

## Date Fifty-Six:

Memorex repeated everything I said. Everything. Repeated. I said it. He said it. Sometimes rephrased. It wasn't a conversation. It was an echo.

## Date Fifty-Seven:

The Two Minute Mexican was the last time I dated outside of my race. Not because of him. Just because I realized I was just more attracted to black men. Give me a minute, I'll come back to him.

A date is a chance to get to know the other person and let them get to know you. Mutuality. Reciprocity. Talking AND listening. Not monopolizing the conversation. Not interrogating the person. Displaying your personality while getting to know theirs. Balance. Balance also means to me not being too aggressive or too passive. Not being too forward or too reserved. It's not easy, but it's probably a major reason there aren't second dates.

So the first five dates above lacked balance in the conversational topics as well as listening and talking. The Two Minute Mexican had a different problem.

We sat. Ordered drinks, His first statement was, "I bet you taste good.

G- O-I-D; good." He looked down as if trying to see my crotch through the table.

I looked at him, stunned for two reasons. I'd never had a man talk about how I taste in public, on a first date, before we even had water on the table. And he couldn't spell a four-letter word.

He waited.

I responded with I don't really consider sex till about two dates in when I see compatibility, chemistry and feel like the interaction has the potential to be long-lasting.

He said that's too long. Two dates could mean we've known each other for weeks or even a month. Emotional attachment may have occurred. Then if the sex is wack, it's harder to walk away.

I replied, you know most women get propositioned or get dick pics sent to their inboxes. You are talking to me about sex. You don't know my last name, if I have kids, my personality, what I do for a living. You know nothing about me.

He replied, "I'm offended you're comparing me to disrespectful men. You have some nerve. I was just being honest. Women say they want honesty, but then they can't handle it. We have nothing else to talk about."

And he left. We never spoke again.

I ordered, ate. The waiter asked what happened. I told him, shrugged, and he walked off shaking his head, passing the story on to the other waitstaff who all came over one by one and asked did that really happen.

Yes.

The manager came over and gave me a free dessert. I laughed and thanked him.

He said, "Damn, I'm glad I'm married. Dating sucks."

I sat there enjoying my meal and my dessert- a deliciously creamy cheesecake, amongst new allies who could not believe this dating scenario. It was a great night.

I posted the whole thing on social media, just as I told it here, and asked:

1. Why do some men think they are so different when they are essentially doing the same thing?
2. Why do some men feel "being honest" should somehow substitute for properly approaching a woman?
3. Why are some men so easily offended when their inappropriate behavior is mentioned?

The comments were interesting. Food for thought.

Balance also means realizing the world is not filled with people exactly like you. I love hearing new perspectives, but others find any alternate viewpoint maddening. I believe variety is the spice of life.

## Date Fifty-Eight:

The Adversary was very attracted to me. When he wasn't arguing with me, that was all he would talk about. I think he thought the purpose of the date was to ask my opinion on topics, and when he did not agree, spend an inordinate amount of time trying to convince me I was wrong. I never have understood why it's so important to others what strangers believe. But it was tedious and turned intellectual stimulation into a silent stalemate. I wasn't giving him any more fodder for the fire he wanted to set under my beliefs.

Dates Fifty-Nine to Sixty-Three lacked balance and common sense.

## Date Fifty-Nine:

Mr. My Kids- His kids lived in England. I learned everything about them. I kept asking about him, but every answer somehow started with my daughter, son, and kids. I love my kids too, but I wasn't trying to date or get to know his kids. To me, it was absolutely inappropriate.

## Date Sixty:

The Jamaican Sex Fiend was fascinated by the freedom in other countries regarding sex. He talked about sexual restaurants and clubs and wanted to know if I would go or had gone. He'd been a swinger but said he was out of "the lifestyle", but I didn't believe him.

## Date Sixty-One:

Mr. $100,000 Houses are Crap- He was a traveling salesman looking for someone to wine and dine when he came to town. She had to be classy, well put together, etc. He was impressed with me but was more interested in my resume than me as a person. It was the first time; I got a glimpse of what that must feel like for men.

How much do you make? How big is your house? How much did it cost? How old is your car? I couldn't figure out for the life of me why a successful man would even care. Finally, it dawned on me that he measured a person's worth in dollar signs.

## Date Sixty-Two:

The Erotic Amateur Poet- He was going to be late for our first date and sent me a poem that I could read while I waited. I wished he hadn't. I write erotic poetry. By this time, you've read some of mine. But first off, I didn't know that's what he was sending. Secondly, I'd never read anything so graphic in my life. And not graphic in a good way.

I lost my appetite.

It was an overshare of Titanic magnitude, and just like the ship, my interest sunk to the bottom of an icy ocean.

## Date Sixty-Three:

The Cop - This was the one, and only time I went out with a cop. In conversation, the ones I'd met online were super aggressive. Angry. Bitter. Judgmental. One wrong word set them completely the fuck off. This guy seemed sweet. We met at Starbucks. He was cute, charming. Then when he walked me to my car, he tried to put his hand down my shirt.

I pulled away immediately, and he said, "I know you're a teacher, and you're probably not into public displays of affection.

You don't want a student, another teacher, or a parent to see you disheveled. But I'm a cop. No one's gonna say anything to you."

It was such a weird statement.

1. I could be a private person regardless of my job.
2. His job didn't change my standards.
3. The entitlement. Geez. What else did he feel he should get away with because he was "a cop"? The question was more than a little scary, and I definitely didn't want to know the answer.

## Dates Sixty-Four to Seventy

These next seven I desired. Every one of them. It was strange to get to this point where the universe seemed to be sending me what I wanted, kinda sorta, not exactly.

### Date Sixty-Four:

Tennessee- I met on Tango. He was just in town for the weekend and invited me out to Sam's Boat to hang with him and his fraternity brothers as they watched an MMA fight. He was handsome, a great date, fun, and gave me a fabulous good night kiss at my car. He came to one of my shows years later, and to this day, we are still Facebook friends. And he is still fine. I would have loved to get to know him better, but he lives in Tennessee, and neither one of us believes in long-distance relationships.

## Date Sixty-Five:

Quinz was a workaholic on a five-year plan, preparing for retirement. I admired his drive, his work ethic, and loved his sex appeal, but he wasn't making time for anything but the Benjamins.

## Date Sixty-Six:

Bern was looking for a wife from back home. Nigeria. A traditional woman, a child bearer, a cook, a maid, someone he could love for sure, but someone who would never consider working outside the home. I had never met anyone so traditional. The man took the idea of being the sole provider seriously. We went out just to talk, to hang, to watch movies. He had one type of woman in mind, and I was definitely not her.

## Date Sixty-Seven:

The Bearded One actually met me at McDonald's, with his son in tow. I shit you not. We had a great talk, G-rated, over fries, shakes, and burgers as his son ran in and out of the indoor playground. We are still Facebook friends to this day.

## Date Sixty-Eight:

Yuk Mouth broke my heart a little. My friend in New Jersey had fallen off the map, and Yuk Mouth had appeared in my inbox. Brains. Wit. Banter. Oh, banter. That poem is coming up soon. I swear if I could fall in love through text and calls. YM would have had me- hook, line, and sinker. He was actually my first connect after Ace left, so we had been talking a long time, months before we actually met. I actually didn't even want to meet him. I liked our conversations so much I was scared to lose them if the date tanked. He alternated residences - here and Dallas- and was only here a few weeks every three or four months. Not the kind of relationship I wanted. But finally, the day arrived when we would meet, and I saw him across the parking lot of Hooters. Yes, Hooters. SMDH. It was an omen.

He smiled, revealing rows of black tobacco-stained teeth. I instantly was transported back to my childhood, staring at actors on *Little House on the Prairie*. I stopped mid-step. As a kid, I thought that was make-up. As an adult, I'd never thought about it. Never seen it. I had imagined kissing this man. Now I couldn't imagine hugging him. How was it possible to have teeth like that?

I entered the restaurant but couldn't stay long. Now it was my eyes ( Tool 3) that were looking anywhere but into his eyes, his face, his mouth. Like with Mr. Cleen and The Musky Mentalist, I made an excuse and left.

**Tool 6: Hygiene** I shouldn't have to elaborate.

## Date Sixty-Nine:

The Pint-Sized Pimp- I'm 5'6, so a man's height has never mattered to me. I like them my height or taller generally, and PSP was eye to eye with me. We met on Tango also. He followed me forever. Liking my posts. Commenting. Flirting. Never hitting my inbox. So finally, I jumped in his. And he asked me to a sports bar. We had had some steamy conversations. And when I arrived, he was already at the bar, drinking, looking as at home as a man could be. I grabbed the barstool next to him, and he complimented me, leaning over casually, whispering in my ear. "Damn, girl. You look good. Smell good. too."

He had all the tools and **Tool 7: The Voice**. In the movie *Dune*, they talk about THE VOICE. This mesmerizing collection of vocals that hypnotize the listener. Whatever is stated, is done immediately, no question. Total compliance. Like magic. I wrote in my journal, "Sound

Sound is the closest thing to God. In the beginning, God said. So the man I love will have a voice that calls to me, not an Urkel, Pewee Hermann voice but a manly timber that beckons to my lobes, that loosens up my loins, so whether he's profound, profane, or purely playful, I will hear AND listen.

Seductive, melodic, masculine, confident you will call to me, and I will answer. Acknowledge you. Honor you. You are the first voice I want to hear each morning; the last one I want to hear each night."

His voice made me look into his eyes, mistake. They were sexy for no goddamn reason. And then he ran a finger along my chin to my lips. I saw myself in my head, in his lap, kissing him. I didn't. I wanted to.

I couldn't tell you what we talked about. He smelled too good. Sounded too good. His words were like a fragrant miasma about my head, making me high.

I . Wanted. Him.

We walked outside, hours later. It seemed like minutes, and he pulled me to him, gifting me the kiss I'd been pleading for subconsciously all night. It was all I wanted but not nearly enough.

Then he said, "You know I want you, but I don't do relationships. Too much trouble. I just do one night stands. Are you down?"

Huh? One night. Oh, hell no. I could tell I would want more than one night. I wanted every night, every morning, every afternoon. And maybe a few quickies in between.

The lump in my throat was so big. I shook my head.

He whispered in my ear, "The offer will always stand. I don't see myself settling down till my kids are grown. Just let me know." He kissed my neck and slowly walked away, his hand holding mine till the fingers lightly let go at the last minute.

I walked back to my car, wet, throbbing, miserable, wanting to change my mind but knowing that would be utter stupidity.

## Date Seventy:

Accent- This Jamaican should have had the voice; he had the accent for it. But the closest thing to his personality was a terrier, jumping, twisting, biting at your heels for attention. His voice matched. We ended up meeting at the same sports bar, though I actually didn't realize it till I drove up and remembered PSP. My body started reacting to the memories. I literally walked into the bar, planning to get a drink to calm myself down. Accent was there. Eager. Friendly. We talked. It was nice. Boring. I glanced around the room, taking in the slot machines, the pool table, the group of men standing there, one intently looking at me. When he caught my eye, he smiled. PSP, Accent noticed me get quiet.

"You know him?"

"Yes, I'm just gonna say hi. I'll be right back."

Some may hate me for that, but I couldn't help myself. I walked over. PSP slid an arm around me whispered in my ear, "Fancy meeting you here. Were you looking for me?"

"No."

"It's all right if you were. I don't mind competition. If I wanted you, I'd have you."

"Cocky ass."

"Nope, just truthful. He can't handle you. I can, and I know you better. The offer still stands."

"I don't do one night stands. I gotta get back."

"Okay. I'll hit you up online. Have fun," He smiled a knowing smile, knowing Accent didn't have my attention or my desire or a chance at getting or keeping either one.

I walked away almost determined to prove PSP wrong, throwing myself into the date with even more attention, more encouragement, hoping Accent could compete.

As Accent and I walked outside, I couldn't help but remember the last time I had stood on this sidewalk, my lips embraced by PSPs, our tongues dancing, his breath like a whisper on my neck.

Accent had his own plans and whipped out his phone. I thought he would take a picture of us, surprising but not completely unprecedented. But instead, he opened a file in his gallery, hundreds of pictures of him, his anatomy. I turned and looked at him.

"What the fuck?"

"You don't like them?"

"You sit around taking pictures of yourself?"

"Yeah. Why not? I like what I see."

"That's weird."

“Not any weirder than women taking pictures of their hair, their nails, their toes. Not weird at all.”

“It's not something you show someone you just met. Good night.”

He spent days calling and texting me. I didn't respond.

PSP called and texted me too. I did respond. But I never went out with him again.

## Date Seventy-One:

Milton- There are some men that I hate putting on this list. Not because they were bad dates, just the opposite. They were life changers. They changed the way I saw myself, the world, my future. JJ. The Muse, Harlee, and Milton. Milton was a musician. Music is magic. Pure and simple magic. It's a spell that captures minds, hearts, and souls and transforms them, uplifts them. Musicians are alchemists who turn base metals into gold. So I should not have been surprised he had such a deep impact on me, but today I still am. We talked for a long time. No plans to meet. Both busy but enjoying the banter.

One night he called me from the studio. "You popped up on my page, a poem," he said, "You wrote this?"

"Yes."

"For real, I mean really, truly, like from scratch, you wrote this."

I laughed, almost a little offended though- what did that mean? I stated more insistently, "YES." *Negro, don't ask me again.*

"Woah. I mean damn. It's good. I don't even read poetry. I never read poetry. I thought the whole idea was hella boring. But I liked this. A Lot. Would you read it to me? Your voice, these words. Shit."

# Banter

*Engage me in a conversation,*
*Witty repartee,*
*Draw me in with witticism,*
*Flirting so subtly.*
*Vulgarity unnecessary,*
*Put your mind on view*
*Intelligence and character should be part of you*
*Talk of only work and sports*
*With me tends to bore.*
*I need mental stimulation...*
*Dig deeper. Give me more.*
*Talk on politics, religion, arts.*
*Debate me casually.*
*Leave me with some food for thought*
*Till the next time we meet.*
*Banter.*
*It's so cool, so lost with texting on the rise*
*But it's step one, gate one, lock one to get between my thighs.*
*And the man who has it,*
*Grows taller in my eyes.*
*Engaged in it, I blush and grin,*
*It raises him above other men*

*That mouthpiece, his rap can snag my soul.*

*Especially if he's masculine and bold.*

*Sexy too (won't hurt a bit)*

*But average men grow more who spit*

*Some knowledge, wisdom, experience.*

*How sexy is some common sense?*

*I'll end saying men without banter bore,*

*I check out and head for the door.*

*They may be "nice," but I won't see if they can't communicate maturely.*

*Three things are pivotal.*

*Not my rules.*

*Sex, money, and communication- tools.*

*Lack one, you suffer.*

*Two? you're "dead."*

*Three? Become a monk instead.*

*But with all three, you earn a prize.*

*Respect, attraction optimized.*

*So dust off your voice box.*

*And begin.*

*Communicate and slide within.*

I started reading the poem, thinking how I felt when I wrote it, the longing, the anticipation and excitement when banter appeared, the total rapture when it connected a young bachelor and me in its erotic dance. And the words slid off my lips warm butter, a caress, an invitation, seductive, perfectly pronounced, playful and poignant, capturing the highs and lows of 70 dates, two failed marriages, and even my boyfriends in high school and college. For a minute, every love, loss cycle was relived and transmitted through the phone that bonded Milton and me together. I finished.

There was a silence.

A long enough pause for me to flashback to my first recitation at The Sugar Hill Lounge, The Muse as my cheerleader, the flurry of publications that followed. I hadn't read to anyone since then. I had never been asked to.

And then what seemed like the loudest noise I had ever heard broke through my reverie. Whoops, and whistles and "Where can I hear you perform?" "When is your next show?" erupted. A cacophony of voices. He'd had me on speakerphone to a whole audience I didn't even know existed.

"They like your poem written. They love it performed. You should be performing. Make people come pay to see you. I would pay you. We've got a radio show. The last season is done now, but I would pay you a thousand dollars to take a fifteen minute segment of our show and perform 4-5 poems. They'd have to be memorized and practiced." He got silent a moment. "You hear them? Still clapping. They'd get everybody they know to tune in, and those people would tell people to tune in. We already have a huge audience, but you would get us to tap into a whole new demographic. And who is doing spoken word on the radio? Nobody. Untapped market. Girl, you are a goldmine. Stop giving your shit away for free; make 'em line up at the door for hours to see you."

Now, I was the one in silence. $1000? Radio? My own show? People lined up for hours? I was relieved when he said they had to get back to recording because I had no response to any of that. I was a poet, not a spoken word artist. Spoken word artists intimidated the shit out of me.

But they thought I was. My mom had said I could be. That I'd memorized Shakespeare, memorized all kinds of lines- Woolf. Emerson, Dickinson, Hughes, Angelou. Why in the world would I think I couldn't memorize something from my own mind and heart?

Because of that night, I practiced for my first spoken word performance, expecting him/them to be in attendance. They weren't. But a mind once stretched never goes back to its old dimensions again. And I kept performing and kept inviting them. They never came. Milton and I met three times and then lost touch, but that night he changed my vision of myself, of my future, and I went on to make a lot more than $1000 for performing poetry. Not in one show, but in two months, I could make that.

I had been on one path and suddenly, dramatically, was shown a drastically different path because he had **Tool 8: Vision.** Many people ignore those signs, those doors of opportunity. Still, for some reason, I never have, and because of that, I am the person I am today.

Besides expanding my vision, I realized my time with Milton had given me one more thing, a demonstration of the law of giving. When I was with The Muse, I had been the visionary for him. He wanted to make more money, and we brainstormed and came up with cyber security, and he had made excuses of how he wasn't good with computers. Just like me and my fears of memorizing, And I had reminded him he was an expert photographer but hadn't always been. I gave him my son's old computer, and we celebrated every little gain together. His income increased by $25,000 through that certification.

Some had tempted me to see him dumping me as him using me to get a leg up, improve his life, and move on, a pattern my mom had experienced when her fiancée broke up with her. But I saw our relationship, I saw me giving to him, as a blessing, not a curse. Now someone had been sent by karma, by the law of giving and RECEIVING to expand my vision of myself. That seed sown in The Muse bore fruit in Laughz and Lyrics, the show I filed my DBA for a month after this conversation with Milton.

**Lesson 10:**

Find out what's in his toolbox. It may be just the right tool for the job.

# CHAPTER 11

# Kindred

## Date Seventy-Two:

When The Young Lion, jumped in my inbox, I'd deleted another dating profile and didn't want to meet anybody. I was depressed. Missing The Muse. I was writing, getting published, and The Muse wasn't there. It all felt empty. The accomplishments resulted in a post on Facebook with a handful of likes. The checks in the mailbox that could pay a department store credit card, a water bill, a Firestone charge were appreciated but didn't feed my soul like his support had.

A week of TYL asking me out in many different ways, while I steadily turned him down, led to him saying, "Let me take you out and take your mind of all that." I pictured his beautiful smile from his profile picture and said yes.

I don't remember if I was anticipating the date, but I was surprised by his height when he arrived. He was much shorter than me, but we sat, drank, and ate, and true to his word, our date was the first time in a long time I laughed that much, felt that light, and absolutely forgot what was bothering me. Before I arrived, I'd been worried. My son had to go to court. I don't know how it came up in the conversation, but he gave me some really great advice. Mature. Wise.

Then on a totally different topic, he said something odd. No one my age or even close would have said it. So odd, I stopped mid conversation.

"How old are you?" I asked.

"Thirty. You're just 35; that's no difference at all," he said. " I know you thought I was 35 because the Facebook group we're in has that as a rule, but I know one of the admins. She was friends with my ex-wife. My ex-wife is older than you; she's 47."

"I'm 47."

"Naw," He stopped and scrutinized me, searching for signs of my age; satisfied he was right, he stated, "No, you're not. You don't even look 35. In fact, I think I look older than you."

"That may be true. But my kids are 24. You're only six years older than them."

We sat in stunned silence for a moment, both disbelieving. I would never have put him a day under 38. Nine years was nothing, but 17? Sheesh.

Then he shrugged, "Well, we're here, might as well enjoy ourselves." And he ordered another Blue Motherfucker.

He was right. I relaxed. What could one date hurt?

The date was fabulous. The kiss at the end exquisite, and we went our separate ways. I thought.

But he kept calling me. Texting me. And I kept answering. Texting back. And soon we were on date two, pool. I hadn't shot pool since college. And then date three bowling, another thing I hadn't done in a decade. And then I was at his apartment, being introduced to his roommate, walking into his bedroom, and being made love to.

I'd never had the whole " I have a roommate" experience. I was too busy being virginal in college to do that. And then I was married. And then I was 40, and I'd never dated a 40 year old man with a roommate.

The Young Lion wanted me. Permanently. Months flew by. The holidays loomed, and all I could hear was my brother-in-law's quip to my sister. "Two boyfriends in four years. Part of the fun of the holidays is seeing who your sister's gonna bring. And what that guy can cook."

I'd laughed. It had stung. My sister had been married 20 years by then. I'd been married 17, if you count both marriages. She was still married. I was divorced. But I was "forgiven" because my boyfriends could cook and were handy. The Muse had built me a desk, custom-made. Harlee had built a fence, and now The Young Lion could both cook (was opening his own food truck, in fact) and had finally re-wired the ceiling light in my living room that had never worked since I'd bought the house.

He fit the pattern. Only problem, he was 30. He didn't look it, but he was. And every now and then, it crept up, fights he was having with his parents. The kind that had long been solved by 33, 35, or 40. His music. His interests. The kinda, sorta desire he sometimes had to have his own kid. And his utter unsuitability as a father figure for my kids.

Try as I might, that was one desire I couldn't shake. I missed having a family. A real nuclear family. 12 years with Drew (including our pre-marriage relationship) and 6 plus months with Harlee. It was something I ached for, especially on the days/nights when my kids seemed lost, and my female brain/words, motherly instincts just couldn't pierce the darkness.

I cared about TYL, but I couldn't commit to him.

We went our separate ways. But stayed Facebook friends. Just like I had with Harlee.

If you had asked me in 2018, "How many times have you been in love?"

My answer would be 5- My first and second husbands, The Muse, Harlee, and The Young Lion.

## Six

*Five times in my life, I looked at a man and said, "He is enough."*

*It didn't matter how tall he was, how dark/light, fat/thin,*

*It didn't matter how much he made or what he did for a living.*

*I looked at him and wanted to spend every free moment with him,*

*to build him, to know him, to just breathe him.*

*Nothing was the same. Everything felt new.*

*We could lie on the bare floor and stare at the ceiling and talk the whole night through.*

*We didn't notice what we didn't have,*

*only what we did.*

*And life was magical.*

*I was ALIVE. Life felt VIVID.*

*And I miss it.*

*So much.*

*My spirit grapples with the empty space left behind.*

*The void like a sucking mouth, a grand canyon, a valley of death.*

*My heart and mind whirl in circles searching.*

*My imagination remembers but cannot visualize another incarnation.*

*My body aches, throbs, trembles- unsatisfied.*

*Ambition. Success. Accomplishments. Money. Possessions. Accolades. All are futile.*

*Piled sky high-*

*they whimper at the knees of love.*

*Six is the number of man. The man. The last, the final, the one to love till my life ends.*

*I wait for six.*

*I wait*

*And*

*I exist.*

TYL reached out to me this year, 2021. Our connection on the phone was almost like no time had passed at all. But when I saw him this year, time hadn't been kind to him. The saying you never step into the same river twice applied. His eyes looked yellow and jaundiced. He'd lost too much weight and looked frail. His hands shook from what looked like alcohol withdrawal.

If you asked me why men came into my life, I'd have an answer for almost every guy. For TYL, my only answer is we were kindred spirits.

**<u>Lesson 11:</u>**

Some connections are inexplicable.

CHAPTER 12

# *Listen*

## The Treasure Trove

*Woke up feeling some kinda way,*
*My body needing sexual play,*
*No partner, it'll go away.*
*I'll go on about my day.*
*But feelings linger, demanding time*
*so I relent and pen this rhyme*
*To channel angst in words and lines*
*Till my release will come.*
*I used to push these thoughts away*
*with hours of running, practice, and weights*
*A perfect figure I obtained till pregnancy ensued*
*Married life is great for sex.*
*Whenever, wherever, nights- no rest*

*I miss all that unfettered access*
*All that unmitigated bliss.*
*But things go wrong with health and such*
*Years pass with barely one hot touch*
*Divorce becomes the state of mind*
*A new lover I must find.*
*My first was a jewel oh so rare*
*Sex, plentiful without a care*
*Passion extraordinaire*
*Like I'd never known*
*43. And now I learn I squirt.*
*Role-playing and tantric work*
*Toys become sensual dessert.*
*I'm multi-orgasmic was revealed*
*What else have the years concealed?*
*I had bad sex a first time too*
*One minute man I'd never knew*
*How my understanding grew*
*Until I reached today.*
*My body still craving release*
*These words were fun*
*But nothing ceased*
*Wish you were here to me unwind*
*My pleasure spots to seek and find*
*But likely the most erotic thing today*
*Will be my words upon this page*

I finished the poem, was reading it.

My phone rang, which was strange. It really hadn't rung much for a month.

"Hey, Stranger."

Gatzby. "Where's your wife?"

"I'm not married. It didn't work out." He paused. He didn't know how to ask if I was involved, taken, married. He didn't want to hear the answer.

I wish I could tell you how this conversation went, but I can't. I don't know what was said, how it was said, or who said it. I only know that we ended up in bed. Again. After almost a year apart.

Backtracking a little, July - November 2018 had been a whirlwind. Summer school. Open mics. And then a life-changing opportunity, a request to organize a recurring poetry show at a local venue. A plethora of research followed, a DBA, a name for the business, the show, a logo, a flyer, booking artists, a DJ, and then a show every week. ***https://youtu.be/_iyxvdMHdw8*** [3]

Dating The Young Lion. My kids. My grandson. Back to the 9-5. Not dating The Young Lion anymore.

S-T-R-E-S-S

Open mics were my release. The show was an even greater release. And sex was always my go-to when I was involved with a man. And now I wasn't seeing anyone. Hence the poem.

And like clockwork. Like he was tuned into my pheromones from across the city. Like Batman responding to my silent Bat-signal, Gatzby called.

---

3 Devall jerome's Expressions

I'm an artist, not a scientist, but I think there's a theory that explains his call. This was beyond think of someone, and they call. I didn't think of him consciously. The last time he crossed my mind, I was washing my hands of him for good. Never going back. Betty Wright had nothing on me.

Yep, Betty Wright said it best in "After the Pain." I may not have written a poem about never taking him back, but I told my sister, my friends, San Antonio, Mo. Whoever would listen.

And I didn't and don't regret that re-connection. If someone asked me how we ended back in bed, I would have said The Muse was the love of my sane life, and Gatzby was the love of my insane life.

For The Muse:

*I never knew I'd log them,*

*They'd be etched into my mind*

*I thought they'd follow their owner like a video on rewind.*

*But they pop up unexpected, make me smile a time or two,*

*And though I have moved on, some days these firsts seem new.*

*The first time he walked up to me,*

*The first call I received,*

*The first kiss, first date, first trip, first plate,*

*a dinner cooked for me,*

*First necklace, first ring,*
*first gift for my home,*
*The first time my car was detailed,*
*The first time I brought him home.*
*They pop up when I hear a song and*
*Sometimes in my dreams.*
*They pop up with a favorite meal,*
*A movie that I've seen.*
*I rarely feel nostalgia*
*I embrace the present time, and*
*I never feel these moments wasted even though he's no longer mine.*
*My life's so richer, almost complete,*
*Through all the firsts I've seen.*
*I'm lucky, blessed so fortunate,*
*No regrets it seems.*
*Not a moment wasted, each packed with the best*
*Good memories, lessons, growth, reflection*
*These firsts made me who I am,*
*In all my intricacies*
*I embrace all the firsts to come*
*Venga my destiny*

When it comes to Gatzby and me, words like “why” just don’t compute. We just are. There was an inevitability about us like we had lived before and were just living out a script written for us, taking our places, reciting our lines, donning, and removing our roles like costumes. When we were together, time ceased to exist, the mind quieted, there was only breath, sound, smell, motion. Our movements fluid as waves in the ocean, crashing, breaking, cresting, flowing. "They became one flesh" was not enough to describe us. We became one heartbeat, one current, one soul. "Brown skin, up against my brown skin, I don't know where yours begins. I don't know where mine ends." India Arie crooned as we melded. But no music could compete with ours, so her melody faded away, just like the laws of physics. We contorted like circus performers, our bodies boneless, our limbs more flexible than at any other time in history.

Afterward, he played in my hair; I stroked his chest in silence. There were no words for what seemed like hours, days, weeks. We floated. Weightless. Suspended. The world could crash and burn, and we would not have even noticed. Slowly, we came back to ourselves, once again reinhabiting our bodies. The dream state/waking state meld receded as reality came back into focus.

Usually, I would rise on one elbow and begin to trace his perfect eyebrows, play in his goatee. He would open his eyes, mocha brown and gorgeous, smile, and ask," What are you thinking?" If he asked too soon, I would shake my head. My brain still stunned into silence, having no syllables, consonants, or vowels to wrap around the ecstasy that was us. If he timed it right, I'd normally say, "Wow," or "gorgeous," and he'd laugh, a warm honey of a ripple and wrap that bear arm of his around me and pull me closer, kiss my forehead.

He'd say something sweet back, "I missed you," or "I love you," or something deliciously erotic.

That day he asked what I was thinking, and I said there was no reason I should have talked to him, kissed him, slept with him.

To which he said, "We always come back to each other."

True. Disturbingly true.

"You should be with me," he continued.

"Maybe. Probably. We tried it, and it didn't work. Nothing changed. You stood me up again." I shook my head. It was old news. So old I didn't want to know why. It no longer seemed to matter why. I'd slept with him, not knowing why, so why ask now?

"How do you feel about me?" he asked.

I laughed. "When? Right now, I feel great. When I'm no longer sex high, I might hate your guts."

"But you love me. I love you."

I shook my head. What did that matter? Love. I loved both my ex-husbands when I divorced them. Love was not what I made decisions on. "I can't talk to you, not now. When we're together, I feel too much. I'm not thinking rationally."

"Just tell me you'll be with me."

"Be with you? Yeah, I mean you call me and end up in bed with me. What more do you want? I am with you, and I don't know why or how this happened. How did it go from you being gone to you being here? From planning to never speak to you to spending an hour making love? You have too much control over me. I can't say no to you,"

"You say no to me all the time. You've said no to me since 2015."

"My mouth has. My body OBVIOUSLY hasn't. And I said yes to you once. You dropped the ball."

"I was scared of getting hurt. I didn't think you meant it. You always pushed me away."

"Well, now, I don't trust you."

"You don't trust me? You trusted The Muse and Harlee, and where are they now? I'm here, but you don't trust me?"

"Why are you here?"

"I love you. I think we'd be perfect together if you'd just let us be. You don't want me with anyone else. You lost your shit when you thought I was getting married."

"Yes, I did."

"What was that?"

"I don't know. I felt you owed me. I was tired of taking losses. The idea of another loss, especially one you caused, just drove me crazy. All the chances I gave you, the times I forgave you, it had to count for something; it had to pay off."

"Chances you gave me? You broke my heart. I stood you up. I think I'm the one owed, not you. But I don't even think that way. I just want us to start over. I've forgiven you. Do you forgive me?"

"I'm mad at you."

"For what?"

"For this. You were supposed to stay gone. Not call me out of the blue. I don't have any defenses against you."

"Why do you always talk like that? 'Defenses? I owe you? You can't say no?.' You made things this way. You said we couldn't be together but let me make love to you. You said I wasn't what you were looking for but called me when you needed advice, a shoulder to cry on, or a man to hold you. I was your crutch, your security blanket, your rebound. After The Muse. After Harlee. And now. But you never let me truly love you."

"Everything you just said is true. But you were a momma's boy with no boundaries. Always on the road. Stood me up. And with the fence, 'our relationship',"

Dramatic air quotes here. "You totally dropped the ball."

"When I met you, I knew what I had to offer a woman, but you made me doubt myself, made me feel insecure, made me feel like I was good enough to sleep with but not good enough to love."

At this point, I was crying. I never meant to make him feel that way. The last thing I wanted him to feel was cheap, used, hurt.

*It was so many years ago, it was hard to remember how things started. Did I do that? Was I the reason?*

"I'm sorry. And I'm still mad. You made **me** feel cheap, standing me up. I feel stupid every time I listen to one of your excuses. I feel gullible, naive and embarrassed when my friends or family find out you're back. I think it makes me look desperate. And I felt so rejected, so shut out that you'd come to my home, but I'd never been invited to yours. I mean, do you know how many guys, strangers, have invited me over? But not you, not my lover?"

"Do you really think I want to have memories of you there, in my living room, my kitchen, my bed, and you not be in my life? I already see you in my head. I don't want to see you in my home too. It would just make me want you more. Just make this in-between shit harder to do."

*That made sense. And yet it pissed me off. Why couldn't I just replace him with someone who didn't make me crazy, didn't stand me up, didn't disappoint, someone whose size and job I was comfortable with?*

*But I admired him. He was patient, a good listener, nurturing, calm. He had never once lost his temper with me or even raised his voice. And sometimes, he had so much hope for us. It was contagious; he almost made me believe we could be.*

*I kept leaving. And he just kept bringing me back.*

"Why are you here?" I demanded. "If I did ALL that. Why not leave me alone? I was gone. We were done. You reached out to me. Not the other way around."

"I can't let you go. Ever. I miss you. I crave you. You did all that, but you are amazing, fascinating, the sweetest, most nurturing, strongest woman I think I've ever known. You're eccentric, exquisite, and so goddamned beautifully sexy. I could wake up happy lying next to you for the rest of my life. And the way we make love- indescribable, irreplaceable. I never want another woman to touch me."

The compliments took my breath away. And I was crying. Sobbing. Weeping. In his arms. Fighting not to. Not succeeding.

"Stop. You just make me cry. I don't want to cry anymore. I don't want to hurt you anymore. I never meant to hurt you. We've done so much damage to each other."

"Yes, but you've also made me feel more love than I ever knew was possible. You love me for me. Just me. Just my thoughts, my personality, my interaction with you. It wasn't good enough to commit to, but the way you looked at me sometimes. I'd never been looked at like that. The way you listened to me. Just letting me talk as long as I wanted."

He ran his hand over his bald head, down his face, and stroked his chin. "You never had to tell me you loved me. It was in every glance, touch, kiss. It was in your texts and your calls and the sweet messages you sent me just because. You know it's true."

*He had a point. Several, in fact.*

*And he felt like THIS after almost a year apart?*

*But none of these revelations changed all the bad history, all the bad blood, the broken promises, the mistrust. How could I ever truly love Gatzby?*

Even writing this brings no closure; there's no 20/20 aha, no certainty I should have done this or that which I can give you wrapped up in a crisp red bow.

To me, Gatzby was unreliable. To him, I was wishy-washy (his actual nickname for me when he talked about me to his friends).

To him, I was textbook indecisive, telling him we couldn't be together, but still saying I loved him (as he said) in every touch, kiss, gesture. To him, me sleeping with him or even the time when I said yes to being his woman, meant we could and would eventually be together.

To me, those things were unrelated. I'd loved both my husbands and The Young Lion when I ended those connections. Love doesn't equal compatibility, and it doesn't equal a healthy relationship.

Was he naive for expecting that love meant we could and would be good together? Was he a hopeless romantic? I nicknamed him Gatzby after all; I couldn't be angry that he had an irrepressible, though totally unrealistic, hope.

And it wasn't wishy-washy to me that I broke things off when he stood me up. He said when I'd agreed to a relationship, he actually hadn't expected me to say yes. And I expected him to jump in with boyfriend actions when I'd trained him to see me as merely a sexual partner, someone he didn't have to be consistent with, stay in contact with, take out. He said expecting a seamless transition on his part was unfair and unrealistic. He couldn't change that fast.

Well, then why even keep asking me for commitment? I replied.

He said he hadn't meant to. He said by the time I agreed, he had already given up, and he couldn't accept that I had suddenly changed my mind.

While on one level, I understood. On another, it sounded like total bull shit. He got what he wanted, what he asked for, and flaked was still etched in my mind.

To me, Gatzby was the person I reached out to, HOPING he would come through but EXPECTING him to fall through. His word meant nothing to me. When he came through, he was the best. But he fell through, enough for the saves to seem like hail Mary's.

I soaked in the tub a long time that night. Wanting to wash away the conversation like I washed away the residue of our lovemaking.

My phone rang again. I didn't even want to look at the caller ID. I answered blindly.

A voice from the past startled me. One I would never forget. His African accent deep, mesmerizing, like a lullaby from the Motherland, Mystique.

The next morning, I called my co-host. Rattled off about 25 show titles, ideas for promotion, artists I planned to book. Suddenly, Kaye was silent.

Kaye was never silent.

We sometimes talked over each other, in fact. Her voice, an animated exclamation point, ended my sentences.

I stopped.

"Aw, shit," she said.

"What?"

"You."

"What about me?"

"You got some."

I burst out laughing.

"And not just regular dick. The GOOOOOOD shit." I laughed harder. "You're always creative. But this. Thiiiiiiiis. No, this is next-level shit. Sex Magic. You ain't gotta tell me shit. Whatever it is, I'm down for it. ALL. It will be, simply, legendary. Bye, sugah." She hung up.

Sex Magic. She was joking. She was still right, though.

I'd seen a book with that title, never read it. In ancient times, I'd heard there were priests and priestesses who had sex rituals. Hieros gamos. Their couplings were said to bring good luck, good fortune to the tribe. I was buzzing. My fingers, toes, hair. If I could look with a blue light, I imagined myself glowing like Bruce Leroy in *The Last Dragon*, able to catch a speeding bullet in my teeth. Invincible still from the sex magic Gatzby and I created.

In my mind, I went back to the previous night. Energy rushed into my body at just the memory. I sat transfixed, lifted, feeling as if I was levitating. They say that one atom smashed against another in just the right (or wrong way) creates atomic energy, enough energy to bomb Hiroshima, enough energy to power a small city.

We were those atoms, smashing, colliding, and now I was that city powered indefinitely. Sex Magic. My brain aflame, creativity unleashed, energy unbounded. I thought about his desire to be with me, his dream of building a committed relationship.

I didn't think it was possible. Humanly possible. We collided then departed, dispelling the energy we created over days, weeks, months, years. Could we survive extended contact? Could we eat, sleep, function?

Hieros gamos wasn't a daily thing. People were initiated for years, preparing them for it. Their minds, bodies, souls, spirits fashioned for the union, the release, the magic. We stumbled on this. Accidentally creating magic. Our own pheromonic spell. Ancient, modern, untamable, unquenchable.

That was why when he called, I answered. When I called, he came.

He was my priest. I was his priestess.

I breathed in. The energy still building, ebbing, and flowing like The Northern Lights. I pulled it back inside me. Shook my hands, arms, and legs.

And picked up the phone. My intuition had always told me he wasn't right for me. Maybe it knew that together we would create this type of combustible chemistry- intensely passionate but chaotic. I once had even searched soul mates online. I got results on twin flames and karmic relationships. The last one seemed to fit us. Addictive passion, red flags, drama, growth, life lessons. The internet said these karmic relationships never lasted. Still, they always altered each partner and made them face their karmic debts, so they could evolve. Well, I had owned up to my part last night. WE had created a cycle. He wanted to continue, but as much as this energy and creativity were incredible, I doubted I wanted to pick up the disappointment and unmet expectations that seemed to follow our continued involvement.

And it seemed the universe was giving me a choice; the clearest one I'd ever seen.

After I was washed and clean and rested, Mystique had called. He had seen me, he said, in a meditation. His ancestors told him I was touched, blessed, spiritually gifted. He wondered if I would change my mind- be celibate with him for a while, date him only. See if we were destined to walk this path together. He said he had never had a woman appear in his mind when he was meditating. He thought it was important.

And I thought the timing was uncanny. I'd apparently performed sex magic, and he saw me in his mind, and was told I was "spiritually gifted." If Gatzby was my karmic mate, one I could never be with, who was there just to reveal my shit and make me deal with it, then what was Mystique? My soulmate? Another dead end? A friend?

Well, first things first, I had to deal with Gatzby. Whatever he wanted to begin, I needed to end. Quickly. Without much talking. I didn't need him using THE VOICE. I dialed the phone and waited.

He answered.

"I've got a question," I stated.

"What?"

"I heard you last night about not wanting me at your place, but I still don't understand."

"What?"

"You say I broke your heart. You don't want memories of me in your place. Still, you know me thinking you're lying about being self-sufficient is a major reason I never wanted to be with you. You could dispel that with one visit. And you know that one day, I'm probably not coming back, and you could take away one reason I have for leaving, but you refuse to? That doesn't make sense."

"You think too much."

Oh, I hate when men say that. To me, it always means women are not supposed to question, just take men's bs and run with it. I also hate that I always get told this after saying something a man said didn't make sense. If a woman's too emotional, her thoughts are discounted. But if she's absolutely logical, she "thinks too much."

"So I'm supposed to invite you over to prove that I have a place?"

"Not just to prove that, but yeah."

"Baby, I'm grown. I don't respond to ultimatums. I don't feel the need to prove myself to anyone. You either believe me, or you don't."

"Fair enough." I don't usually believe in tests, but I'd given him one last chance to prove he'd changed, and he failed with flying colors. He'd made this easier.

I told him that our hookup had been a mistake. There was too much bad blood. Too much fucked up history. He was hurt. Again. But also angry. Said I was used to men doing whatever I asked. That I was a control freak, as most teachers were. Asked how I could move on so coldly when the bed was still warm. Said if he were a stranger, he'd get a chance. That I gave my husbands too many chances and him not enough.

This time, I was sure that there was no coming back. Ever. He had borne his heart to me, and that hadn't been enough.

But after almost a year apart, did he really expect it to be? He hadn't come with bouquets, and gifts, and a slew of apologies. He had made love to me and given me pillow talk. Pillow talk I was sure was real, but that didn't mean anything about him, about us, had changed. And I had reached my limit of replaying this merry-go-round with him. He had a chance to show me something different, open up, give me more than pillow talk, dates, and great sex. He could have chosen to share his home with me as I had so often with him, to reciprocate. He didn't.

**Lesson 12:**

When words and actions don't match, listen to the actions.

CHAPTER 13

# Mooring

## Date Seventy-Three:

Mystique and I talked every day, then met for a brief bite. He was driving his daughter's truck, a bumper sticker read, "Something witchy this way comes." It startled me. I mentioned it. He shrugged and asked what I knew about witches. I had no answer, sensing that anything I said he would nix as dogma rather than research. Well, I wasn't trying to date the daughter. Did it really matter?

His vibe, mellow and relaxed, led to a nice lunch date. We had talked about family. He said it was really important to him. He had six kids. Three lived with him, and he had no problem being a father figure to my sons who at 23 still needed a man's guidance, he said. I agreed. In fact, my heart was singing. It looked like a great start.

He called as I was taking my son Elijah to Bush Intercontinental to rent a vehicle the next day. I answered my phone's ring but then proceeded to tell Mystique I'd call him right back.

I was excited. This was no everyday drive. This was a rite of passage. Elijah and his college friends were going on a short road trip. I would drop them off and pick them up when they returned in a few days. They didn't want to drive their unreliable cars or board them at the airport. As I helped my son make sure he had everything for the trip and didn't leave anything in my car, I could barely restrain the joy I felt at the little part I played in helping my son have an experience I never had.

But when I called Mystique back minutes later expecting to share my excitement, he was fuming. How dare I prioritize helping my son over his call. He wanted to see me - tonight. I should be available to him, waiting on his call, wanting to see what he had planned for my/our evenings. These kids, whose mothers coddled them, always checking to see if they had handled their business, were immature, and it was the fault of women like me.

I wasn't offended. His words and behavior were so far off my grid of acceptable that I simply said, My kids and I are obviously not what you are looking for, and I hung up, mid rant, and blocked his number.

I was proud of myself. I wasn't that girl from 1995 rebuilding myself for a man's approval.

I had my flaws, but helping my son be prepared for a trip wasn't one of them.

I was a little disappointed. I'd thought he was more evolved, not a Neanderthal in disguise. And I had partially, not really, stopped dating Gatzby to be with him. But Mystique was not the only reason. I could have written a book on reasons Gatzby and I shouldn't date.

November was here. Thanksgiving, around the corner, and my mom was sick. Sicker than we ever could have imagined. Turns out she had hepatitis which had gone untreated for about 30 years, and now the damage was showing, in her organs, showing all throughout her body. She was given three months to live.

With a diagnosis like that, you go through all the stages of grief: denial, bargaining, anger. I took an intermittent leave of absence, my sister did too, and I told mom I'd stop doing the shows.

"No, you won't."

" I have to."

"No, you don't. I spent almost my entire life as a businesswoman, as did your grandfather, your great uncle. It's in your blood. I sent you to the high school for business professions."

*I remembered learning nothing about business there.*

" I tried to get you to sell Avon, Mary Kay, insurance, lingerie, pre-arranged funerals, Amway, and Tupperware. You never would. You've had your DBA for four months. You've already done 11 shows. Sold out a few times. Got a buzz. Maybe it's beginner's luck. Maybe you found an unserved niche. Maybe you've found what you were born to do. If you stop, you go back to less than zero. You won't be able to pick back up where you are now. You can cut back, but it took me thirty-odd years to get you into business. You will NOT quit."

"Yes, Ma'am."

"You will do what business owners have always done, separate personal and business. Be fully present when you're there, setting all this aside. And be fully present when you're here."

The first show I'd stated rule number one of Laughz and Lyrics. Leave the outside, outside. The show was started as my haven from stress, an artistic cocoon from the outside world. In those four walls,

I welcomed, nurtured, and vibed with my tribe- young and old, all races, ages, and creeds, all backgrounds tied by one thing love and honor for laughs and the lyrics of comedy, music, and poetry.

Now that rule took on a whole new significance, a promise to my mother. The entrepreneurial spirit in our family would not die with her; it would live on through me. It was a high bar and a hard promise to keep. Conversely, it also provided self-care. For at least two hours a month, I could forget the debilitating signs of her disease, the side effects of her medications, the deterioration of her health. There are no words to express watching someone vibrant- a powerhouse of energy, a force in the community, an entrepreneur with eight DBA's, an involved grandmother and doting mother- wither and decay. It's even harder to express the personality changes that occur as the liver and kidneys fail and toxins flood the blood, temporarily causing mood swings, violence, confusion, and chemically induced dementia.

It was even harder because I'd seen it before. When my son was shot, he too went from the body of a 22-year-old to a bitter, PTSD ridden, paranoid shell. He was out of his head on pain meds, saying things, doing things, remembering nothing. Now that screaming, raving, fighting person was my mother. Not understanding why she had an IV in her arm, why she was getting a shot, not understanding the treatments, begging, pleading, crying for us to stop, not knowing who we were.

My sister dealt with it more than I did. She lived five minutes away. I lived almost an hour distant. But there were days when the memories, the screams wouldn't stop playing in my head. Nights when they invaded my dreams and woke me up. There were days I sat at her bedside in the hospital or hospice or her home. I would suddenly see nothing, hear nothing, feel nothing. I was floating above my body watching the scene, or floating off in the clouds, or just in a field of gray emptiness. Disassociation, they call it.

In my twenties, when my flashbacks of rape came back, I disassociated. Spacing out. Losing time. I spent six months in therapy learning how to feel the flashback coming on, prepare for it, change something in it to make it less terrifying so that I didn't disassociate.

I went back to therapy. Images of the Jennifer Lopez movie *The Cell* felt like a very real possibility. Trapped in my head. Catatonic. Unresponsive. Disassociated.

It's kinda scary to distrust your own mind, your own subconscious, to know that if things become too intense, they can and will leave you. Awareness gone. Your identity submerged in nothing for a moment, or ten or an hour. To lose time.

November faded into December, and then New Year's Eve at the stroke of midnight, 2019, my phone rang.

"Happy New Year, stranger."

"My mother's dying," I replied and hung the phone up on Gatzby.

And fell into his arms when he rang my doorbell thirty minutes later.

# Messy 1/3/19 (Dedicated to those like my mom, who face a terminal illness)

*I crave clean lines,*
*cream walls with paintings in frames.*
*But sometimes, life is messy.*
*Bipolar, insane,*

*I crave a fresh fade and cologne*
*with a goatee to match,*
*Stylish and classic, and swagger that's brash,*
*A seductive wink, a smile 1000 watts strong,*
*A masculine voice, some good taste in songs.*
*A head bob to rhythm,*
*Some smooth feet and then,*
*Lovemaking breathless, no need to pretend.*
*It's all pristine and spotless,*
*But don't you run,*
*If some messiness seeps in while we're having some fun.*

*A hospital visit,*
*Skilled nurse, no less,*
*A few payday loans,*
*Some gray hairs from stress,*

*I'd promise just good times*
*But that'd be a lie.*
*Both bitter and sweet fragrance this pie.*

*Life is messy, confusing.*
*Overwhelming, it seems,*
*Some false starts,*
*Some pipe dreams.*
*Some laughter.*
*Some screams*
*But it's also beauty and hope and loving galore.*
*Don't let messiness keep you from what's in store.*

*I used to think life could be carefully designed,*
*Planned like a blueprint, all sketched out and lined.*
*But so little has gone the way that it "should"*
*But maybe the messy is what makes life good*

I didn't have any expectations when I said those words. I think I partly said them because I couldn't deal with all that was going on and Gatzby too. I hadn't said those words many times. In fact, I wonder if I'd said them ever. The announcement just happened. And that night/ morning, I can't tell you what happened. I was not myself. I'd spent over a week at mom's. I'd come back, and my house had been burglarized sometime between Christmas and New Year's Eve. Items taken. Damage. It was too much.

I'd been invited to so many places to bring in the New Year, but I felt fragile. As if one touch, one word, and I would shatter into a million blubbering pieces. As if I would crumble like a Jenga tower.

My body felt upside down. Tears in my throat, my chest, my belly, longing to rush up to my eyes. They waited like a million moths for the flicker of light to swarm and engulf it.

I sat in darkness.

He came. He left. He came back. He left. He called and texted. And I was at my mom's and home and work and a show once a month. And The Shrine and Baba's class almost every Saturday. I slept little. My hair shed. I wrote.

She was given three months to live. She lived six months till May 19, 2019. The day she transitioned was magical, a tale for another book.

The weekend that we buried my mother, Gatzby disappeared. He was supposed to come over and didn't. He stood me up.

I couldn't tell you if Gatzby called, or I did. I just know that I told him standing me up after my mom's funeral was unforgivable, that her parting gift to me was showing me clearly in a way I couldn't overlook the type of man I had been dealing with. I told him never to contact me again.

The month after the funeral seems like one day. One heavy, dark day where I woke up every morning, sat on my bed, and waited for the grief to become bearable enough for me to stand. By week six, It took fifteen minutes. Then I could stand, dress, and go through the motions of life.

## "How are you?" May 22, 2019.

*I wake up in the morning, tears in my eyes.*
*They don't fall, stuck in corners; my eyes tight and dry.*
*I see beauty around me, hear the stirrings of life.*
*But feel pain, loss, confusion, sometimes peace is in sight.*
*I reminisce greatly with family and friends*
*and laugh loud and long at memories of kin.*
*I still don't know how to answer,*
*"How have you been?"*
*I've been angry, overwhelmed, felt selfish, in fact.*
*I've cried at harsh words spoken from the disease's attack.*
*How to deal with conditions that steal the person you knew.*
*The words she says, the way she looks, is strange and untrue.*
*Her body discolored, her mind warped and cold,*
*She takes leave of her senses without a minute of notice.*
*It's rational to say it's just the disease,*
*Don't listen to the words that cause you dis- ease.*
*But it's impossible when they're spoken in a tongue that you know.*
*From the mouth that raised you, though it's twisted and cold.*
*When you should be pulled closer, you're rejected, attacked,*
*told you are not wanted, and your actions all lack.*
*That you do the wrong things and make her feel pain inside,*
*But you're doing the best you can to care and provide.*

*You doubt yourself, your motives. Want to run away and hide.*
*But you have to return daily to be by her side.*
*You have to call and run errands, clean her, help her stand.*
*Rush her to the ER and hold her IV filled hand,*
*You have to feed her, comb her hair, dress her, put her to bed,*
*You have to ignore all the hurtful words said.*
*There are glances asking, "Is what she said true?"*
*As the hospital staff bustles with questions for you.*
*"is she always like this?" "Can you do x,y,z?"*
*You have to hold her much stronger, she won't stop fighting me."*
*"Did she take all her meds?" "She is how old?"*
*You become a reporter, objective, and rote.*
*And still, you have to get up, go to work, pay your bills,*
*Act like you are normal when that's not how you feel.*
*So now it's over a death, funeral at hand.*
*People asking how am I, where do things stand?*
*I don't know how I am. I lived. I survived.*
*I don't know who I've become because of this ride.*
*I don't know how to proceed except to do the next task.*
*I don't know what normal looks like after the fact.*
*So don't ask me, "How are you?" I haven't a clue.*
*I'm alive. I'm breathing; that's what I'll tell you.*

I thought I had lost myself after each divorce, that I didn't know who I was and lacked confidence, that I had to rebuild me. One of my favorite book series was *Game of Thrones*, an amazing tv series too. There's a scene in the episode "A Man Without Honor" that sent ripples through me when I watched it, " You think we're savages because we don't live in stone castles. We can't make steel as good as yours, it's true, but we're free. If someone tried to tell us we couldn't lie down as man and woman, we'd shove a spear up his ass. We don't go serving some shit king who's only king because his father was. No. No, we serve Mance Rayder, the King-Beyond-the-Wall. We chose Mance Rayder to lead us. He was a crow, same as you, but he wanted to be free. You could be free, too. You don't need to live your whole life taking commands from old men. Wake up when you want to wake up. I could show you the streams to fish, the woods to hunt. Build yourself a cabin and find a woman to lie with at night. You're a pretty lad. The girls would claw each other's eyes out to get naked with you. I could teach you how to do it," Ygritte said.

" I know how to do it," Jon Snow replied.

"You know nothing, Jon Snow."[4]

This was fiction, based on a fictional land of thousands of years ago, but growing up religious, following the rules of others just because they were older, "authorities," being taught that my honor lay in not having sex, in following rules… was bondage. They try to teach you it's the way to freedom, but that is a bald-faced lie.

In the book, Jon Snow turns his back on all that and finds the love of his life, the purpose of his life. But at that moment in the barren wasteland and ice, Ygritte's words had to be the scariest thing on the planet. Throw away all you know and start over. Think for yourself. Question everything you were told. Be your own man.

---

4 "A Man without Honor" David Benioff and D.B. Weiss

When my mother died, it felt just like that. There was no one to check up on me, to keep me in line, to live up to, to dishonor by not following their standards, rules, expectations. There was no advice, guidance, support system. I was now the matriarch. I could be my own woman. But who was that? I had asked "who am I" when I wasn't a wife or a daughter-in-law. But who was I when I wasn't a granddaughter, a daughter?

I was not ready to ask or answer that question. I'd always thought I was independent, self-sufficient, a grown-ass woman. But I suddenly felt so lost, so much loss, there were no words for it. Every death had been difficult, sad, painful.

But unbeknownst to me, my mother had been my anchor. She had made me feel sturdy and secure. Just knowing she was there, a call or text away, gave me a rock, irritating, nonsensical sometimes, overbearing and controlling, but steadfast, sure, un-shakable.

Now, I had no rock.

I was moorless.

Drifting.

Tossed. Turned. Swept away.

Losing my mother was different from every death before it because she was the last person above me. My grandparents, two sets of in-laws, my father, and now my mother, gone.

Who was I without them?

What allegiance did I owe to their memories, to the lessons and roles they taught me?

And there was also the idea that she was the epitome of what men used to scare women. She died with my sister and me in her hospital room. My sons had spent most of the day, my brother-in-law, nephews, her friends there also. But, there was no man. She'd wanted love after my father died. Dated a few men. Even went on one trip and had us meet one guy, but ultimately, no one stuck, and her desire for love, true love, deep love, not just a marriage of duty and longevity, went unfulfilled.

It haunted me.

The only reason my father married my mother was he saw my grandfather punching her. My dad did his duty, side-eying my mom; they barely knew each other. My mom felt trapped too. My mother was a duty wife. She wanted to be a love wife.

I couldn't ask if she'd ever made peace with it. Still, I knew on that last rebound, when it seemed she might actually make a full recovery, that she'd spouted all the things she wanted to do, hadn't done, and that was one. Love.

Not the "I grew to love him" love that she felt for my father, but the "I couldn't help myself I just fell, kind of love" that I don't think she ever felt she had been given. She wanted to be the love of someone's life. She craved it, wanted it, dreamed of it. It eluded her.

I'd had so much love in my life that it made me feel guilty in contrast to my mom.

When I pictured myself her age, dying alone was the greatest nightmare I could imagine.

But I wasn't that girl of 2015, so eager for approval and lacking in total confidence. I wasn't the woman of 2016 who knew I'd get hundreds of hits and was looking to wean the herd with a perfectly written profile. I wasn't the woman of 2017 heartbroken after two failed relationships. I wasn't the woman of 2018, super happy and content single.

It was 2019.

I was vulnerable, lost, alone.

I had no one above me anymore. No matriarch. No patriarch. Bereft of the supports that had guided me 48 years, which had made me feel stable, helped me know who I was in the world.

And I was desperately afraid of dying like my mother, surrounded by family and friends, but single and alone.

"You don't need to live your whole life taking commands from old men [or women]. Wake up," Ygritte's voice sounded like the voice in my head. Calm, sure, derisively mocking my whole and entire life, all the decisions that had seemed so right, so righteous, so unquestionable. That voice questioning everything I had been, everything I was - was utterly terrifying.

I'm a thinker. You might have guessed that. Knowing things gives me comfort. It probably gives most of us comfort. That's why we can get angry when our long-held beliefs are challenged. It can be why we fear uncertainty.

Well, I had lots of interesting thoughts after my mom died. I was thinking about her, my grandmother. They were married almost their whole lives, but in the end, as they neared their deaths, there was this frenzy of "I wish I had," "I hope I might still," "I regret I didn't." I had been living my life on their standards, their guidance, their rules, and The Rose Doctrine and church.

I was 48. I was the matriarch now, and I was suddenly questioning everything. Cognitive dissonance was in full effect. See, I'd been trained a certain way, but for the last four years, I hadn't been living by those rules. And while there was definitely some fear and trepidation about stepping out of my comfort zone. The pain of two failed marriages had made it a necessity. And suddenly, I realized, before my mom died, I had never been happier.

Now, I was grieving. I was lost. My heart ached terribly. But even after the funeral, when those emotions receded, I had never been happier.

It made me angry. It seemed like so much time wasted, running in circles trying to fill society's expectations of me as wife, mother, daughter, Christian woman.

I had never once asked whether this would make me happy. Does this make me happy? Instead, I blamed myself for my unhappiness. I must not be sacrificing enough, unselfish enough. I must be greedy. My expectations must be unrealistic.

Now I felt as I had at seven when my aunt told me on Christmas Eve that I was old enough to know there was no Santa Clause-cheated, bamboozled, led astray, run amok, utterly and completely deceived.

The last tenuous hold on the girl/woman I had been was unraveling. It was terrifying. I was grieving the loss of my mother, but I was also grieving the realization that she had been the last thing holding me to tradition. I knew the person that emerged from the dark chrysalis I was entering would be radically different. That I was about to melt, reform, and emerge someone totally different. I could feel it. A little piece of my former persona slipping away every day. Who would I be? I had no idea.

In the month after the funeral, the grief seemed complete. My whole world. My whole outlook on the world. It was my breath, my food, my drink, my anchor to reality. All-encompassing and heavy. I'd lost my mother. I was losing myself.

Then Saturday, June 15th, 2019, I went to The Shrine. They were having their Juneteenth Buy Black Market. I had attended class. Felt some relief and then plastered a smile on my face so I could network and invite people to that month's show. I walked by a table, and a woman waved me over.

"My, you have an amazingly beautiful smile," she said.

"Thank you."

"But there is so much grief. It's pouring off of you in waves. Look at the table. What calls to you?"

I hadn't even noticed her table. It was full of crystals and essential oil roll-ons. I picked up a black stone, wrapped my fingers around it. It felt solid, but not just physically. I felt instantly bonded to it. It belonged to me.

She nodded, "Your soul is guiding you to what you need. That's tourmaline. It grounds and centers, helps balance all the chakras. It can even absorb negative energy, clearing the way for more beneficial energy and beliefs to arise. You need that. What else?"

I tried not to register shock at her words. They seemed prescient but actually calmed me. I picked up a long rectangular stone, almost completely translucent.

She smiled," Had I been trying to guide you, I would have given you that one next. That's an angel stone. Extremely high vibrationally. It's the perfect stone to help when one may feel emotionally unstable or distressed. It provides inner peace, mental clarity, heightened intellect, and joy. On your worst days, it lifts. It clears mental fog and assists in transforming a life that feels stuck or stagnant. It'll push you to take action and do what you truly love, to follow your goals and dreams and embrace your pathway."

*Damn. Nah. I don't believe it. A stone can do all that? Well, what did I have to lose? They were only $5.*

I picked up another, and she told me about it, and then I bought the three stones

And two roll-ons. $31. Nothing if they helped, even a little.

I finished networking. Went home. Left the stones in my trunk. Remembered them at bedtime, retrieved them, Sat them on my dresser. Admired them. They were beautiful. Brilliant. For that alone, worth the price. I slept.

I woke up the next morning and sat up, waited. Waited for the grief that always came. Heard the birds chirping. Waited. A neighbor cutting grass. Waited. A car driving by, then another. Waited. My stomach growling. Waited.

If I'd continued waiting for the grief to arrive, heavy, all-consuming, overpowering, I'd still be waiting till today. It never came back like that. It came back in waves and left. But the heaviness was gone. The only thing that had changed in my room, in my life, was the crystals.

Once, long ago, I would have never bought them. I was trained to believe anything outside the Bible, outside church- horoscopes, tarot, palm reading, crystals, yoga- was evil. Those beliefs seemed a million miles away.

Many mornings after that, I sat up waiting. Thinking maybe it was a fluke.

The grief never came, but one day an equally strong impression did.

And I didn't have to wait for it. One morning, the first thought I had was, "I love myself." A nice thought. A beautiful thought. A random thought. And an ironic thought because suddenly it dawned on me that The Rose Doctrine had taught me NOT to love myself.

That morning, the totality of me was beautiful- my thoughts, my values, my talents, my heart, soul and spirit, my actions, my body. The Rose Doctrine had taught me none of that mattered. My total and complete value lay in my abstinence or lack thereof. My purity was related totally and only to sex. And suddenly, so many things made sense. Women in relationships, in marriage, punish men by withholding sex. Why? They were trained it's a valuable commodity, and he should earn it. If he isn't, why would they give it?

Women in marriages/relationships give sex as a gift on a man's birthday on Valentine's. Men question why would something I can get other times when it's not a special day be a gift now? The Rose Doctrine. She's still giving you, and only you, her precious flower petals. The men are FOREVER supposed to be grateful for this "gift." Women trained this way often don't see sex as a way to bond, strengthen the relationship, have fun, and release stress. Instead sex is some diamond ring, Rolex, Holy Grail that men have to jump through hoops, 90 days of proving themselves, a marriage proposal, or stellar spousal/partner performance to get and/or keep.

And there's a darker side to teaching women NOT to love themselves but to see their value only in their pure virginal state. What happens when a woman trained this way is molested or raped? Some blame themselves. Some have lost their "only value" and feel they are worthless. They become promiscuous. Some hide the "shame of their worthless state" in drugs, alcohol, reckless behavior, and even suicide. I know of women who did this.

I was in therapy and had been ever since my mom's diagnosis. But my therapist changed practices, moved to a whole other city, and the new therapist and I just did not click. So that was done. But getting another one wasn't an urgent necessity. I wouldn't even want to calculate how much money I'd spent on therapy, and it was worth every cent. But in that month, the crystals had made a bigger difference, and I was content to go without the weekly sessions.

Besides, my former dates had become sort of a support system by now. San Antonio, Bern, The Young Lion, The Bearded One, and the long-distance three musketeers whom I'd never met were my entertainment, sounding boards, counselors, and friends.

I'd come a long way. 2014- May 2019. 73 dates. But that word really doesn't encapsulate the totality of each experience. As you can tell from the last one hundred pages, these men were not a free meal to me, or a diversion, or my chance to reject one after one because I think I'm Ms. Perfect. They were my teachers. My mentors. My guides in learning how to shed roles, beliefs, habits, and mindsets that were stifling, toxic and unrealistic for me.

And do not for a second think that all these dates mean I don't want or value love.

Dating is not a game to me. It is just like life- unpredictable, precious, enlightening, frustrating, an encounter with what it means to be human, a woman, and need love.

Love is a risk, a beautiful warfare on the senses. It is one of the most dangerous, exhilarating, fulfilling, devastating adventures one can undertake. Men have given their lives for love, built Taj Mahals for love----killed for love.

And yet many people treat love so flippantly

Nonchalant.

Cavalier.

Downright callous.

They act like 2 people + job, house, car= happy relationship.

Me, I need love. Passion. Magnetism that keeps me thinking about him day and night.

For that, I am willing to risk my heart. Not for his credentials but for his ability to make me feel loved.

I'd created and deleted at least four dating profiles on at least as many apps. I'd joined Facebook singles' groups, and I'd felt first meeting exhaustion. Thinking about this conflict between wanting a man and hating the process to get one, I penned this.

## Call Me What You Want.

*I wake up in the morning with a smile on my face,*
*Punch YouTube --affirmations emanate.*
*Comb my hair, brush my teeth, lotion down, dress fly,*
*Grab my stuff and some grub, clean up, wave goodbye.*
*On my way, all smiles, do my job very well,*
*Respect, accolades, and a paycheck that's swell.*
*Errands done, my commute was pleasant enough,*
*Drag my ass to the gym to keep myself tough,*
*Shower, cook, eat, and clean,*
*Load up Facebook and friends*
*And the first thing I see is a bitter accusation.*
*All I do day to dusk is live at my best*
*And a relationship is desired, a nice place to rest.*

*Share my day, share my food, share my body and mind,*
*But where in the hell a man will I find?*
*They accuse me of judging before I say a word,*
*Accuse me of pushing them off to the curb.*
*I'm just living life, and I smile all damn day*
*But when they see me, that's not what they say.*
*They say black women demand too much,*
*Won't submit*
*Can't show respect, always trying to get.*
*That black women are whores,*
*I just shake my head,*
*Why is it my brothers can't see me, just RED?*
*Instead, they paint me much worse than other races do.*
*it's me they call bitter*
*No matter what I do.*
*Man, I'm tired of proving myself every day*
*Tired of countering the words that they say.*
*My face hurts from smiling*
*I can't bend anymore*
*I've been complimentary from eons before*
*The script has been written*
*My die has been cast*
*I can be Pollyanna and still get called ass.*
*I can be Dorothy and get painted a witch*
*I'm tired of overcompensating to show*

*I'm not the only image you know*
*You don't see*
*Won't see me*
*And when I sit quietly*
*Nothing left to say*
*You still won't buy it.*
*I'm hanging up my cleats*
*For me, the game is done.*
*You're right. I'm wrong.*
*There -- happy?*
*You've won.*

2019.

I was all over the map. I'd pen a poem like the one above. And then go to The Shrine and write.

## Remembering who I am

*I am infinity, divinity.*
*I am the universe in human form.*
*Serenity, tranquility,*
*Unbound by social norms.*
*I am melanin-infused.*
*I may have been misused.*
*But still, I cannot lose,*

*Because I am.*

*Unfathomable.*
*Unconquerable.*
*I am.*

*Indomitable.*
*Indefinable.*
*I am.*

*More than meets the eye.*
*I am.*

I was going to bed one night, and I happened to pick up an old journal. It fell open to a page I wrote on 1/4/14. I think this was the day I filed for divorce. Simply titled THE LIST, it was my dream, my goal, my fantasy, my prayer to the universe for my lifelong partner.

1. Intelligent and articulate
2. Good listener
3. Self-sufficient
4. Attractive, well-groomed and hygienic
5. Confident
6. Complimentary, charming, and/or fun
7. Sexually compatible, skilled, stamina
8. Spiritual
9. Easy going
10. Loyal, faithful, trustworthy, honest

11. Reliable
12. Someone who stays in contact with me
13. A good kisser
14. Has money to take me out, likes trips on occasion
15. Generous and helpful
16. I feel safe and comfortable with him
17. Nice voice, smile
18. Location provides reasonably easy access
19. Older children or no children
20. Limited baggage
21. Desires a committed relationship
22. Supportive

## Date Seventy Four:

The Vegan- I don't know if him meeting every qualification on the list was the reason I invited the Vegan to a Juneteenth open mic with me. In fact, I don't even really know if it was a "date." I invited so many people to so many poetry events that it was a habit. But I include him because he was my first foray back into male - female interaction in months. And I thought he was gorgeous. I would have loved to date him. I don't think he had any interest in me, though. He said he thought it serendipitous, a sign from the ancestors that I invited him out on Juneteenth. He'd had no plans to celebrate, and that made him feel bad. It was like I picked up on his guilt and offered. I'd been at the show an hour. No one had performed. Everything was running late. But I drank and relaxed and waited, and he walked in, looking cool and fresh and utterly delicious. We sat and talked, and he saw me perform, and we talked more, And I introduced him to half the poetry world in attendance. So much fun and I hadn't realized how much I'd missed my poetry family. How normal all this felt, how good.

I could breathe.

When my mom was sick that whole year, I had one ear infection after another, one asthma attack after another. I hadn't had an attack since I was pregnant in 1995. Still, suddenly I was getting breathing treatments that did not work, steroid shots, carrying inhalers. The doctors thought I might have walking pneumonia, but I didn't. And finally after X-rays, and so many tests, I lost track. It was found out I had scarring on my lungs from pneumonia in 2015. Allergies were aggravating the weakened lungs, and I went on a treatment program to strengthen my lungs and lessen the effect of atmospheric allergens.

It's hard when you can't breathe because of emotions, and then you literally can't breathe because of health issues. It was also ironic because spoken word artists NEED breath. We all do. But breath to us is part of our pacing, our rhythm, our performance.

*Sometimes it hurts when I breathe.*

*And as much as I'd like to blame it on smog, or asthma, or allergies.*

*It's the indentation, the devastation, the exacerbation of fatigue.*

*Sick and tired of being sick and tired.*

*It's the crater left by molestation,*
*Rape and its alienation.*
*The observation of a nation of gangs and their devastation.*
*Too many COLORS.*
*Too much death.*
*It's the drugs, tobacco, endless crime.*
*It's fines and court dates, lawsuit land mines.*
*It's spam email and junk mail too.*
*It's debt unfolding, bills past due.*
*It's baby mamas with no class.*
*It's baby daddy's jailbird ass,*
*It's stereotypes I've seen come true.*
*It's feeling I'm screwed no matter what I do.*
*It's dreading the start of another day.*
*It's wishing singleness would go away.*
*It's too much poor sex. And too much loss.*
*It's dreading another year of my boss*
*It's no vacations yet in sight.*
*And kids that try but don't do right.*
*It's feeling I can't even be the kinda person I wanna be.*
*With poor decisions dogging me*
*It's tiring being a garbageman.*
*I take a breather when I can.*
*But it's yet another meaning of*
*I Can't Breathe.*

## Asthma

*Louis Hay says asthma symbolizes being stifled,*
*I agree.*
*Restrained, checked, suppressed, denied*
*Has often described me,*
*Black and woman,*
*Of two underclasses, I be*

*And then the South has its own oppressive litany,*
*To smother the balance in me*
*Labeled too much yet not enough,*
*How can that be?*

*My reaction?*
*Introversion, asthma,*
*I gasp for air you see.*
*Looking for permission to be,*
*Like some cosmic inhaler that can set me free*

*For me, that inhaler.*

*Be*

*Poetry.*

I was coming out the other end, seeing the light at the end of the tunnel. I'd attended one open mic, And my ex-husband Drew, husband #2, and I were on the best terms we'd been on since our divorce. I'd reached out to him when mom got sick, and he'd called her. He called her all the time. Like a son would. Checking on her. Giving her comfort. I could never thank him enough for that. And he checked on me after she passed, and he called the boys, our sons. We were back to being partners, completely platonic, like two old grandparents rocking on the stoop, steady, familiar, warm. He played with his grandson and had even come by the house. He was transformed. Those years of avoiding the doctor had taken their toll. The first time I saw him, he looked 70 though he was 52. Frail, unable to walk without a walker. My son Joseph gave him a bath and then cried in my arms afterward. My kids were angry with him. How could he have been so reckless with his health, so stubborn to not treat his symptoms? But they loved him. I did too.

There was not one ounce of bitterness in me. Just gratitude. Concern. Hurt, and a little anger too, because things did not have to be this way. They could have been different.

He asked two weeks after my mom's funeral could he live in one of the rooms the boys had vacated. His living situation was precarious. He couldn't work. Was on disability. Without missing a beat, I said yes. He said he had to have a procedure done. It was nothing, minor, a few hours at the doctors, and he would call me afterward. I waited for that call. Called him when it didn't come. No answer. A week went by. Another.

I got a little worried, shrugged it off. I hadn't known where he lived in years. It wasn't like I could drop by and check on him, and it wasn't like we had even kept in contact daily. It was a weekly thing. I was overreacting. I calmed down.

Then I got a call out of the blue. Musclehead Barbie missed me, wanted to take me to lunch. I accepted. I'd felt so lonely lately. Isolated. Withdrawn. It seemed serendipitous. He took me somewhere new, the name escapes my memory, and then mentioned he was getting a massage, did I want to come with. Oh, now that sounded like heaven.

We drove fifteen minutes away, waited a few minutes while they prepared side-by-side tables, couples massage- we both laughed. I closed my eyes and relaxed for what seemed like the first time in an eternity. Spa music, oils, warm hands kneading my body. The smoothness of hot stones. It felt like rebirth.

It was July 11. We walked outside and hugged, and my phone rang. I was tempted to ignore it, but I didn't. It was my nephew. There was a post on Facebook saying RIP for my ex-husband. Was it true?

My knees buckled. My friend caught me, opened the car's door, and sat me down. Talked to me, his voice a soothing whisper stream of nonsense words. I steadied enough to drive home to call my ex's friend through Messenger because I did not have his number and be informed, yes it was true. We've been looking for you. He took you off his emergency contacts. Complications of diabetes (the very thing he'd refused to treat in our marriage) led to complications in the procedure. He was gone.

It was 22 days since my mother had passed. And now I had to inform my sons that the man who raised them was gone. I wanted to be anyone but me. My feelings could wait. Theirs were the first priority.

It was back to therapy. Looking back on July 11, I felt my ancestors had so cradled me, pampered me, soothed me. The invite. The massage. The call that I had not had to answer alone.

There are no words to tell how much this death impacted me. At one time, this man was my very best friend. I always told people we skipped from best friends to husband and wife and never dated. It was true. The moment we kissed, he became my provider, changing my oil, bringing groceries, taking the kids to school, picking them up. We moved in together a month after sleeping together and were married five months later. And we stayed married for almost 11 years. I had loved him. I had loved the family we built together. I was so grateful for the love, the attention, the utter devotion he had to his boys. Though not his biological children, those were definitely his boys. I often thought he wanted to be a father way more than a husband. I was not on birth control for eight years, hoping to conceive. It never happened. But we rarely had sex, so that's probably the reason.

Another gift my mother gave me was reconnecting with him as my confidant, my advisor, the friend who knew me better than any other had or ever would. When he died, that is who we were to each other. Sometimes I thought we should have never married. We should have loved each other as friends. Because that love rekindled like it had never died. He wanted a life with me, with the kids, but had no idea how to be a husband to me. But he knew how to be my best friend, how to be their father. And in the end, that is what he will always be and what we - my sons and I - can never replace.

**Lesson 13:**

When you've lost everything, find a place to moor yourself.

# CHAPTER 14

# Nature

Two months passed before I emerged from my isolation. At that time, my wedding anniversary to Drew came and went. Needless to say, I was not back to normal by any stretch of the imagination.

My son and his pregnant girlfriend had moved back in with me with a one-year-old in tow. Adjustments you do for family. Just when we all seemed to be finding our groove, my son burst into my bedroom, pacing, rambling, shouting, crying.

I grabbed him, not knowing what was wrong but knowing something was very, very wrong.

In between sobs, shouts, and nonsense words strung in a line, I pieced it together. His best friend had shot himself in the chest. 8/30/2019. Best friends actually don't do this relationship justice. Victor and Joe were born a week apart. They had lived across from each other, attended the same schools, had sleepovers, and had done almost everything together since 2003. This was 2019. Joe and Victor got along better than Joe did with his twin brother, Elijah. While my sons had had their moments of stupidity and recklessness that had resulted in tickets and accidents and even arrests, Victor had avoided all of that. He was the one everyone looked up to. And he'd even been on my show. He'd done more in the poetry world than I had- an album, no less. A Ted Talk. He was a boy prodigy, and he took his own life.

I was stunned. Victor's life flashed before my eyes. I remembered how I had described my sons' childhood in an essay that had been published twice in 2016, "Mothering a Member of an Endangered Species."[5]

> "See, no kid grows up in a vacuum. And my sons were popular and involved. Football, basketball, track, band, debate team, lyricist society, Black student union, mock trial team, choir— keeping up with their schedule was a huge addition to my full-time job. And by the time they hit ninth grade, they had a local pack of companions, ten, in fact, a few a little older, a few a little younger. As parents, we had cookouts and sleepovers, carpools, and birthday parties with this dozen in attendance. They pictured graduating together, going to college together, doing the same things they were doing now as friends, with their kids. When graduation came, of that dozen, two were dead- one stabbed by a Hispanic classmate at a high school my kids no longer attended, and one killed in a home invasion. Four were in jail. Six walked the stage—four friends and my two sons. So 40% of my sons' friends made it to 18. Six in all, including my sons, were alive and un-incarcerated. So, even graduation was bittersweet."

5 https://usfblogs.usfca.edu/switchback/nonfiction/mothering-a-member-of-an-endangered-species/

So many friends my sons had lost, and this one by suicide, a month after my sons had lost their dad. It felt inconceivable. Unbearable.

And my son felt like he should have seen it coming, stopped it from happening. Survivor's guilt. And it wasn't like my son didn't have a lot on his plate. His pregnant girlfriend was due on 9/14/19. They were preparing for baby #2.

I got him through that day and the next. Taking off work to be with him. He could not be left alone. And then as 9/12 came, just past midnight, ironically two days after Suicide Prevention Day, I was trying to get my son to sleep. Victor's funeral was that day. Joe was a mess. I'd taken off work to be with him. And then Treasure's water broke. Joe was inconsolable. What was he supposed to do? How could this happen? The baby wasn't supposed to come today. How could a new life begin when we were supposed to be celebrating the one that ended? It's the Circle of Life, I told him. I asked if he had decided on the baby's middle name. He answered no. Any ideas? He said he wanted to show the bond that he had with Victor, but he couldn't think of a way. I said, why don't you combine your names. Jericho's middle name could be JoCyrus. Now you have to bring him into the world and put into him all the love he deserves, all the love you have for Victor, and the lessons the two of you learned.

I told him, '"You're going to the hospital. And whatever happens, however it happens, will be God's will."

9/12, that morning dawned, and I wrote this poem as I brought them breakfast in labor and delivery.

# Light Bringer

*Life is a circle of twists and turns.*
*And ancestor leaves and then returns.*
*I can't doubt that as I sit and wait*
*Anticipating a new life mate*
*My grandson is named after my son's best friend,*
*17 years strong, brothers, just like kin,*
*Jo'cyrus will be ... his own man.*
*But he's coming in sync with Cyrus' homegoing.*
*It's sad that we lost another black man.*
*It's a blessing a new life will begin.*
*Life is filled with joy and pain.*
*You rise and fall, lose and gain.*
*Today affirms the circle of life-*
*birth and death, dark and light.*
*Energy transforming state.*
*Never lost. Never gained. Just spread like fate.*
*The universe is stressing this circle to me.*
*As I leave labor and delivery headed to a mortuary.*
*As I return, I'll be headed where life begins.*
*Having just left where it ends.*
*Twelve months in a year.*
*Twelve hours in a day.*

*Twelve hours in a night.*

*Twelve disciples of light*

*12 is completion.*

*12 a circuit makes.*

*Life ends in death.*

*But impact remains.*

*Victor Cyrus, your physical journey is done.*

*But your light will continue to shine like the sun.*

Finally, the time came when a decision had to be made. Was my son going to the funeral or staying in the hospital room? Both his girlfriend and I agreed as much as Joe was torn, he would never forgive himself if he missed the funeral. My son never stopped crying on the way there. Getting him through the door and then into the actual ceremony was one of the hardest things I have ever done. And at the moment my son held Victor's son's hand, promising to be there for him, he received a call that his son was born. Don't tell me there's no order to our lives. As painful as life is, there is often a poignant beauty in its symmetry. These 24 hours reminded me that death and life are a circle, the natural order.

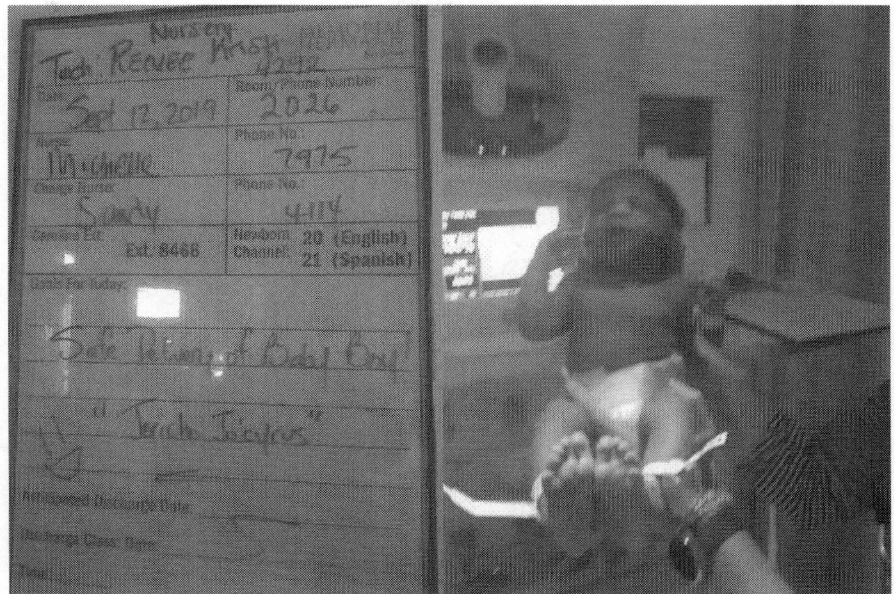

**Lesson 14:**

Nature: Life goes on.

## CHAPTER 15

# Opposition

September 21 was my birthday. A Saturday. No excuse not to go out and do something. Anything. So much death. And I was alive, another year, 49. But, I actually told no one.

The Facebook group OG 35 was where I'd met The Muse in 2015. We'd gone to some of their outings together. Now there was a new event. On my birthday. It seemed like the perfect no stress scenario to ease back into social life after being booed up with grief for months. It was a Wine and Topics party. Each person brought a bottle of wine, and the host had a list of topics or questions equal to the number of guests. All the bottles were opened. Everyone got a glass. Each guest would read a topic, and the host would pour a small sample of wine into our glasses as we discussed. If you liked the wine, you could drink the whole sample. If not, there was a huge punch bowl in the middle of the table where you could discard the unwanted elixir.

It was great. A night full of spirits and spirited conversation. And the man I happened to sit next to on the sofa was a tall drink of chocolate liquor. The night was amazing. The chemistry building between us palpable. My mind wasn't the only thing whetted. But at the end of the night, I went home, and he had not said one word to me privately.

But the next day, there was a dm asking me out. A movie date. I'd only had one of those in the last four years. In fact, I usually suggested we do something else. You can't really talk or get to know someone at the movies. But I accepted his. I didn't need my head filled with any more of his brilliant thoughts, his timbre. I didn't need to stare into his eyes as we discussed whatever topic filled our fancy. The date was great. And then he dropped the bomb.

## Date Seventy-Five:

Even though I didn't consciously remember the list of qualities I desired in a man, my subconscious must have because invariably, the men I dated had all these qualities but one.

Des lacked quality 19, grown children or no children.

He was 39 with a 3-year-old, a 2-year-old, and a newborn.

My interest went from infinity to zilch immediately. I was currently living with a newborn and getting no sleep. Not a wink. Sleeping in fits and starts between feedings and changings.

My interest in a relationship was absolutely over. I told him so. But it only took him leaning in and his breath touching my ear for my interest in him sexually to re-awaken.

"I figured you would say that," he said, "I just wanted to shoot my shot anyway. I want you."

I explained that I didn't see us as compatible, and I didn't think it was a good idea that we continue to see each other because I wanted him to.

"You can have me," he smiled suggestively.

"That's a horrible idea. I've been too long without sex. I get a little wild and intense. It causes problems."

"Problems?"

"The last person I had sex with in this state said I was addictive. That I should have warned him."

"Consider me warned," he laughed. Then paused when I stared back serious as a stone. "I'm grown. This isn't my first rodeo. Let me worry about me."

I shrugged.

Now I have to digress for a minute to introduce you to my alter ego, who took center stage in this fling. Meet Minx.

Minx is always there, just quiet. (I also called her Zena in chapter 3). But at the two-month mark, she gets LOUD. And if I have sex at or after that point, she feels that man is hers. She plans to mark him- for life, to erase any memory of any other woman and claim him head to toe as her personal playground. Some people call this marking "snatching souls." In other words, providing such an intense sexual experience that you become the standard, the benchmark. So that you are unforgettable, no matter what happens in the future. So that he/she feels like they've never been loved this thoroughly before.

Sometimes she invades my poetry when I won't let her play. In lieu of a blow by blow of Des and I making love, here's a poem narrated by Minx.

# Dick Sucking

*It's been a day. That's much too long.*
*I miss the way you writhe and moan.*
*I lick you from your tip to base.*
*Savoring the bliss upon your face.*
*Your thighs caress, lick, suck inside*
*just where your legs and groin collide.*
*My mouth slides up*
*and down one side,*
*the next I kiss; my lips just glide.*
*Upon the head, I twirl my tongue.*
*then briefly suck, not close to done.*
*Sweet and salty glides within,*
*I play with pre-cum. Lick again.*
*My hands are moving all around, your legs,*
*your balls, your shaft surround.*
*It's time for the dance to begin.*
*You can't sit still,*
*My mouth opens.*
*You gasp. I deep throat.*
*Grab my hair.*
*Push face and hips together where,*
*you moan, once, twice, gasp once again.*

*Start muttering nonsense, words blending.*
*"Don't stop. So good. Damn what was that?"*
*I've got tricks. You're shocked at that.*
*I'm kneading softly, bobb around*
*I'm licking, tounging up and down.*
*So fun. I smile. I'm wicked though. I tease a little.*
*Go fast then slow.*
*Go faster. But won't let you cum.*
*I'll let you know when I am done.*
*I want that stunned look on your face.*
*When all your limits, I erase.*
*Cuz I'll make you cum. then cum again.*
*It's what I do, once I begin.*
*I know I've marked you; you can't forget.*
*My soft lips wrapped around your dick.*
*My smile when I saw your surprise.*
*The mischievous twinkle in my eyes.*
*Dick sucking is an art. That's true, and I'm a maestro.*
*Thought you knew.*
*Enjoy it like my favorite song.*
*the taste, the smell, the gasp, and moans,*
*You calling my name, soft and loud.*
*You begging, creaming in my mouth.*
*So luscious, filling, just askin',*
*'Babe, can I suck your dick again?"*

That poem perfectly describes relationship sex, but Des and I used protection. Still, when we were done he said, “You need to be mine. Be my woman.”

“Huh? That was NOT the deal.”

“But you just made love to me like that. I mean. I need you to be my woman.”

I shook my head, “I warned you.”

“You should have tried harder… Well, how often can I have it? Every day, every other day, twice a week? You can’t just break me off like that, and then, that’s it.”

I don’t know what we agreed upon. Still, whatever it was, this conversation played out exactly word for word every time. One day, he said that he couldn’t sleep with me and not have me, that he was falling in love with me. I don’t think it was me he was falling for at all, but I was glad he was moving on. I felt guilty having sex with him, no matter how much he begged for it, precisely because he begged for it. It was the second time I felt that I had unintentionally altered a man’s behavior. First sapping Gatzby’s confidence. Then swapping Des’s detachment for clingy desperation. Desperate to leave. Desperate to stay.

I encountered desperation of another kind when I met Devoted Daddy.

When I think of him, the word winsome comes to mind. Charming and alluring in an old-school kinda way, gorgeous with no clue that he was. Mature but still retaining a sort of childlike innocence.

We'd been wining and dining when he suddenly fessed up he was married. My mood changed.

"Don't leave. I know you don't date married men. There was something I just wanted to ask you in person."

I shrugged, annoyed, "What?"

"How do you make staying bearable?"

It was such an unexpected question that I sat silent. I took a deep breath and stated, "You have to have a compelling why. For me, it was my sons. My ex-husband was a good father, the only involved father that my kids could really count on. I felt if we split, my kids would spiral. I loved them enough to stay. I figured when they were grown-18- I'd still be young enough to begin again. I felt I owed them that."

He nodded, exhaled and confessed, "It didn't start out like this, empty, cold, pointless. We loved each other…once. Now, we don't. She changed," he paused. "But I can't stand the idea of another man raising my children, of not being there to guide them. It's just sometimes I feel so lonely. I almost feel insane."

His words took me right there. Back to that miasma of solitude, that fog obliterating a glimpse of anything hopeful, happy, healthy in my past marriage. It felt like sitting across from myself, as if suddenly I was transported back to my first date, freshly divorced, loneliness streaming off of me like some perfume I put on by accident that I vowed to never wear again. It took me back to my total disbelief that Drew, my best friend, my confidant, my unconditional supporter, was cold and uninvolved as my husband. I had spent nine years trying to understand that transformation, denying it. I had never understood it.

So although I was the ideal person to understand his conundrum, I couldn't solve his problem. All I could do is tell him that for me, staying was worth it. And I had been right. My kids, 18-year-old young men, had completely acted out the first two years. I even wondered at times if the divorce led to my son taking my car without my permission, feeling I owed him. But now, we were all in a really good place. And the difference between my life now and then, well, I could write a book. Damn, maybe he'll pick up this one and read it.

He was the only married man I met that I felt sorry for, for many reasons.

1. People tell spouses like us, "If you're not happy, just leave." If we reply- We have kids. They'll be hurt. Their response is, "Kids are resilient."

True. That doesn't mitigate the damage that can be done as kids try to implement that resilience.

Their other response. "The kids are better off. Who wants to be in a house full of tension and arguing?"

Well, every couple's bad marriage isn't full of tension and arguing.

If these people were honest with themselves, some of them would admit when they became adults and looked back on some of the marriages of their parents, grandparents, or other relatives, they realized how unhappy those people were. As kids, they didn't notice a thing, and those unhappy marriages provided a stable environment.

Those same people shouting JUST LEAVE are also often the same ones putting these long-lasting and often unhappy marriages of our parents and grandparents on a pedestal and asking why relationships no longer last. They don't seem to realize they can't encourage people to leave **and then** complain people don't stay.

2. People assume bad marriages happen because the spouses "rushed," "didn't get to know each other," or confused "lust for love." In his case, he grew up with his wife. They'd known each other since age10, and they waited till marriage for sex. They couldn't know each other any better, and they couldn't avoid acting on lust any more than they had. Turns out sex and sexual satisfaction are not a given. And people change, sometimes drastically. It was devastating to hear how this woman that he had known 35 years was now a total stranger living in the same house.

3. People harp on being friends first, building a foundation. Friends first? No, thank you. Up to this date, I'd spent 25 years of my adult life, married or in committed relationships, and 6 years of my adult life single.

I do not now, nor have I ever believed in or desired the friend's first approach to relationships. It did happen for me with Drew, and I believe that was a big factor in the demise of my second marriage. And it almost made me lose the best friend I ever had and the best influence my sons ever had.

A. To me, If we are satisfied to be just friends, there's not enough interest and passion.

B. Friends and romantic partners have different roles and expectations. A great friend could make a horrible romantic partner.

C. This friends first idea is why people get their feelings hurt in dating. You start off casual, get to know each other, hang out, and build a bond. Still, one person becomes romantic faster or loses interest because the connection doesn't seem to be progressing. Then either someone else who was never seen as a "friend" enters the picture, or one person starts asking the "what are we" question. Either way, somebody gets hurt.

D. And women often get upset when a man they wanted to be "friends first" with introduces them as or calls them "a friend." They get upset when he wants to go Dutch or doesn't plan dates or just wants to chill or doesn't "pursue them," but I never heard of men doing any of that to their female friends.

When you start dating with a romantic intent squashes all that confusion. Either the dates become progressively more intimate in conversation, and affection, and deeper compatibility is explored, or you stop seeing each other. Clear. Simple. Effective.

I think friends first is also what caused Gatzby and me to have so many problems. When I met him, I just wanted to date. He believed close friendships with chemistry evolved into romantic relationships. I could feel that expectation in him, beaming off him, and so I kept telling him I didn't see us together, every time hurting him. Had he not expected us to evolve, I think our interaction would have been clean, simple, and satisfying like the encounter I'd had with JJ.

Facebook is fascinating. So frequently, people complain relationships don't last like our grandparents. Still, then they seem to be able to just turn off their feelings once a relationship ends. I saw some older people fall in love once and make no secret of the fact that they would always love their husband or wife or ex- divorced, dead or absent.

So is this cutting off feelings part of the problem that people post about?

And then there are the people who claim they start as friends and make their partner their best friend. You mean you guys have no feelings after the breakup too?

I can't relate to emotional coldness like that. A part of me will always love the schools I went to, the friends I had, the jobs I held, and the men I committed to, both officially with a title and unofficially with my heart.

Just like I'm not going back to the schools, some friends, and those jobs, I'm not going back to those men, but I still have a fondness for them.

So the idea of no feelings, none at all, like we have no history, no memories, I don't understand that.

And I think this double-mindedness is kinda crazy.

But I can't really fault people. Being human is kinda crazy. We try to make sense of it by coming up with rules, boundaries, guidelines, social constructs. They provide us structure and calm us. They are helpful and harmful and often if we're honest, illogical.

As I sit here typing these words, I wonder who I'm writing to, who I'm writing for. Myself? To make sense of all that happened? To the men I dated? My friends? My family, alive and gone? Strangers? Or even life itself?

Sometimes these all seemed in opposition to me, making my life harder, not easier. Sometimes, I just felt opposition. Other times, total support. It was kinda crazy.

Sometime in between dates 75 and 76, my mom's birthday came, and there were other responsibilities: sorting through her papers, filing paperwork, the things you do when someone passes on. I had mom's medical power of attorney. I was responsible for all the medical decisions while she lived. My sister had the financial power of attorney.

Sometime in the span after the funeral in June and my mom's birthday on October 3rd, I drove to the south side of Houston. I was supposed to be going to my sister's house, 45 minutes away. I drove to the hospital where my mom passed. By accident. On autopilot. Those fifteen minutes of extra driving did not exist in my mind, not until I was driving into the parking lot and realized where I was. Realized there was no reason to be there. Mom wasn't there. And I parked and cried.

I told you during 2019, I wrote a lot. I did. I wrote poems about my mom.

But I also didn't. What I remember most about that year is feeling I couldn't think.

I'm a thinker.

Thinking is what I do.

I evaluate, analyze, sort, categorize, make sense of, explain.

I could do none of that.

Mom died May 19. Then Drew. Then Victor. Three deaths between my sons' birthday 5/7 and mine 9/21.

I couldn't think.

Sometime after my mom's birthday, I stopped going to therapy.

I couldn't think.

I couldn't respond to the questions.

I couldn't talk about my feelings or my thoughts.

Sometime in that period, a guy (don't ask who, I don't know) texted, and I wrote this:

## Not at all Okay

*He texts, "How are you?"*
*"Ok," I reply,*
*Shake my head, it's only half a lie.*
*I'm employed and stable,*
*Money in the bank,*
*Nice clothes, nice car,*
*Jewelry in sync.*
*Educated, healthy, networking linked.*

*I'm articulate and beautiful and accomplished, see.*
*But singleness sometimes gets to me.*
*Swipe right one hundred times and yet,*
*it's been a month since a new guy I met*
*Two years, in fact, since date 3 held intact.*
*People are fickle. Unreturned texts.*
*Say they'll call, haven't heard one click.*
*Life is busy, I understand*
*Doesn't stop me from feeling forgotten.*
*These men don't know me, don't realize,*
*I am a beautiful, intriguing prize.*
*I don't know them. I feel the loss.*
*No masculine energy making me soft*

*I'm all hard edges, too intense,*
*Driven. Focused. Relentless.*

*All good things, no doubt it's true.*
*But I wasn't created to replicate dudes.*
*I was created with softer skin,*
*some vulnerability and feminine whims,*
*But like an egg in a boiling pot,*
*I've hardened, toughened, all thugged out.*

*It helps me to succeed, yep that's true,*
*But dollar signs can make one blue.*
*They cannot hug, or kiss or thrust,*
*They cannot stir me with one touch.*
*They cannot make me laugh and smile.*
*Alone they don't make life worthwhile.*

*I'm ok, yes, but want to be-*
*happy, fulfilled, satisfied completely.*
*I want to spoon and fork, gyrate.*
*I want my drought, sodden and sated.*
*I want to reply to how I am,*
*"Mmmmmm. Damn. Baby.*
*Damn Damn. Damn."*

Opposition. I felt angry sometimes that Gatzby wasn't here. That I shut him out. I know you're reading this book, and it seems I'm always meeting someone new, going out. Well, the time from June 19 to September 21st seemed like a lifetime of loneliness to me. And I didn't know what to do with it except perform or write. And I know Gatzby let me down, but I sometimes felt I should have asked why. Was there a reason? I never let him explain.

I knew his thought process about me missing him. We'd discussed that once before when we connected, and he expressed surprise that I felt that way. First, he would call me Cray Cray. That was his second nickname for me because he said it was crazy that I would push him away and then later miss him, that I would refuse to commit to him but somehow feel he was important. Then he would relent and say he understood because he was my "crutch, my security blanket."

All I knew was that I wasn't angry with him anymore, just hurt and missing him. But I also couldn't go back. I really did feel my mom had shown me how unreliable he was. (He would scoff at that, saying I was the one expecting reliability from a man I said I was only going to have sex with, that I was unrealistic. I would respond with I was only expecting him to do what he said he would do.)

At times like this, I was angry with myself. Sometimes people seemed to want things from me- commitment, attachment, some emotionality as a woman I was supposed to have, and I just didn't. It was a bridge too far. I felt in opposition with the person I was and the one society, my sister, or Gatzby wanted me to be.

## Apologizing in Advance, lol.

*There is this thing that's called EQ,*
*And I don't always have it.*
*Sometimes I'm so in touch, just psychic,*
*Compassionate empathic.*

*Other times I blunder in, all Taurus straight ahead.*

*Those times, I might leave broken china bits in my stead.*
*I've gotten better as I've aged, but sometimes I still see,*
*A little girl scratching her head, chagrin a little tardy.*

*It doesn't help I overthink the words once they are said.*
*It doesn't help I worry my texts will be misread.*

*I mean no harm, disrespect or foul.*
*I seek a life of Zen.*
*And thus many times my art speaks for me*
*Because my literal words seem sin.*

*If I offend, not intentional*
*It's just an act of fate.*
*It's why I let so few get close.*
*So I don't have to retrace.*
*My words, my texts, my acts all day.*
*Exhausting it can be.*
*Easier to seclude myself within my artistry.*

*The stage and the pen, they are my security*
*But the world at large is often my purgatory.*

*And so many times, I sit quiet when I have lots to say.*
*And many times I work, instead of rest or play.*
*And sometimes, men have called me blunt, intimidating.*
*It's why when I make a friend, I never do lose them.*
*And so, tonight, I bore my soul maybe you learned a bit.*
*At least now you know the meaning of* EMOTIONAL QUOTIENT.

Sometimes I wished men could read my mind. I wasn't a pet owner at the time, but I'd had both cats and dogs, and I felt my life would have been better if Gatzby, The Muse, or Harlee had been more like dogs.

Dogs are loyal. They're your best friend. They give you tons of attention. They follow directions well and are easily trained. They're easy to please and forgiving. They're protective. They read moods very well and reach out when you're sad. They like to cuddle. They're approachable. They're trustworthy. They're good listeners. They are the poster boys for commitment and want to grow old with you. They love unconditionally.

Instead, many men are like cats- aloof, distant, unresponsive, passive, self-centered, flippant, rude, nonchalant, destructive when they're bored, territorial, and easily distracted by flashy things (like half-naked selfies or big asses). Cats don't listen. They feel and act superior or condescending. They contribute very little but their presence yet want to be pampered. Cats are fickle. They think they can sing very well and don't mind showing off. They expect to put people on the shelf and deal with them only when it's convenient. They disappear and reappear without warning. They're secretive yet nosy. They seem to take pleasure in being underfoot and tripping you up when you're busy but avoid you when you're free. They almost make you feel like you're imposing on their free time. They're overly dramatic when they're sick. Moody and picky.

I'll even go one further; most people like dogs. You never hear them say dogs ain't shit. Most people dislike cats. And dogs are even better communicators; Timmy could interpret Lassie's barks with ease. Cats just meow, purr, and hiss- I want something; I'm good; leave me the fuck alone.

Oh, don't think I dislike men. Like Kermit, the frog says- "You can't live without em. There's something irresistible-ish about them. "

If what I said in those last paragraphs offended, it was metaphorical. I was in my feelings. Hurting. Lonely. Lost and missing, more deeply than I'd admit outside my poetry, Gatzby.

## The Question

*The heart isn't logical. It wants what it wants.*
*It glimpses a future*
*And strides forward with force.*
*So damn optimistic,*
*It doesn't get hints or clues,*
*That the one it is chasing is*
*Distant, aloof.*
*He may not be malicious,*
*Just cold, uninvolved,*
*But the heart still will crave him like he is the boss.*
*Can't turn off the craving.*
*I damn sure have tried.*
*Distractions and busyness lend places to hide.*
*But every spare moment, he creeps in my thoughts.*
*So fucking annoying that I haven't moved on.*
*While I'm fretting and feening, he hasn't a clue.*
*So fucking annoying since I'm usually aloof.*

*I'm usually the one who doesn't feel a thing*
*Not because I'm cold, but because most men*
*are trifling.*
*The ones I've met bore me, shallow, unprepared.*
*But those that ignite me seem unattainably scarce*
*Consumed by work or by hobbies, by family affairs.*
*Can't get a call or a text; communication is rare.*

*So much like Murphy*
*The law that just states.*
*What you want, you can't have but will send in its place.*
*A million friend requests, a dick pic or two.*

*But the one you want,*
*Nope, he won't want you.*
*Oh, he may say he does, may even deign a kiss,*
*But on a daily basis, weekly even, his attention you'll miss.*

*You'll regret you met him because before he came,*
*You were coping better, pursuing fortune and fame*
*But ever since his smile, it's like love is all you seek.*
*But it takes two to tango and a halfway meet*

*You lay at night in bed alone, only craving him*
*And solace fantasies with porn, and throw poems in the wind.*

*Even writing this seems silly, pointless,*
*Just hearing yourself vent.*
*Guess it's time to wrap it up.*
*Damn, what's wrong with men?*

Now, as I finish pasting that poem into this manuscript, I picture a person out there reading this, pointing at the book and saying, "See." His or her finger right on this page, "Now THAT is why I don't believe in these situationships."

Well, hold on a minute there. Let's examine that thought process. What are you objecting to? Feelings? People who say they save feelings for a title are not honest with themselves. Although you may let yourself go " all in" with a title, there were feelings, or you wouldn't want the title in the first place. It's kinda like someone suited up for the third round of tryout saying, "I'll only care about this team winning if I get a slot." If you didn't care, you wouldn't be trying out.

Are you objecting to longevity? Stability? Well, I'd dated Gatzby from 2015- 6/2019. Even including the three breaks- The Muse 10 months, Harlee 6 months, and Ace 3 months, that's still two years, longer than both my post-divorce relationships COMBINED.

And still I could not explain why I was so attached to him, yet so unable to commit to him.

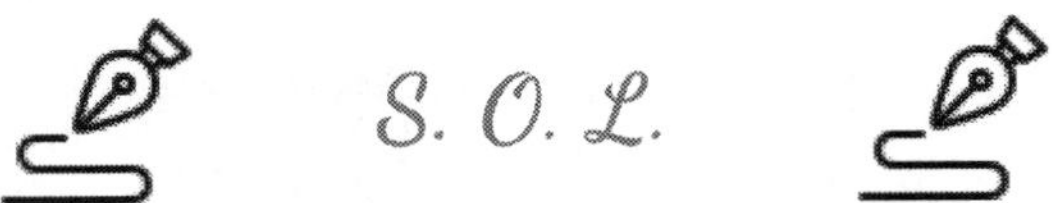


*Just breathing in,*

*Without a clue,*

*Cause all I want tonight is you.*

*I'm tired, lonely, horny, bored*

*Should've hit the gym, made myself sore.*

*I didn't. I came home instead.*
*In minutes I will hit the bed.*
*But first I'll try to purge this pain.*
*Singleness is such a drain.*
*Dates that turn into demands.*
*Heads half-buried in the sand.*
*Sloth, entitlement, childishness too*
*It's what I face waiting on you.*
*An insult here, stood up again,*
*Can't open up to two-faced men*
*So charming on days 1, 2, 3*
*But say one wrong word, and fangs I see.*
*Nothing to count on.*
*Not one line.*
*Can I just wake up to love sublime.*
*A man I can relax around,*
*Who's not whining all over town.*
*A man sensual, intelligent, true*
*A man who makes love like I do.*
*I never thought I'd say it here*
*But I'm so done with searching dear.*
*Disgusted, damn near gave up hope.*
*I'm tossing my last length of rope.*
*Tow me in from this abyss.*
*Pull me out of all this mess.*

*Let your caress just ease my mind.*
*Let your kisses my lips find*
*I give up.*
*Wave the fucking flag*
*I'm done, kaput, gave the last fuck I had.*

**Lesson 15:**

Opposition- Sometimes it feels like everything and everyone is against you, even yourself.

# CHAPTER 16

# Power

## Date Seventy-Seven:

Rhett- Brewingz was the place where I met him. I call him Rhett because I was Scarlet. Not Scarlett, like *Gone with the Wind*, but like *The Scarlet Letter*, at least to him, that is. I could have called him The Inquisitor because he seemed to do what so many men complain women do, see our first date as his personal interrogation room. Only he really shouldn't have asked me these questions. He wasn't ready for the answers.

He didn't like the answer that I got divorced because my ex-husband and I grew apart. He wanted details. We lived like coworkers. We never talked except about the kids, the bills, or the house was not good enough. But when he learned part of the reason was my ex was impotent and refused to treat it, he was incensed. "You left your husband over a medical condition?"

"No, I left because, among other things, he put his pride above his health and our marriage."

"So I've had problems with impotence. Would that stop you from dating me?"

"Maybe. Have you tried any treatments?"

I might as well have said that I jumped on stage with Ozzy Osbourne and drunk blood from a recently decapitated live bat.

"You sound like a nympho," was his answer, which did not answer my question at all.

I laughed. "I doubt nymphos saved themselves for marriage or would go almost 9 years with no sex while married, but ok." The Muse who had considered sex once a week extreme had called me that too.

"So, when is the last time you had sex?"

"Nosy," I shrugged. "Not sure. If I'd known you wanted dates, I'd have brought my planner." That stunned him to silence and was only partially an exaggeration. Given my two-month window, I had more than once written when I'd had sex in my calendar.

Rhett was so scandalized he wanted to go Dutch. I paid for my food. He for his. We parted ways.

Once, long ago, it might have bothered me that someone, anyone, thought my sex drive was a problem, unladylike, hedonistic, wanton, untamed.

That girl was dead.

She died when an epiphany took her place. The Rose Doctrine had told me sex outside of marriage would make me feel cheap. But the cheapest I ever felt was when I learned my first husband had slept with his baby momma while married to me and when my second husband didn't think enough of our sex life and marriage to even let the word impotence drift from his lips in the privacy of a doctor's office. I felt worthless. Unwanted. Unwomanly. Undesirable. With a ring smack dab on my finger, a marriage license filed cleanly away, and my husband's name stuck on the end of mine.

By this date, I had slept with JJ on the first date and had four other FWB's- Gatzby, Ace, The Young Lion and Des. I hadn't felt cheap or used; actually, I'd felt more loved (emotionally, mentally, and physically) than I could have ever imagined. Not having rules like 90 days or commitment made each situation feel like a gift rather than a contract, like a loving interaction and not duty.

And unlike the warning all the people on Facebook and in my past had given by asking, "Why would a man give up his freedom if he can get the milk for free;" every one of these guys had offered me his farm- his love, his commitment. **I had turned them down.**

And most poignantly, there was a part of me that screamed my first husband might have been faithful and my second more motivated to get help had I embraced my sexuality, my sensuality in the way I had learned to in the past three years.

If I had known how to seduce, arouse, pleasure, excite, entice, and satisfy my husbands in the ways I had Gatzby, Ace, The Young Lion, and Des, I don't think I would have reached 43 before learning I was multi-orgasmic.

The Rose Doctrine and The Angel in the House, which equated passion with promiscuity, all desire with lust, and sexuality with sin, had robbed me.

Of pleasure. Of freedom. Of being comfortable in my own skin.

I had been married 17 years and still wasn't sexually free.

And this wasn't about regretting my divorce or wishing I was still married. It had taken me three years of singleness, three years after a divorce, to give myself permission to fully enjoy sex, to revel in it, to explore, finding in this journey self-love, empowerment, and much greater intimacy.

If I had to wear a scarlet A, it would mean Amorous, Ardent, Aroused, and Artful.

And I just felt it was a total shame that that woman had not existed when I was a wife.

Every time I hit the bedroom now, I painted my name on his body, signing my work with my signature.

And every time that masterpiece bloomed in his mind, I knew he would stop, and smile and nostalgia would fill his heart.

And if that scared Rhett, scandalized Rhett, stupified Rhett, so be it.

I think part of him expected me to ask for his absolution. Not me.

I suddenly flashed to two contrasting scenes.

One from Honor, a book by Elif Shafak. In it, a Turkish girl runs away with her boyfriend expecting him to marry her. He doesn't. She returns home and is greeted with a basin with a rope in it. To hang herself. She has lost her honor and is as good as dead. She does so.

I'm not Turkish, and my honor is not wrapped up in my abstinence from sex. Instead of killing my physical body, I killed the part of me that found sex dishonorable.

It was like the scene in Monique's movie "Phat Girls" when she shows up at the same bar that she'd slunk in sheepishly before, garbed in her new confidence. The man who turned his nose up at her before, now made a beeline to buy her a drink, to ask her to dance. Her name, height, and weight were the same. But that old personality was long dead.

My old sexual shame, apologizing for my needs, wants, desires, feeling "lust" was dirty and sinful had been replaced with seeing sex as a natural human desire for intimacy and connection that was as pure as crisp water on a sunny day

If Rhett needed me to be ashamed that, as a single woman, I was having sex, he would die waiting for that shame to surface.

As a high school student, I wore my letterman's jacket with pride. I had earned it. I could don my A with just as much pride.

Some readers may instantly know who I refer to, dusting the cobwebs from the mental attic where tomes on feminism and Virginia Woolf are stored. I am not a feminist. I think few pro-black women are. I'm about the progress and freedom of both men and women. After all, I had spent the last three years killing the "Angel of the House." But in this particular instance, after meeting Rhett, I felt like Virginia Woolf's ghost was by me. Even in writing this book, as a woman, a formerly Christian woman talking so bluntly of human relations, morality, sex, of killing off The Rose Doctrine, I felt as if The Angel of the House were a demon on my shoulder.

How could an angel become a demon, you say? She was the voice telling me that no one would take my work seriously if it included erotica; if I had sex outside of relationships, if I admitted that I sat at a restaurant table and didn't immediately storm off when I learned a man who asked me out was married.

If I wanted to write about dating, the Angel would say, I needed to be sympathetic to every man I described, or I'd risk being called a man basher. I needed to be so chaste, I blushed if a man even hinted at seduction. I needed to be passive, letting him make all the moves, or I might be thought unfeminine, controlling, demanding, too independent. I needed to drop my metaphorical hankey and wait for my knight and be ever so gracious, "Woe is poor little old me. What would I do without your big, strong, handsome self? I have no mind of my own, you know."

First in that date and then in the writing of this book, I did as Virginia Woolf said, " I turned upon her and caught her by the throat. I did my best to kill her. If I were to be held up in a court of law, my excuse would be that I acted in self-defense. Had I not killed her, she would have killed me. She would have plucked the heart out of my writing."[6]

Though I killed her, I think it was just temporarily. I think she's like Jason or Michael Myers. I think the Angel is alive and well, especially on Facebook. In singles' groups, I often see women comment that they won't do or say X because men might think they're a whore. This comment is very strange to me because

1. No one can control what another thinks, no matter what she/he does or doesn't do.
2. These same women don't care what men think about their hair, nails, job, education, weight, clothing, or other areas. In fact, they would probably be pissed if men commented negatively about any of these things.

So, why care about men's opinion, especially a usually inaccurate opinion, about your sex life?

---

6 Killing the Angel in the House by Virginia Woolf

My answer- it's the Angel in the House prompting these thoughts.

Writing. I was doing a lot of it in 2019. A lot. The loss of people, of familiar roles- daughter, granddaughter, daughter-in-law, wife, Christian woman- had me re-establishing my foundation, searching for what I KNEW, what was REAL, solid, sure. ("You know nothing, Jon Snow.")

It felt like being back at high school, the first day, so lost that I did not realize I already had a schedule since my mom had it set in stone before my arrival. So I needlessly sat with new enrollees in the auditorium, waiting my turn to be processed. Walking into class late, already feeling like others knew, had known what I should have long known.

Long forgotten snippets of literature seemed presciently applicable now, at 48, when before they had just been clever turns of phrase. Now they were mantras- *Killing Off The Angel in the House*, proudly wearing *The Scarlet Letter* and this gem from Walt Whitman.

"There was a child went forth every day, And the first object he looked upon and received with wonder or pity or love or dread, that object he became, And that object became part of him for the day or a certain part of the day . . . . or for many years or stretching cycles of years."[7]

In other words, for the first time in my life I was able to see the lessons I had been given as "objects" I had become "for many years." They were not part of me. They were not mine. They were just

---

7 "There was a Child went Forth Every Day" Walt Whitman

objects to be kept or discarded. And for the first time in my life, I realized what I kept and what I chunked, was totally up to me.

I was becoming more discerning. I determined as Whitman would say to "re-examine all you have been taught in school, in church or any book, and dismiss whatever insults your own soul."

I was finding a lot that insulted my soul. And discarding those outdated ideas was making room for new ones. New ones often supplied by the men I met on dates. New ideas I turned over in my head, examining from all angles before discarding or storing them for future reference.

I think the universe has a sense of humor. It tests us to see if we've really changed.

## Date Seventy-Eight:

Test of Faith- Looking back, I think he asked me out to pick my brain. He said he was open-minded in matters of faith. That he understood I'd left the church. That he, too, had done his research, and his beliefs were evolving. I smiled at all that. Dating in Texas and trying to find a man who isn't spouting that he's God-fearing and wants a "good Christian woman," " a woman of faith," is hard. The men my age seemed mired in tradition. And those who aren't, like Mystique, are still foreign because they're often vegan or vegetarian and uninterested in a meat-eating plus-size woman. So open-minded was good. Very good. Except he was the opposite.

Every statement and question on this date was really a challenge, an altar call, an admonition on the error of my ways. And the more I shrugged and gave facts, research, church history, incidents of how paganism had infiltrated the church, the more adamant and angry he became. He was a living, breathing backfire effect. The backfire effect is the inclination to resist accepting evidence that conflicts with entrenched beliefs. Rather than working through the initial discomfort of cognitive dissonance, the person barricades themselves behind confirmation bias, remembering all the people who agree with them, clutching onto tradition and experience more tightly. It's why facts rarely convince true believers because when people are presented with that conflicting information, they will cling to an illogical but comforting paradigm ( even admitting its flaws) rather than question it or shift to a new way of thinking. His was an extreme case. People with his level of backfire effect react to new information as if it were a physical threat, becoming angrier, louder, and sometimes even violent.

Years ago, had I met someone like him, I would have backed down or even questioned my new revelations, my way of thinking. But on this date, I was unperturbed. I said my piece and let him have his feelings. His feelings were not my problem. I wasn't trying to change, challenge, or contradict him. I answered his questions with what I knew to be true. He could take it or leave it. Of course, he chose the latter and physically left and then called apologizing. I accepted the apology but told him there was no reason to communicate further.

Test passed.

## Date Seventy-Nine:

Test of Worth- Back at Brewingz again, I'd been invited to watch a game. Strange date, I thought. But what the hell, a new experience. I arrived. We chatted, ate. It was pleasant. He was distracted. Half his attention on the game, half on me. I'd figured as much. As we finished our meals, he said something interesting, a statement that could have come from my head at one time. "I'm really glad you came out. I really liked your profile. You were my #1 this week. Now, when I go home, I will have new greetings in my inbox, and one may stand out. She may become my new #1. Singleness is so amazing. I never knew there were so many single women, beautiful like you, smart like you, sexy like you, accomplished like you. And all interested in me.

So you may not be my #1 next week, and you might not hear from me again."

I acknowledged I understood and walked to my car as he turned to watch the game.

Two things struck me as I left. 1. His reasoning was exactly why I was currently NOT active on any dating profile. He had been my last connection before I deleted the last site. That idea of there'll be another hit later tonight; I don't need to invest much in this; the conveyor belt mentality that had slowly started creeping in smacked of an arrogance that I could not stomach in myself. People shouldn't be that disposable like stations we switch when a commercial comes on, or the current show gets boring. But dating sites could make one feel they were. I didn't want to feel that, think that, or act that way.

The second revelation was that had I met him when I first divorced, I would have been angry, insulted, hurt. I would have felt dismissed and wondered what was wrong with me. Why men found me undesirable. Now when that idea popped up in my head for a split second, it rang so false that it was immediately discounted.

His statement was not a valuation of my worth. No man could determine my worth; that was not in his control. My worth existed outside of whether I got a date, or got a second date, or was so absorbing that a man forgot about the game blasting on the screens around us or his inbox possibly filling up with - well, hello there's. He made a choice that was his to make, and I had a nice outing, and we both were moving on.

Test passed.

*I no longer accept society's scale.*
*My worth's not set by their intel.*
*My weight, my kids, my length of hair,*
*My past romantic or business affairs,*
*My elocution, my degrees, my credentials all can see.*
*My travels, credit score, money gained or lost*
*No longer determines my self-worth's cost.*
*I realized something new, you see,*
*These scales can drive a person crazy*
*On one, you shine, another fall.*
*A third barely register at all.*
*So weigh and sift and label at will,*
*None of these numbers my value tell.*
*And those who judge me by these means,*
*Just might miss my truest gleam.*
*Spirit, soul, and energy*

*so much better define me.*
*You can't measure that global reach.*
*The lives I touch because I teach.*
*The words I spoke, not dead but seeds.*
*The landscapes filled by all my trees.*
*You can't capture upon a scale,*
*The hearts I lift by stories regaled.*
*My purpose is not to meet your stakes,*
*But to become the person I was fated.*
*So numbers and statistics, I see, no sighs.*
*On something much stronger I rely,*
*My heart, my intuition, my certainty,*
*My calling unfolding hourly, daily,*
*My judgment seat, my feather scale,*
*MAAT confessions, negations I upheld.*
*I lift my head at peace inside,*
*My worth indelible breathes, abides.*
*Beyond time. Beyond space, beyond current norms.*
*I am the ALPHA and OMEGA'S home.*
*And interestingly enough I see,*
*You valued Him little, not just me.*
*Called him names, accused him, vilified,*
*Upon a cross he bled and died.*
*And now we've renamed history,*
*in the year of our Lord, BC, AD,*
*So is it any wonder society misvalues me?*
*No matter, all that matters is my worth, I SEE.*

## Being in the moment.

There was something I learned in that last year with my mom. Something so vivid it was seared in my consciousness. Be in the moment. We all have those moments of presence. At the beach, watching your kids in the waves, knowing that their floaties belong to a very small window of time. Homing in on that moment, taking mental snapshots to pull out and flip through at a later date. Enjoying that perfect Fall or Summer or Spring day knowing the weather will change. Dating was like that to me now. There were moments within every date that could be savored like fine wine, mulled over in a lonely moment, burrowed away like a nut or like fat for a winter hibernation. Just because I had had a date every weekend for a while didn't mean that would continue. In fact, I was waiting for them to peter out since I had closed down on my profiles.

I was searching my heart. Where was I in relationship to wanting a relationship? Did I want another FWB? Did I just want to be single? Forever? I often didn't have an answer, so I removed myself from the pool of eligible subjects. I didn't inbox, pursue, flirt. If some man wanted me, he'd have to come after me. Not because I was "all that" or out of some sense of tradition, simply because I didn't want to send mixed signals. My life was still re-arranging itself. I still felt…

## Lost/Loss

*I woke up this morning and felt loss/lost.*
*Started taking roll- body, soul, mind intact. Nothing happened as I slept,*
*Not even dreams.*

*It could be growing pains,*
*Change is so dis-comfortable.*
*So out of the norm, inexplicable.*
*And so utterly lonely.*

*I felt loss/lost*
*As the sun rose,*
*And birds sang.*
*And breezes caressed tender blades of grass.*
*Like I'm losing part of me and*
*don't know what will take its place.*

*Like good enough is*
*no longer GOOD ENOUGH.*

*I felt this way in relationships before*
*In church before*
*At jobs before*

*And I closed those doors and opened new ones.*

*Sometimes life moves too fast,*
*When you evolve.*
*All things revolve.*
*The only center, elusive.*
*Like the eye of a storm,*
*Constant but moving.*

*I felt loss/lost*
*As I opened my eyes to my day.*
*My choices await.*
*My future at stake.*
*My goals in the making.*

*The only thing to lose is*
*All my status quo*

Healing! People post about healing before starting a relationship, before having kids.

As a person who has been "healing" on and off for 22 years, I agree with these ideas to an extent. But I also wish people would stop acting like healing is a destination. It's a journey. We heal. We get injured and heal again. We grow and realize we didn't heal everything. To me, this idea that you can't move forward till you "heal" is ill-informed. It's like saying you shouldn't love till you're successful. What's success?

As you grow, the goal post changes. At 18, success may have been getting into college. At 22, it may have been graduating. At 26, it may have meant a house. Healing is like that.

No one's life should be on hold because they "should be healing."

**Lesson 16:**

Healing is a journey, not a destination, and that journey may require the voyager to kill old beliefs, patterns, and dogmas as they keep moving forward. Take back your power..

# CHAPTER 17

# *Qualify*

### *Damn* 

*I had a man text me he missed me,*
*ironic because he never met me,*
*but something about my words made him not forget me,*
*ironic those who met me can.*
*And you can call it game,*
*It's a shame*
*we doubt the best but believe the worst*
*about our fellow man.*
*Me, I took him at face value,*
*Though not the way he intended.*
*He missed his musings of me,*
*The me that could be*

*If I fit his image of femininity.*
*Of Christianity.*
*For he didn't know enough of me*
*To miss the totality,*
*Can he handle my brutal honesty?*
*My reality?*
*My complexity?*
*He missed the me he made up from syllables he might have misread,*
*Fantasies I half said, so he filled in the gaps with images in his head.*
*But we all do this,*
*Infatuation, fixation, elevation*
*Of a love interest to a pedestal they never*
*Asked for.*
*So I smiled and said thank you,*
*Grateful someone missed even the very thought of what I could do,*
*For this world can seem so cold that a random*
*"I miss you" can actually make a difference.*
*Damn.*

## Date Eighty:

I read in my journal, "It's 8 in the morning. I'm about to go meet L at Golden Corral for breakfast. I think it will go well. Apparently, I stayed on his mind for five months. Then he texted me, "taking a chance" (small) at being rejected. He knew he "wanted me" and put his "pride and fear aside to pursue me." I like that."

His kiss was awkward. I think it's the big lips. I think sometimes they even get in the way of his conversation. He's so traditional. It seems like every time I run into Texas-born and bred men, they are. His drawl is thick but also disconcerting because his yalls and fixin to's and ima's contrast with his street slang. I found myself silent just listening to him, contemplating the linguistic anomaly that sat before me. He noticed. "You don't lak how ah talk, do ya?"

I didn't know how to answer. "It's interesting. Unique."

"Nobody laks how ah talk. But I don't especially know how ah would change it."

I shrugged.

"Ah really laks you. Ah really do. You so smart."

My eyebrows rose. "Thank you."

"Ah knows you gots lots of interests, and that's good and all, but since we now seeing each other, you can put all them away."

"Put them away?"

"Of course, our relationship needs to be yo priority. Making time fo me."

"I do make time for people I'm dating, but I won't stop writing, performing, or developing my business to do that. If you want me, if you like me, that comes as part of the package."

"Well, see now that's the whole entire problem with you career women. You forgot what's really important. Love. Security. Connection. That should be yo focus. Not money, fame ah status." He counted on his fingers and pointed to the table like they were objects in view.

"1. I have security. 2. Connection and love shouldn't require me to become less of who I am. It should enhance, not detract."

He shook his head, "What's detract?"

"Subtract. Take away."

"Well, why didn't you say that? Yo vocabulary is intimidating. Do you always talk lak that?"

"That was a two-syllable word. I use much longer ones. But yes. I use the words I know. I use the words that best express my ideas. I'm a reader and a writer. I know a lot of words. I just talk, not necessarily thinking about how big or hard or sophisticated the word is. If I was talking to a kid or a teen, I'd probably consider whether they might understand me and use smaller words. I don't do that with adults. Detract is just an everyday word to me."

"I feel like I'd need to tote a dictionary around to date you."

I was really in awe. I couldn't believe we were having a whole conversation about my "inappropriate" vocabulary. It made me think of what my grandmother once told me when I was in elementary school and was reading The Scarlet Letter that I found on her bookshelf, "You know that's a high school book, eleventh grade?"

"No, Ma'am, I didn't. Really? It's not that hard. I've only had to look up a few words. The sentences are long and written funny, but once I got used to them, it's just like any other book."

She smiled but looked worried, "Boys don't like girls that are too smart."

"Boys? What boys? Why would I want boys to like me?"

She laughed and patted my head. "Enjoy your book, girl."

It had been a long time since I had been called intimidating. In fact, my first husband being utterly unintimidated was one of his top-selling points. He seemed so masculine. I felt so feminine. It was one of the reasons I fell in love with him. When we had met, nothing I did, could do, said, or accomplished made him feel challenged or inferior. It never occurred to me that later he would be the man trying to control and diminish me, literally beat me into submission.

But this week, that label for me had popped up twice. Once before an interview, (a radio personality had called me for a panel on domestic violence and also wanted me to touch on male-female roles in Ancient Kemet, what Africa was called before it was colonized. Kemet meant the black land). He said I know you're single. I bet you intimidate a lot of men.

And now on this date. It was such a turnoff. And as much as we like to think we've progressed, Kemetians had gender roles much more advanced than this conversation I was having. They believed male and female energy needed to be balanced. If there was a meeting, a gathering, a celebration- a woman and a man should organize and create it. The perfect example of this was in the movie Wakanda, when the king appeared before the queen mother. The women said, in essence, we understand you are king. Still, you will also understand, respect, and uphold our vital role as queen mothers. We submit to you because you have earned it, and we will only continue to submit to you while you walk in wisdom.

Getting back to L, he'd taken me to breakfast, then putt-putt golf and batting cages. We'd had a blast till this conversation at the table and his ultimatum at the date's end. And when he kissed me, I was unprepared. I was definitely not feeling him like that anymore.

"Ah still laks you. Ima good man. You really should consider putting all that unnecessary stuff aside. I knows you was bored, lonely. You filled yo time. You didn't run the streets or club. That's real good. I'm proud of you. But I'm here now. You don't need that stuff. Ah'll take care a you. You take care a me. Just the way it's posed to be."

I just blinked. How was I supposed to respond to that? I was speechless. I shook my head and walked away. Was this what my mother dealt with? My grandmother? This was what she warned me about.

Out of the corner of my eye, I saw him watch me, then raise his hand and wave it, not in a goodbye wave, but an absolute wave of dismissal. He shook his head and peeled out of the parking lot.

And although I do believe he was "a good man" and that he had every intention to "take care a" me. I call him L. L for loser. Because he wanted me to lose everything I had gained the last several years, so I could "take care a" him.

I'm sure there are some women and men who think of all the men I went out with; this was the one I should have committed to. They think this offer of a life with my only responsibility being to "take care a" my man is heaven on Earth. Not me. I grew up watching Cicely Tyson and Miles Davis, Ossie Davis and Ruby Dee, and others- beautiful, black, married couples. ( By the way, Davis and Dee had an open marriage). Cicely Tyson never remarried after 1989. Oprah has never married. Shonda Rhimes says she never wants to marry. To some men, these women are statistics. Those who will or did ( I laugh as I type this) "die alone" and were "leftover."

I should be so lucky. To die - alone. Legacy intact. Talents fully utilized. Self-actualized to the max. But my ultimate fantasy is to be a part of a power couple.

I don't fear marriage, as one video by Kevin Samuels hinted that so many of us women are walking around scarred and scared of marriage.

It's just less important than those three things above- talent utilization, self-actualization, legacy creation. Every woman was born with a purpose, gifts, a calling. We all need interaction, intimacy, love. None of those require committed relationships or marriage.

Being part of a power couple is definitely on my list of "Man, that would be the most amazing thing ever." But so is dying with every dream fulfilled, every goal realized, every talent explored. Depending on the day, if you ask me which I'd rather, who knows. Relationships bring so much, but they cost too. Time. Money. Effort. Sacrifice. and more. As some would have us believe, the choice is between love/relationship/happiness and singleness/loneliness/ unhappiness. For many of us, it's a choice between a life spent building a union and a life spent building an amazing life.

One of my favorite writers is Zora Neale Hurston. She said, "I do not belong to the sobbing school of Negrohood who hold that nature somehow has given them a lowdown dirty deal and whose feelings are all worked up about it. Even in the helter-skelter skirmish that is my life, I have seen that the world is to the strong regardless of a little pigmentation, more or less."[8]

I'd like to adapt her quote. I have seen that the world is there for the taking regardless of relationship status. I do not belong to the sobbing school of womanhood who hold that a dearth of men is a lowdown dirty deal and whose feelings are all worked up about it.

8 "How It Feels To Be Colored Me" Zora Neale Hurston

I don't know if men talk about their dating lives. Some do on social media. But I wondered after this particular date what L would say about me. It was the whole good men thing that he harped on over and over. I wondered what his complaint might be if he had one. Maybe it would have been- nice guys finish last.

Men post women like bad boys. Women post men like ratchet hood rats. Some people reading these posts think both are true for some men and some women, but no one likes whiners and complainers. Painting good men/good women as victims is unattractive and actually plays into the very scenario the posters say they hate. Very few people are attracted to those who paint themselves as overlooked, ill-treated, or unwanted. And bad boys/ratchet women never come off as whiners and complainers because they don't post these- "nice people finish last scenarios."

Thinking about L again later, I also wondered, did he really like ME.? I've wondered that a lot in general. Do the men in singles' groups like women? Not only are they attracted to us, but do they like us? I mean, men crave boobs, ass, thighs, lips, and sex, but do they crave the women attached to them? I left three singles' groups in the past few years because I couldn't remember seeing one positive post about women. Every single day was a barrage of complaints.

Me, I like men. I have a lot of good things to say about them. I don't post tweets, memes, etc., regularly, just complaining about men. It would have been totally random to ask this on the date, but I almost want to call L up and ask him. Do you like women or just what women can do for you?

And before I leave L, I have to mention this whole "good men" thing again. I post on Facebook. I've probably responded to this complaint of men more than any other. I wish I had saved them because my exasperation with the sheer ridiculousness of this idea makes me not even want to write about it. Good is an opinion. An adjective. That means it is subjective. Ever-changing, depending on who you ask and when. So it is not a standard for making a choice as important as a relationship partner.

Also good is a low bar. If given the choice of a good, great or amazing meal, who would choose good? The only reason you would is if you hated the items in those other meals, were allergic to them, the places were inconvenient to get to, or the meals were too expensive. We all want the best if we love ourselves. Good is not the best.

Good has no bearing on the rightness of something. An F150 is a good vehicle for someone. Not for me. I would HATE hauling myself up in it daily. I'd find it difficult to maneuver. It does not fit my personality, lifestyle, or vision of my future.

People understand someone wanting the RIGHT car or house, but those same people think someone should settle for a GOOD man or woman. It's nonsense. A person can have much more influence on one's life than a car or a house.

Finally, "good men", "struggle love" and single women. I've heard men say and saw men post that single women need to be willing to struggle and build with "good" men, even in groups for people who are 35 and up. Singleness for some women is like a comfortable retirement. We wake up when we want, don't have to punch anybody's clock, no rush hour traffic or road rage. Just peace. Every now and then, some boredom or loneliness.

And these men want us to trade that for going back to work on a commission job with no benefits and doubtful chances for advancement? Many of us would gladly leave retirement for a job that was truly compatible with us. But just leaving because we get any offer? Unlikely.

Now, does it make sense?

And there's also past experience. Not "all men are alike" because of past experience complaints, but the ability to compare singleness with being in a relationship.

So I've spent 25 years of my life married or in a committed relationship. And I've been single for 7 years total of my adult life. And I fit into that 70% of wives who filed for divorce and 75% of girlfriends who initiated the break-up.

So I have a question. Given the stats and the resulting conclusion that women seem more than twice as likely to end a relationship, even though doing so may make them single, why do many men act like women dread or fear singleness?

By the way, do these men know how they appear? I sit in singles' groups, sometimes reading, sometimes commenting, sometimes just observing. So many singles groups/dating sites seem filled with single men whose posts make them seem petty, cheap, insecure, stupid, lazy, entitled, immature, inarticulate, short-sighted, inappropriate, and just generally undesirable.

1. Why do these men think (in light of this) that most women are freaking out about being single?

2. And how do these men reconcile their belief that no woman is "truly single," that we all have a "food guy, a shoulder to cry on, or a friend zone buddy who wants more" with this idea that single women are lonely and desperate for companionship?

Guys say women make no sense but think it's completely logical to hold onto two paradoxical male beliefs ( women are afraid to be alone, but no woman is truly alone).

To be the "more logical " of the sexes, these assumptions of women's views on singleness seem completely illogical.

If women need to kill off The Angel in the House, men need to kill off Prince Charming.

We want men to be princes of charm.

Still, Prince Charming is built on the assumption that a woman, all women, are stuck, Cinderella's slaving away, or Rapunzel trapped in loneliness, or Sleeping Beauties unable to lift a finger to save themselves.

Without Prince Charming, these women are doomed to lives of drudgery, abuse, and helplessness.

Women love helpful men, valiant men, romantic men. But we are not helpless. You are not our only hope. We can and have often chosen and created lives we like or love and just want you to add to our already vibrant lives, your love.

There's this meme I've seen daily for a while. "A man will change his behavior for the woman he wants."

Do women really believe this? That night I believed that L believed it. He was convinced if I wanted him, I would change.

If I had, did he really expect that change to last?

I'm unconvinced. I believe people choose their behaviors based on the roles they intend to play. A man is different as a brother, friend, employee, boyfriend, husband, etc. That's not a change.

Those characteristics were always there.

They're just now being expressed because he is active in that role.

I believe relationship dynamics can change people, but most of those changes are reactionary, not planned, and thus are stimulus-based. For example, a person stimulated by alcohol may become the life of the party. A person stimulated by infatuation may become romantic. Neither is a lasting change.

I treat people/men like the weather most days. I see how the sky is/they are and act accordingly. If I get annoyed or disappointed, just like with the weather, it's a fleeting moment of wishing things were different, then I accept what is and move on. It's helped me be less emotional and much more logical. People will be who they are, reacting to whatever they are reacting to. Sometimes they may change their behavior for me, but they probably won't.

And this is why I believe even more strongly; as Maya Angelou said, "When people show you who they are, believe them the first time."

Part of me wished I could tell all this to L. But I couldn't, and he probably wouldn't hear it anyway. There are plenty of women who will give him what he wants and be happy.

Which leads me to my next date.

"You're famous," The message popped up in my notifications. Messenger. I clicked the pic of the guy who sent it to see more.

Handsome. My age. Single according to his Facebook status. Caramel, about 5'9, compact, a running back's build, a soldier's stance, "chin up, chest out, shoulders back, stomach in." This should go well, I thought. Military men love me. Harlee, The Muse, and the three musketeers are ex-military, all branches represented. I hit the back button on the phone and messaged him.

"Clever. Nice opening line."

"Nope, just true. There are 3000 people in this singles' group, but only 20 people post. Mostly admins. And you. So you're famous. Everybody has to know you in this group."

"Naw. I doubt it. I don't post that much. I don't comment that much. Just when I have something to say."

"I get the feeling you could comment on everything if that were the only criteria. What are you doing tonight?"

"Tonight? I don't know. Why?"

"Zydeco night at Zum Barrel. Your page says you're in Spring. It should be like 15 minutes from you. I live on the south side. But I'll drive to catch a drink and some tunes with you."

"Really? That's kinda short notice."

"C'mon, it's a beautiful day, perfect weather. It'll be an even more beautiful night. Swing through. One drink. 7 pm. Here's my number. I'm ________. " He gave his name.

"I'm not saying yes. I'll text you by 5:30 if I'm coming."

"Cool. Later."

"Bye."

Well, that was the fastest I'd ever been asked out. But I did remember him. We'd gone back and forth dozens of times on dozens of issues. I liked the way he thought. Loved the way he communicated. I'd even been tempted to jump in his dm after a few of our exchanges, but I hadn't. Once I had direct messaged a guy in that same group. Just dropped a line, "I enjoyed your comments. I'd love to chat sometime." and he posted my message in the group, calling me forward and unladylike. That didn't go as he planned.

After a second of being embarrassed, I actually became amused- The Angel in the House happened to have bass in her voice today.

I responded to his post. "So I gave you a compliment and wanted to have a conversation? Most people would say thank you and accept. Or thanks, but no thanks. 'Forward? Unladylike?' Hardly."

As soon as I wrote that, the flood gates opened. I'd never seen a post go viral in this group, but that one did. Men chimed in. Women chimed in. And every single person was on my side and had some choice words for him. He ended up quickly apologizing to the group and me and pulling it down after about 200 people went off on him. But still, that exchange left a bad taste in my mouth, so I refrained from reaching out, and now this new, more interesting, and possibly interested guy was reaching out to me.

I'd never heard of Zum Barrel, so I googled it, checked out the website, the Facebook page. I was impressed. And sure enough- Zydeco tonight, a whole Creole invasion. I felt a pang of homesickness. I'd grown up with dual citizenship- fall, winter, spring in Houston, but every summer and holiday in Baton Rouge, and that was a whole other country. I'd been back once since Hurricane Katrina. And I'd never known till that moment that I missed it: the food, the music, that time in my life before...

As my excitement built, The Angel in the House perked up (she's such a killjoy) and dredged up some dogma I had read maybe in some book on dating rules about not being too available, not accepting spur of the moment dates. But I wasn't listening. Now that I had had a few minutes to think, I was looking forward to going. A new place. Music. Zydeco. Live.

I was born in Baton Rouge, so Zydeco conjured up good memories. Crawfish boils. Cards and dominoes. Pool playing. Lazy days and endless nights. Good food. Good company. Pure bliss.

I texted I'd be there, finished my errands, showered, dressed, and drove up. The parking lot was full. The music already playing. And as I walked up, he was waiting.

## Date Eighty-One:

The Fig looked just like his Facebook profile picture. We headed in, got drinks, headed outside. A trail ride company was there. Swinging out. Loud talking. Louder music. But the vibe was perfect. The sun was setting. The breeze slightly kissing my locks. Damn.

Although I was surrounded by strangers, every face I looked at was friendly. Some greasy with food. Some already slightly tipsy. But all smiling at me, at us, like we were some gorgeous happy couple that just lifted their hearts to gaze upon. I've always marveled at the arts. At its ability to turn strangers into sudden friends when you're swaying in time with everyone else, belting out the words to some melody you feel deep down in your soul. It makes me wonder what Woodstock was like. Three days of that, non-stop.

We stood awhile in the back, him leaning over whispering in my ear. It was the only way we could hear each other. Time passed. We danced. Drank. Talked. Danced some more. Finally, I wanted to sit down. The sun had set. It had to be about 3 hours after we'd arrived, but the party showed no signs of winding down. His hand on the small of my back as he led me through the crowd was comforting and protective. Suddenly, my sandal caught on an uneven patch of ground, and I started to fall, and his arms were around me, righting me. I stared into his eyes. Warm, ablaze. A moment. Then his mouth was on mine, his tongue dipping and swirling. His mouth was succulent. My hands were on his shoulders as he deepened the kiss, and my mind went back to the last time I had tasted something this rich.

I was in Baton Rouge, up a fig tree, my hands sticky, my mouth full of the best thing I had ever tasted. It tasted like liquid sunshine, thick, honey-smooth, so sweet it was sinful. I had never tasted anything else that good till this moment, this man.

He broke away, whispering in my ear, "I've wanted to do that all night. Don't hate me."

"You're good," I smiled.

Inside, the party continued; the band had passed out instruments to the guests, washboards and tambourines, and things I had no name for.

"I'm glad you came," he said. "I had a blast. I'd like to see you again. But I have to tell you I'm not looking for a relationship."

"Oh, ok. That's cool. I wasn't thinking about one. But is there any reason why, if I might ask?"

His face darkened. " I just got back from Afghanistan in 2018. I was in a relationship. I have nightmares sometimes. When I woke up once. I was choking my girlfriend. Needless to say, that was the end of that relationship. So, I'm in treatment. I don't trust myself to stay overnight with anyone. I don't know if I ever will."

"I'm sorry." I took his hand, held it, caressing each of his fingers with mine.

"I haven't told anyone that," he said. "You just seem approachable. I was lonely. I wanted to forget and feel normal."

"I understand." And I did. I knew what it was like to have nightmares and flashbacks to not trust my own mind. I knew what it was like to wonder if they would ever stop.

"Yeah," He paused, searching my eyes. "I think you really do. It's something in your poetry sometimes. A hauntedness. Like the past visits you, and it's the only place you can exorcise it."

"Hmph. That… is an apt description, Insightful. I think you've been reading my diary."

He smiled. "No, just your vibe. A fellow wounded warrior. Music is my exorcist. I come here alone. All the time. Well, whenever I can. But I wanted to share this with you. I knew you'd understand."

We didn't talk much after that. We ordered some food, sat side by side, eating from the same plate, holding hands, laughing at the little dramas unfolding around us. At the end of the night, he walked me to my car, kissed my forehead, and patted the door.

We went out twice more, the last date ending with him sitting in my car, talking tearfully about his past, future, and present. We never kissed again. Never saw each other again, and he disappeared from the group, Facebook. His number suddenly changed. I think about him sometimes. Pray for him. Send him positive energy. And I wonder…

I see the term "real relationship " on many Facebook and Instagram posts. And I'm not sure what that is.

I was married twice. The first husband cheated, but people would still call that a real relationship. The second was an amazing father and friend, but a lousy husband- no romance, no sex. But people would consider that a real relationship.

Since my divorce, I've experienced things I never did in any of my "real" relationships.

1. A guy who walked 4 miles round trip to spend the day with me after I was depressed my car was stolen and totaled- Ace.
2. The man who showed me (at 44) that I was multi-orgasmic- JJ.
3. The guy who stayed on the phone with me when my son was in the ICU, and I was all alone- Mo.
4. The guy who first encouraged me as a writer, becoming my personal cheerleader - The Muse. (Although we were committed, some people think any “relationship” lasting less than a year isn’t real. We lasted 10 months, so I included him in this list.)
5. The guy who drove 3 hours and rented a hotel suite as a surprise to whisk me away on the anniversary of my dad's passing, who also made my first logo- San Antonio.

None of these were "real relationships," according to some people, but they all changed my life, made me feel incredibly treasured, and showed me, love. And then there was The Fig, my fellow wounded warrior. He was full to bursting with goodness: life, love, friendship, good humor, but once bruised, he seemed unable to heal. I think about our first date sometimes. His kiss in the moonlight, like summer itself, blossomed in my mouth, spreading its warmth and goodness from my head to my toes, and how quickly that illumination dimmed when he remembered his past.

We too, shared something intimate. So intimate that it almost seemed like we became each other’s confessors, participating in something so sacred that after the first date, we almost never touched.

To me, commitment is great, but discounting dating interactions or "situationships" as not "real" denies the fact that although short-lived, these interactions can be valuable and life-changing.

**Lesson 17:**

Only certain princes need apply. You define your qualifications for real and fake relationships.

# CHAPTER 18

# Revelation

Now, you've read enough to know that I, like probably many women, love gorgeous men. But that doesn't mean that's all I've dated. If I could place a picture of dates 1-81 here, you'd see 6'6 to 5'2, 185 pounds to 400 plus, jet black skin to white enough to pass, early 30's to late '50s, so gorgeously perfect that some woman probably walked into a pole staring back at him, to so ordinary he could fade into the woodwork.

## Date Eighty-Two:

Cinder could never fade into the woodwork. He was too big for that. Body builder big. We'd first met in 2002, between my first marriage and my second at the workout room in my apartment complex. I was working out, alone. He came in. After that, we often timed our workouts together. We went on a few dates. I was 32. He was 27 and a virgin, saving himself for marriage. I wasn't about to touch his abstinence with a ten-foot pole.

He was sweet, totally inexperienced with women, and I worried about him because he seemed so gullible, innocence beyond all explanation for a black man in America. The one time we kissed, I realized I'd found one body type I disliked. I'd dated athletically built men before, and my body sunk into theirs as we kissed like a hand into memory foam, firm but cushiony. Big guys were of two types, the teddy bear, soft but solid, and the bean bag, feeling like a decrepit pillow that, no matter how much you fluffed it, just sagged flat.

Body builders, it seemed, were a cinder block, unwieldy to hold, uncomfortable to cuddle with. I was surprised.

I was equally surprised when I ran into him at Kroger's 17 years later. He exclaimed I had not aged a day, and he would have known me anywhere, and took me out around the corner to Chili's where we caught up.

I was happy to hear he was no longer a virgin. Sad to hear, he was still single. And we were just as platonically attracted as we had parted, friends, never anything more.

## Date Eighty-Three:

Triste is the one guy on this list who makes me sad when I think about him. Next to Gatzby, I had known him the longest. I had met him my second time at The Shrine, which by this time was probably two years before our date. We had been friendly, chatting at The Shrine. I had purchased several of his necklaces and earrings.

The day my mom had died, he had unexpectedly shown up at a gathering partially in her honor. No one there knew she had yet passed, but he arrived bringing gifts from The Motherland. To me, it was a sign that she had been accepted into the ancestral realm. To walk into the gathering and see it decorated like an African village was breathtaking. It gave me more comfort than he could have ever known.

We began to talk much more privately after that gathering, with him checking up on me as I grieved but giving me six whole months of as much space as I needed.

I was grateful to him and hoped something would develop between us. In December, he attended one of my shows. It turned out to be an amazingly special one. I and several of my fellow artists were honored with Congressional Awards for Activism.

He said we **had** to celebrate and took me out afterward. Although he'd worked all day, and the show had lasted two hours, and it was probably after 10 when we entered the restaurant, he acted like he had all night to spend with me. I was touched.

I'd been overjoyed to see him at the show. It was such a surprise and the fact that I received an award, and he was there to see it, felt serendipitous.

But our date was awkward. We always talked freely, but not that night alone at Papa's BBQ. I chalked it up to exhaustion and shook it off.

We finished our food. He walked me to my car. And at the door, when I turned to thank him for the night, for coming to the show, for the late dinner, he kissed me. He was the tallest guy I'd ever dated, 6'9 and big in a way that I hadn't noticed till we were face to face, and he was staring down at me.

The kiss was awkward, almost like a movie kiss between virgins. The only thing missing was the bumping of heads. The hug afterward was the most awkward physical contact I'd had with another human being. I had imagined memory foam or teddy bear. He was the flat pillow.

If I believed I could grow to love someone romantically, I would have seen him again. But while I could feel his desire for me, all I felt in the end for him was gratitude and appreciation.

He felt I had led him on, but I never meant to. I had wanted to explore our connection. I hoped it would deepen. But somehow, this man who had been so kind to me, so gentle with me, in my mind was more like a father figure than a lover. And I had no idea how to reverse that.

Every time I thought of that date, of him, I was saddened.

## The Magic Penny

*I think it's broken,*

*My wishing well.*

*It's hit or miss*

*Haphazard as hell.*

*It's protected those I love a lot,*

*But Mr. Right, I cannot spot.*

*I've met some alternates.*

*They stand-in.*

*Pinch hit a game*

*Take a spin.*

*I get frustrated.*

*Why can't they be,*

*just a little more right for me?*

*It's like I search for Clorox 2,*

*Not wanting bleach to dim my hue.*

*Instead, I find ammonia, Windex,*

*Men that I struggle to accept.*

*Red flags a plenty,*

*The wrong vibe,*

*I want to ignore just to give it a try,*

*But I can't deny the inner me,*

*It screams aloud, jealously.*

*See, the problem isn't just their flaws,*

*But my soul won't compromise at all.*

*No budging, hemming, sacrifice,*

*It wants chemistry, compatible lifestyles,*

*Great conversation, and ultimately.*

*That eureka, this is it, finality.*

*Without it, I'm restless, inconsistent,*

*It's not playing games but my soul's insistence,*

*They he is not the one for me,*

*That he can't satisfy my inner safari.*

*I think it's broken, or am I that rare?*

*That for me there's no match, no pair?*

*Or am I too picky, honestly?*

*If I can't love a man just because he loves me?*

We stopped speaking privately after that day. And things went back the way they had been before, chatting in passing, giving cordial greetings like we had never had any history at all.

If there is any date I regret, any date I felt should not have happened, this was it.

**Lesson 18:**

All revelations aren't pleasant. Some are downright painful.

# CHAPTER 19

# Standards

Robert Frost said, "Way leads onto way." That was true about poetry. I performed. I started a business organizing poetry, comedy, and live music shows. That "way" led to my one Facebook page with 638 friends becoming 3 pages with over 8,000 followers. I moderated another page as the nonprofit organizer of an activism group. Plus, I now had an Instagram, LinkedIn, and Twitter page, all with followers.

I kept my phone on silent because notifications of comments on my posts, past show clips and flyers were frequent. One commenter began to stand out, Cleveland.

Physically, I have no type. But those I've committed to since my divorce have one thing in common. They inspire me.

I seemed to inspire Cleveland. He got progressively flirtier in his public comments on my posts till one day I said, "I'd like to see you in my office."

Immediately, I got a dm.

“So are you really interested, or just flirting?” I asked. “And if the latter, why? I looked at your page. You’re a minister. I would think I’m the last thing you’re looking for.”

“Well, that was direct. No, hi, how are you? How was your day?”

I sent a shrug gif.

Then a hi gif.

“Lol,” he responded. “Just joking. I like your directness. A man would always know where he stands with you. No games. I’m interested. I know you have non-traditional beliefs; that doesn’t bother me. I’m more open-minded than most ministers. I’m not much of a texter. Here’s my number if you want to chat more.”

Well, he’d scored brownie points for the number. Texting. I don't mind texting people I know for short messages. I'd rather call, though. I miss texts daily. I don’t see them till much later. Because my phone is sitting on a table in another room while I do whatever I'm doing, I don’t hear the notification that I’ve received a text. That seems crazy to some people. Like they think I'm lying. I tell people, you're likely to get me faster if you call.

Then these dating sites. From 2015 to 2018, I’d pull one out of the moth balls every so often, just to say I hadn't given up on finding a mate. I’d forage, scavenge, search, and finally, I’d message someone.

Ugh.

"Hi. Nice pic. How are you?" I guess everything has to start somewhere, but somebody needs to develop a better method.

I feel I have no personality in a text, and others rarely do either. I'm never bored, except if I have to read texts. So I will ask if we can talk instead. That request goes over like a lead balloon half the time.

If a guy says he'd rather text than talk, I'm not giving up. Still, I definitely have lost 95% of my enthusiasm for continuing the process. So I ask how many kids he has and their ages. That's usually the end. Not what I'm looking for. Or work schedule might do it.

If we talk, I'm much more flexible. Good conversation is hard to find. Intelligent men are gold mines

I thought I was a unicorn in hating texting. But maybe Cleveland and I shared this. We also shared being plus-sized preacher's kids. But I didn't knock Cleveland for his looks. He looked just like the cartoon character, a sturdy teddy bear

I called. A great conversation followed. And he asked me out to a Thanksgiving church concert. My first church date. I accepted.

## Date Eighty-Four:

Cleveland asked me to arrive at Fallbrook Church at least an hour early to make sure I could park, and there would be seats. There were plenty. In fact, we spent the hour sitting in two separate rows. He sat in front of me, turned around, talking to me in the row behind him.

"You're too gorgeous and intelligent to be single," he said.

I burst out laughing, wagging a finger at him. A few days before, he shared my post about this very statement men make.

I'd written the compliment in that post and then stated that the statement was often posed as an accusation that the woman (me) was either lying or hiding some egregious flaw that wasn't immediately visible. I'd posted that I used to hate the other question that was used instead of the "compliment" - "Why are you single?" And then I'd confided to Facebook my change of heart.

"Once, I couldn't picture being single longer than 6 months. Singleness was just a breather in between relationships. Now, I remember all the amazing things about relationships while I think of the perks of singleness:

1. I love controlling my life, time, and money and owing no partner any of it.
2. I'm building an empire.
3. I like variety and options.
4. I love freedom
5. It's time for a break from monogamy.
6. It's fun.
7. No one's been compatible enough
8. No one's added to my life in a way that makes me want to commit to them
9. I've done the relationship thing; now, I'm trying to fulfill myself completely without a relationship.
10. Have you ever been in a bad relationship? I'll take singleness instead.
11. I protect access to my heart and my life."

The belly laugh this memory caused was a great icebreaker. I'd only been in church three times since The Muse- two funerals and my grandson's christening. So I'd felt out of place, awkward, but not anymore. He'd suddenly gone from a "stranger" to the guy I'd chatted digitally with for months. Now that rapport had become physical.

We chatted till he had to move next to me to accommodate people coming in, and then we enjoyed the concert side by side. Afterward, we sat in the vestibule chatting. It was nice talking with someone who'd been following me long enough to get a gist of my personality, thought process, and preferences. He didn't ask me what I was looking for. He knew I'd always say chemistry, compatibility, and great conversation, and secondly,  a nonsmoker with his own vehicle and place, a job/career, and grown kids or no kids.

So I was unprepared when he said out of the blue, "You need to heal your triggers. You're eliminating possible partners who might be good for you because of past romantic failures."

I looked at him. Smug. Having sized me up, he thought he had my number. I sighed. "My preferences aren't based on triggers. They're grounded in triumphs," I paused, looking for a response, none forthcoming. I continued, "I've been in therapy five times in twenty years. The clinical definition of a trigger is something that affects a person's mental state so significantly it causes extreme overwhelm or distress, possibly flashbacks. A trigger influences one's behavior because of fear and pain.

Let me paint a picture for you. When I was a kid, I spent my summers in Baton Rouge. My grandmother had a three-bedroom house with a window unit in the living room. That was the only room that got cold in the stifling weather. The others sweltered. We got used to it. I got used to seeing the sweat beads pop from my grandmother's head as she cooked or cleaned. When the sun went down at night, we sat on the steps as the whole house cooled. When I look back on those days, I don't think of the heat, but the love, the fun, the food, playing checkers with my grandmother, badminton with my cousins, and watching cartoons and kung fu movies on

Saturday mornings. Me now choosing to never live in a house with no central AC is not because that past triggers me, but because I can choose a better option.

It's the same way with my standards or preferences, whatever you want to call them. Out of all the available houses for rent or sale, men in this analogy, why would I choose the one that's going to make me sweat when I can be cool and comfortable?"

"You have to take a man as he comes," he replied.

"No, I don't. That's the thing you don't understand. I don't. The choice is totally mine, and I would rather be single than sweat. That's a triumph, not a trigger. I'm not my grandmother who had no choice."

He was flustered and excused himself to the restroom. I took out my phone. I had so clearly heard the voice of the Angel in the House in his claims that a new idea rose in me. I thought the concept was one created by Virginia Woolf, a woman, to give a name to the demands placed on women. I **had** encountered the phrase in her writings. But suddenly, I realized, and an internet search confirmed, that the phrase originated with a man, Coventry Daughtry, in 1862. Slavery was still in full effect when he wrote his poem, "The Angel in the House."

Slavery, the ultimate representation of the denial of choice.

While I don't think Cleveland or any sane modern man wants to enslave women, I do get the feeling that some men, like Cleveland, are very uncomfortable with the idea of women having choices.

The choice to date or not to date, to have sex or abstain, to accept a man where he is, or say, "No, I want someone more established." Once in history, women had few or no choices. Their lives were planned by their fathers, brothers, uncles, matchmakers.

Women were chattel. Now we speak our minds. We live lives of our choosing, unapologetically.

When he returned, I continued my thought process. “Standards. Some men, maybe you, think women set them too high. They think when we were younger, we women let more things slide. I agree with the second conclusion. That's called growth. It's called refinement and shows that women can and do learn from our mistakes. It doesn’t mean I’m triggered. Some of these same men scream about women taking accountability but don't realize this is how accountability shows up. If I was once a party girl and dated guys who drank and smoked all day, and then I saw how destructive that was, I probably now would only date men with more self-control in that area and exhibit more myself.

Sometimes it seems that men want it both ways. They want women to take accountability WITHOUT those standards applied to the men they date.

Is that laziness? Is it unrealistic? Is it a desire to have the new and improved woman but still be the same old man?” I stopped talking, expecting him to answer.

He didn’t.

Cleveland had stated that he was open-minded, that he enjoyed intellectual debate, that he wanted to “pick my brain.” His withdrawal into almost complete silence when he returned from the restroom showed that he needed some evolution in this area of free will. But religious people often do. Sometimes their dogmas have narrowed their vision to the point that being shown other choices exist is disconcerting.

I’m sure that he had expected me to hear his assessment of me and be ashamed, unsure, apologetic. He hadn’t expected me to dismiss it immediately.

But that’s what happened after I learned myself. I knew my triggers. And they weren’t the seven things I wanted from men. Five sessions in therapy had made me intimately familiar with my triggers. I was also intimately familiar with our patriarchal society with its many Hydra heads. Cut one off, and two more emerged to take its place.

As an English major, I’d once learned that myths were used to reinforce cultural taboos and codes of behavior. For example, in Greek culture, Cassandra’s beauty prompted Apollo to give her the gift of prophecy. But when she refused to sleep with him, he cursed her so that no one would believe her divine wisdom. I sometimes feel I understand her. Men give their compliments and gifts but cannot accept that I know my own mind to see what is best for me. I am only a woman, so choosing anything in opposition to them results in their curse.

Although, I didn’t exactly expect a love connection with Cleveland. I had expected a friendship with this man who seemed to value my words and my mind. The last thing he should have said to me was - “You have to.”

As many people say, “the only thing I have to do is stay black and one day die.” But accepting a man, settling for what I don’t want, is not something I have to do.

Now, I MAY choose to.

There is a truth that many don't like to hear. They feel it's unfair. Different women/men bring out different reactions. I'm a woman, so I'll speak on men. I'm really easygoing (nicknamed Zen for 25 years). But still... there are men in my life who get "yes Daddy" treatment and those who get "boy, please."

I prefer dating men who provoke the first response in me. Why do I submit, want to please, and even often cater to the first group? I don't have a clear answer. Maybe it was the sex appeal, his swag, his confidence, his "man's man" aura, how he radiated masculine energy. I don't know.

I know that the first type makes me want to do things that I actually have to work on desiring to do for the second type. The first type I'm patient and helpful with. I serve and respect him. The second type I expect more from. He has to prove himself, and sometimes that's not good enough.

The first type checks all my internal boxes of what a man should be. I'm proud to be with him. I want to keep him. The second is in my inbox/ear complaining I won't give him a chance.

The same holds true for how many men react to different women.

I don't have a physical type. But there's definitely a type of man who attracts me. Society tells women we should change that (and I actually tried once or twice. It never sticks). Now I'm okay with the fact that my inexplicable preferences remain firm.

I like who I am with guy one. I love our interaction. It's a pleasure in itself just to be with him regardless of how long the interaction lasts. No regrets.

I meet two types of men, and I know them within the first 3 or 4 encounters whether things with us progress or not. Unfair? Maybe. But that's facts.

And sadly, after this date, Cleveland was nowhere near being in the first group.

**Lesson 19:**

I have the right to decide what is acceptable or desirable for me, regardless of whether any man or society at large agrees.

CHAPTER 20

# Triggers

If you've ever done yoga, you've probably heard an instructor say that modern society keeps us tense, breathing shallowly, barely expanding our lungs. It can be such a relief sitting on that yoga mat in comfy clothes in Lotus position. Then you close your eyes, and as Terry Mcmillan says, "It happens. You exhale." I always thought her book was powerful, from the title to the imagery, *Waiting to Exhale.*

In 2018, I had three musketeers; by 2019, only New Jersey was left. He was now in New York. But to me, he was Breath. Our conversations, his voice, his advice, his verbal kick in the ass, his potty mouth, his cheerleading. He made me feel invincible every time I pushed forward in my business. He would say these three words so convincingly that I could hear them like a mantra. "You got this." He made me believe I did.

# Breathe

*Breathe. Slow my mind. Inhale again.*
*Damn, your smile popped into my head again.*
*Inhale twice, make me smile,*
*Do some work for a while,*
*Antsy like I had espresso,*
*But it's just the effects of your style.*

*I'm so calm, cool, and rational, nicknamed Zen,*
*But my stomach goes all fluttery when I think of him.*
*Love songs fill my head, romantic fantasies ensue,*
*And the crazy thing is - I've never even met you.*
*But I feel like I am blossoming.*
*R. Kelly's "I can Fly."*
*I feel like I can reach up and touch the goddamned sky.*
*I feel like I'm floating "Dream Lover" you rescued me.*
*I wanna "Rock with You," " Islands in the Stream."*
*"I Call your Name" in my head as I send my next text,*
*I think my brain orgasmed, but we never had sex.*

*I mean, your fantabulous, mesmerizing, unique,*
*I feel like I ramble whenever I speak.*
*A little lightheaded, I breathe deeply again.*
*So honored that I can call you my friend.*
*But hopeful for more, I'd feel lucky it's true,*
*If one day I posted pics with you as my boo.*
*Ella Mae's in my head, Janet Jackson's there too,*

*Cuz honestly whatever you want- "It's all for You."*
*I'm "Nutty for You," with a big kool-aid smile,*
*What the fuck did you do to drive me this wild?*

*I keep holding my breath, like I'm under a spell,*
*I keep thinking, he seems to understand me so well.*
*I want to give you the best, exalt you as my king.*
*I mean face it, I want to give you every damn thing.*

*You're a thousand miles away, so distant like a speck,*
*But you make me feel my life is "Golden" like the best hasn't happened yet.*
*"There is Beauty in the World," and you,*
*"You're the Best Part"*

*You captured a corner of my heart.*

Neither of us believed in long-distance relationships, so we'd text and call and video chat and continue our own single lives.

Texting can only tell you so much. It can hide how a person breathes.

## Date Eighty-Five:

I met Darth Vader. He was handsome, intelligent, witty. I'd gotten used to looking forward to his texts. He asked me out to Pappasitos, and then at some point in the date, his breathing drastically changed.

"Are you all right? Something went down the wrong pipe?" I expected him to cough uncontrollably any second now.

"What do you mean?"

My eyebrows rose. "Your breathing. It sounds like you're having an asthma attack, laboring to inhale and exhale."

"I'm just breathing."

THAT was not breathing. I flashbacked to high school, freshman year 1984, in front of the tube, watching sci-fi. An actor, who looked absolutely human, blinked, and the audience saw the lizard pupil emerge for a second. His human disguise was perfect, except for one flaw, a small V behind his ear where the skin could be removed and reapplied. I wanted Darth to turn, so I could check his ears.

Cleveland was right. I had a trigger, and it was breathing like Darth Vader.

Suddenly, his breathing returned to normal. And I exhaled. I hadn't even known I was holding my breath, but I had been. Tense. Nervous. Out of sorts. Who breathes like that? Why?

I've never had a poker face, so whatever I was thinking showed all on my features. The date ended swiftly, and I can't even tell you the details because as much as I just joked. I watched both my mother and father struggle for breath. I watched my father take his last breath. I kept vigil in hospice while my mom and sister slept. I heard every catch and shudder and wheeze and the whisps of breath so slight you almost thought you imagined them. And the very last ones, gasps, like someone who was drowning and finally broke the surface…

Breath. I had held my breath so many times that night. Waiting to breathe till he breathed. Unconsciously. Then there was no more breath.

When my mom got sick, I already told you there were so many problems with my breathing. I think I breathed the best the day we purged her house.

Hoarding is the persistent difficulty discarding or parting with possessions, regardless of their actual value. The behavior usually has detrimental effects—emotional, physical, social, financial, and even legal—for a hoarder and family members.

My mom was a hoarder, not the kind you see on tv where no one can move around in the house, or there are stacks of items that could topple and kill someone. But the kind where once Medicaid and Medicare got involved in providing nurses to visit the house, my sister and I were warned that we had to get rid of things because they were a fire hazard and could make EMT's getting to her and treating her, more difficult.

We spent hours purging the house. And it felt different afterward. She hated us for it, feeling betrayed, disrespected.

But I felt something when I looked back on that time, a lesson. Life is supposed to flow. We are 60% water. Our heart is 73% water. If the flow in our bodies stops, we die. Money, time, love all are supposed to flow. But when it comes to experiences, people and objects- we want to hold onto them, grasping them tightly, controlling them- we think. But we are often working against nature. Against the natural order, against nature's desire to flow. We are often tight, turbid, and tense.

When Ygritte confronted Jon Snow, she was asking that he flow. That he understand that the way he had lived was one way, one option, one alternative, one lifestyle. Not the only one, not even possibly the best one for him or his people. But his people were not her focus. He was. He was a prisoner. But he could choose to become freer than he had ever been in his life by taking his thoughts, his beliefs, his habits in his hands, like squirming fish, and setting free whatever would not nourish him, setting it back into the stream of life. By releasing that tension, moving through the confusion, the turbidity that would follow, and understanding that tightness is a sign of constriction, repression, limitation, the opposite of growth, and expansion, he could gain a new life.

I set out to embrace people, situations, experiences, objects, and money that came into my life with joy, appreciation, even wonder; to let them freely flow in my vicinity, and then when they chose to go, when our time was ended, to release them with the same joy, appreciation, and wonder. I thought that I had removed tension.

But this date with Darth had shown me that I was still fragile, that a sound could trigger me back to a clear night in Missouri City, the night of 2/2/2013.

**Lesson 20:**

Triggers reveal what makes us tense, what freezes us, what represses us and stresses us.

CHAPTER 21

# Unbound

If my life was a boat on the sea of circumstances, bobbing up and down with the passing waves of happenstance, being an artist who put on shows was my mooring. There was something comforting about that date on the calendar each month, like a lighthouse in the fog. The nearer it got, often, the better I felt.

*You know it when I hit the stage.*
*The words and ink once on the page,*
*Drip from my tongue and gaze.*
*My words imbue my melanin.*
*I live through the tip of my pen.*
*And what you hear when I begin,*
*Is the heart and soul that beats within.*

*It's hard for me to stay away*
*from the spotlight that's upon that stage.*
*And not cuz I crave fame or wealth.*
*But on that stage I'm MOST myself.*

*Away from it, I fear and doubt.*
*But upon it, the words GUSH out.*
*The energy within the room*
*Becomes the fuel I must consume.*

*Addictive is that center stage.*
*Addictive more the listeners' gazes.*
*A snap, a clap, a standing O,*
*Is music that just calms my woes.*

*I stand erect*
*A pilgrim true*
*To words that stain me through and through.*
*Like tattoos etched upon my skin.*
*Like freckles on my melanin*

*I must perform*
*It's not a choice.*
*Even to the point my voice gets hoarse.*
*The words have a mind of their own.*
*Till they have made YOUR minds, their thrones.*

On 12/9/2019, someone asked me what would make my show different from other poetry shows. I said, first, it will house poetry, comedy, and music. Second, it's meant to be a refuge, an oasis, a pit stop from the chaos of life.

Why?

Because I had experienced so many deaths in so few years

Because my job was stressful beyond words

Because I had almost lost both my sons to more than one car accident and a gunshot wound…

Because...

Because...

Because...

Because poetry and music and comedy made all that bearable.

Come stressed, leave relaxed.

Come worried, laugh like you have no cares.

Come broke, feel rich because of the beauty and energy flowing all around you.

Come lonely, leave feeling like you have a family that gets you.

All that is what I called Getting Zenned.

That's why I created Laughz and Lyrics.

To give relaxation, joy, a great vibe, and artistic family to everyone who wanted it.

And after days that shook me, like my date with Darth, it was the perfect place to go to "leave the outside, outside."

Once I pictured the show as a decontamination chamber like I'd seen in movies. Showers cleansing toxin of stress, the virus of grief, rinsing them clean away

My hands almost feel like they're buzzing as I type. I was so excited. That night would be show #38, and four more were coming in quick succession: Seasonz Greetingz, Winter Solstice, Kwanzaa, and New Year. Four, three, two, and one week away, respectively. They were all close to selling out; almost 640 tickets would be sold or given away. They were all joint productions with other artistic communities. However, still, it's hard to put into words the feeling that happens when you know before you hit the door that there won't be an empty seat in the venue. There is no other feeling like it. *https://youtu.be/Bevkf7rDu0A* [9]

Having been in the audience and on the stage, I know both sides. I know staring up at a performer and thinking. "I could never do that." I also know the nervous butterflies, the walk onto the stage, the moment when everyone quiets and waits for the first word from my lips. Expectant. Hopeful.

There is a moment before I speak when I open my heart, and I think, "This is my tribe," and I welcome them. One of my friends calls the stage "the bully pulpit." the energy in the room is like a bath, ebbing and flowing, warming and cooling, lifting and rising. We, the performers, can hype it up. We can feel it wane, We can build it ever higher, like an impending orgasm, and then there is the afterglow.

It is magic.

## Date Eighty-Six:

Companion showed up on time, ticket in hand; I sat him next to my seat, front row, right. I manned the door, got the show started, and took my seat next to him, enjoying his pure enjoyment of the

9 BeeTap Speaks

spectacle in front of him. The music was superb, the comedy uproarious, the poetry sublime. I'd never been prouder.

This was only the second time I'd had a date to my show. (Tennessee had once attended one.)

The one thing, the only thing, I hated about performing was coming back to normal. On stage, in the venue, socializing with the crowd before and after the event was electric, addicting. And then I packed up my merch (oh, I had t-shirts and totes with all kinds of sayings from my shows by this time) and headed home.

I was on a performer's high, buzzing from the vibe, and there was no one to tell. On my luckiest nights, I would call Breath, and he would answer, and I would pour into him every detail as he hung on my every word. And then he would tell me about his day.

But often, it would be late, and he would be asleep. And that drive home to an empty bed would seem like the loneliest trek on the planet.

But tonight, that was not the case. Companion and I sat and had drinks in the venue, rehashing our favorite moments of the night. It was magical.

The shows were too. Standing room only, electric, life-changing. I almost felt like we should have had a fire walk outside because after the Gospel music on 12/8, the smudging on 12/21, the Winter Solstice, and drum circles during the Kwanzaa show, we literally could walk on hot coals and not be burnt.

It was awe-inspiring, humbling, and engendered in me the most profound gratitude to see the growth and to know that my mom telling me not to stop having the shows was one reason all this was happening. And it was more than just the numbers, the artists, the shows themselves. Through the shows, there were opportunities to give back. September, a school supply drive. November, a toy drive. December, a coat and blanket drive.

And there was also the idea in the back of my head of helping those like me, those for whom the arts were a balm.

I grew up in this atmosphere of tension: my mother was a brilliant hustler, my father an artist/ singer who gave up his craft to get a "real job." They sent me to private school a few years, whereas one of 5 minority students, I was ostracized and found my only escape in books and writing. I received my first writing award on that elementary campus. I repressed memories of being molested by my great grandfather, married one abuser, and then one rejector.

Then 5 years ago, I rebuilt myself, even while constantly losing people- 6 deaths, then 3 more this year.

Through it all, writing had been my escape. Words are my Zen. But not only poetry, the stories captured in music, in comedy. All art.

When I was suicidal as a teen, Mrs. Kroiss, my 5th-grade English teacher, made us journal every day. She saved my life. I could get my ideas out and look at them. Cut my problems into pages, paragraphs, sentences, words. Rearrange them to make something better. Because of the fact that I continued to journal for the rest of my life, you have been able to read an accurate account of these 86 dates.

I am Zen Ase. And I create escapes- from pain, from stress, from monotony. I bring a rainbow of color in the form of art. I provide release. I do this to honor my mother - the entrepreneur, as I provide a platform for vendors and my father, the artist who needed a platform.

My mission, my calling, my purpose, my peace all were funneled into Laughz and Lyrics.

Get Zenned! Stay Zenned! Spread Zen!

People say Christmas is the most wonderful time of the year. For me, it was seeing Jazzmeia Horn live.

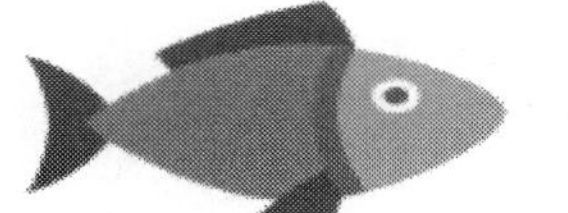

## Date Eighty-Seven:

DJ- The only sparks that happened were between me and the stage that night. DJ, who is an actual DJ, invited me out, "saving me from Cleophus," the guy he said I was destined to end up with since I was still dating and single a year after we had first encountered each other on the dating app POF. We both fell too in love with the performance to even notice each other.

## Brillianz

*I listened to a songstress tonight,*
*Dancin among riffs like they were raindrops landing softly,*
*smoothly, gliding down.*
*Her fingers wrapped round her waist, then snapping, clapping,*
*Undulating, punctuating every melody that hung in the air like*
*starlight, magical.*

*The horn blew, the drum pounded,*
*The keyboard jazzed through melodies*
*so pure.*
*distilled magnificence.*

*I sat, poet I am, saxophone sounds embracing me,*
*Thinking of the audience enraptured,*
*Captured,*

*That's what gifts do*
*When they're unfolded.*
*They mold us, lift us, transfix us.*
*As they were designed to.*
*So bring your brillianz,*
*Your wordz, your songz, your art.*
*You were born with brillianz,*
*In brillianz,*

*Don't fear to shine.*

In college I was engaged to a bass player. He wrote a song for me. I sat on the floor of his living room as he plucked the strings that told our love. I didn't have another piece dedicated to me till…

## Date Eighty-Eight:

Composer- We'd known each other for 15 months, chatted casually, performed on the same shows. For Christmas 2019, I got a poem- the first poem about me and performed to me, privately, and he asked me to enjoy the seductive percussion of the Pedrito Martinez Group as his date.

**Dates 87- 88** are fond memories. Colleagues, fellow artists. We run in the same circles, still, see each other at gatherings, still. Comment on each other's posts, still. Not enough there to fully breach the line between friendship and more, we left it at one date.

Midweek dates rarely happened when I was working my 9 to 5, but with two weeks off, I had one each week of Christmas break.

## Date Eighty-Nine:

Philosopher - This date was very interesting. He met me, to cross me off his list. In the middle of our conversation he blurted out, "I was right."

I looked up from my plate, fork halfway to my mouth, and lowered it, "about what?" I sipped my drink instead.

"I'd never date you."

I choked on my wine, and coughed out, "Why?"

"You're too together."

I laughed, "Oooooooookkkkkkkk. Can you elaborate?"

"You don't need me. You don't need a man. See, men are basically pimps or providers. A man looks for a woman because he needs her to take care of him (pimp), or he feels purposeful because he's taking care of her (provider). Going to work, paying bills, fixing things that all has more meaning when she needs you to do it. You got it all taken care of. I need a woman who's needier."

"Hmmm, Pimps and providers. That's an idea I've never heard of, and I will never forget. But you're wrong, I do need a man. Companionship. Emotional support. Damn, remember Mahogany. 'Success is nothing without someone you love to share it with.' I was five years old when I saw that movie. It's one of two memories I have before age six. I'm 49 now, and I understand exactly what Billy Dee meant. As a performer, leaving the venue after one of my best shows and having no one to tell, no one waiting on me at home… Some nights it sucks almost all the joy out of the accomplishment.

And there are two things, two HUGE things you're overlooking. Partnership and reciprocity. I grew up around nothing but married people. I didn't always see love and compatibility, but I damn sure saw partnership and reciprocity. I was taught reciprocity, the golden rule, give 100%, put your best effort forward. I was taught anything (including a relationship) that's worth doing, is worth doing well and wholeheartedly. And that it should be mutually beneficial. " For a minute, my mind went on a tangent, and I thought:

I was taught when two people decide to commit to each other, there should be a discussion of what that relationship would look like. A discussion. Not a set of demands. Not ultimatums. Not a gripe session on what the opposite sex usually does or gets away with.

The older generation got some things right.

1. They valued the differences between men and women.
2. They believed in hard work, sacrifice and partnership.
3. They generally held the idea of manhood and womanhood in high esteem.

What I see now is a lot of jealousy between the sexes. Women angry at what men get away with and vice versa. A lot of feelings of entitlement.

After that long pause, in which he seemed to be waiting for me to finish, I said, “Sorry, there’s a lot of ideas swirling in my head. Tonight, I’ll tag you in a poem. I’m not exactly sure what it’ll be about because the dust hasn’t settled yet, but you can tell people you inspired it.”

He smiled.

A month later, he was married. He’s still married now, and we’re still Facebook friends. And we still tag each other on postings.

That night I wrote this:

## Why I Need a Man

*A man holds masculine energy.*
*Which transforms the intensity of me*
*from fire that burns*
*to a glow that heats.*
*An interchange, a brief exchange*
*Can inspire, motivate and galvanize change.*
*And better yet as I reflect,*
*I relax and soak in his manly wealth*
*Of experience, of insight, of confidence*
*True*
*And I remember I'm woman*
*with my own Virtues.*

*To know light, see dark.*
*To know up, see down.*
*I become my most feminine*
*when I surround*
*myself*
*with*
*His traits, his smell, his thoughts, his sound*

*By myself*
*I am a BEAST.*
*But in his presence, I calm, at peace.*

*By myself,*
*I overthink,*
*But in his presence, I laugh and drink*

*In moments that would pass me by.*
*I soften, bend, flexible and pliable.*
*I lose the outer shell so hard.*
*I let down all my walls and guards.*
*I may have bank, status, acclaim*
*A man may say I need NOTHING*
*But I NEED masculine energy to be*

*Relaxed, balanced, UNCONTROLLED.*
*To release burdens I often hold*
*To release the other side of me,*
*That's playful and sensual,*
*Nurtures effortlessly.*

*And THAT is why a man is Key*
*Whether I'm single or committed,*
*He releases me*
*To be the best and happiest version of me.*

That date was unique in the fact that I got lost in my thoughts for a moment. Normally, my thoughts wait till the drive home to pounce. But that night, nope, no waiting.

Now phone conversations and texts are different.

I have written more poems than I can count, after texts that made my creativity pounce.

It could be a word. A phrase. An image he brings up, and then… I'm not responding to his text. I'm typing….

*He asks me, "Is it shaven?"*
*After one intermittent conversation as we both pump iron in the gym,*
*After two phone conversations,*
*Before our first date.*

*Before he knows my middle name, last name, birthday.*
*My favorite food.*
*My zodiac sign.*
*My TV show.*
*My favorite song.*

*Before our first kiss, our first hug, our first walk holding hands.*

*He asks me if it's shaven.*
*And I don't answer.*
*Though a million retorts fly through my head.*
*Because the answer is he hasn't earned a word.*

*The answer is I am enigma.*
*Not a woman you box*
*As shaven, trimmed, bald or bush.*

*My body, like a treasure hunt,*
*Requires a concerted effort.*
*A careful exploration of the map that leads to x*
*Marks the spot.*
*And if you fumble, stumble,*
*You will tumble,*
*Break your stride.*
*Lose the prize.*

*You are unworthy.*
*Common.*

*He asks me, "Is it shaven?"*
*Like this is not misbehaving.*
*Like it's not the pervert's craving of an almost peeping Tom.*

*Oh so bold and brazen,*
*But oh so all mistaken.*
*My interest in you shaken.*
*I go back to square one.*

We never made it to a date. But there's his poem. And this one:

*I ask how you're doing. You reply- bored*

*I simply shake my head.*
*Your imagination's DEAD.*

*I try to let you slide. Maybe it's your pride,*
*Bored is easier to say than*
*lonely, horny or tired.*

*But still it's disappointing. It's 2019,*
*Rise up lazy head. Unbury your dreams..*
*Do a rep. Take a walk.*
*Pick a pen up, TALK*
*Call a long lost friend,*
*take your kids to Pizza Inn*
*Stop killing time spitting out a quick line,*

*Take a class. Take a hike. Jog or ride a bike.*

*"I'm bored" is a sentence to shelve.*
*Do whatever it takes to better yourself.*
*Being bored is just boring and kinda annoying*

*when there's millions of things you could do.*
*Don't let thoughts vegetate, instead cogitate on where*
*you could go that is new.*

*Have you seen a museum, a painting, a play?*
*Have you learned your own history,*
*Feng Shui'd your place?*

*Bored can be the beginning of something that's new,*
*But only if you realize bored is NOT for you.*
*It's a cop out, an excuse, a sign you should dig in.*
*For in the world we live in, with everything changing,*
*The bored will be obsolete before they understand.*
*It's the thinkers and doers who are making bold plans..*
*Because if you're going nowhere, you're a speed bump on their route.*
*You're a waste of time to talk to. You're not what they're about.*

*If I ask how are you today and all you got is bored,*
*You need a jump start bad because this life is short.*
*Don't let it pass you by because you're standing still.*
*You weren't born to kill time, but to make time yield.*
*Fruit and harvest and progress galore.*
*To leave a legacy for your family and friends and more.*
*So being bored on the daily is kinda selfish of you.*
*Cuz frankly, the world needs fewer bores*

*to improve*

Sometimes I think I'm the opposite of most people. I've seen a lotta people bored by life. But you give me time, I'll fill those minutes, hours, days with interesting experiences. Life never bores me. I can entertain myself with projects and goals. My mind is my playground.

But over half the people I meet ...bore me. If they're not intellectuals or artists or passionately driven... I'm bored with their conversation.

I think there are two categories of people- those bored by life (maybe extroverts) and those bored by humans (introverts).

That being said, I know this book is unusual. Narrative. Poetry. Inner Dialogue. As you read it, I hope the narrative flows. I'm a poet. I don't control the muse that bursts inside my head and begins to flow through my fingers onto the page. It shows up unbidden, and I am thankful. I've tried to capture that in this book. To show you my life, in its true form, and this inner dialogue, these artistic interruptions are a part of it.

One thing is said or happens, but in my head, a web spreads of interconnectedness to the past, to the arts, to social media. I think like that. I'm glad I do. I think it's one thing that helped me break free from my past and create a new future

It was down to the last two days of 2019, and I was looking forward to 2020 with so much optimism. It's hard to put into words, but the word that best describes it is Unbound: I felt as if I was acting and speaking more freely than I ever had in my life, as if I was at liberty to explore, to choose, to become. I felt like the caterpillar that was transforming, and I had no idea of what I would look like when I was done or if I would ever be done.

**Lesson 21:**

Question everything. Explore your dreams. Challenge your mindset. Grow. Then Grow again. And again. Ad Infinitum.

# CHAPTER 22

# Vibrancy

There were only a few days left in 2019, I was glad. It had been a rough year.

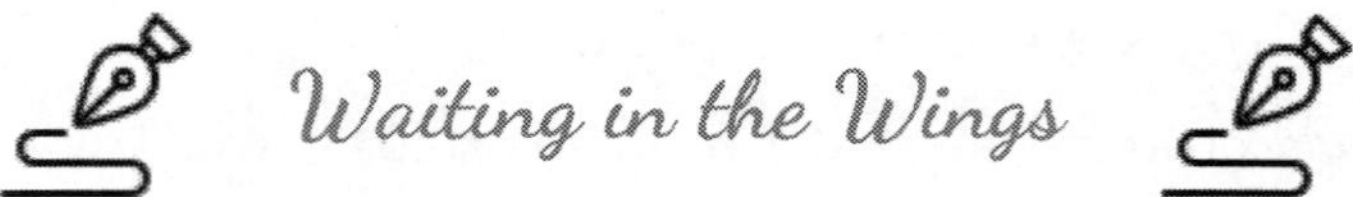

## Waiting in the Wings

*I've been 20, 30, 40,*
*Been divorced two times; it's true,*
*Inhabited the space between size 8 and 22.*
*I've been the preacher and the heretic.*
*A sinner and a saint.*
*So when you meet me now, understand*
*I'm no blank slate.*

*Molested, abused, cheated on, fought back*
*and yes beat one man's ass,*
*Broke a few hearts that broke mine first,*
*Got one hell of an amazing past.*

*I've been completely celibate and sexually risqué,*
*The nun and the Jezebel.*
*I've turned my back on church, now rock ankhs,*
*No more lies Christians tell.*

*I've been a doormat a time or too, so my boundaries stand firm.*
*So understand when you see success.*
*Every bit of it was earned*

*I've got dreams so big they'd scare you.*
*I'm not scared to walk alone.*
*But I'd love to have a man beside me on my ascending throne*

*And it's a tall order, I'll confess because he's gotta be alpha like me.*
*He can't be just nice and good and milk toast*
*He needs an edge I see.*
*Sensual, dominant, articulate, stable, intelligence sublime,*
*Not a runner, a liar or insecure, but an equal but masculine mind.*

*I go to bed thinking of him, wake up there too.*
*But I shrug it off, got shit to do.*

*Wanna build an empire that I can share.*
*Wanna man with his own, a matching pair.*
*I guess you're out there, sometime, somewhere*

*But for now I'm alone.*
*Solo. Just waiting to say,*
*"Well, hello there."*

It was eerie to open my POF inbox and read, "Well, hello there." I'd just typed that as the last line in my poem. When I calmed down, realizing it was just a standard greeting, I read, " I have a grown-up Christmas wish." *Shit, he had posted this at least a week ago.* " I haven't had a date all year. I'd like you to be the one to break that trend."

Hmmm. Direct. Not whiny. Kinda flirty. A little sad. Grammatical. I called him. By then, POF had a phone feature for those who had the app. The convo was nice.

## Date Ninety:

We set an early evening date for that night. I was actually excited. He was a chef and met all my standards. I dressed, drove, and walked into Chili's. Five minutes later, I knew why he hadn't had a date all year. I wasn't going to be that date either. I walked out of the vestibule, got in my car, and called my co-host for Laughz and Lyrics.

She picked up immediately and said, "Hey, girl."

"Kaye, I just got catfished."

"No.....Was he fine online?"

"Yeeeeeessss."

"Looked at his profile he was sexy and fine."

"Ooh, ooh, I gotta go. I'm gonna write this up as a poem."

"Wait. Did you at least eat?"

"No, I said one thing - you lied to me and left."

"Girl, I woulda ate. He owed you a meal for the inconvenience and the drive."

"I had no appetite. Talk to you later. Bye."

"Bye."

## Plenty of Fish

*Looked at his profile he was sexy and fine,*
*Got excited to meet him over a glass of wine.*
*Walked into the place,*
*Stepped right through the door, a Black Danny Devito was smiling…*

*So sure my date was beside him, I looked to the side.*
*He tapped me on my shoulder, said, "I'm your date for tonight."*
*I stifled a cringe, studied his face for a clue.*

*Where was the man from the pictures I knew?*
*Much shorter than me, balding, ashy brown skin.*
*He had the nerve to ask what I thought of him.*
*I tried to be polite, avoid answering,*
*but he pressed forward so clueless and asked yet again.*
*"Sir, the problem is this, to be frank and true.*
*You said you were 6'1.*
*It looks more like 5'2.*
*You boasted of fitness but look stout and round.*
*In fact, not a single detail from your pictures I've found.*
*I don't want to say more. I don't mean to be rude, but*
*I've never seen nose hairs so boldly protrude.*
*Your hair's all gray, not black.*
*There are teeth that you lack.*
*And surprisingly, there's hair on the top of your back.*
*Your beard is unkempt. It looks moldy and old,*
*and you smell slightly like muenster cheese, or black mold.*

*I came out for some wine, but have no appetite.*
*I think I'll bid you adieu for the night.*
*But before I depart, I must ask, be open,*
*May I have the name and number of your friend*
*Because it's obvious you borrowed a picture from somebody you know, but*
*I understand if you'd rather just go.*
*A blind date does not mean that I cannot see, and*
*It's pretty obvious you catfished me.*
*Wasted my time, but*
*Not all is amiss,*
*You inspired a poem Mr. Plenty of Fish."*

I didn't say any of this to him. I just said, a connection can't be built on dishonesty, have a good night. I deleted my POF profile, removed the app from my phone and never went back to POF again.

The next day I was doing my first New Year's Eve show ever. The show would finish way before midnight, and I'd be home before the revelers took to the roadways. I was also planning to do something I had never done, debut a poem I had just written. The POF poem was so raw, real, and practically burned into my psyche it felt memorized, although it was less than 24 hours old.

Then I got a text from someone I'd never met but who had been my Facebook friend for a long time, Caretaker. We'd bonded over one of my posts on caring for my mom. His mom was dying. He was her sole caretaker. I couldn't even imagine the strain, the loneliness, the overwhelm.

"I saw your flyer. I'm coming to the show."

"Wow. Really?" I was shocked. He never went anywhere, just work and the grocery store. He didn't feel he had the time or energy to. But I was glad he was getting out, and I really wanted him to have a good time. From time to time, I knew he activated his POF profile. His situation popped into my mind when I saw people in singles groups complaining about someone trying to date-

1. With an ailing parent
2. A newborn
3. Unemployed or starting a new job
4. Having just arrived in a new city
5. Starting a business
6. Going back to school

I understood. It was a question of priorities, availability, energy to invest in a new relationship.

But on the other hand, life rarely gives anyone perfect timing. People find love in every one of these situations, and some found love during Covid. I think every person is an individual. Some could make a relationship work during one of the transitions above. Others couldn't. There are no hard and fast rules to love.

Someone could be retired and have all the free time in the world and put none of their time, effort, or money into dating.

Another could be going through hell and be the best partner ever.

Judging based on a situational description does not tell what this person has as far as skill set and resources.

I arrived well before show time. Parking was already non-existent, not just there but at venues up and down the street. I texted him that fact.

## Date Ninety-One:

Caretaker arrived. 6'1, not 5'2 and hugged me. My eyes closed, breathing him in: clean, fresh, manly. He squeezed my hand, and we climbed the stairs up to the roof. There was no ceiling above our heads; it was beneath our feet. To my left, the bar, in front of me, the stage, all around me, seating.

The night was gorgeous, crisp, clear; cigar and cigarette smoke wafted in the air. The skyline behind us was breathtaking. I enjoyed sitting there, no need to check on anything; this wasn't my show. I could just enjoy and perform.

It started. Then it was my turn. I was announced. Heard the ripple in the crowd as heads turned, and they realized I was a performer and not just another guest. I took the stage, did piece one, and then asked how many were single and had used dating apps. Almost every hand went up. Perfect. I paused, shook my head, took a deep breath, and said, "Plenty of Fish."

Someone burst out laughing. Another said, "Oh Damn!" A third yelled, "Catfish" I nodded or pointed conspiratorially to each. They were with me. 100%.

Each line, I paused, taking in the widened eyes, the mouths that gaped, those who slapped someone beside them or ribbed them mouthing my last phrase. The guy with his hands wrapped around his belly laughing raucously. The keys that jingled on lines they liked. The snaps. The claps. The taps on the table, and when I got to the last line, they were ready. I started the line, "You inspired a poem Mr." and they finished it with me:

"Plenty of Fish!" in unison, so flawlessly we might have been reading each other's minds. The applause was deafening. The energy electric. The moment was flawless. I was grateful.

It's hard to explain the feelings I had felt the night before, the disappointment, disgust, disillusionment. I don't know whether it was the holiday season, or the fact that it was date 89, or the fact I had now been dating 5- FIVE- long years, but there was the slightest hope that this guy who checked all my boxes, might be him.

The waiting to exhale, scared to hope, cross your fingers, tiptoe in excitement had preceded the date.

Walking back to my car felt like the hardest fall I had ever taken, the most shocking, the most dramatic upset in my whole dating history. I desperately needed to turn that tragedy into triumph. To take the wondering if I would ever meet HIM and flip it. Forever in my mind, their smiles replaced his gums, the scent in the air negated his odor, the connection replaced that moment of hurt and loss.

I looked around in wonder as I took my seat, and Caretaker beamed. He hugged me, then slid his arm around me, then put his hand in mine. He looked like a different person. So relaxed. Gone the furrowed brow, the clenched jaw, the hunched shoulders. He looked peaceful, relaxed and cozy. I smiled. We laughed at the comics, reveled in the singers, and clapped and snapped with the audience celebrating the rest of the poets gracing the stage. Briefly, I noticed that the show organizer had expanded his show offerings from poetry and comedy to include music, which was my format and had only been my format among the shows I'd seen in Houston. But I shrugged it off. It was a compliment. It was needed, and there were more than enough people in Houston to entertain. This wasn't a competition. This was an opportunity to provide in mass what had happened to me and to Caretaker personally, for people to find in art a release. What we were doing was as ancient as drum circles, as griots on the African safari, as Native Americans around a campfire.

The moon was a waxing crescent, 1/4 full. I'd heard that phase of the moon encourages positivity and faith, so even the most steadfast pessimists may be more likely to leap without a net. Maybe that was why I had performed a poem I'd written 24 hours before. Maybe that was why I remembered a poem I wrote the second time I took Gatzby back. It played through my head.

*You leapt,*
*You trusted and were burned, ignored, devalued and deceived.*

*Now you stand at the ledge,*
*And see the rocks below the cliff.*
*The bitterness, the painting everyone with that same hue of deception,*
*The desire to retaliate,*
*To do onto others BEFORE they do onto you.*

*The doubts creep in, insidious whispers that you were naive,*
*That you missed obvious signs,*
*That you deserved to be used because you trusted that skunk, yet again.*
*The leap has you at the ledge*
*And you wonder how many more times*
*Before you fall over*
*Before all faith is dashed on the rocks,*

*all hope is shattered,*
*all capacity to love sinks into a sea of disgust and disillusionment.*
*And yet against hope, you do hope.*
*You do pray.*
*You do imagine*
*that the leap leads not to the ledge*
*or to the loss of your faith in others,*

*but to love.*

As I remembered, I didn't feel the fear I had when I had penned those lines. I felt wonder. I looked around at the audience, this beautiful group of strangers, who would sometimes turn around and laugh together like they were old friends. This young, old, male, female, gay, straight, single, taken, multiracial motley who now shared one night, one set of memories, one journey into artistic expression. This beautiful group of strangers, who was for this moment in time, one people, one tribe, one unit, with one purpose to enjoy this moment, together,

For this moment, politics, race, religion, economics did not matter.

And I was one of the artists who created that bond by giving them the truth in a poem that was so good, so funny, so healing.

And it was also humbling. I knew that each artist now resided in a tiny part of my brain, in a cubby in my heart, and I did in theirs. There was a trust in that.

A rebirth. A renewal. This was the real alchemy. Taking problems and creating a way through.

In the last few hours of 2019, I reflected. The year had been harsh, but I was resilient. I had fallen, but only so far, not to where as

I put it in my poem, "my faith was dashed on the rocks." I had angelite and black onyx crystals in my purse, teachings from The Shrine that strengthened me, art, and a community of artists. I felt rich. Albert Einstein once said, "There are two ways to live your life. One is as though nothing is a miracle. The other is as though everything is a miracle." On this last day of 2019, I chose the latter.

I couldn't control everything, like the date from last night, like the three deaths this year. But I could control my attitude and how I reacted.

I could choose to focus on the simple pleasures of life. The smile of the man beside me, the praise, the breeze, the glass of wine, the moonlight. I could see it all as a miracle.

I'd come to the show hoping to reframe my POF date.

I'd needed that more than anything. And I'd gotten it and more.

I was no longer hurt, demoralized, devastated, depressed.

I was ebullient as Caretaker sat beside me downstairs as people came down, got food, complimented me, and bought tickets for my next performance.

There was something magical about having him there, on that night, after the night before.

It reminded me of being a kid on the basketball or volleyball court and looking up and seeing my dad in the stands. Proud. Supportive. Engaged. His eyes were shining. Admiring. This was date 91, but the men who had seen me perform- The Muse, Companion, Composer, Tennessee, Triste, and now, Caretaker- were few.

I hated to think this, but I wondered why Gatzby, Harlee, or the others still hanging on the periphery of my circle had never come. If

Caretaker could take time away from his dying mother and choose to relax with me at my show when there were hundreds of other recreational options in Houston, what did that mean about these other men?

But the way I was feeling, so hopeful, so blessed, I just let that question roll off of me. A problem for maybe another day, or maybe one I didn't need to concern myself with at all.

The night ended with us cuddled up outside by my car, sharing a few long lingering kisses. We both knew this would go nowhere. We both didn't care, and that fact did not mar the perfect moonlight, mood, and company.

It was a gorgeous way to bring in 2020.

**Lesson 22:**

Death can make you feel more alive, make you appreciate the moments, rare moments of conversation, of music, dance, poetry, comedy that make life this unpredictably vibrant experience.

CHAPTER 23

# Wonder

There are no guarantees. Period. Point blank.

1. Wait, don't wait.
2. Commit, don't commit
3. High standards, flexible
4. Patient, in a rush
5. Perfect candidate, settling.

There are no guarantees.

Anybody spouting off a recipe for finding or creating the perfect relationship is full of it.

No relationship is perfect.

All relationships take work.

No relationship comes with a guarantee.

Ring or no ring.

Take your chances or delude yourself.

So decide if the person is worth the risk.

## Date Ninety-Two:

Poet decided I was worth the risk and pursued me intensely. And there were risks, not just rejection, but we performed together, and there was a significant age difference. Still, he was the smoothest person to ever seduce me with his words.

Kudos.

He did that shit.

The sweetest. The most open. Bared his soul like a full page and said read till your heart's content.

The intimacy was an aphrodisiac. I'd never had a man open up to me, full lotus flower. He didn't pretend to be anything at all. He just was. Himself. Take it or leave it.

I took it.

Being with him felt like riding on the open road, top down, wind in your hair, nothing but space and opportunity. Timeless.

Poetry was everywhere in my life, big, bold, bodacious, personified with a distinctive style and a wicked smile. I could spend pages telling you about the places we went, how romantic he was, how he pampered me. Instead, I'll share my poems.

## Month one:

### Buckle Your Seat Belt, It's Started

*I smile every time I think of you.*
*Tall, strong, but soft and cuddly too.*
*A dichotomy, an interesting brew.*
*Somewhat like me,*
*But different too*
*I'm tired, on many levels stressed.*
*Want safety and a place to rest.*
*Want a new place to build my nest,*
*Or at least a place to recoup; shred stress.*
*I feel last year was a war.*
*I lost so much stopped taking score.*
*But I gained so much, experience galore.*

*I'm still getting acquainted with the new me.*

*So who you're getting, shrug, I don't know.*
*I've cocooned, and my wings still don't show.*
*I feel ugly, scarred and vulnerable.*
*I really haven't let anyone close.*

*But around you, I tend to relax.*
*And open slightly. Walls half-cracked.*
*I laugh. I smile. I cogitate.*

*But only on the love we'll make.*
*Lol, I typed that? My mistake,*
*I'm supposed to be demure and wait.*
*From you, I want it all and nothing.*
*I want passion conversations, fucking.*
*I laugh as I type.*
*I picture combusting.*
*But I picture freedom too.*
*That's a good thing.*

*I don't trust relationships,*
*Or promises.*
*I don't believe hardly a word that's said.*
*But energy, that guides my head.*
*And yours is good, so I'm prepared.*

*I've no questions to ask.*
*My mind's a blur...*
*I might forget your words for sure.*
*I'm distracted, yet you have the cure.*

*Center and ground me.*

*I need that balance - bring it on.*
*I need that oneness, isolation gone.*
*I need that outlet, one on one.*
*Pure happiness you see.*

*But don't expect me to make sense,*
*I feel tears and joy in one sentence.*
*I'm broken and whole.*
*I'm smart but dense.*

*Do gather me in your loving arms,*
*If you wish, and silence all alarms.*
*I'm all safe danger. Non-conformed.*

*I'm fire and ice combined.*

*Our unity is overdue.*
*You know it. It's 100% true.*

*I have no idea what will ensue.*
*But I'm signing on for the ride.*

## Month Two

*As a poet, I'm rarely tongue-tied,*
*But you make me ooey- gooey inside.*
*Butterflies and giggles reside*
*in what used to be seriousness.*

*Relaxed like a hammock,*
*You're my blunt,*
*Want one more hit,*
*No, hits abundant.*

*Like I lose track of minutes.*

*They turn to hours spent entwined,*
*The time apart, you're on my mind.*
*Your laugh, your smile, your dope ass lines.*

*We write. We kiss. We dance..*

*You seem so integral,*
*Fuck that's new.*
*Your calls, your texts, my mind just blew.*
*Our conversations epic too.*
*Like priceless gems and wine.*

*You're deep and goofy.*
*I just stare*
*and run my fingers through your hair.*
*And trace lazy circles on skin bared.*
*Your kisses? No one else compares.*

*FWB, and so much more,*
*I wonder if at night you snore,*
*I was too knocked out to notice before.*
*See you, did that, to me.*

*So quickly you're under my skin.*
*Mind blowing, how'd you do that again?*
*I reminisce on the times when*
*you've made sweet love to me.*

*With you, it's almost bearable*
*That I spent so much time alone before.*
*And now I laugh and moan galore.*
*You bring my minx such glee.*

*Your eyes are pools of luminance,*
*Your smile mischievous beneficence.*
*Your hands, skilled, strongly intent.*
*The rest I will not name.*

*Your lips, won't forget.*
*They bring me joy.*
*You truly are a golden boy.*

*And I bask in your sun.*

## Month Three

I had two dreams. One I was in Africa. He was there as my husband and father of our two kids. The other, I was in ancient Greece. In both, I was a priestess, and he was a warrior. They were interesting and felt so real that I woke up looking for the food we were eating in the dream. Then I realized it was a dream. I'd never dreamt of living in a different century before. It was definitely interesting.

## His Name is...

*He spiced one nipple with nutella,*
*Licked it off. I sighed.*
*Body trembled, unexpected*
*I thought we were done for the night.*
*We'd loved four hours, all positions.*
*I'd lost track of time.*
*This cub played lyrical seductive games with my body and my mind.*
*But this cougar turned him out,*
*"Wore him out," times two.*
*We lay on semi soaked bed sheets,*
*Catching our breath*

*Resume.*

*We learned each other once again,*
*Experiments sublime.*
*I love a man who can seduce,*
*Knows how to take his time.*
*But when I say, "Now."*
*Then he thrusts.*
*He times himself to me.*
*We roll and tumble,*
*But never fumble, erotic ecstasy.*
*I'm grateful for him*
*This he knows.*
*In that, we share one mind.*
*Connecting on all levels- body, soul and vibes.*

*He is my match and that I love*
*Brings me variety.*
*It's never the same when we join seductively.*

*I smile, a Cheshire cat, full purr.*
*Where will this rabbit hold lead?*
*Not sure, but this adventure is one*
*I sorely needed.*

*He makes up for the mess,*
*The false starts,*
*of love with no success.*

*With him it's simple.*
*One plus one, infinity creates.*
*He truly can handle all of me,*
*And impressive thing to state.*

*Honest. Open. Playful. Fun.*
*Ambitious. Seductive, one on one.*
*Talented, more ways than one.*

*He is my erotic fantasy.*
*Whose name is...*

## Month Four

### It's Complicated

*When you meet, your soul is torn*
*Feel the love, but were forewarned.*
*Incompatibilities alarm,*
*but not enough to abdicate.*

*Together... the world is silenced.*
*Heart, mind, body- all compliant.*
*Finally, found your one reliant,*
*Dependable, trustworthy boo*

*Your paths have interwoven,*
*Ready.*
*Visions all aligned and steady.*
*Yet, the future probably heading,*
*For a fork in a year or two*

*For now, at least, the honeymoon.*
*Someone you trust through doom and gloom.*
*Someone who is your sun and moon*

*and stars.*

*His smile and laugh can make you beam.*
*Within his arms, life is a dream*
*Time melts away,*
*The world is green.*

*But nothing gold can stay.*

*But still the future is unknown,*
*Who knows, my heart may have its home.*
*To live a life, never alone.*
*My soulmate next to me.*

*But honestly, I am conflicted.*
*Fwb? Open relationship? Shifted,*
*Dating? In love? Fucking misfits?*

*Labels don't fit. It's true.*
*What do you call your every breath?*
*The man you came to after death?*
*The reincarnation of your gift?*
*Your husband from another trek?*

*You dream*
*See glimpses of the past.*
*Cassava trees, and huts and staffs.*
*And centuries already passed.*
*A world inside his eyes..*

*You wake.*
*And feel the pull within..*
*Towards a man once just your friend.*
*Like a novel written, you're starring in.*
*It's complicated to begin again.*

Life has a way of forcing decisions. One, by the first week of May 2020, Covid had put Houston in lockdown. Two, we were falling in love. Three, he wanted kids, had actually already named them, in fact. And I wasn't having any more. So we slowed down on seeing each other, and then we stopped. We still talked, texted, and seven months later, when the world opened back up, we still performed together. But the age difference ultimately meant we were in two very different places in our lives, and that was something neither of us could change.

The other thing that happened from March 8 to April 26, 2020, is I went through an initiation. I had weekly three-hour meetings, readings in three texts, journals, guided meditations, breathing exercises, dietary changes, and abstinence. Coming face to face with my belief system in nine areas, examining each area, changing what needed to be changed were some of the hardest things I'd ever done. The process changed my life. I started an herb garden, cut off all my relaxed hair and went natural, and forgave so many people, including myself.

It was a spiritual house cleaning. I didn't agree with everything I read. I didn't become a vegan or a raw foodist, which were both recommended. I didn't give up wearing pants and shorts, which were also pushed. But I did deepen my connection to myself, to my ancestors, to nature, and to my purpose. I did see patterns in my life that had been hidden from me. And I learned that the name I had chosen to perform under, Zen Ase, was not random but destined. I was on my path, fulfilling my purpose. The seven other women initiated with me received new names, Kemetic names; I already had mine. It was blessed and recognized by the village.

Initiation was one of the best decisions I'd ever made.

Going natural was another great decision. I'd always feared it, feared being a "bald-headed chick." But suddenly, paying someone to pour toxic chemicals on my head that burned and sometimes left scabs in my scalp for days so that my hair could go from its natural texture to straight somehow didn't seem natural or normal or necessary. It seemed very unnatural, defying the natural order for my life, abnormal, like one more form of self-repression.

My hair being straight did not make me better.

All my life, I thought that men would find me unattractive natural, but when I mentioned to Poet that I was considering it, he almost begged me to do it.

I chopped my hair off in three stages, months apart. Each stage made changing easier. The woman looking back at me from the mirror looked vastly different from my former self, so it only felt right that I was making new choices, trying new things.

Some people say the hairstyle change took ten years off my appearance. It definitely made me feel as if any change was possible.

I sometimes wonder at the timing of things in my life. When I went to the interest meeting for the initiation, I actually did not know all it would entail. I certainly did not know that abstinence was going to be involved. But then, that decision was made for me. Covid burst into the news, and I was dating an avid weed smoker who was STILL sharing blunts. We stopped seeing each other immediately. The entire time I was going through initiation, we talked, texted but were never physically in the same room, much less in the same bed.

He did stop taking risks like that, and we did see each other after my initiation, but it was serendipitous how that happened. How the choice was almost made for me.

When Easter came, I wrote in my journal, "Today many celebrated Easter, and like any celebration that comes with food, certain foods were expected, anticipated, longed for. The same way sex is longed for on holidays, special occasions, and celebrations. I was glad I wasn't in a relationship when I went through initiation. Being in a relationship and asking someone to be abstinent is almost unthinkable to me. It's like expecting a person to give up celebrating every holiday and offering nothing in return. Holidays can lead to memories and bonding. Sex does too. Holiday traditions, especially those involving food, can become part of a person's identity. Being a great cook, baker, having a specialty. Sex can too. A person can live without meat, but that requires lots of discipline and retraining. Abstinence does too. Then there's the idea that the abstinent person is also trying to reassure the partner that when meat/sex is reintroduced, the person who's made a lifestyle of going without will

1. Have an appetite
2. Be a good cook
3. Like the same kinds of dishes.

All of which is total speculation.

So when people say no thanks to abstinence, it's not always that they don't care about the person they're dating. They're choosing the life they love with all the delights of food/sex and the comfort that comes from knowing there is true sexual compatibility over a forced restriction for a reason they may not even believe in."

# Perspective

*Perspective is like magic.*
*It changes all you see.*
*I started off a teen, an obsessed athlete.*
*I didn't eat junk or sugar, worked out incessantly.*
*Then I left home and became the darling of a fraternity.*
*I'd never seen myself as popular,*
*Not one with the cool kicks,*
*But suddenly I ran a pack, a part of the clique.*
*Years passed, serious I became,*
*Consumed by spirituality,*
*Abstinent and studious,*
*headed for the ministry.*
*Then married and parenting,*
*maternal all my days,*
*Degree in hand, done lesson plans,*
*A molder of minds I became.*
*Each shift a new perspective,*
*a metamorphosis,*
*Laying aside old identities*
*Like finished to-do lists.*
*Page poet, playwright, essayist,*
*Spoken word artist,*
*Each shift a change in vision*
*An exploration of gifts.*
*From married to divorced and single.*
*From dating to grandparent prime.*

*From employee to entrepreneur,*
*Each step, a renewed mind*
*To recreate oneself is fun, and scary all the same.*
*Leaving behind shorelines to lay an explorer's claim.*
*I've cut off relaxed hair,*
*Been initiated too,*
*Flipped from black and white to gray,*
*My insight all brand new.*
*So see me now, and take a pic,*
*I guarantee you'll see*
*a much different person a year from now,*
*Kaleidoscope, that's me.*

Sometimes a reader pops in my mind, we'll call this reader Scroog. Right now, I'm hearing Scroog say, "Four months wasted with this Poet fellow. Nothing to show for it. Meaningless sex." Now I don't know if Scroog would have actually gotten this far in my book, but I'd like to ask Scroog, have you ever taken a walk in the woods or on a trail? In the end, you end up back at the beginning, walking home or driving home in your car. Was it wasted? You exercised. I exercised. You relaxed. Me too. You fed your body, mind and spirit. Me too. You lived in the moment. So did I.

Those four months would have passed regardless, but I now have memories I will treasure for life.

And if Scroog thinks sex wears the vagina out ( I would hope Scroog is more informed than that, but…), I'd like to say kegels are wonderful things.

Life is meant to be lived. You can't save days for later. You can't cork time up in a bottle. And it's absolutely unwise to put happiness off for someday in the future when Mr. or Ms. Perfect comes along.

If Scroog is a Puritan, then call me a Transcendentalist, following in the footsteps of Thoreau, whose words I memorized long ago

"Live in each season as it passes; breathe the air, drink the drink, taste the fruit." And to go back to our little metaphor, "I went to the woods because I wished to live deliberately, to front only the essential facts of life, and see if I could not learn what it had to teach, and not, when I came to die, discover that I had not lived. I wanted to live deep and suck out all the marrow of life." For Thoreau that meant solitude in the woods. For me it meant dates, writing, performing, and initiation.

I was learning to live deep.

And living deep is living in wonder at the choices life offers and where they lead.

And I was feeling grateful to have this life, the ability to choose at all.

## Battle Fatigue

*Open my phone to drum circles, chants,*

*And fluted notes that ripple and prance.*

*I'm gonna put on my ankle bracelets and dance*

*As tears roll down my cheeks.*

*Dip my finger in shadow and draw designs down my face, down my arms,*

*Round my waist and spine,*

*Gonna pound the ground*

*bare footed, calling out the divine,*

*Because I live, some died, I grieve.*

*I will not call the angels, but they'll see*

*The lineage lost resurrected in me*

*as I sit on the ground in ceremony,*

*It's not back to business for me.*

*I'm gonna bend and bow,*

*Meditate, allow,*

*Emotions to flow,*

*words to quake,*

*Libations to pour,*

*smoking sage,*

*My aura purified, no hate*

*Will remain in me.*

*Chakras unbound,*

*Qigong ensues,*

*Crystal water drink,*

*Infused,*

*Breathe deeply, slowly as I muse*

*Let Nut have her way.*

*My endurance I have reached,*

*Now is time for full release.*

*I live, some died, I grieve.*

By May 1st, 2020, all the world seemed to be talking about was:

# Covid- 19

*Woke up.*
*Took a minute.*
*Thought of what I need to do.*
*My mind went blank, confusion...*
*For a moment or two.*
*I haven't cried a tear*
*but suddenly felt the urge to...*
*And I wondered why because tragedy is not something new.*
*But as I thought and reminisced on personal inventory,*
*I realized 9-11 was one day, Katrina and Harvey one week,*
*And the loss of many relatives was solely a personal tragedy.*
*I realized never had I seen the world attacked at once,*
*Mourned with an Italian, an American, and the Chinese, just for starters.*
*Seen most I know lose jobs in mass*
*Essentials risk their lives.*
*Worry whether a trip to Walmart may actually cost my life.*
*Been almost afraid to scroll my phone*
*or click on the remote*
*because of yet another tale*
*of loss and hearts lay broken.*
*Nature, so beautiful,*

*once a constant friend,*
*Suddenly makes me wonder on whom I can depend.*
*Nothing seems certain,*
*I'm unused to mass uncertainty.*
*Unused to life daily retarding productivity.*
*I take a long cleansing breath*
*My hands dab at my eyes*
*And even these moves so basic underline my plight.*
*That breath I took- someone just lost*
*That gesture brings to mind*
*The fact I'll wash and sterilize my hands probably a million times.*
*Because I'll grab my mail. Have kids.*
*Not one surface is safe,*
*I'll sterilize and wipe all day.*
*Clean incessantly.*
*These are my first Covid stanzas.*
*Downloading all my brain.*
*But numb inside and feeling like I'm failing all the same.*
*I check on people, call, and text.*
*Stay busy as can be.*
*How is one supposed to deal with a GLOBAL catastrophe?*

May 7th was a special day for me, but that morning, before I could wish my sons a happy 25th birthday, I turned on the news and watched the story of Ahmaud Arbery. I cried for the next three days. But that day, I hugged my sons tighter, grateful beyond words. There are moms who didn't get to celebrate their sons' 25th birthday. There are young men taken from us too early.

I planned to join the run for Ahmaud that Friday. My son ran most mornings before I got up. He was a track star in middle school, a football star in high school. I couldn't help but picture my son as Ahmaud, and was so glad he was celebrating this milestone, 25.

I'd written an article, published twice about my two kids being harassed since the age of 12 for living while being black. I remember as a kid my dad telling me, "I had to make you hard because I didn't know when I might be taken from you." My dad worked 12-hour shifts in a plant in Pasadena, came home, ate/showered/slept, went nowhere but church and family gatherings. He still expected to die young. Just because he was black.

I remember posting an "I love you, black man" meme on all my social media pages and calling and texting all my male friends.

Then I got a text.

"When's your next show?"

I was sitting in the McDonald's drive-through, so stunned I didn't hear the cashier asking for my order… again. I rattled it off, picked up my food, and parked.

I looked again at my phone, certain I had to have accidentally scrolled backward two months. Next show? There were no shows. I'd had eight in the planning stages- March-August, my busiest season. Then the Ides of March hit, and like some flawed Shakespearean comedy where the soothsayer warns, and no one heeds, the entire entertainment industry was assassinated.

This was the worst joke anyone had ever played.

By this time, I'd been performing since 8/2015, 57 months, almost 5 years. It was my primary coping mechanism, my escape, my pressure release valve. Losing it was like a death, another death after so many.

I called the number about to light into whoever this crazy person was.

"Hullo," It was Gatzby. He had this unusual accent, part Cali, part Jersey, part Texan, that showed up in certain words. And that was one. I was shocked. I never expected to hear his voice again. I forgot about the reason I called. Instead, I was instantly relieved. He was healthy, alive, safe. "I wasn't trying to bother you," he said. "I know I'm probably the last person you want to talk to. It's just my friends are bored senseless, sitting at home in quarantine. Are you doing any online shows?"

"No, that's not my thing." There was a long pause. Static crackled on the line. "I never thought I'd hear from you again."

"Well… You did tell me to lose your number."

"You stood me up, after my mom's funeral."

"No, I didn't. I called you and said I couldn't come, and you cut me off. You said I was unreliable, and if I couldn't be there for you after the funeral, I should lose your number. I was trying to tell you my uncle died, and I had to fly out to Cali. You were rude and selfish, expecting me to be there for you when you couldn't even be there for me in return."

I tried to rewind in my head. The scenes of that day almost a year ago exactly scrolled backward like an image from a VCR recorder. But when I pushed play to revisit our conversation, a white blotch spread over the canvas of my mind consuming the images till all that was left was a blank screen. I tried again, going back even farther, revisiting that whole six months. The night I blurted out my mom's diagnosis, him coming over, the nights when I couldn't sleep, and he would stroke my hair till I fell asleep, and stay for an extra 30 minutes or an hour, just so I could sleep; times he brought me food because I hadn't grocery shopped or ate; the time he asked what I needed, and I replied to forget anything exists outside these four walls, and he'd made love to me so tenderly that for those moments, I had forgotten. He had done all that, and I thanked him then, a lot, but I felt something now, a tenderness deeper than any connection I ever remembered feeling for anyone.

My voice softened, grew quieter. "You say you told me your uncle died? Did I respond?"

"You asked if I would come over to your house after your mom's funeral."

"Did I respond to what you said about your uncle?"

"No, that's why I'm saying you weren't there for me.."

"I didn't hear you. If I did, what you said didn't register. For me, it feels like this is the first time I'm hearing this. What I remember is you didn't show. We talked later. I told you to lose my number. Nothing else. I'm really sorry for your loss." I started crying. "I probably couldn't have done anything but cry with you, grieve with you, but I could have done that. I just don't think I even heard you. I think I was too lost in my grief to hear anything. I wish I could give you a hug. I feel terrible."

He started talking, pouring out his anger, his disappointment, his hurt; what I heard was- I was there for you, and then the universe gave you a chance to reciprocate, and you slammed the door in my face.

I'd gone from expecting nothing from him to getting used to him being there, to demanding he be there. I suddenly felt like bridezilla exposed on camera, watching myself through his eyes. Our last conversation I had made him feel like his pain was invisible, and his only purpose was to serve my needs.

I wanted to turn back time and do things over. I'd always been the giver in my relationships. I'd always felt I'd gotten the shaft too. It had never occurred to me there would or could ever be a time when I would make someone else feel that way. And the worse thing was I made him feel guilty for not being able to be there for me and for his family too. He bore a burden of feeling as if he had failed, as my friend, as my lover, as my support system.

It was one conversation, but suddenly it felt like the worst thing I had ever done. And he hadn't understood why I hadn't just listened, why I wouldn't let him explain. I didn't have an answer for that. I just knew that day in my head; the only thing I wanted to know was that he would be there for me after I went through one of the worst days of my life. And I just felt there was no justifiable reason for him to say no. Was that logical? Who the hell knows. I wasn't thinking logically right then.

I apologized over and over again till finally he stopped me and said, "I could use a hug. I haven't really been around anyone, touched anyone in what feels like forever."

When he came over that night, there was a lot of awkwardness, and hurt, and distrust, and then the longest hug I'd ever had in my life. A hug that bridged six months and two funerals and all the tears we had both privately shed. He forgave me, chalking my reaction up to grief, but I still felt the need to make things right. I don't think I ever consciously realized it till now, but inside and outside of the bedroom, I softened to him, opening up, reciprocating his affection, his "I love you's." The next four and a half months, I saw only him.

When I thought about his "When is your next show?' text weeks later, I concluded my poetry (shows, performances) had made Gatzby text, and I wrote this:

## A Poem Made Him Text

*I wrote you off as finished,*
*Through,*
*And moved along with no adieu.*
*Ten months passed, and out of the blue,*
*You texted.*

*I was shocked, so unexpected.*
*Damn near ghost now resurrected.*
*Will I respond? I'm so conflicted.*
*What's a girl to do?*
*I didn't think, straight in the moment,*
*Phone in hand. My thoughts I vomit.*
*Lines, and rhymes, it's no damn sonnet.*
*Erotica for true.*
*My muse sees you in one light,*
*Playground, masseuse, my acolyte,*

*You write. I'm famished.*
*I'll take a bite.*
*You offered. I'll receive.*
*I write the lines, explore the thoughts.*
*Down memory lane I dance,*
*Am caught.*
*Enticed, seduced, your words have wrought*
*A chain reaction in me..*
*Up to the mind this choice is not.*
*Your birthed words, my soul is hot .*
*I burn with lust, brain cells are shot.*
*I text, reply complete.*
*We catch-up, find there a place*
*Where we misread each other's states,.*
*And now the distance is erased*
*For you more than me.*
*A poem can do a lot, that's true,*
*I vent, examine, get seduced*
*Re-evaluate from a different view,*
*But not enough to make me love you.*

Performing was gone for now, and it took A LOT to replace it as a coping mechanism.

- ✧ Meditation and Journaling, I was doing both a lot. I'd even created an ABC list, titling my journals by topic, exploring one concept after another that COVID, racism, Trump, 2020 had not stolen from me.

- ✧ My to-do list and Passion Planner. I was busy building my business, trying desperately to engage with the followers I'd amassed in the last five years. I created a hashtag- CreativescombatingCorona, and I was posting uplifting, funny, motivational messages regularly. It lifted my spirits and seemed to lift others' hearts as well.
- ✧ Walking. I'd hit the trail almost every day for a mile or two or three.
- ✧ Podcasting preparation. I'd always been told I had a nice voice, a radio voice, that I should record a podcast. I was taking a podcasting class and planning to turn the concepts I'd been journaling about, my own personal ABCs of Zen into the weekly episodes. I'd call it Zennurgy, the urge for more peace and fulfillment in life. That was absolutely the quest I was on, and I figured others could relate.
- ✧ From social media, it seemed peace and fulfillment were both in short supply.
- ✧ Social media and conversations with Breath.

Before 6 years ago, I had no social media accounts. Then I joined Facebook, and about 4 years ago, I started joining Facebook groups. Then all of a sudden, there were all these new ideas I'd never heard of, never seen outside of social media. Breath and I would laugh when I read them to him: Women searched men's phones? They wouldn't date a guy who had "too many" female friends online?

People thought dating was exclusive from day one? Women stalked their man's pages to see who he texts and whose pics he comments on?

Now I can add a few more to this list from a post in mid-May:

1. People see a man's excitement about sports and question why he doesn't pursue women that way? I never thought to compare those two things.
2. Women, supposedly, brag on inboxes?
3. And finally, men won't take a woman seriously who hasn't cleared old numbers, texts, and dms from her phone? Do guys actually ask women this?

We debated if 1-3 were real things. Were they generational or regionalized?

Another day I told him that certain posts made me wonder was reciprocation just talk?

Some women say men should be in contact because that's important to build connections. But does what he feels builds connection matter? What if that's sex or being fed a meal? Some women consider both wife duties.

Then there's sex. Some women want great sex. Do they give it? Do they reciprocate the effort? The touching, the kissing, the foreplay. Every time he thrusts, does she thrust in time with him?

Some women want gifts. Do they give them?

There was this post I'd seen a half dozen times no, and it annoyed me. IF HE CAN'T PUT MONEY IN YOUR PURSE, HE SHOULDN'T PUT HIS DICK IN YOUR PUSSY.

## Pros to the statement

I agree that every adult should be self-sufficient. I agree a woman should not take care of a grown man and that a man should have money to date. He should have the ability to help a woman out, but although this post said "can't," every woman I ever saw reply to it, read it as if it stated if he ISN'T PUTTING money in your purse, so I responded to it that way when I posted on social media and when I discussed it with Breath.

## Cons to this statement

1. It reduces sex to a financially based interaction versus one that results from multiple areas of compatibility.
2. It sets women's rights back to the days of doweries and choosing a man solely for his ability to provide.
3. It gives other races an advantage. Statistically, black men make less money than men of other races.
4. Putting money in her purse is something the man has to do ON TOP OF paying for dates and gifts for special days.
5. It requires nothing of the woman but keeping her legs closed
6. It's frankly hypocritical; the same women shouting amen to this restatement of no romance without finance are likely the same ones stating they are independent and don't need a man
7. I think it's a departure from the strong marriages of the 60s and 70s. Simply put, if my mom had thought this way, I wouldn't be here.

At 16, My dad chose to stay in the U.S. when his family was stationed overseas in Germany. My mom met him his senior year at Southern University. They dated. And I can guarantee he never "put money in her purse." He did impregnate her, marry her, took his degree and a fearsome work ethic, and together they bought a 3 bedroom house that they turned into 6 bedrooms. They bought several cars, started a few businesses, helped put 2 daughters through college, and stayed married 43 years until he died in 2013.

So obviously, she saw value in him beyond his ability to put money in her purse. Some today would say her choice meant she was naive or had no standards. I call b.s.

What my mother lacked was the sense of entitlement that some women today have. They feel entitled to so much, and some are willing to do so little. So let's take sex off the table. Because I wasn't referring to it right then. There are women who expect a man to put money in their purses who would be insulted if he asked her to do his laundry or vacuum or cook him a meal or even give him a massage, fix him a plate or bring him a cold drink. That annoys me. THOSE WOMEN FEEL TOO ENTITLED.

I'd seen posts where people didn't care at all that some people aren't big phone talkers or texters or are homebodies. they expect those people to "put in the effort" if they want the resulting relationship, But those same people seem unwilling to move out of their own comfort zones when demands come from that person they just pushed to "step it up."

I do not believe men and women are the same or should act the same.

But I believe humans need the same things to feel loved, appreciated, and special.

Bread and I discussed what we'd given in relationships and what we expected and concluded that we both valued RELATE-ion-ships, rather than one-sided dictatorships.

I'm not saying people in the second group are only takers. Dictators give too. They just set all the rules and only give what they want, when they want.

And people wonder why situationships are on the rise? Right here is one answer. Some people are done pretending they want to put in the effort of a real RELATE-ion-ship.

Talking to Breath brought out a craving I hadn't had in years:

## Oh, So Horny.

*Sex is great that's true*

*But I'm horny for the stuff that couples do.*

*The holding hands, the pillow fights, binge watching all night long.*

*Driving, going nowhere, belting out our favorite songs.*

*Running my hands through his beard.*

*My neck crooked under his chin.*

*His hands knead my shoulders, ass,*

*Waking up next to him.*

*Sharing a poem or two, meeting up with friends.*

*Just breathing in his essence, uncaring where the day ends.*

*Silence isn't awkward.*

*Talking is sublime.*

*I wake up and I go to sleep with him on my mind.*
*I feel so honored, grateful to know that he's all mine.*
*Cooking, cleaning, chores and life*
*Then special days come through.*
*Yes, sex is hella gratifying.*
*But I'm horny for the things couples do.*

I was 45 before I ever met anyone I talked to every day (San Antonio). I saw people do that in high school and wondered what was wrong with them. I had never craved contact like that and couldn't fathom it. Also, I played volleyball and basketball and competed in choir and extemporaneous speech, as well as participating in our church's youth group. It would have literally never occurred to me to call anyone daily.

Although I've dated many people, there were only two I talked to daily. I'm an introvert; maybe that's why. I like to miss people. And for the most part, it's more than a day before I miss them. So every time I see these memes about calling or texting daily or several times a day, I just shake my head.

I literally didn't know this was something anyone expected or thought was normal till 5 years ago. I and the people I dated- we called when we called. Maybe daily. Maybe every other day. Maybe a few times a week. It was never an issue.

So is this an age thing?

A thing created by cell phones being used constantly?

Is it an extrovert thing?

Is this for people who let themselves get bored?

Sometimes I wonder if it's a small talk thing. I don't really know how to small talk. I like to talk about life, art, books, thoughts, and philosophies. A good conversation could leave me satisfied for days, mulling over what we talked about. I generally date great communicators. We crave quality over quantity.

But Breath and I did talk, A LOT.

I would read Breath my poetry like the piece below I wrote about Gatzby.

*Kismet, chance, dumb luck,*
*Stuff and happenstance.*
*I remember the very first time I saw you,*
*Your eyes captured my glance.*
*So nervous when we met, I was,*
*A thing I never am, I'm Zen of course,*
*Chill at all times,*
*Cept you make me shiverdance.*
*So challenging you seemed.*
*I didn't trust you, not one bit,*
*But still I felt so magnetized,*
*Drawn by vibrational current.*
*You'd make me mad. It shocked me so,*
*How you delved under my skin.*

*I'd walk away.*
*Try to forget all this ever happened.*
*Because something so random as a scroll had brought your pic to me,*
*An inbox on a dating app,*
*A call or maybe 3.*
*So many problems followed.*
*Most you claim, my fault.*
*Because you defied*
*every single lesson*
*I'd ever been taught.*
*I thought you arrogant and stubborn,*
*And a workaholic to bat.*
*I thought everything I needed,*
*you absolutely lacked.*
*Chemistry, we always had.*
*Communication's come.*
*Is compatibility in the cards?*
*Don't know even after 6 trial runs.*
*Tried to sever ties and dip and push you straight away,*
*But each year brings you back again.*
*Serendipity at play.*

Breath didn't understand Gatzby. He said if I had allowed him to be my man, I could post his pic to my heart's content, that he would never stand me up. In fact, he said if he lived in Houston or I in New York, we'd be married.

I told him, you’ve never met me.

He said, “You've wanted a house, car, this certain career, a certain type of relationship for years. You've researched it, journaled, visualized, even told people about it. Then you go to that one open house, even if it’s virtual, that one online interview, and sign on the dotted line. You're all in. You love it. You know that you don't know all its quirks and inner workings, that problems will arise, that nothing is perfect. Still, your dream has become flesh. People are happy for you. No one tries to talk you out of it. So why with relationships is it so different? Why do people feel there can't be that speedy recognition of chemistry, compatibility, alignment? Why can they accept a house closing in 30 days but rail at an engagement in 6 months? The idea that you don't know enough is always spouted. To me, you never know enough. You just follow your heart.”

I could relate. A Lot. I felt I’d been at least five different people in my life. If you met me in high school/college, one person, during my 1st marriage, a different person, 2nd marriage, different again; stepping into my writing/performance career, different yet again. And becoming an entrepreneur, once again different.

You could know me my whole life and not know me at all. Or meet me 6 months ago and understand me perfectly.

So knowledge is helpful but not the end-all and be-all. There's intuition; there's chemistry; there's synergy- and all those can happen extremely quickly.

For me, it's heart over head. 51%/ 49%. I have definite standards and things I need to know, but my heart and gut are the final judges. I told him we’d have to have sex before I would commit.

He said why.

I replied, “I heard this story, and I want to give my own version of it. The animal kingdom decided to make a school with climbing, running, and swimming as subjects. All the animals had to take all the subjects. The rabbit failed swimming. The eagle failed running. The otter failed climbing. Tutoring didn't help. It just made each more stressed and self-conscious. Now, let's apply this to humanity, specifically human sexuality. If we replace those three subjects with foreplay, sex, and stamina, a pattern emerges. Human beings, like animals, have strengths and weaknesses. While some can be taught to improve in a weak sexual area, others can't and would be better off finding a rabbit, eagle or otter they are already compatible with. I wanna know what I’m getting.”

He laughed, “You’re getting a BEAST, king of the jungle, baby.”

He had me rolling.

I had him rolling when I told him I logged back into POF on 7/10/2020 and kept getting asked, "What do you do for fun? What do you have planned this weekend?" and I replied, “It's Groundhog Day, mofo.”

“Give me your phone,” he said, laughing. “Give it up.”

“Why? You’re not the only one who can cuss. Every time I tell you I’m worried about the podcast or the e-commerce site, here come the expletives.”

“Get the fuck outta here with all that fucking negativity. You. Got. This. Babe. Your brilliant, sexy ass-”

“See, see what did I tell you. New York accent strong than a motherfucker.”

“You know it.”

He made me smile and forget everything. Everyone. Covid. Money problems. Kid problems. Work problems. He was my breath.

I told Breath what I would do. I told Gatzby when I'd done it.

Breath was my New York confidant, my confessor, my sounding board. Gatzby was my Jersey boy turned Houstonian:

## Unwinder

*My hair's not long,*  
*But still I'm tied in loops and snags and tangles*  
*I've been so tightly wound,*  
*all my curves are jagged angles.*  
*I can't think straight.*  
*I can't relax.*  
*I wake up feeling tired.*  
*Can't sleep, eat, drink, talk enough*  
*To smooth out all these tangles.*

*I need a dark secluded room,*  
*Some music, just us two.*  
*I need your voice next to my ear,*  
*Your pants soon to undo*

*I need your kisses raining down.*  
*Your skin upon my skin.*  
*I need your hands roaming around,*  
*My legs slowly parting.*  
*I need to gasp and moan and shudder,*  
*Nonsense words all I can mutter.*

*I need to cream and scream and stutter.*
*Till I'm almost sore inside.*

*I need that Mona Lisa smile*
*That Cheshire cat arch now my style.*
*I need your slow stroke for a while.*
*Unwinding all of me.*

*You say you have what I want.*
*Say you are skilled, a true savant.*
*I care less and hope you will flaunt*
*Your prowess, my request.*

*I just need what you can give.*
*No expectations, make me live.*
*No titles, just your thrust, my give,*
*No promises, just consummate skills.*

*Be you, Fuck me, want nothing more.*
*Mr. Feel Good.*
*My sex explore.*
*My heart, soul, mind, body you tour.*
*Unwinding all of me.*

*For I have reached my breaking point.*
*One straw away from quitting point.*
*I need a reset.*
*A respite.*
*A reason to not give up the fight.*
*and sex seemed nowhere in sight,*
*Till you popped up you see*

*So let's meet up,*
*I'll take your hand.*
*I'll lead you to my promised land.*
*I'm yours for the taking, dive right in.*

*Unwind. Unbind.*
*Let us begin.*

What was it with me and these Northerners? The South was definitely losing compared to everywhere else.

Facebook is interesting because there are guys from everywhere. In the last 4.5 years, I've had conversations and met guys from Cali, Indianapolis, Ohio, DC, New York, and Detroit. Gatzby was born in Jersey and raised in Cali and Detroit.

In five years, I'd never heard a single one of these complaints from any one of these northern guys.

1. Women expect too much because they want a man with a job, a vehicle, and his own place.
2. Child support is a scam women use to drain men of money.
3. Men shouldn't have to pay for dates.
4. Bills should be split 50/50 if the man moves in, or he should only contribute to the bills he made increase since she already had those expenses.
5. Black women are too strong/opinionated/angry/intimidating.

I asked all my guy friends and Gatzby about this difference between Southern men and men everywhere else, and their theory was it's a remnant of slavery and Jim Crow. Southern black men, according to them, faced more discrimination and difficulty in staying employed, so they started leaning more on women and became more sensitive about spending money on women because they feared losing what little they had and saw women as competition. In the North, East, and West, there were more opportunities, and black male and female relationships were more traditional and long-lasting, so there's less distrust and antagonism.

Interesting.

On July 19th, I opened my Tinder app, fooling around, curious, and swiped right on this gorgeous man, RJ, dark like the night, clothed in all white, chest out, massive biceps. Delicious. He responded immediately, meaning he'd swiped right on me too. We had matched. And then he texted his name and information. I hadn't expected that. We chatted. I liked him instantly. He. Was. Suave.

We exchanged numbers and started talking. Then I found out he wasn't looking for a relationship. I was disappointed. I didn't need any more male friends. I had Breath and San Antonio, long-distance, and Gatzby. I grew distant. But he kept texting. Checking on me. Asking about me. Being interested and being interesting. I told him I didn't see a point in our meeting. He still kept texting and calling. I told him I didn't see this going anywhere. He still kept texting and calling. He said he didn't have many friends here, and he found me sexy and fascinating. By September, he had inspired this poem:

# Harem

*I have an intellectual harem*
*Varied flavors under the sun,*
*Flirting with intellectual stimuli so*
*Luscious, I could cum.*
*A bass voice with clear thoughts*
*And reason,*
*Intellect divine.*
*Let's have a debate baby,*
*See if you can blow my mind.*
*I like militants, and politicos and*
*Those who ride the fence,*
*Play devil's advocate.*
*I'm on my toes.*
*Razor sharp wit,*
*I wince.*
*But parry,*
*Duck and volley*
*and return the blow.*
*My intellectual harem keeps*
*My rhymes fierce, watch them flow.*
*I love men with facts and figures.*
*Worldly, street wise G's*

*Bursting with some elocution*
*Mac like old school MC's*
*I like 'em confident damn near cocky,*
*Eloquence within. The kind that chooses*
*Fists or words and can win with both of them.*
*I got an intellectual harem.*
*Foreplay between the lobes.*
*Got my mind intrigued,*
*Entranced.*
*Got my juices flowing.*
*Intellectuals are sexy, at least the kind I seek.*
*Give me a TI vocab, a Method Man*
*A David Banner, king.*
*A Malcolm X, a Martin,*
*Just to name a few,*
*All colors, all sects, all flavors,*
*Just brilliant, sexy too.*
*I got an intellectual harem.*
*Langston, Baldwin, Countee Cullen,*
*I guess you figured out now,*
*One major draw for me in men.*
*So if I approach to banter, I just want to see your mind.*
*It has to turn me on first*
*Before limbs intertwine.*
*I could tell people I'm picky,*

*They probably wouldn't understand.*

*If I said I'm sapiosexual,*

*That's even more confusing.*

*So I write this poem to elucidate what draws me in for sure*

*Big vocabularies. Deep thoughts. Minds complex and Mature.*

*The Harem*

Rj asked me questions about myself that I had to pause and answer. Questions no one had asked me before, like, what's your writing process. Sometimes, I couldn't answer, and I would text or call him later, like when I replied,

Poems hit me sometimes, and I have to catch them, and they start coming fast and furious and are done in minutes.

Other times, a topic comes and sits in my head, or in my gut, or in my heart. I feel it churning. I zone out sometimes thinking about it. It's growing, breathing, becoming one thing then another, then going back to nothing like the liquid Terminator when it died.

Then one day, it announces itself- a little knock, not an explosion. And I coax it out slowly, like a scared child. And sometimes it's done. On the page, full and finished.

And sometimes, it sits on my shoulder, coaching me through a few drafts.

My literary nonfiction is often like this. Timid, adolescent, wallflowerish, till the last draft, when its bold, ballsy self sits on the page, arms crossed. Satisfied.

I journal, but my pieces rarely come from my journals. My writing process seems to be a different mode.

I also need silence to write, most times. I can write to paintings. That's me.

I didn't know this then, but he was seducing me mentally.

I was in this very strange place mentally and emotionally in September 2020. As I said, I'd been performing for almost five years, but I still was extremely introverted. I called myself a behind-the-camera person. I had put on 45 of my own shows and guested on probably a hundred others. Still, I never set up my camera to film myself. I didn't run around post-show taking pictures. That was probably bad because some performers who did had much more enthusiastic fans. But when I decided to do the podcast, I felt it had to be video and audio. I had to be able to post clips on Youtube, Instagram, and Facebook. I had no followers elsewhere. How would I get them to follow me onto a streaming platform without video? That seemed impossible. So my comfort zone had to expand. And there was Breath and RJ, encouraging me. Breath would say, "This is light work." It was something about the WAY he said it, acknowledging that for everyone in the world, talking in front of people was hella scary, but because I had already overcome so much, refashioned my life, left behind domestic violence, overcome flashbacks, dealt with multiple deaths and heartbreak- ---- THIS was light work.

For years, I had missed The Muse because no one, not even my parents, and definitely no friend, had believed in me, seen me as he did. But Breath was on a whole different level. I could be scared shitless and ready to give up. I could feel like I was trying to do too much- teach, build an e-commerce brand, write and publish essays and poems and podcasts, and he would video call me and give me a loving swift kick in the ass, with his potty mouthed self. I loved him.

I saw a meme one time that showed a lioness and a lion. She was in front. It read, “She doesn’t fear what’s in front of her because she knows who is behind her.” I sent it to him.

The faith he birthed in me, I’d only felt one other time, as a staunch Christian, believing what I was taking on: finishing college, attending seminary (one whole year), and being a youth pastor was my destiny. I felt I couldn’t fail. I didn’t. I was great at it.

Likewise, Breath made me feel invincible, formidable, a force to be reckoned with. When my house had been burglarized in December 2019, he’d been angry, actually wishing he could fly here to take care of me, of the damage.

He told me he “stalked” my page. Every post, he read.

He gave me this feeling I’d never felt before. Unconditional love, support, encouragement. And I tried to give it right back. He was the epitome of “yes, daddy” treatment. I wondered why the universe had placed us half a nation apart. But I was just grateful to have him at all. When I looked at him, at RJ, it seemed that my affirmations, my mental and emotional changes, were resonating out into the universe, changing my vibration. It seemed my vibe had FINALLY attracted my tribe- mature, stable, brilliant men. It just sucked that RJ didn’t want a relationship, and Breath didn’t live here to give me one. But still, having them in my life made me feel different.

# Feeling Myself

*People say my voice is sexy.*
*You should hear it when I first wake,*
*Deeper, sultry like a sax,*
*Screams out "fuck me", telepathically.*

*People say my eyes intense,*
*Deep and languid, like incense,*
*Stare in them and lose your senses,*
*Hypnotic mesmerizing glances.*

*People say my lips so full,*
*So soft, so warm, just all but pull,*
*A kiss to mind that makes men drool.*
*Imagining them around their tool.*

*People compliment my pretty feet,*
*Muscular calves, thighs taut and sleek,*
*A core so tight and wet and deep,*
*Addictive with its Southern heat.*

*My breasts, DDs, spill out of cups,*
*My nipples, sensitive, succulent,*
*So pretty, just beg men to suck,*
*So full, their hands ache for the touch.*

*My skin, so creamy, like pure silk,*

*Soft and womanly,*
*Then*
*There's that dip,*
*That arch, that ass, that knowing smile,*
*That innocent wickedness drives men wild.*

*Madonna, maiden, sex siren,*
*My energy vibrates, undulating.*

*I'm nurturer,*
*Zen for sure,*
*An ancient priestess at my core.*

*But I'm also woman, purely bold,*
*Behind closed doors where one man knows.*
*I'm virginal it seems, but then*
*Unfold the kama sutra when,*
*The right man approaches with his pen.*

*The poems we make- magnificence.*
*The love so sating, elegant.*
*But raw and primal.*
*Uninhibited.*

*So when you see me, be forewarned.*
*I'm layers. I'm fathoms. I'm not for boys.*
*I'm addictive. Unforgettable.*
*And I just might toy.*
*And fuck your mind, if you're disloyal.*

*A woman like me, you'll never meet.*
*Cavalier as a man, I can be,*
*As understanding as a mother, nurturing,*
*And as naughty as a hooker, but very discreet.*

*I've stopped being perplexed by my various sides.*
*I've got layers, embrace them,*
*A never boring ride.*
*I'm evolving, for sure,*
*Set your ego aside.*

*I'm feeling myself.*
*(Single now, destined wife).*

I don't know when I started talking about my 50th bday coming up. But I did, In fact, I posted about it on 9/13. "9/21 will be my 50th bday. I have no idea what I'll do after work. I was on the phone with [Breath]. He said if he were here, he'd make a candlelight dinner for me. I realized I've never had a man do that, and I've been married twice.

Sometimes I wonder about this marriage thing.

Sometimes I think single women want to be wives, and wives wanna be spoiled like some girlfriends are. Two of my former boyfriends talked a lot more about goals to spoil me than my husbands ever did. Ultimately the result was the same. Being transparent

I've never

1. Had a man plan a trip that wasn't to see family
2. Gone on a vacation

3. Gone on a cruise
4. Been bought expensive shoes or a purse
5. Had a man pay all the household bills
6. Been taken to a bed and breakfast
7. Been given a spa day
8. Had a man throw a party for me

All these, except #4, are my relationship bucket list. I think they've happened for many women, but not for me. I'm kinda close to just making this a list of goals to do for myself. I wrote this list four years ago. I'm no closer to it today. I don't know if that even matters. It's just a list.

Do you have a relationship bucket list? Have you done everything you wanted to do in your relationships? Do you feel you've missed out on certain experiences?

I guess I'm just reflecting on this because I'll be 50 and never had these things happen and because someone posted a meme saying women equate things like this to love. I disagree. I've never had them, so how could they mean love to me?"

September was weird. Laughz and Lyrics had its two-year anniversary on the podcast, not in a live show. It was an emotional reunion. Kaye, I, and the other three artists had not seen each other in six months.

Gatzby and I were in this weird place too.

In May, I'd given him that hug which, of course, turned into sex, which led to us picking right back up, but not exactly. We had both grown in those ten months apart. He had been on a church retreat. I'd gone through initiation. He told me that I was in love with him. I refused to believe that. I should know, right?

I said I thought I was addicted to him somehow, like a drug, a bad habit, a fix. I said I know the brain releases feel-good chemicals when we feel love and a hormone-like morphine when we feel pain. Maybe I'm hooked on the release of both you give me," I pulled out my Rick James voice and belted out, "PAIN AND PLEASURE."

He laughed, "Is it that hard to admit that you're in love with me?"

"Yes... Yes.... Yes!" But I said it grudgingly, "Ok, I'm in love with you."

"Was that so hard?"

I stared at him. "Hell yes,"

We both laughed.

"I didn't think me not showing up after the funeral would hurt you so much. I wasn't your man."

"You were the man in my life, the only man in my life, the only one I saw, kissed, made love to, cried about my mom with...." I trailed off, not wanting to go there in my head.

" I was the ... man... in ...your...life?" He sat there taking that in, understanding what all those words meant. I was a strong black woman. No one was supposed to see me crack. Not my sister. Not my sons. Only him. It was one thing to let a man have a title: boyfriend, husband. But it was quite another to actually let him occupy that space when all the walls come down, and you are a woman, completely fragile, feeling helpless, overwhelmed, weak.

To let a man see that.

There were no words I could have said.

I wouldn't have even put into words the fact that that was what had happened in those six months.

To say it is impossible. To admit I needed him like that.

All I could say was what I said.

But he got it. I thought.

So the level of betrayal I felt when I thought he stood me up after the funeral. There were no words to explain it. I told him, "I wanted to flay your skin off and lie you in a pile of ants. And still, you wouldn't have hurt like I hurt."

"Damn," he looked at me as if he was a little worried I'd do something to him.

"I'm not violent. You know that. I just felt that way. And now, you're still that, The man in my life. I don't know if I'm in love with you. But that's the position you have. My 50th birthday is coming up, and I can't go anywhere to do anything. There won't be a party. But I want something from you, two gifts."

He asked what and said done.

That was all I needed.

There was anxiety surrounding my birthday. It was the same day my high school would open back up. I would no longer be working from home. I would be at work, mask on, surrounded by strangers. I looked forward to that last weekend of safety, the last weekend before I went back to work. Thursday, Gatzby and I were supposed to meet up. Some of his relatives came into town, he postponed it to Friday.

Then Friday, he was supposed to come by with my gifts. He was "ten minutes away," but he had to pick up someone from the airport. Then he didn't show. I got a text saying. "Let's get together early tomorrow. Like 10."

I awoke at 10, disoriented. I thought I had set my alarm to wake up and get ready. We were supposed to spend the whole day together. I washed my face, brushed my teeth, took out clothes, and debated what to wear. I didn't know where we were going, what we were doing. I texted- What should I wear? No response.

It was 11. My birthday weekend. 50 was two days away.

I called. No response.

I put the clothes down. Sat on the bed. Surfed the web. It was 12.

I pictured the day ahead of me. I had cleared it- for him. Put all my tasks aside, so we could go and have fun, do "couple" things, eat, talk, laugh, make love.

12:30.

So many times I had waited on him like this, for him like this, clock watching, stuck in limbo, dress? Make-up? Call again? Text some more?

Now I was 50, almost. And suddenly, this seemed ridiculous. Utterly, completely, fantastically ridiculous. To tolerate this. I thought back to the night before, on Facebook, some guy had posted that today's women did not submit. I replied, "We do. Women do submit. Not all. But many. In fact, they submit much more often than men seem to want to admit.

They submit in positive ways. They also submit by making excuses for bad behavior, doing more than their fair share, and lowering their standards.

In fact, that negative type of submission is more to blame for the success of a poor relationship than the lack of submission is to blame for the failure of good relationships.

The problem is that the latter were ways women should have never submitted to begin with.

But some men expect total submission, and like an adult getting mad when momma and daddy stop paying the expenses, they blame women when the relationship's gas tank hits e.

Each person in a relationship has his or her responsibility, and too often, women have done too much out of a desire to "submit."”

It suddenly felt as I remembered typing that that I was talking to myself. That it had been a psychic message for me, for this morning, this missed meeting with Gatzby.

I called again. He answered. “Good morning.”

“It’s afternoon, as in **AFTER NOON.** You said 10. I’ve been waiting for two hours. And had I not called, I’d probably be waiting all day.”

“I was just about to call you.”

“It’s ok. You didn’t even have to call. You could have just shown up. At 10, whether I was ready or not. For once, just once, I wanted a date between us to go well, not to be sitting clock watching. It’s my birthday weekend. I don’t even want to see you now. I feel…” What did I feel? Too many feelings. Too much history. Too much disappointment. Like I couldn’t have one nice thing in a year of horrible things. I wouldn’t go out with RJ because of this? Because of Gatzby? Because I felt I owed him loyalty? Reciprocation? I was a fool. “It doesn’t matter what I feel. I’m done. I’m hanging up. Moving on. “

“You always assume I’m gonna stand you up. That’s why we split last time. You assumed I stood you up. Why won’t you see the best in me? Give me the benefit of the doubt?”

"I have given you the benefit of the doubt for four years. I've never seen your place. I don't know a woman on this planet who would sleep with a man when she can't even go to his place, doesn't even know for sure he has one. That is a hell of a lot of benefit of the doubt. You wanted the benefit of the doubt for that area; you got it. I have no more ability to trust your word than that. You knew how I felt about clock watching, knew it for four years, but here we are. I'm 50 almost, arguing with a man about why he made me wait. I'm done. Stay gone this time. Don't call me. Don't text me. Don't show up. I don't have the gifts I asked for or the day I wanted. I'm too old for this shit."

"Fine. I cleared my schedule for you, but that doesn't mean anything because things weren't done on your timing.'

"You set the time. It passed 2.5 hours ago. That's something you never seem to understand. What you say matters. What you promise should be able to be relied upon. You're 49. I shouldn't have to explain this, any of this. Whatever we have. Whatever this is. I'm not doing this anymore." I hung up.

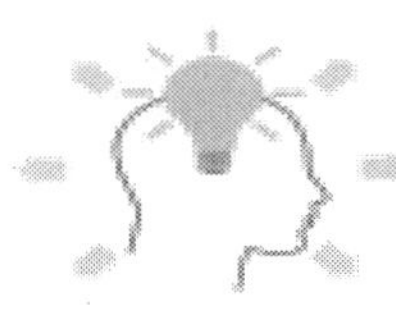

**Lesson 23:**

Wonder- We may not be able to answer all the questions we wonder about. But we can choose to grow, to move on, to try something new.

# CHAPTER 24

I cried. I was about to turn 50. I had pictured being married again at 50 when I got divorced, and now I was single, single. Gatzby, the man in my life, was gone. He had been my crutch, my security blanket. It was time to grow up and go it alone.

Nature abhors a vacuum- even a one-minute one. Because my phone was buzzing. A messenger inbox. “Happy birthday.” I frowned. Who was this? I looked up his Facebook page. My age. Handsome. Single.

“Thank you.”

‘It’s your 50th. What do you have planned?”

“Nothing.”

“I know you have a man; somebody’s treating you.”

I sent about a dozen laughing gifs.

“I know you don’t know me but let me take you out. I’ve been following your page for a while. I hope that’s not creepy. I’d really like to meet you. I don't expect anything. I hope we might click, but it's ok if we just grab a bite.'

"Okay, when?"

"Okay?"

"Yes, I'll go out with you. When and where?"

## Date Ninety-Three:

Lick- We met up at Cheesecake Factory. He brought flowers. I smiled, thanked him, and we had a great meal and walked along the Woodlands Waterway. I was thinking about all the women who posted on Facebook that you had to get the joker out of your life for a king to arrive, and feeling very grateful, almost in awe. He suddenly stopped walking and pulled me closer, looked me in my eyes, and LICKED MY FACE. From chin to eyebrow, on the right side, like some version of a Jim Carrey movie. I stood there, stunned for a second, and then walked off.

He licked my face.

I climbed the steps back to The Cheesecake Factory, went in the bathroom, got a handful of sanitizer, and slathered it on. Then washed my entire face over and over and over again.

I picked up my phone, blocked Lick on social media, and got in my car to drive home. My phone rang. He couldn't call; we'd only talked on messenger. It was RJ, asking how my day was.

I told him all of it, from waking up to the current moment.

He said, "I know you didn't want another FWB situation, but just let me take you out. I promise I WILL NOT lick your face."

We laughed. I told him to let me know when he was free, and I'd love to go out with him, no promises on where it would lead. The last thing I wanted to think about right then was the disappointment of a man who wasn't my MAN, but I wanted to treat me well.

My mind doesn't really let me feel sorry for myself. As soon as that pity bug rears its ugly head, all kind of other images appear. On 9/19/2020. as I bathed and once again scrubbed my face, I thought of a dinner my uncle hosted when I was around 13. He had rented a back room of Landry's seafood. The entire family, his wife, two kids, my cousin, my other aunt and uncle, my grandmother, and I sat at a huge table in this room. They brought out appetizers, raw oysters (gross), salad, wine, the entrees. And I heard my grandmother say she had never been to a restaurant before.

I was stunned. She was married with grown kids and grandkids. And she had never been taken out on a date at a restaurant or had a meal that she or someone she knew hadn't cooked.

I decided then that wouldn't be me. The marriages of our grandparents lasted, but I never saw a healthy one. The quality of marriage is based on the quality of individuals. We have a society that beats down the individual, especially in religious circles. People are taught to live in fear and shame and judgment when faith, trust, and acceptance are the bedrock of good relationships. So first, we create more holistic institutions that support more healthy individuals. Then those individuals join in mutually supportive marriages.

As I thought back on the night. I realized even with the uninvited lick on my face, I lived a life my grandmother could only dream of. I don't think her husband had ever brought her flowers or walked with her beside a waterway with ducks gliding past and

Christmas lights already strung as mood lighting. I don't think she's sipped wine and held a menu and picked not only an entree but a decadent dessert that she requested the waiter cut in half in the back and serve on two plates.

No one has a perfect life. Man, woman, child, single, married, elderly- every category comes with challenges. If you actually think about putting yourself in the shoes of any of those groups you don't belong to, you could probably see what I am talking about. And while the past had beauty, there was also darkness there too. So let's not sigh nostalgically for the era of our grandparents.

Instead, as RJ would say, "Let's approach each other with empathy. Let's realize no one in any of these categories is our enemy. Let's lighten the load for each other. Let's love. Let's forgive. Let's give people the benefit of the doubt. Let's first treat others as we want to be treated and expect the universe to supply our return in divine timing."

*As a little girl, I feared my fate.*
*I wanted to avoid the workload my grandmother ate.*

*She woke up, cooked from scratch, cleaned, gardened, cooked again,*
*Cleaned, watched a show, fixed more food for her kin,*
*Then after cleaning once more, tucked us in.*

*Cyclical. Like a clock. Like moon cycles or tides.*

*Forgotten.Unacknowledged. Did what felt obliged.*

*Tethered. Limited was all that she seemed.*

*But I didn't realize the resources she'd gleaned.*

*She could live off the land. Could can and preserve*
*Didn't need the grocery store, just two hands, and nerve.*

*There's something to be said about the old ways, for sure.*
*Biscuits that you crave a dozen years later.*
*Pot liquor and holidays that were magical.*

*I regret I'm not that kind of grandmother.*

*She seemed so old. A beautiful crone.*
*Strong for so long. Did some things right. Some things wrong.*

*Womanhood, meant something. Not all the right things.*
*It meant duty and honor and responsibility.*
*But also looking the other way and timidity.*
*It meant poise and grace and sacrifice.*
*But also keeping a man at almost any price.*
*It meant faith and devotion and seeking security.*
*But also equating the fairer sex with inferiority.*
*It included biting your tongue and making up beds.*
*And not pursuing the dreams in your head.*
*The kids came first. Hubby did too. Maybe a morsel of energy left for you.*
*I saw the good and the bad, See how far women have come.*
*We've got new jobs, degrees, our own incomes.*
*We've got anthems, and pampering and sisterhood lines.*

*I hope one day we'll balance the best of both times.*

*The strength of the old with the flair that is new.*

*The confidence bold with some humbleness too.*

*Accomplishments yes, but a less selfish view.*

*A worthy result of our ancestors' dues.*

The next few weeks were busy. I bought an air purifier for my classroom and turned the bedroom my son had moved out of into a podcasting room and bought an air purifier for that. I'd hired a videographer/sound editor to record and had already recorded and broadcast my first live podcast interview. 296 people had tuned in. Most importantly, I was getting even closer to RJ and getting closure from Gatzby.

*I don't even know why we met,*
*what brought you into view,*
*just in hindsight, I can bet,*
*the universe sent you.*
*I learned who I wasn't through your eyes,*
*And that helped me define me.*

*Because love it seems has x-ray vision of who we're meant to be.*
*I learned my faults, and needs and likes,*
*My boundaries renewed.*
*Fell in and out of love,*
*Moved on once we were through.*
*I've come to realize we are mirrors,*
*A living looking glass,*
*And holding onto a faded love,*
*Is living in the past.*
*Flames can be rekindled, but most often it is true,*
*your vibration has evolved.*
*It's time for someone new.*

Prior to Covid, I went to lots of popups and farmers markets promoting Laughz and Lyrics, and had a mountain of business cards that I was now cataloging into an email list. I picked up one. I remembered this guy, from my last show on March 15th. He'd made a point of giving me his card, touching my hand as he did, asking me to give him a call. I noticed his flirtation, but I hadn't acted on it. Then I was with The Poet, not officially, not committed, but in all the ways that counted.

I dialed the number, introduced myself. He remembered me instantly. I asked, "Did you give me your card for business or pleasure?"

He answered, "Both. What are you doing tonight?

"I guess you're going to tell me," I said, smiling.

## Date Ninety-Four:

Job and I met at La Madeleine, mostly because it was outdoors, and neither of us was doing anything outside of going to work, working out outside, and hitting the grocery store twice a month. We'd gotten used to quarantine.

As we ordered, he told me this was his favorite place. Ok. He began talking, and talking, and talking, All work. No pause. No breath. And suddenly, I felt my head bob, and caught myself and looked around, and at him. No one had noticed. Not even him. He had droned me to sleep. Literally. Our food hadn't even arrived. We'd been there just 30 minutes, but I told Job that I liked conversations in two parts, give and take. I didn't feel like we were connecting, and I didn't want him to spend money taking me out when the chemistry, in person, just wasn't there. He stood up as I left, still a gentleman, and I went home.

I had some flames on my phone, in other words, hits on Tinder, so I opened up one message and chatted. He seemed nice till he told me a price. Pay for sex? I sent laughing emojis. That was the last thing in the world I ever had to do. Women did that? I deleted the app.

I had a bunch of messenger icons also.

*Their Eyes Were Watching God* has been my favorite book for years. But I had an epiphany after reading some of these messenger messages and chatting with a few guys. Let me give you a tiny summary of the book first. Janie is married off to a much older man because her grandmother, who's raising her, caught her making out with the neighbor's son. This older man has a big house, cattle, and lots of land. Janie is worried about not loving him and the fact he stinks and doesn't cut his toenails. She works hard as a farmer's wife and is always dusty with no nice things. Janie runs off with the first man that shows her attention (who also happens to be a rich black man). He marries her. Together they build the first colored town, and she becomes the mayor's wife. He also forces her to cover her hair because someone touched it in public, and he beat her when he felt she disrespected him. When he dies, the good men of the town have decided she has to take up with one of them. They size each other up, and one has decided he's the logical choice. She ignores him. In the scenes with him, the audience can tell he sees her money, status, and beauty but not her as a person. Then a drifter, Tea Cake, comes to town, doing odd jobs, staying in the rooming house and talking to her, noticing her, listening to her, treating her like a person. The men in town are furious; he's a nobody. The women in town feel she's being led by her lust. Janie and Tea Cake run off together, and Janie has never been happier. She returns to that town after his death.

What I realized that night about this book is there are a lot of modern men just like the men in Janie's town. These modern men size a woman up and decide what she SHOULD want, often without even seeing her as a person. They see a body, certain skills, status, education, or money. But just like Janie, a lot of women want to feel important, listened to, respected. Those women, many of whom, like Janie, might have been with someone their family approved of, someone respected and stable, later really just want to feel real love. Not the *idea* of two people fulfilling a role or a man covering them up because their sexuality or personality is too bright.

These Janie women get accused of not wanting good men, of craving bad boys.

This book shows for some women, it's not that at all.

Whenever I see a video of a white person losing his/her mind because black people are selling water/lemonade, in a pool, sleeping in a dorm, using coupons, swimming, doing a job, or sitting in Starbucks, I think they really haven't embraced racial equality.

Likewise, when men complain about single women having preferences, I think these men have not evolved.

Decades ago, a male relative picked a young girl's husband. More recently, young women picked their own mates, but looks, love, WANTS still weren't really part of the choice either.

Then birth control became prevalent. Women entered college and the workplace in droves.

And men, just like Pool Patrol Pete, who was the latest male KAREN in the news, started getting angry.

Almost every day, I had some guy jumping in my inbox telling me I HAVE TO choose him, date him, give him my number because he is a good man.

When I tell him,

1. You're old enough to be my father (or young enough to be my son). He gets pissed and pushy, and I block him from contacting me further through that app. Or
2. You're a smoker. Not interested. Pissed, pushy. Blocked
3. Or you live states away, I don't believe in long-distance relationships. PPB.
4. Or you have small children. I'm done with that stage of my life. PPB
5. Or I cannot understand a word you're typing. PPB

Every one of these men ignores what I say and tells me- someone whom he's never met-

1. That I'm just scared
2. That they know what I need
3. That I haven't had a real man
4. That I'm wrong for not giving them a shot

In short, they assume they know a complete stranger (they don't), and they are angry that I can choose.

I'm a woman, and some genetic throwback in their brain wiring tells them I'm supposed to agree. And be quiet.

Well, it's 2020.

A woman does not have to do what a man wants.

That doesn't mean she hates men or doesn't desire a good man. It means she no longer has to let MEN DECIDE WHAT IS GOOD FOR HER

The last guy who messaged me was an interesting dichotomy. He poked me on Facebook. I poked back. He said he looked at my page, and like 70% of women ( not sure if he meant black women), I was single. I wasn't sure where he got that statistic.

I responded, "Maybe. Not here to debate your stats. Here's what I know-

1. 70% of divorces are initiated by women.
2. Women are known for friend-zoning men.
3. Women are also known to be single and
   - serial daters
   - part of a situationship or mistresses
   - or celibate/abstinent by choice

So from this, I conclude that unlike the lonely, nobody wants her picture that some men are so fond of, modern singleness is varied and often CHOSEN by women for various reasons. It is as likely to be full of companionship, sex, dating, and friendships as it is to be lonely, sad, or bitter.

So what's your point in posting that statistic?"

He replied, "I think you may be interested in me. What are you offering?"

I replied, "Lol. I don't know you. I don't know anything about you. Why would I offer anything? You poked me."

He responded, "Well, there's 8 of you single women to one of me, an eligible single man."

I sent a shrug gif. Then typed, "Again, maybe, but not my problem. I just got back from a date, and I was working on clearing out my inbox when you poked. You seem to have the mentality of the last five guys I blocked. So I'll tell you the same thing I told them. Maybe guys should try to find out what type of single woman they have met rather than assuming

1. No man wants us.
2. We can't handle a real man/real relationship.
3. We're desperate and should accept the first man that shows us attention
4. We all want a title/marriage/kids
5. We all are gold diggers or have unrealistic standards.

Maybe we just like singleness, and the guy would have to be amazing to change that."

And then I blocked him and was done with my inbox.

But I posted the following before I closed down my social media for the night.

Great communication for me was a non-negotiable. Some people didn't seem to understand that.

"Both men and women post incomprehensible statements in text or video and then get mad and complain about being "judged" when people say:

1. Your grammar is problematic.
2. Communicate with more care.
3. Realize that people can and will be turned off by what appears to be immature logic and communication skills.

For me, intelligence and great communication are two of 5 non-negotiables.

I feel nothing- not one conversation or date - can begin without them.

Questions-

1. Why does there seem to be an idea that people "have to" or "should" accept a person as is?
2. Why do some people believe others should get to "know their heart"? In fact, how would a person even think one could get "to know their heart" if communication is almost impossible?
3. How does a person unable to communicate expect to be taken seriously? This does not just reflect carelessness but a lack of understanding of the world. I.e.. If you can't spell a place, it's almost assured you know nothing else about it. Extend that logic to a very limited view of the world, in general.

I find it very amusing that people accept that others know what they need in a car or a house, but when it comes to a relationship, people like to post things like this: "Have any of Y'all figured that the Person You Don't Want, Just May be the Person You Need in Your Life?"

Is that type of post some people's method of criticizing the type of person who is overlooking them?

In a small percentage of cases, that post is true. But it's equally true that A LOT of cheating and breakups happen because people settle for what they don't want out of loneliness or frustration.

Getting someone shouldn't really be the focus. We could all most likely get someone. Longevity and fulfillment should be the focus, and that's what these posts overlook.

Most of the time, we reject people because we can't see longevity with them, not enough attraction or compatibility. Or equally important that what we offer isn't what we see them bringing to the table."

On 9/21, my actual birthday, The Poet called. He was sitting in the drive-through at a fast-food restaurant. He belted out a stanza of Happy birthday to ya when I answered. Stevie Wonder style. I laughed, "Man, I love you."

"Love you too," he mumbled.

Through the phone, I heard the cashier at the window say loudly, "I hope you said it back."

"Huh," The Poet replied.

"I love you, I hope you said it back," she repeated, defiantly. I pictured head rolling and lip smacking, and I smiled.

"I did. I did." he stammered apologetically. When he drove away, we both fell out laughing.

"She was SERIOUS," I blurted out.

"I know. I gotta check my food."

"Thanks for calling. It's not been a great birthday."

"I'm sorry to hear that. I wish things were different with us. I would have made it special."

"I know. You would have. Good night."

"Bye, birthday girl."

I thanked the universe for the cosmic lightness, the utterly needed comic relief. The Universe gave me another birthday gift on 9/23, the publication of my essay "Those Women."[10]

## Date Ninety-Five:

RJ- His schedule was busy like mine, so I had recorded another podcast episode and actually launched the podcast before we actually met. The date, a late birthday, podcast release celebration was wonderful. Incredibly, he had waited from July 19 to October 17th for our first date. We went out, ate at Applebee's, chatted. Went out again to Razzoo's a week later. Then we shot pool.

I got approached to record a song whose proceeds would fund a domestic violence charity, so I wrote and recorded my portion. My lyrics are below.[11] RJ and Breath inspired them.

---

10 https://herstryblg.com/theme/2020/9/23/those-women

11 https://highvolumemusicrecordings.bandcamp.com/album/i-feel-the-way-a-woman-should-2

# I Feel Like A Woman Should

*I opened my eyes, feeling good,*
*You're not here, but I feel like a woman should.*
*Respected, important, recognized, understood,*
*It took a lifetime, never thought I would*
*Meet a man I loved, who loves me.*
*Intensely, correctly, sacrificially,*
*No half measures,*
*you come correct*
*With you, I know what to expect.*
*You make me laugh, challenge my mind.*
*When I am down, help me unwind.*
*When I am up, you always be,*
*lifting me higher miraculously.*
*To say I love you is so small.*
*I need new words just to extol,*
*Your resilience, your swagger and your grace,*
*Things you've done for the smile on my face.*
*I could go all day, tell a million rhymes,*
*How you studied and learned me by design.*
*You apologize when wrong,*
*Correct your way,*
*Sent me digital flowers to make my day.*

*You amaze with devotion,*

*Consistency rare,*

*No doubt in my mind, you'll be there.*

*All I asked for,*

*I got,*

*You are all that's good.*

*Blessed not stressed*

*I can relax,*

*Exhale*

*as a woman should.*

My phone rang; it was Friday, November 20th. RJ blurted out, "Babe, I wanna see you tonight."

"Sure. Wait. I signed up to do a networking event."

"I'll come with."

"Really?"

"Are you kidding? I'd love to see you in action. In fact, I'll rent a room. We can make a night of it. No expectations." We hadn't slept together yet.

I packed a little bag and drove about ten minutes from my house to a Holiday Inn I'd never even noticed. Put my overnight bag down and hugged him. He looked and smelled delicious. He kissed me. I kissed him back and pulled him towards the door.

"Don't start anything," I said. "We got somewhere to be."

We piled in his black truck. Mood music played softly. "Thanks for doing this."

"My pleasure."

"So it's cuddle season, but we're not cuddle buddies. What are we?' I asked.

"You're my bae."

My eyebrows went up. "Me? I thought that was a girlfriend title."

"Not to me. I call you every day, text you, bring you a bottle of wine each date to take home to unwind after work. And tonight, you're getting a full body massage. You know I'm a licensed masseuse," he smiled.

"Damn, for real? Alright, looking forward to that. So, you're my bae?"

"No, I'm your boo."

I bust out laughing, a huge smile on my face. "My boo. Heyyyyyy boooooooo."

"Hey bae." He winked at me and grabbed my hand.

The restaurant was beautiful. Empty. Two impeccably dressed black women sat outside in the perfect evening weather, a tray of appetizers and a wine bottle in front of them. I walked up and asked if they were with the networking group. Yes. We sat. Everyone introduced themselves. The host told what she did. Her friend went next. Then me. And then they looked at RJ. "What do you do?"

He was retired military, 1 year, working on his real estate license.

"I'm her bodyguard," he said. My mind instantly went back to The Last Dragon, so I was Vanity, and he was Taimak.

"Really? She's famous enough to need a bodyguard?" the friend asked.

"Yep," RJ replied.

The host asked, “And if there were a threat, what would you do/”

He shrugged, “For her. I’d take a bullet. I’d die.”

We took pictures, exchanged cards, and left.

“Wow, “ I said. “Where did that come from?”

“It was my first thought. It was the truth.”

I didn’t know what to say, so I asked what he thought of the networking session. I’d expected it to be a lot larger, but of course, Covid was always a factor. He’d replied, “It was black girl magic all up in my face. Made me feel like I needed to get my shit together. Three black women- impressive, powerful, motivated, movers and shakers in your fields. And then there’s me, starting over.”

I loved his description of the three of us. I hated his description of himself and told him so.

He changed the subject. “Those appetizers were nothing. Let’s eat.”

We ended up back at Applebee’s and were seated in the same seats as our first date. We both burst out laughing. Then we returned to the hotel. He dimmed the light. Poured some wine. Set his playlist playing and led me to the bed, where he took off my heels, slacks, and blouse. He washed his hands and filled them with oil and started on my neck and shoulders, undid my bra, and did my upper back, my lower back, thighs, calves. I had never felt anything that good.

I turned over, my bra falling away, and pulled him into bed. We kissed. He wiped his hands on a towel nearby and slid down my body, kissing every inch. Worshipping me. My hands gripped the covers. Then my panties were gone, replaced by his lips. I hadn’t had oral sex since May. It wasn’t something Gatzby did.

"Delicious," he murmured. "Sweet, just like you."

And just when I was about to cum, he rose, put on a condom, and slid into me. And we made love for hours. No exaggeration. Hours. We lay afterward, cradled.

"You didn't stop me," he said.

"Stop you?"

"You didn't complain I was taking too long. Women always do. It makes me kinda nervous about having sex with someone new. I take too long. And I sweat."

"You didn't take too long. I loved every minute. And I know how to use a towel. Your sweat is clean, like water, not sticky. Everything was perfect."

He pulled me tighter. Our arms wrapped, our legs wrapped. And we fell asleep. Before the sun rose, we made love again. And then he woke me up to breakfast in bed.

I trundled off to the restroom, washed my face, showered, brushed my teeth, ate, and then we kissed and were back in bed, making love again. No, I think we were on the duvet that time, coverlet thrown across it.

We eventually had to shower AGAIN and leave. I smiled when he texted later," had a great time last night… AND this morning."

Me too. Me too.

I was almost kicking myself. July 19 to November 20, those four months seemed wasted for a moment. Then I realized it wasn't. We actually had done something I hadn't done since my second marriage- truly learned each other, built a solid foundation. It was actually ironic. I kept seeing these 90 day, make him wait posts. How long does lust last? I know, according to Steve Harvey, ugh, a man shouldn't get sexual benefits before he'd qualify for insurance benefits at a new job. But that logic sucked. One, the job is doing that to save money. Celibacy isn't about saving money. The job also is fully using the services of the employee. The celibate person is not. In fact, the celibate person is avoiding the very thing that probably drew him/her in the first place- sexual attractiveness. It just made no sense to me.

But he had actually waited 120 days. Wow! I had told him I didn't want another friend with benefits situation. I had referred to Gatzby as "The Asshole who treated me like shit." I'd said it would be foolish to make the same mistake. But I still refused to date RJ out of my attachment, my "love" for Gatzby. Looking at how my birthday turned out, I couldn't fathom my reasoning. Gatzby had been back in my life five months after ten months apart and STILL couldn't do right by me?

RJ said, "With me, it won't be the same. I'm different. We would be different." It took him a whole month after my birthday passed to convince me.

*There's something gracious in knowing someone could say,*

*"I told you so," but doesn't,*

*Something like a gift never wrapped but handed to you all the same.*

*There's something sexy in patience,*

*Listening, waiting,*

*there undemanding,*
*Knowing somehow that someday*
*the fire alarm will sound,*
*The glass will break*
*and your hose will be better*
*and more long-lasting than any*
*Extinguisher,*
*Dimming the flames till*
*Only a puddle remains.*
*There's something languid in the seduction*
*That needs no title,*
*Just here, just now,*
*Just passion and ultimate bliss.*
*Something decadent.*
*Tantalizing.*
*Lick your lips delish*
*Better than a Harlequin romance*
*you are,*
*Put Zane to shame,*
*Luscious,*
*Dark chocolate.*
*Good for me but only in moderation.*
*For the mature.*
*Those who know the power of now,*
*The pull of memories,*

*The ambience of afterglow.*

*My gift, you are,*

*Friend and so much more,*

*A key to my independence, but also*

*My place of rest.*

*I exhale after waiting so long,*

*Too long,*

*You breathe life back,*

*Make me strong again when I've felt weak.*

*Wise. A good listener. A true alpha.*

*I submit.*

*I can call you many things but one is*

*Friend with Benefits.*

He'd text "Good morning, beautiful." or "Hello beautiful, thinking of you." or if we hadn't talked for some time, "Hello beautiful stranger."

I appreciated so many things about him. But one of the biggest was he was NOT one of those people who judged my level of interest or sincerity SOLELY by if I called or texted. That never made sense to me. I missed calls or texts when my phone was dead or on silent (at school, recording podcasts), but for some people in the past, that was a crime. They felt I should always be accessible, always checking for their missed calls or texts. That just wasn't me.

There was also, "Hi beautiful, how are you?" "Hey beautiful, what you doing?" "Hello, sexy." "Good morning, sexy." "Hey baby girl!" "Hey beautiful baby girl," "Good morning, delicious sexy boo." and "Good afternoon sunshine."

When I was young, I was raised that it took a relationship to get romantic and sexual needs met. I think many people were raised that way. Then we lived, and some experienced getting what we wanted outside of relationships; others didn't.

I think for some people the idea that a relationship would meet those needs became the ideal, but the practical and temporary solution became dating, fwbs and situationships.

I think maybe it's just evolutionary. Once there were only houses, inns, and rooming houses. Then came apartments, condos, and townhouses. Some people in houses can't imagine renting an apartment. Some people in apartments can't imagine taking on the hassle of a home.

I don't think America will ever revert to married/taken, courting and single/unattached being the only arrangements. Maybe it was never that way, to begin with, and we're only fooling ourselves that anything has changed.

And after hanging out with RJ, whether we were or were not having sex, I wasn't sure I wanted another relationship. I loved who I was becoming.

- What do you want?
- Why do you want it?
- What does it take to make you happy?
- What do you have to give to others?

I was journaling about those things. I looked at the world saw people on motorcycles, eco cars small as a go-cart, two-seaters, SUVs. I saw people who only wanted a condo and would never want to own a home. We recognized people wanted different vehicles to transport them, different types of castles to call home.

But when it came to relationships, marriage seemed to be the only goal pushed. Marriage was also a vehicle; it's also a huge impact on the hominess of one's home.

Lots of people were no longer buying into the idea that marriage is for everyone. Percentages were down. More people were dating-longer, living together, choosing singleness in one form or another.

Marriage is amazing. But so is singleness. They each have pros and cons. And for the first time in my life, I didn't see one as better than the other.

No man is an island. But that does not mean no man/woman can be happy single.

As 2020 turned to 2021, I reflected on the past year and uncovered a new reason I was single.

It was safe. Love, commitment, settling down are risky.

I admitted to myself that although I'd done and still do the work on my habits, mentality, triggers, flaws, there was a part of me that wondered had I gotten more selfish, less trusting, less forgiving, less supportive, more critical, more jaded than I once was in relationships. Single me might say no. I'd healed. I'd be better. I was more mature, more stable. I knew myself better. My common sense said if I'm better, healthier, wiser, a better listener, more reflective then I must be a better partner. But only time and opportunity could verify those theories.

And some days I was glad that

1. I didn't have to see whether the new me was better at passing the tests and trials of a relationship
2. I didn't have to see whether I retained or regained everything heartbreak stole

Other days I knew that if HE appeared, a man like RJ who wanted a committed relationship, I would take the risk, even if I/he/we might fail miserably. Because love is worth that risk. At least that hadn't changed.

I could always tell when the holidays were here. My dry inbox became inundated. I was guilty, too; I sent two hey, big head texts and a couple of ✋s feeling playful just before turkey day. I was stuck in the house being a good quarantiner. So it was amazing when I planned a Christmas show and even more amazing when RJ walked through the door.

December 18th, I was nervous. I hadn't been on a stage since March 15th. I was glad RJ was there. I was kinda nervous because The Poet was too, and we hadn't seen each other since May. I knew he'd been looking forward to seeing me. I had no idea RJ was going to show. I think it was for moral support. He knew how nervous I was. Like San Antonio, who had driven three hours to make sure I was okay, RJ would drive an hour just for moral support.

But unlike walking into my job on the anniversary of my dad's death, the stage was a long-lost lover, and this was our reunion, and it was beautiful. And it was even more beautiful that this man I nicknamed "Perfect" was sitting next to me.

The next week, Poet and I were on another Christmas show together. I apologized to him privately because I felt he might have felt blindsided. We hadn't been dating for a long time, but still, I felt he had wanted a heads up and wasn't prepared to see me there with someone else. Composer was there with his new girlfriend, who now is his fiancée. Two shows in two weeks. Life felt like it was getting back to normal.

The next week I spent in front of the computer writing Zennurgize Your Life, Volume I, Edition 1. The revised version of that book is now a best seller on Amazon, and as of the day I'm typing this- 12/27/21- has been on the best seller's list for 12 days.

2020 had been a good year. I'd accomplished a lot, as you can see from the icons on the following page. I also was:

## Single… and in Love.

*I woke up this morning,*
*a feeling rumbling around.*
*The longer I stay single,*
*the less I see settling down.*
*At first, I cried, forlorn,*
*like life was on attack.*
*But after I dried my eyes,*
*I looked back at the track.*
*I've loved hard and deep and strong,*
*And I'm so blessed for that.*
*That still is true today*
*although "a man" I lack.*
*My relationships have shaped me*
*like I'm on a potter's wheel.*
*My muses, my lovers, my boyfriends and husbands,*
*The dates .... so unfulfilled..*

*I've had the best conversations,*
*mental ecstasy divine,*
*I've had the best intimacy,*
*like strawberries dipped in wine*
*I've had support and challenge and heartbreak,*
*I'm grateful for that too.*
*So at 50 plus,*
*I now care less about being cuffed anew.*
*So far from jaded, I'm sublime,*
*I realize*
*life's not black and white for me.*
*And lonely I am rarely,*
*I'm actually where I love to be.*
*A nexus of creativity,*
*A ball of sensuality,*
*A whirling dervish spinning through the buffet of what can be.*
*I date sometimes and have such fun.*
*I have to genuflect*
*to those with conversation,*
*those men who still can "mac."*
*I didn't know this world existed,*
*The in-between you see.*
*I spent all my life committed,*
*Never imagined singletry.*
*But 6 months passed,*
*no boo,*

*Ensued a year or two*
*And what I found was me.*
*Recreated, refined, and FREE,*
*Making so much damn money.*
*Three business and GLEE.*
*And who ever knew*
*that I would date more in 6 years*
*than in the past 32.* 😮
*That I would learn more sexually than marriage taught me to.*
*For divorce, I'm oh so grateful.*
*For singleness, too,*
*You see.*
*I take a huge breath and puff my chest,*
*Damn, I love being*
*With Me.* 🥰

**Lesson 24:**

X is pronounced Z, jumping ahead in the alphabet like Y doesn't even matter. And sometimes, why doesn't matter. The unknown can be scary or exhilarating. It's all a matter of perspective. What we think we know, may be wrong. "You know nothing, Jon Snow." In the words of another famous author, I heard on a Ted Talk. "The cave you fear to enter, holds the treasure you seek," Joseph Campbell.

2020

THIS YEAR, I

1. Completed 52 new goals
2. PAID OFF 8 DEBTS
3. READ 35 BOOKS
4. SURVIVED WORKING FROM HOME & ONLINE LEARNING
5. WALKED 155 MILES SINCE 5/15/20
6. RAISED MY CREDIT SCORE AND INVESTMENTS
7. COMPLETED KEMETIC INITIATION & WENT NATURAL

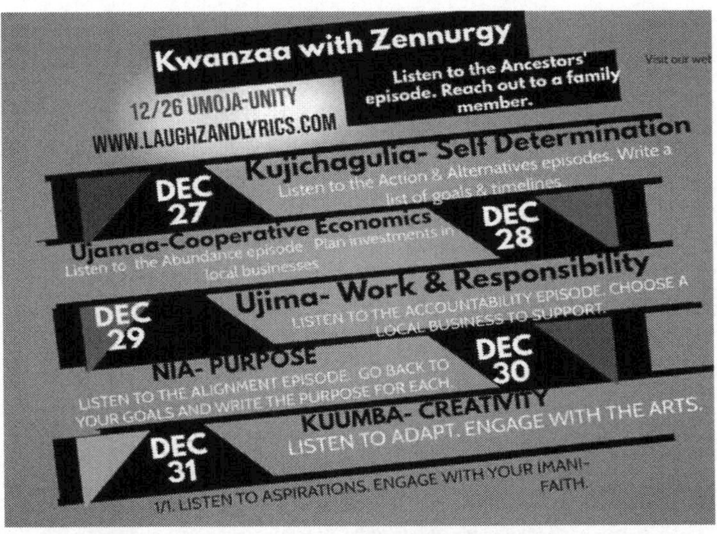

CHAPTER 25

# Yearning

January 2021 was busy. 1/1 was my Laughz and Lyrics show Flow. 1/2 was my Zennurgize Your Life workshop. It was exciting to transform my personal journey, my personal journals into a workbook. I had nixed everything I hated about guided journals- their length, their repetitiveness, their lack of cultural resonance, and their dependence on mostly visual learning. Mine was short- 20 pages, not 365, 5 different types of prompts. My book pulled in role models, books, movies, songs, vision boards. It was the kind of guided journal I had wanted and needed, and I sold out within weeks. Then sold out again. And again. Then people were asking for Volume 2. I set a date for July to have it written.

The podcast had been the impetus for all of this. One step, one idea, and now I had two books written. I was selling a line of inspirational materials- bookmarks, affirmation cards, keychains.

Every week I was dropping a new episode and clips from an old episode. I recorded three new episodes this month and guested on two other podcasts. Podcasting was becoming my life. And because my podcast focused on personal growth; it was stretching me, pushing me, challenging me. The teacher is always the student too. I had learned this from 26 years in education, and it was proving once again to be true. And the podcast had brought me one other blessing. In 2020, I ran across my former college roommate on LinkedIn, sent her a message. No response. Then she appeared in the people I might know on Facebook, and I sent her a friend request and inboxed her. A month later, she accepted, and we caught up. It was great gaining someone I had lost instead of always losing people through death or disruption.

When I told RJ about my conversation with my ex-roommate, he just shook his head.

"Another you. You haven't spoken to her since 1990. She has multiple businesses, is an author and a book illustrator, a pianist, singer and composer, an essayist, and s curriculum coordinator. She's another you. I wouldn't even want to read the bio that you'll write on yourself when you finally release your book to Amazon. That shit would make me feel embarrassed about what I've done with my life."

I frowned, "You're impressive. You did over 20 years in the military. You're retired. You should be proud."

"I am, but still. That shit was inspiring, this conversation with your ex-roommate, the networking event. I'm glad I came. I've never been around a group of black men doing what you guys were doing. In fact, whenever I get around men in Houston, all they do is complain- about women: that women pick the bad boy; that women don't want to build with a struggling man; that women's expectations are unrealistic; that women are single because they're loose- literally and figuratively; that women seem to have lost respect for themselves; that women don't know how to treat men; that $150 is too much to spend on child support in one month. We're focused on women, and you women are focused on goals and growth, and impact. We used to be the builders. Now, most new business owners are women. Why is it women seem to know how to buckle down and get their shit together, but men suddenly seem to be lost and stuck and always looking for that ride or die to push/pull them through the hard times?"

I was stunned. But as I looked at the women who were buying my book, I was face to face again with Black Girl Magic. I remembered how that conversation had ended.

He had grabbed my chin and said, "When I swiped right, I didn't know if I was getting an ax murderer. But you," he paused. "I was sitting on my ass, taking care of my kids, my mom, my little brother- yes, but totally directionless. I'd been retired a year and dabbled here and there. And then this spitfire came into my life, and she was pivoting. I watched it. I watched you get depressed and make a solution. Lose all your shows, your whole summer plan, and launch a podcast, merchandise, an e-store. And I listened to every episode, watched every guest show you featured on. I wanted some of that to rub off on me. And it has. You have. You keep asking me why I stuck around when you wouldn't date me. So many reasons. You deserved better than you were getting, and I deserved a woman like you in my life."

He'd leaned over into my seat and kissed me, and then held me to him, like I was so precious, like he loved me. And that hug and kiss somehow stayed with me. I would feel it sometimes, like when I was nervous before that first workshop or when we hadn't talked or seen each other in a while.

## Date Ninety-Six:

His comment about male-female roles reversing popped up in my mind again when I went on Date Ninety-Six

T had been my Facebook friend for years. He'd been involved, and looked me up when they split, said he'd always wanted to meet me. So we met for breakfast. I wasn't prepared for his demeanor, and he wasn't prepared to date AT ALL. He spent the whole time talking about his ex, a woman who happened to be separated from what seemed like the ultimate jerk. T had started off a friend but ended up more and fell in love, and then she had felt it her "Christian duty" to take her philandering mate back when his affair fell apart. T was devastated. I felt for him. The brunch date was sad and very awkward.

It was worse still when he walked me to my car, we hugged, and he started to cry. I felt for him so much. He apologized, stating that no woman had touched him since her. And I told him it was alright. It was grief. I know grief intimately. We talked till he calmed down, and then I left.

I had a lot on my mind. Divorce causes so much pain. So does infidelity. My mind flashed back to posts I'd seen and written on divorce. I've been divorced twice. Facebook posters often seem to spout ideas that seem strange to me. Marriage is a HUGE commitment. Really the biggest commitment one can make in life. Some people seem to think because there is a high divorce rate, that means marriage means nothing in general or nothing to the people who get divorced. I don't understand thinking this way.

Would you say that because 50% of freshman college students flunk out, college has no value?

Would you say that because there's a high rate of foreclosure or repossession, no one should buy a house or car, just lease or rent?

Divorce, for most, is much more traumatic than a repossession or foreclosure or even the loss of a job. In fact, the only thing I could realistically compare it to is starting a business.

85% of businesses fail in the first seven years. But people start them, pouring their heart, soul, blood, sweat, tears, time, and money into them- just like marriage. Changing their whole lives- just like marriage. And the arrogance of someone who has never worried, never had the sleepless nights, never been exhausted beyond belief, never kept going when all seemed hopeless, the arrogance of their flippant criticism is mind-boggling.

People can try their best and still fail.

Most people do not marry, planning to divorce. They really want it to work.

There are so many reasons divorces happen, but at the core, I think many of us don't really learn how to make a relationship work day in and day out till we live with someone. And the bad habits, flawed thinking, entitlement, selfishness, and immaturity that we bring into the relationship take their toll. We don't protect the relationship at all costs. We don't spell out ground rules and really know each other and exhibit absolute transparency.

But none of that is because marriage means nothing to us.

We've been sold fairy tales of happily ever after that magnify the wedding and honeymoon rather than preparing us for married life.

I applaud those who get married and stay married, especially those who have built happy, thriving relationships. But I wish some myths would die - today. Staying married isn't a "duty." It shouldn't define one's faith, and it has nothing to do with being a strong woman. When I heard T, for TEARS, date 96, say this woman's husband had told her that "God made women so strong so they could hold their families together and get past hurts like infidelity." I was livid.

I also felt a flash of recognition. It sounded just like something my first husband would have said about his cheating and his inability to keep a job. It mirrored something my second husband said about dealing with his impotence and his refusal to treat it.

I remembered that day in therapy back in 1999 when my counselor had asked, "Why is it your job to keep this marriage together? Didn't two of you take vows?"

Those two questions stuck with me for life and kept me from defining my faith or my strength by what I did for a man. Men need to stop thinking they can define what women need to be, and women need to stop thinking they can define what men need to be. Define yourself. Get yourself together, and then seek partnership. No one should seek to be carried, raised, or groomed by the other sex. Partnership is reciprocation, not parenting. If you don't know yourself, haven't developed yourself, can't control yourself, and carry your own weight in a relationship, then why are you in one? I hated when dates pissed me off. But this one did. Not Tears, I had nothing but empathy for him. But the whole system that made women so easily manipulatable by playing on these roles we were supposedly supposed to fill made me want to wring someone's neck.

As much as RJ talked about role reversal, the roles hadn't reversed enough on that date for that couple. But here's an update, everything worked out. A month later, they were together, and she was filing for divorce. They've been together ever since, and we're still Facebook friends.

This date also made me think about this idea of being "ready." So many people would say neither of them, Tears and his lady, were ready for a relationship. That's not for me to judge. But the idea that two "ready" people equals a functioning relationship as easy as putting gas in a car and pushing the ignition button is bullshit. It's along the same lines as the fallacy of thinking," If we "have to work at it, it's not working."

Relationships take work, whether two people are "ready" or not. And this whole idea that two people can somehow link back up later when "the time is right" is so arrogant. Who has that much control? We can't control tomorrow and do not know what it will bring. There used to be many sayings acknowledging this- "God willing," "If the creek don't rise." "Hopefully," "If all goes to plan/goes well," but now people just feel like they know that everything will magically fall into place.

It also makes me wonder if one of these two "ready" people is looking to be a taker rather than an investor. It seems to put all the emphasis on the work done before getting into the relationship. It reminds me of the guy who asked me, "What are you offering?"

Well, to the right man, everything.

Every damn thing.

To the wrong man, nothing.

Who are you?

I don't know, so I have no answer for that.

I think each person has a choice. Love should come with a disclaimer like a carton of cigarettes: known to cause heart ache, sleepless nights, deep pain and depression, self-doubt, binge eating, loneliness. If you know that and accept that there will be ups and downs, and you have prepared as best you can, then step forward and begin. Realize that the unexpected will happen, and no one can perfectly plan for the future and decide if that person is worth that journey and the sacrifices and adjustments that come along with it.

I think maybe that's one reason dating is harder now. It's become transactional. If I come ready, and he comes ready, we should be at x point by y time, at Z point by A time. And when that person doesn't react as expected, we feel they're playing games or wasting our time.

Everything else has become simpler, faster; you can car or house shop online. Sign and drive.

But relationships still are the same. No shortcuts. And I think it's hard for some of us to deal with. We don't have the patience.

**February 2021** was busy and unprecedented. I got invited into some new Facebook singles' groups, joined, and left before the end of the month. I have a low tolerance level for negativity. The first group seemed to be a group of men who wanted old school women but wanted to be new school men.

Sometimes the posts that showed up in the first group made me think that those men thought that there was some golden age of relationships, and if everyone went back to pre-marital abstinence, it would return.

There is no such age.

The battle of Troy, a thousand years before Jesus, was supposedly started over adultery. Solomon had 300 wives and 900 concubines. Songs like "Papa was a Rolling Stone, "about a player and "The Clean-up Woman " about a side chick played on the radio in 1972. We have always had premarital sex, infidelity, single motherhood, lust. It is human nature. It is not an invention of modern society. Shame will not stop it. Disease will not stop it. Nor will laws or memes or Facebook posts.

These men would harp on promiscuity endlessly. Finally, I got tired of it and wrote, “What is promiscuity? Depends on who you ask. In fact, to someone, you probably are promiscuous.

1. Promiscuity can be someone who didn't wait for marriage
2. Someone who lusts after multiple people
3. Someone who watches porn
4. Someone who practices what some call deviant sex, meaning anything, not missionary style
5. Promiscuity can be someone who has sex with no plans for it to lead to procreation.
6. Promiscuity can be someone who talks dirty or dresses provocatively
7. Someone who dates more than one person at a time
8. Someone who has had sex on the first date or had a one night stand or a threesome
9. Someone who has cheated
10. In Islamic countries, a woman showing her face and arms or with a man unchaperoned is promiscuity. And kissing and touching in public (PDA) is illegal.

In someone's religion, 99% of the population is promiscuous because it's a matter of perception.”

They also hated women who dated more than one man at a time or who had been on many dates. They assumed she was sleeping with every guy. So I commented, "Men,

1. Do you expect sex at the end of a date?
2. Do you understand that a date is a mutually agreed upon time to get together to enjoy the company of another person?
3. If the answer to 1 is no, and the answer to 2 is yes, then why does it seem so many of you think women who date multiple men sleep with them all?

A. Is it that you lied about #1?

B. Is it a cover for your dislike of women taking control of their romantic lives by not depending on one man for everything?

C. Is it a cover for your sense of offended tradition and a desire to hold to the idea the man controls a woman's relationship options?"

So I've shown you the traditional side. Here was the ultra-modern side. See traditional roles have women as the virginal till marriage wife and homemaker, men as the provider. These men wanted the first part but would post that they wouldn't help pay with bills (even while living with the woman), and they wouldn't pay for nails, hair, make-up because "she would do that anyway if I weren't here."

That was the most illogical statement I'd ever read. Many single women do or hire someone to do everything they need done. So if that's his plan. He plans to do nothing.

NOTHING.

She drives her car single. So he would not pick up a woman in his car? She eats and goes on outings, so no restaurants, concerts, movies, etc.? I could keep going. Let's flip that. If he has that mentality, and she treats him the same way, no cooking, no cleaning, in fact - no sex. He knows how to climax, right? Did it before meeting her, right? So that one statement makes a man coming into a woman's life pointless.

Leave her alone then.

Much of dating and being in a relationship is gifting to another person what they can do and usually do obtain for themselves. If you don't plan to do that, don't make up illogical reasons for why.

Just state you're not doing it.

So, I left that group. I'd been surrounded by a great group of guys for a while- RJ and Breath and San Antonio, and these dudes on Facebook just annoyed me and reminded me of years ago, of so many pointless dates. I wrote this:

## Give Yourself a Hand

*I woke up this morning, grateful as hell,*
*lonely as fuck, is that normal?*
*Counting all my to-dos.*
*Smiling at my things done.*
*In an empty bed with a boyfriend pillow*
*and no one.*
*All the hellos and gm beautifuls result in tumbleweeds on my line.*

*Attention spans lacking.*
*Consistency slacking.*
*Say you want a woman but you're jacking*
*off seems quite sufficient for the moment.*

*Otherwise seems you would follow through.*
*Not chasing you.*
*Got too damn much to do*
*and although you're cute*
*not breaking my neck for you boo.*

*Silly thing is, I'm amazing,*
*so worth the time you are not taking,*
*So you've lost my focus,*
*Duly noted,*
*You are all talk and zero motion.*

*Thanks for the false hope*
*But I didn't expect much.*
*Too many men have mastered the bluff.*

*I breathe in,*
*Exhale again*
*Too much to do*
*To wait in suspense.*

*A day awaits with tasks galore..*
*Grateful I am for opportunities pour*
*in writing, performing, networking too.*
*Would have been nice to share all with you.*

*But we all have our priorities.*
*And obviously your hand is more important than me.*

In the second group, one of the admins helped me experience something I'd heard men complain about for years. He so spectacularly misinterpreted both my comments and posts that it was actually entertaining. It made me understand the argument I'd heard guys have with women.

Him- What are you talking about?

Her- You said y.

Him- No, I said what I meant to say- x.

Her- But your hidden agenda was y.

Him- I didn't have an agenda. I said x. I meant x

Her- But men always say x and mean y.

Him- How can a woman tell a man what men always mean?

Her- see, that's why you're a chauvinist (in this case, feminist). You never listen when we share our feelings.

Him- Huh, who was sharing feelings? We were discussing x, which is an issue, not a

feeling.

And on and on

Now, I

1. 1. Have more sympathy for men.
2. 2. Wonder what is wrong with the world that roles get reversed like this so much more often.

So I went out on a date in early February, and afterward, I immediately left this second Facebook group. I felt the group must have changed my vibration because he was the physical embodiment of the mentalities in that group.

## Date Ninety-Seven:

70's Guy showed up looking like he was in costume for a Blackploitation film. Gaudy jewelry, shirt open to his navel, hairy chest. I almost expected the waiter at Olive Garden to ask him to button his shirt because it was such an egregious violation of any decent dress code. We had the usual small talk, and as he asked about my life, I flashed back to a conversation with RJ. He had called me " a boss, on my game, constantly evolving," and I'd realized then that I crave a dude on that same path. He'd said any man meeting me would be "motivated or intimidated. There was no middle path." His assessment mirrored exactly what I'd experienced for the last 32 years of my life. I used to try to make myself smaller and hide my accomplishments.

Not anymore. I be who I be. Boss up or Bounce. Not sorry. Just free.

The longer 70's guy and I kept talking, the farther apart our mentalities grew. He had the nerve to tell me, "See, that's why you can't keep a man."

I laughed out loud and shook my head. "1. I can. I have. I'm the one out of the two of us that spent 25 years of my adult life in committed relationships. I'm the one of the two of us who filed for divorce and whose exes tried to come back multiple times. I'm the one of the two of us also, who has an active dating life. Men can't keep **me**. Not the other way around sugar. I don't want to be kept by the men I've met. Your thinking is as outdated as your wardrobe. Thanks for dinner. Good night."

I'm not usually that blunt, but society and men without a leg to stand on need to stop with this rhetoric, and for once, I wanted to state that.

That month I recorded two podcasts, guested on one, and got to host Breath on my Valentine's day episode.[12] We had a great talk about CONNECTION. I'll always be grateful I did that episode.

That morning I had found it hard to sleep and penned this:

*It's 1:00 am on Valentine's Day.*
*And I'm happy,*
*Resurrected*
*By a tub fragrant*
*with bath beads,*
*dried and tucked in warm sheets,*
*cocooned while outside freezes.*
*Drowsy, placid, pleasant*
*Languid like a cat,*
*My fur silky, smooth,*
*moisturized- all that.*

12 https://pandora.app.link/xtPlXkjHhnb

*Once this day plagued me,*
*worried about haves and have nots*
*Which would I be?*
*Now, I have all I want,*
*for now,*
*My time, my space, my own pace.*
*My every day a blank page*
*I fill.*
*It feels miraculous, limitless,*
*No regrets,*
*Just peace and happiness.*
*No stress.*
*One life I have,*
*One body, mind, soul.*
*Intoxicating and trepidatious,*
*This sense of control.*
*Being single means taking FULL responsibility,*
*For choices, moods, and habits,*
*And yes destiny.*
*Things I'd abdicated,*
*Left untended on the vine,*
*Now I'm weeding, pruning, fertilizing*
*To brew the sweetest wine.*
*It's interesting the fairy tale always ends when damsel gets the prince.*
*Because he's always touted as the answer,*

*Heaven sent.*

*But it's really cool to take the throne*

*And do most things on my own,*

*To bask in my unfettered zone,*

*And reach inward my dreams entone.*

*So grateful, I now close my eyes*

*My dreams await like lullabies.*

*Happy V day to me.*

Then the winter storm happened. It was scary, traumatic, unprecedented. It was a Covid like experience. It came with little warning, isolating everyone, making them feel helpless and unprepared.

As we were storm prepping, my phone rang. It was Gatzby. I was expecting RJ, although we'd already talked that day and on Valentines.

Gatzby was checking on me in more ways than one. He was concerned about my preparation for the storm. Sweet or Opportunistic? He was also checking on my status and specifically asked if I was sleeping with anyone. He never had done that before when we were separated. I didn't lie. He was not happy.

I felt a lot of emotions.

Nonchalance. His behavior had led to us splitting, so he earned whatever happened next.

Surprise- I actually hadn't expected to hear from him again.

Relief- he was healthy and safe.

And confusion- Why was he still calling me? Why was I still picking up?

I'd started dating again because being 50 and single did get to me some days. I was looking for that last date, last kiss, last sexual partner for life. Stability.

And Gatzby just kept showing up.

Did that mean it was supposed to be him? That we were supposed to work things out? Was Gatzby's strategy of giving me time to cool down and then calling in a moment of crisis a sound idea? Would it work this time? Did I even want it to work?

Before, I had always walked away and not looked back, even if we remained friends, like Harlee and JJ and The Poet. We said our hi's and byes and kept it moving, but Gatzby was different. The chemistry was deeper.

**Why?**

Our interaction was the textbook definition of it's complicated. And I hated that one call from him made my simple life complicated. It made me wonder AGAIN if somehow I was addicted to the drama- the highs and lows, the unpredictability. Our interactions were never routine, never boring. Could that be the draw?

And there was also so much history. A call from him brought to mind him checking on me during Harvey, but also the fence, his care for me as my mom declined, but also my birthday when we never went out, and he ended up dropping my gifts in my mailbox, the amazing sex, and his refusal to let me see his place. For every HIGH, there was such a devastating LOW. He seemed to be able to forgive me and move forward in a way I could not. Kaye said it was because I was a Virgo, and Gatzby had committed the three unpardonable sins in a Virgo's eyes: fucking with our schedule, making us doubt our decisions, and making us feel we trusted the wrong person.

Part of me said he was a "good guy," and other women wouldn't have the hang-ups I did with him. The other part of me said he was an undependable workaholic with too many secrets and too many friends/family depending on him, and other women would have never stuck around as long as I did.

I loved him. I hated him. Nope, I absolutely did not hate him. If I had, I would have moved on long ago. I think part of the dilemma was I had no name for what I felt for him: the limbo, Twilight Zone, not yet awake, not asleep either zone we occupied, like our spirits, souls, and bodies connected, but our hearts and minds repelled each other.

At one time, I'd even researched twin flames and karmic soul mates just trying to figure this shit out. How could one man alternately make me feel like the luckiest girl in the world and the most conflicted?

And it had nothing to do with him being my FWB. I hadn't felt this way about any of my other FWB's.

No, this was a situation unique to Gatzby. His calling felt both right and wrong. When I had called him after my break-up with The Muse, he had called it the "lovely dreaded call." He'd talked about telling himself that we would just talk, nothing else, and then seeing my smile. He called it the - oh the things I will do to you- smile. Lol. It sounded like a Dr. Seuss title. Then he said that I would come close, smiling bigger, and one kiss would turn into twenty, a thousand, infinity, and we would talk…. after we made love.

He was good at asking questions that made me think I'd missed something, misread something, not seen what we could be. When he talked, new worlds appeared before my eyes, worlds of us and eternity. It was beautiful captivating. I should have nicknamed him The Hypnotist.

Leaving his presence sometimes felt like waking up out of a trance. It was relaxing as hell, but how do you get close to a person like that? How do you love him or trust him when you don't even trust the ground under your feet when he's near?

That first kiss years ago had buckled my knees, and he had caught me, held me, stared into my eyes. I think a part of me got lost in that embrace that day, and I never got her back.

At the end of the day, thinking about Gatzby and our on-again, off-again, Twilight Zone love affair just made me tired.

I ended the call, but I didn't shut the door behind me. It was cracked, and he knew it. Maybe it was because I didn't have the mental or emotional energy to deal with him and the physical ice storm on its way. Maybe because, like the time before, I still felt he owed me for all the disappointments that I'd suffered because of him. Maybe I felt I still owed him.

Maybe I was worried no one was coming, that time was running out to find love. Maybe I believed, deep down, eventually, he would Urkel me ("I'm wearing you down, baby.") into a relationship, not a three-month one like before, but one for life.

This was year six of dating. I was heading into triple digit outings. How much longer could I do this? How much longer would I want to? How much longer would I want to date RJ before I wanted more? Could I truly be content being his "boo" forever?

I ended the call because I didn't want to argue or rehash the past, and I'd fully answered his questions about how and when in a way that angered him more. He hated that RJ had gotten a hotel, something Gatzby had said often he would do, something he said he hadn't done in the 14 years he'd lived in Houston, something he hadn't even done with his ex-wife, but he planned to do with me.

That stung. He always had this way of making me feel like I had hit him below the belt, stolen something from him that he really wanted, needed, and had earned. I didn't want to be that person who did things like that.

He went on to say I should have waited for him to make good on our overnight trip and claimed that had been his plan all along for my birthday.

Bringing up my birthday was not smart. I went from feeling guilty and sorry for him to feeling absolutely justified. RJ didn't make me wait. I didn't have to beg him for the attention, the gifts. And NONE of this was about GATZBY and me at all. Not one bit.

That tiny getaway was my gift from a man who didn't need a title to feel comfortable taking me on dates or renting a room. I was enough, more than enough for him to want to spoil me.

I started off the next week feeling out of sorts like my brain was still lagging in last week trying to process the hours of cold, no electricity, the ice and snow for days, the crazy call from Gatzby. I journaled, wrote poetry, danced to the drums and flute, did Qigong and hydrated, cleaned up, and hiked. It took weeks to feel normal.

## March 2021

March 2021 was busy. I recorded a whopping seven podcasts, guested on four shows, performed at a new nightclub, and did three Zennurgize Your Life workshops. I was getting glowing reviews, like this one from *Shanta Powell,* "Zen Ase dropped this gem for me 😁 😁. This is an EXCELLENT podcast that gives great perspective on setting boundaries and why BOUNDARIES ARE A FORM OF SELF-LOVE AND CARE. I highly recommend listening to her either on your commute to work, working out, or doing chores around the house 😊."

I was exhausted, but feeling really powerful.

## Sleeping Women Rise

*I took a nap today, but it wasn't long enough.*
*I wanna sleep so long, Rip Van Winkle's stumped*
*Won't toss and turn,*
*Rumple the sheets,*
*But float and flex and melt so deep,*
*Into slumber,*
*I find myself,*
*The version, gone, left on a shelf.*
*The one so fearless, bold and mighty,*
*Strong and supple Aphrodite,*
*The one, comprising uncut will,*
*Who'd never bent, unbroken still.*
*The one with stars, and rose colored glasses,*
*Hopeful, tactless, not for the masses.*
*I've tempered her.*
*Made her voice nil.*
*But at 50, I'm lonely for her for real.*
*There's a love I desire, no testosterone,*
*She pulls me, seductive pheromones.*
*I wanna sleep so long, I meet her in my dreams.*

*My memories feel like wakeful scenes*
*I want to sleep so long… when I awake,*
*All those who knew me do double takes,*
*For I wake with a mindset, a stance, a style,*
*Where the new joins the old, renaissance WILD*
*So don't be surprised if one day you see*
*me*
*Benjamin Button majestically,*
*Shake off years like snakeskin,*
*Arise renewed.*
*Emerge like a butterfly from a cocoon.*
*We grow older and wiser, but along the way,*
*Some of US gets lost, but I say NAY!*
*I'm gonna sleep till I meet her in bed.*
*And we join in rhythms in my head.*
*And we meld in my heart, a syncopated song,*
*And my muscles drink in her all night long.*
*And the marrow in my bones infuses with flare*
*her rhythmic interludes undulate there.*
*And my style grows younger, younger still.*
*I wear bolder earrings, higher heels.*
*And drink deep of the draught of Nut on old,*
*The Metu Neter shall unfold.*
*A reincarnation never seen,*
*From crone to maiden.*
*Evergreen.*
*Sleeping women AND MEN, RISE!*

Writing Zennurgize Your Life Volume 1[13] had made me delve into my past. Memories were still swirling, thinking of who I'd been, how I became who I now was. Getting on a mic every weekend ( sometimes more often than that) and talking about principles of self-development led to more introspection than I'd ever done. And I had probably done more than most, and it was so strange being this person, talking so openly about the past, the present, the goals for the future.

I was an introvert.

I used to have social anxiety as a teen.

I literally would never make eye contact. I would rehearse greetings, good morning, afternoon, evening, how are you, remember to say thanks for asking, ask about their family or something.

Saying good morning when it should've been good afternoon left me mortified.

It took years and pretty much developing an alter ego as a spoken word artist to bring me out of that.

Speaking to strangers is very difficult for some people. Speaking to people we know but aren't close to is less difficult but not easy. Speaking to people is STILL something I have to remind myself to do, and if I'm stressed that day, it's almost definitely not gonna be done.

Being social is classified by many as politeness without realizing for others being polite has nothing to do with how or why they do or don't speak.

---

13 https://www.amazon.com/Zennurgize-Your-Life-Zen-Ase/dp/B09MYXXCD2

And many of us introverts and former introverts KNOW you think we're rude, but that is FAR PREFERABLE to worrying about you thinking us WEIRD or AWKWARD.

Podcasting, journaling, doing the workshops was a form of awakening for me. I did a podcast on that topic. But it went much deeper than one broadcast.

Awakening. Being woke. Wokeness. We use these terms to mean so many things. Some philosophers say most people sleep through their lives. The 5 percenters say 15% of the world is trying to deceive 80% of the world, and only 5% see the world as it really is. Those 5% are awake and have a duty to awaken others.

The Bible says, "awaken thou who slumbers." It talks about having eyes but seeing not, having ears but hearing not. And it says revelation is divine.

I wake up with mini awakenings. Epiphanies. Revelations. Some become poems. Some become designs for merch or products. Some change the decisions I'm making.

My awakening in March was how much I'd lived in fear. Once upon a time, I feared writing like this, having a show like I had where I discussed a topic like awakening.

I was raised there's only one type of awakening, accepting Christ. I no longer believe that. Still, it's hard to deny there are many who believe people awake in only one way. And those people judge others- harshly.

I decided life is to be explored. Perspectives are to be considered. And that I want to be continuously and progressively awakened.

Some call this raising your vibration or ascending, or just plain growth.

Anyway, I believe it's one of the purposes of life.

## The End All and Be All

*Wanna let my thoughts drift just a little,*
*Emotions crest, shift, and just settle.*
*Life, turbulent but unforgettable,*
*has definitely been my lot.*
*Wanna breathe deep, stretch, massage my bones.*
*Oil, lotion, fingers,*
*Touch alone is sensual, needed*
*Is a home*
*that grounds me to my cornerstones.*
*Wanna dance to music, light a wick,*
*Stare in space for just a bit,*
*Journal, question and reflect*
*Till all is calm in me.*
*2021 has been a beast.*
*New challenges bring new release.*
*Family. Environment. Health. Increase.*
*Weather and stress, a search for peace.*
*Darkness then light,*
*Now harvest season,*
*All the past erupts, no reason.*

*Seeds sown years ago have spread,*
*Blossomed, festooned, don't fear to tread.*
*The jungle looms, vibrant and red,*
*But I machete hold.*
*Fearless I be,*
*Secure you see,*
*I know the WHO that you call me,*
*I know the WHAT I choose to be,*
*I know the WHY that's driving me.*
*Then WHEN and HOW, that's not my job.*
*My pulse*
*I listen, hear it throb.*
*I move, synchronous, on top.*
*Nothing will subjugate.*
*Wanna let my thoughts swirl in the ether,*
*Breathe in, join with other seekers,*
*My body, just a Travel Keeper,*
*Storing all within.*
*Life IS. It's true.*
*Is many hued.*
*Is multitudes*
*unfolding interludes..*
*Like music rich, like flavors strong,*
*Like sex, a rapture- hours long.*
*Like nature, a peacock, feathers shown.*

*Love IS. It's true.*

*Is pain and lift.*

*Is growth and death*

*Allegiance shifts.*

*2021 has been a beast.*

*But I choose life, love and PEACE.*

*I choose full expression, RELEASE.*

*I AM. This IS.*

*That's All.*

I am. The two most powerful words in the English language. But only if they are used correctly. "I am creative."- correct.

"I am unemployed." Problematic. You are probably employed in a side hustle or a job search, so saying “I am unemployed” can actually reinforce what you don't want. "I am pursuing new job opportunities" would be much more empowering and just as true.

Then there are statements like, "I am not the kind of woman who approaches a man.' This statement is even worse than the first example. It's a statement tied to identity, which could also position the speaker as being "right" and others as being "wrong" and thus cause her to judge and separate from other women.

What happens if this woman decides she wants to change? She may feel great inner conflict. Identity conflict. And there's no need for it.

What we do is not who we are.

It's a choice. When she became a woman, that behavior did not come with her womanhood.

It would be more empowering to say, "I am appropriate. I am guided." Then if she felt it was appropriate or she felt guided to shoot her shot, she would. That's how Ruth got Boaz. 😊

## Magic

*It's not good man is alone;*
*he needs someone to share his throne.*
*This no tale of rib stealing be,*
*And to some it might be blasphemy,*

*But a man is pure magic,*
*Masterfully*
*woven into skin.*

*He walks in purpose, confident; bold*
*Broad shoulders, troubles built to hold.*
*His gray hairs speak of wisdom older*
*than his years.*

*He listens, patient, supports with ease,*
*Takes calloused hands to carefully knead,*
*A shoulder, back, legs, sometimes feet.*
*He buys a meal or two.*

*He sees through bullshit,*
*Sets it straight,*
*Takes away the need to masturbate,*

*Makes sure to take off of my plate,*

*What he can safely hold.*

*I exhale deep when he is near.*
*Love his laugh, his glance,*
*Deep and sincere.*

*The bass that ripples strong and clear,*
*Like fine wine is he.*

*I play in his beard, lie on his chest,*
*Spoon skin to skin,*
*So deeply rest,*
*I wake renewed and so refreshed,*

*The fountain of youth I call our sex.*

*I feel ageless, matchless,*
*breathe in deep,*
*Throw back my head, and grip the sheets,*
*Arch, grind in time as he thrusts deep.*

*The earthquake he caused wanes.*

*He is magic three times I've said,*
*Short, tall, thick, thin, black or caramel red,*
*Gentleman hood, spit game so deft,*
*I poet tonguetied be.*

*I walk down memory lane tonight.*
*Grateful, paying homage rightly*
*earned,*
*Deserved*
*though I may be*
*as single*
*as a Soul can be...*
*My memories are bold and free.*

*And full, so full of*

*MAGIC.*

## April 2021

April 2021 was busy. I recorded five podcasts, guested on two shows, vended, and did a workshop at the Harriet Tubman Wellness Day at The Shrine.

Zennurgy had its biggest month of downloads ever‼ 6 new cities and 3 new countries. 42 cities and 11 countries were now subscribing. And Zennurgy had ALL 5 star reviews.

Every day that passed, I talked to either Breath, San Antonio or RJ. Gatzby and I were talking too until I said something that pissed him off, and he said he was over me and lost all feelings for me.

We'd argued about my birthday, his intentions, my reactions, my standards, and my preference AGAIN. Rehashing the past again.

But why?

I remembered feeling exasperated, tired of justifying myself. I remember feeling like all his complaints were just typically chauvinist reactions that I'd seen one too many times, heard one too many times, tirades I was sick of. And I wrote this:

## Make DATING Great Again

*I never was sensitive before you see,*
*But 50 years defeats the stoic in me*
*Too many deaths, too many trials,*
*Too many heartbreaks while I smiled.*
*Too much pushing higher still,*
*Through gritted teeth and by sheer will.*
*Too many years of doing it all,.*
*Single motherhood takes its toll.*
*Too many years on the back shelf,*
*Now I'm front, how does this feel?*
*Criticized in both positions,*
*Neither right as others mention.*
*The bar rising incessantly.*
*Be better, stronger, faster,*
*Leap*
*Over tall buildings in one bound.*
*Display that S, and never frown.*
*Because while you shine, no man can see*

*That anger bubbles strong and deep.*
*Keep your list small.*
***No preferences at all.***
*You're past your prime,*
*Invisible.*
*You better be grateful,*
*Feminine. Pleasant. Cool.*
*Fun. A great cook. Ass that's full.*
*Big breasts. Soft voice.*
*A masseuse no less.*
*No drama, never bring him stress.*
*A sex kitten, but on the fly*
*a shoulder on which he relies.*
*No kids. That makes you worth much less.*
*No debts. Be independent but silent.*
*No scars, no baggage. No sign you see that*
*You've lost one inch of ecstasy*
*In love, in men, in hope, in prayer.*
*No sign for another man you've cared.*
*I hear the complaints, read them online.*
*The woman that's desired- fine.*
*Not "run through," virginal?*
*But not a prude, versatile.*
*We're told we're picky,*
*Cannot see how grateful we should really be.*

*Just "average" or worse "overweight"*
*Not "high value," our mistake,*
*We think we're something, cannot see*
*Men don't value what we be.*
*They want the 50s not modern women,*
*for grandma they yearn.*
*The home-cooked meals, sex and silence.*
*The spotless house, his word is binding.*
*They want the throne but not the sword.*
*Adoration, admiration, no discord.*
*They want patriarchy 101,*
*A world where women's lib is done.*
*No criticism, just praise.*
*Nostalgia for the by gone days.*
*Make dating great their unvoiced cry.*
*When was it great? our sole reply.*
*When we were chattel with dowries?*
*When we were voteless on our knees?*
*When we made half on every check?*
*When sexual harassment bloomed unchecked?*
*Abortion was illegal?*
*Birth control only thought?*
*When we were like big children,*
*our voices unsought?*
*I'm Zen, but sometimes rage within*

*At the arrogance rampant among men.*

*Mansplain to me, once again,*

*And watch my smile thin and rescind.*

*Not all are bad, I've found a few.*

*A Breath fresh air, New avenue.*

*But the south, it seems to me,*

*Is stuck in patterns of inequality.*

*And those patterns like yokes are placed on me.*

*I'm not cattle, can't you see?*

Preferences was the word of the month, all over my radar. I couldn't escape it. One man told me it was a red flag I'd been married twice. He was the same age as I was but had never been married. In my mind, I dodged a bullet.

He had no idea of what it took to make the marriages I was in last 17 years total. In fact, he'd never had a relationship longer than 3 years, but he felt he had the right to judge.

I thanked my lucky stars and moved on. He was entitled to his preferences.

I wondered if people like him ever consider the other side. What being married and divorced can tell you is-

1. That person can fully commit
2. That person thinks long term
3. That person believes in investing in someone else
4. That person also knows when a situation needs to be ended and can walk away

5. That person knows how to start again, knowing exactly how difficult the process can be
6. That person has also been judged marriage worthy twice

And someone who has never been married demonstrates none of that. They want the benefit of the doubt that they can do all of the above, but some are not willing to give that same benefit of the doubt to others. Hmmm.

On social media, I'd seen men complain that women want an established 6-foot man with bad boy swag, conversation, and sexual prowess. I'd seen women complain that men want a coke bottle Tabitha Brown (personality, cooking), who has sex like a porn star but is almost a virgin.

So should these people

1. Accept the opposite sex has preferences they may not fit
2. Try to change what is changeable to meet these preferences
3. Evaluate and possibly change their own standards
4. Stop caring about these expectations altogether
5. All of the above

Why do men/women like/date X type?

1. Because they can
2. Because of that person's confidence/strength/sex appeal
3. Because that person feeds their ego
4. Because that's always been their fantasy
6. Because they're rebelling against societal norms
7. Because of chemistry or pheromones or the person's reputation
8. Because of the person's lifestyle/assets/achievements

9. Because the person convinced them or stimulates them
10. Because the person makes them feel comfortable/reflects the environment they know
11. Because the person matches their self-esteem and vibration

    ETC‼

I concluded that anyone not in that relationship or situationship does not know why. Also, it's not an outsider's business to know why.

Curiosity is human nature. But stating as fact that all men/women pursue X type of person for only one reason or that all men/women overlook Y type of person for one reason is illogical. There are as many reasons for attraction and involvement as there are people.

Part of maturity is seeing the world as it is and not whining because it's not as one feels it should be. That was something I told myself. Except for the occasional rant poem, I felt I did pretty well in that area. I'd accepted no one owed me their interest, time, or an opportunity; neither did I owe that to anyone.

Each person has a right to his/her standards and preferences. They didn't have to make sense to me.

I'd had 2 husbands. 4 boyfriends and only spent 5 years of my life single since the age of 18. I now was 50. That was 27 years of committed relationships.

So I definitely believed in monogamy, but dating, with all its frustrations, had allowed me to explore more sides of myself and get different things from different people.

Intellectual stimulation, romance, decency, and sexual attraction were all high on my list, but some guys had one and not the other. And some of the most compatible people I'd met in personality were the most incompatible in lifestyle.

It seemed there was a cost to everything: relationships/ singleness; abstinence/sexual activity

The cost I was willing to pay varied- depending on my current priorities and needs.

The one thing I felt I needed that I didn't have was a committed relationship. I knew it would cost me cutting off my romantic connections, but I was willing to do that for the right person.

Although I looked for ways to build with any person I was spending time with, physically or just over the phone, ways for me to enhance him, there was something about knowing that forever was in the cards that still called me.

But I had my preferences:

What loving me the way I want to be loved DOES NOT look like-

1. Just being a good man
2. Being a constant homebody
3. Wanting me to stay the same
4. Being distant and unaffectionate
5. Having little to no sex
6. Ignoring special days
7. Little quality time

What loving me right does look like and what I absolutely planned to reciprocate

1. Chemistry, compatibility, and great conversation- being the right person for me
2. Planning outings, having a stimulating life of art, and other activities
3. Pushing for personal and relationship growth
4. Close and intimate relationship with lots of touching
5. great and plentiful sex
6. Making special days memorable
7. Quality time

I wouldn't settle for the former. Singleness was preferable to it.

## Date Ninety-Eight:

Pores -We talked. We vibed. We met. He had the sweatiest hands I'd ever felt. The vibe was over. But he's married now.

## Date Ninety-Nine:

Water -We talked. We vibed. We met at a Mexican restaurant that he had picked because they had live music that night. He ate nothing, drank nothing but water, and said that he didn't eat or drink in restaurants at all. He just went there for the vibe, the music; he didn't trust the kitchens, the cooks, didn't know what was going into his food. His reasoning was kinda flawed to me. He could have said the same thing about the grocery store. In fact, he could have his own garden or raise and slaughter his own cattle and not know what was in the soil, the rain that fell on the soil, the air that the plants and animals breathed in that became part of their cells. He didn't like me pointing any of that out. Vibe ended.

I started therapy again in April. I'd been sad on and off since Easter. It was mostly related to my mom. My whole life, she'd wanted me to start a business, businesses. I wasn't ready- at all. I hadn't found the me that could be that person. And now that me was here, but she was not. I was grateful she saw my first year in business. Yet I still wished I had learned more from her. But I knew I needed to be divorced, for my kids to be grown, for me to start the process of recreating myself.

It still made me sad.

*Some say it comes in cycles,*

*Like items in a cue.*

*Triggered by almost anything,*

*Something old, deja vu.*

*They say time heals all wounds,*

*I wonder about that.*

*How much time it takes to not be floored*

*by grief's impact.*

*They say it teaches patience,*

*Forgiveness, valuing life more.*

*I say maybe that is true if one can get*

*up off the floor.*

*I say it leaves one stymied,*

*Tongue tiedness on display.*

*And causes embarrassment,*

*Years gone, yet healing delayed.*

*They say it makes one wiser,*

*In tune with the divine.*

*I say it's at grief's hands I almost lost my mind.*

*They say it's for the best;*

*They're in a better place.*

*I say we're all connected and there is no*

*Other space.*

*Grief.*

*It lays one bare,.*

*Defenseless, no reprieve,*

*The only thing I've found is prayer, breath, nature, sometimes sleep,*

*Meditation, exercise,*

*Journal time or two.*

*Just close your eyes, fantasize*

*Dream they're here with you.*

*One day you move beyond tears,*

*They just remain unshed*

*The space inside your ribs feels raw, ripped open,*

*Bleeding red.*

*And yet you do not say it,*
*You've long put away your black.*
*You've gone to work already*
*Everyone feels you've bounced back.*
*I understand Victoria, England's longest queen,*
*She ritualized her grief so everyone could see*
*The Shah that built the Taj Mahal too appears to say.*
*There is no moving on, not really,*
*Just motions you display.*
*You eat, and work and sleep and talk*
*Finish goals, it's true.*
*But the spectre lurks unseen*
*Just slightly out of view.*
*I've stopped expecting it to vanish,*
*Go for good as one might say.*
*Grief, I no longer fight you.*
*Just another emotion, I display.*
*Grief has left me changed.*
*That's okay, it's true.*
*It just proves that I love deep and thorough.*
*It proves that Me merged with You.*

## May 2021

I found a new therapist, a blessing, the best one I'd ever had. She asked me why I was in her office. I said grief. She said, who've you lost, and I listed, and ended with, "I think this is mostly about my mom though. I can't celebrate the holidays anymore. She was the only religious one left in our family. The days seem hollow."

She listened and questioned me deeper than anyone ever had. I was used to thinking, but now I was examining, pondering, musing, and she assigned books for homework, one a week. Seven books in seven weeks. I read them all, but the first three were a blur. I remember reading them, but not their titles, not because they bored me or were useless. I was just distracted.

I suddenly sympathized with my students in a way I had never had before. I'd never read a book and immediately forgot what it was about. It was as lost to me as if you had asked me what I ate for breakfast last Wednesday. Food.

I'd read words, a book of them, and I retained nothing. It was quite astonishing.

My therapist asked what I knew about the stages of grief. I said, "Denial, Bargaining, Anger, Acceptance."

"You're missing some."

"Ok."

"First comes shock. From what you told me, I think you spent about a year there."

"A year?"

"Uh-huh. And you flew through denial and bargaining. Did you feel anger two years ago?"

"No."

"Are you angry now?"

"Yes. A lot. I'm angry with the stupidity at pointless work meetings. I'm angry my son hasn't moved out yet. I'm angry with

Gatzby. He's never effectively planned anything, always wants to 'go with the flow and let things develop organically.' 'Too much' thought and discussion is 'making things complicated,' micromanaging, a sign of a control freak, which is what he calls me. He says I interrogate him and make him want to do nothing. He says planning sucks all the fun from dating, and he just feels judged."

"How do you feel?"

"I don't plan everything. I do like some surprises. But everything in my life has a purpose, a role. Time and effort are my most valuable possessions, and the idea of wasting either is unacceptable. Too little thought is recklessness, indecision, and disorganization. I feel insecure and directionless without clear answers to my questions. I can't relax. It's one reason I've said he and I shouldn't date. But people say opposites attract. So I've tried to compromise and work on our communication, but the situation makes me so angry."

I pulled out my phone and read the poem I'd written about the fight.

*I made it to 2020 never hearing*

*You're tripping, slipping, flipping out over inconsequential nothing*

*After all, I've always been the measured one, controlled, unflappable.*

*Who knew condescension was one of my triggers*

*Time- it changes us all.*

*You blame my words, my feelings*
*On a bag lady stored within*
*Because you want to, need to*
*Neutralize my accusations*
*You call my statements sensitivity.*
*I'm an artist*
*What the fuck did you expect?*
*But I'm human too, marred, imperfect.*
*Get a blow up doll if you want perfection .*
*Me- I'm real. I'm honest and I'm smart.*
*Out of the abundance of the heart, the mouth speaks.*
*And yours spoke callously.*
*So I'm re-evaluating who I thought you were; who I thought we could be.*
*Because suddenly, I see myself as china.*
*And you,*
*You're the bull*

"So you feel breakable around him?"

"Yes, but he always acts like I'm the one with no feelings. It makes me so mad."

"We have to wrap up today's session," MC said. "But I want you to write about what else makes you mad. It's part of your grief process. People think the anger part of grieving is about being mad at the person, but it can manifest in being mad the sun is shining, that people are loud, that God let this happen. Anger can manifest in a multitude of ways. And I want you to read The Energy Bus. Decide who's driving your bus, who the passengers are, and if you need to ask some riders/drivers to get off your bus. See you next week."

The Energy Bus. It sounded interesting.

It was interesting and very helpful.

And just a minute to ponder what I was angry about produced this:

## Date One-Hundred:

### Boy Toy

*I didn't ask how old he was,*
*He was old enough; that's true.*
*We chatted a little while online,*
*Exchanged numbers, called in a few.*
*The convo was fun and flirty,*
*Pure stimulation.*
*He had my imagination workin'*
*Wondering what would come.*
*We sat on the patio to not have to shout.*
*The convo wasn't quite the same,*
*He was starting to dick about.*

*Being a little demanding,*
*Sometimes even rambling,*
*Asking pointed questions - boxes*

*That I didn't want to fit in.*
*I started to excuse myself,*
*The fun was gone, you see,*
*In fact I felt he was immature, and*
*I couldn't be ME.*

*I walked away a little confused,*
*Thought things would go better than this.*
*I didn't get what I wanted,*
*not even one passionate kiss.*

*But luckily I wasted few hours,*
*Not much time, in fact,*
*Between the texts and phone calls*
*And the face to face contact.*

*I crawled in bed alone and slept,*
*My dreams a mess of quirks.*
*I woke up feeling out of sorts.*
*Disoriented at first.*
*I thought back over the night,*
*Ruminating.*
*And although I cannot say his stage,*
*That decade plus difference was the demon.*
*the date wouldn't have happened*
*Like that with a man my age.*
*It was all fumbles and clumsiness and*
*Cockiness misplayed..*

*The men my age seem jaded, bored, inactive and entitled.*

*But this younger guy was just as troublesome,*
*Unskilled and unbridled.*
*He couldn't dance the dance of love that moves in rhythmic beats,*
*Where you feel the vibe, react in kind and*
*Become one in your heart and your speed.*

*He was bold when he should've been silent*
*Coy when he should have spoke up.*
*He strangled dead my interest,*
*Till I had had enough.*

*So back to the drawing board I go,*
*Back to step one again.*

*Singleness sucks.*
*But it's a new day, I shrug and grab my pen.*

In therapy, we'd talked about the first two stages of grief.

1. Shock and Denial
2. Pain and Guilt.

I'd felt so much shock, pain, and guilt; I'd been in therapy for almost a year.

*Part of me lost in the past-*
*flashbacks of what used to be.*

*PTSD holding me*
*Inner critic scolding me.*
*Tired, lost, not insecure,*
*Grab the reigns and detour,*
*Flash forward present now endure,*
*There's pain there too you see.*
*Grasp the future, walk around,*
*See the details, write them down.*
*My destiny I now have found*
*Unfolds inside of me.*
*I travel daily back and forth.*
*Past, present, future,*
*Circle course.*
*Sometimes exhausting,*
*Sometimes I'm forced*
*to*
*Anchor here and now.*
*So if I drift*
*please do excuse,*
*I time travel ,*
*Time I lose.*
*I get lost in my own musings*
*Introvert you see*
*Maybe a legacy of stress,*
*Of disassociating from unrest.*

*Of seeking always bliss and rest*
*Respite, for pain to cease*
*"What are you thinking?" I get asked.*
*I'm stumped, no reply,*
*I wear a mask.*
*I was lost -present/future/past*
*Doesn't make sense, I think.*
*But it is true,*
*Hard to explain,*
*A seer, prophetess, time's a chain*
*I travel like a circuit,*
*Brain*
*Can slip stream in a second.*
*I walk 'tween worlds*
*Cuz I can see the past/present/future all clearly.*
*Like mirrors of reality.*
*Like differing versions, all of me.*
*The Twilight Zone is real you see.*
*I live it,*
*frequently.*
*I feel it,*
*Daily.*

3. Anger and bargaining was supposed to be next. And that's where I seemed to be now. Angry, and bargaining with Gatzby, not wanting to lose another person, trying to forgive and make peace.

May 1st he'd texted apologizing for saying he "had no feelings for me and was done with me." He said he didn't want that to be the last thing we said to each other. I'd replied with "yes."

Yes? What the hell did that mean?

I texted him back on the 2nd and said I'd felt cheated. Nothing turned out like I expected it to. My

job, my kids, my marriages, dating. I wanted the image I saw in my head, and the older I got the more unattainable it was. I'd made peace with my two divorces, neither of my kids graduating a four-year college ( Joe did have three certifications. Elijah was back in college.), being a grandma three times by age 50, and losing all my elders. I was excited about leaving education in 2025 for the new career I was building. But my romantic life was the one place I was still angry and grieving. Usually, I would have said I'd put up with/tolerated a lot from him and felt frustrated, annoyed, disappointed. But that day, I wrote I'd **invested** a lot in us, and I still didn't know how I felt about that.

But as I put down the phone, I realized my word choice had changed. Tolerated was a victim's word. Invested meant I chose. That small change made me smile. It made me proud. It reminded me I hadn't lost the ability to hope, to try, to give.

At one time, I thought I might lose hope in love, the desire to try for love. I'd wanted this image I saw in my head. Sometimes that was an image society put there. I lived a different life than the one I'd imagined for years, the one I'd imagined all my life. But this discrepancy wasn't actually bad. Nothing was what I planned. But I had an amazing life.

I was employed, healthy, active, loved. I was tired of being angry about the past. I remembered once hearing that stoics felt there were only two types of emotions- useful and useless. And suddenly, the anger felt useless.

Then there was the disappointment in the present. That felt useless too.

Now gratitude was useful. Love, absolutely useful. I could love the life I have. It wasn't worse than the one I imagined. It was just different.

And for the first time in my life, I thought that ALL those differences might be a blessing.

My life might even become better than I imagined. But only if I stopped being angry, disappointed, and scared.

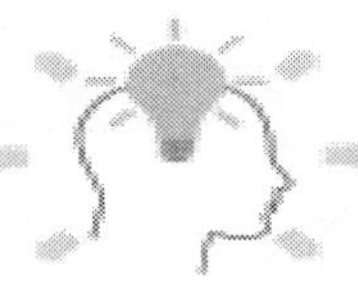

**Lesson 25:**

Let your longings lift you rather than being weights to the past.

# CHAPTER 26

# *Yearning*

## *May 2021*

May is in two chapters, 25 and 26, because there was the before and the after. Therapy is this thing, like leaving the safety of the shore on ice skates, and the ice seems rock solid right near the edge, but the further you go, the blacker it gets. You don't even realize how dark and murky and cold that lake is till you hear the ice crack, and you realize you can literally get sucked under. Forever.

Dramatic. I know. But it felt that way sometimes. So I was tender in May, inside myself and with others. Gentle. Soft. Yielding. Questioning everyone and everything. Seeking. Finding. Seeking again. And to me it was no wonder that May was the month my sons had been born 26 years before and the month my mom had transitioned two years before. It was a 30 day reminder of the cycle of birth and death, beginning and ending.

## Becoming

*As I almost sleep, as I almost dream,*
*I fling soul outward from its fleshly seams.*
*Eyes closed. I drift, yet feel at one*
*with past with future*
*My being comes.*
*Gone limits*
*Gone time.*
*Gone flaws.*
...
*Divine I feel.*
*Connected too.*
*The beat of the Earth*
*My breath renews.*
*Breathe deep,*
*I dance.*
*Inside I sing*
*Erotic uplift.*
*I love being.*
*I love its breath and depth and swag.*
*Unlike ego, no need to brag.*
*I love its float and poise and ING*
*It's timeless. No end, no beginning.*
*Awakened by art or breath or sex*
*Or anytime the mind will rest,*
*Lonely no more, now at peace.*
*Meditation or day dream, soul release.*

*In that clear state it seems to me,*
*I become enlightened momentarily.*
*I accept what is, feel peace that lasts.*
*Feel immersed in the flow*
*Limits blasted.*
*I am love, peace, choice.*
*I am all things.*
*The all, the one, the source,*
*Nothing*
*And yet something.*
*I can feel the oneness and so much more.*
*Love, inspiration galore.*

*As I almost sleep, as I almost dream,*
*I become much more than what I seem*

*Now let's wake and*
*Become the dream.*

April was Easter. May is Mother's Day. I cried the day before Mother's Day, all day. So Mother's Day was good, so much to be grateful for. So many memories. So much invested that continues to pay results. Motherhood is so many things. Being a daughter is so much too. I think about my mom constantly, and so much of what I do is in memory of her and represents her. I re-read this journal from 2020, "This will be my first mother's day without my mom. She would be proud of me. A new grandbaby, healthy and strong. My son back working on his college degree in business (she would love that). She wanted all of us to be entrepreneurs. My sister found eight DBAs going through my mom's things. There was probably nothing legal my mom hadn't sold.

And she was involved in community activism, always giving. So I know she would be proud of my stores, my websites, my following, and my work with 100,000 Poets for Change.

She would be proud of me shining light on the good things going on worldwide and locally with #creativescombatingcorona and #ihealwithart

As I type, and I cry. I know that everything I do is so much bigger than likes or dollar signs. It's about legacy. It's about carrying the torch.

To whom much is given, much is required. And my mom damn sure gave it her best. So I can do nothing less."

I performed and vended on Mother's Day to a sold-out crowd, vended at a Business Expo the next Saturday, performed and did a workshop for 218 sorority sisters, and guested on a radio show, and of course, podcasted and watched the downloads grow.

I took off work on May 12th to meet with a contractor. One day my home will have no scars from the storms it's been through.

I hope to say the same for my mind and heart. I still dealt with flashbacks of my mom's battle with her critical illness, my son's car accident, and the other one's harrowing recovery from being shot. Too many deaths. My two divorces. And then just life.

I'd built my life around coping skills, inspiration, and the arts. And according to a few therapists, that was probably why I was still sane and hopeful, and someone else would be crazy and despondent.

But as much as May 12th was a practical break, it was a mental/emotional one too.

# *Dichotomy*

*I'm no gardener, just two plants*
*One needs shade, the other light.*
*But why with humans- more complex*
*So many act like only one way's right?*
*I laugh for I 'member a time*
*That "many" would've been me.*
*Raised to judge, pontificate*
*and condemn unilaterally.*
*Grown so much, no dogmatism,*
*Shed off all restraints- religion.*
*Now my eyes can see,*
*the beauty in the nature of life*
*The symmetry of dichotomy.*
*None to convince.*
*No one to change,*
*Each journey is unique*
*I understand age brings a change, for me*
*45 / 50 - peaks.*
*I shrug and smile,*
*Debate a while, just cuz it's hella fun,*
*And a mind once stretched seldom resets,*
*Its boundaries undone.*

*I love the pure variety*

*of lifestyles and philosophies.*

*It makes life stimulating, sweet*

*An ever unfolding cerebral treat.*

*To those who puff and scoff so sure that*

*No one. .*

*None...*

*It never could ...*

*I say keep living*

*Overstood.*

*Life speaks for itself*

My favorite song of this month was "Jerusalema" featuring Nomcebo. I couldn't understand a word because it is sung in Zulu, but the melody, the melancholy joyfulness spoke to me deeper than words. It felt like it was rejoicing in spite of loss, in spite of pain, in the face of devastation. It felt humble and exultant at the same time, just like me. It was like the ultimate- the devil can't steal my joy tribute.

One man's trash is another man's treasure.

Artists see art everywhere. Optimists can see the good in almost anything. Pessimists see negativity everywhere. Although I'm sure, we all struggle at times, finding joy, beauty, and music in life is one of the gifts of human imagination.

Singleness, loss, stress can be annoying or can be the foundation for one's next creative endeavor. It's all about taking your skills and making something better of what you've been given.

This song was the epitome of a philosophy my mentor taught me- both/and. I'd learned in rhetoric that either/or was a logical fallacy many times. Baba Fana reminded me that life, most times is both/and.

I can want a man to be as established as I am and still build with him.

I can believe in a woman having choice over her own body and believe life is precious.

I can be an independent woman and still recognize there are things I need a man for.

I can be a giver and a receiver.

Conflict is often unnecessarily created when people live by either/or rather than both/and.

In fact, I think it's one of the major sources of conflict worldwide, the source of competition.

If it's either you succeed or I do because there's only one pie and your slice diminishes mine, we become adversaries.

If instead, I see the world as a place where we bring our resources and make as many pies as we need or want, we become partners.

I saw a post quoted from some guy in an interview, "I don't want a woman who wants to be taken care of. I want a hustler like me."

If there ever was a hustler, it's me. But this quote was a HUGE turn off. I couldn't even see going on a second date with a guy who said this. Why? Because I want a man who sees me as both.

If he only thinks in black and white, this or that, that's hella limiting. I can both love being pampered and spoiled AND hustle like a heathen. In fact, the ultimate turn-on would be for him to take care of me after one of those hard hustling days or because of one of those hustles that paid off.

Both / and was leading to more flexibility in my life, in my view of the world, my view of romantic interactions. I'd done a vision board that had eight areas- love and marriage was only one part of this pie. There were seven other parts that had nothing to do with romance. There were finances, career, family, community, knowledge and skill-building, friends, travel, and talents. I could both be single and be completely fulfilled. I could know what I needed and be flexible in how it showed up.

I had been looking for peace, joy, fulfillment, then limiting what I thought would make me feel that way when other things could be equally viable sources. And then I realized that happiness was largely a choice, not based on any THING at all, but a pure decision to react with joy.

It's hard to put into words the kind of shift that was happening in my brain, in my heart, in my soul, in my spirit. But suddenly, a lot of things that had bothered me just didn't seem important anymore.

## June 2021

Father's Day, Summer Solstice, and Summer. I was vending, podcasting, taking two small business classes ( my first ever) through distance learning with University of Houston Clear Lake. I recorded two podcasts, and continued to read books, one a week. I'd decided, unlike 2020 when I'd read 37 books, this year I was reading 52.

I was done with therapy. And happy. Like cloud 9 happy. I'd get texts like, "Good morning, you beautiful sexy deliciously sunshiny mf!"' from RJ.

Gatzby and I talked frequently. Breath was constantly there. In fact, he told me I should blog my journey, this dating, healing journey I'd been on. San Antonio had said that since 2015, but Breath echoing it seemed to make the idea hit even deeper. I was starting to ponder it.

Then I couldn't walk.

I'd been walking miles, and one day the pain in my knee was such that I could only limp. I was glad it was summer. It turned out I had several meniscus tears and arthritis in my knee. I got steroid and cortisol shots and some anti-inflammatory meds. I had to slow down and heal; I think both physically and metaphorically.

I had three men in my life, all friends, all close. Two who lived in Texas. The first was Gatzby; there was a tentativeness in our conversations, a rehashing of old events, a trying to figure out how we got here and why both of us were still here. Why couldn't we just stay away?

And RJ- well, I'm just naturally attracted to men who bring out the best in me. And he did. He was like a good photographer who helped me catch the light and knew all my angles. He was such a good listener, a great sounding board, and knew everything about everything. Literally. Like a walking encyclopedia.

And Breath? He was my sun, moon, and stars, the only man I ever considered moving cross country for (after I retired in 2025). I wanted us to meet and see if we vibed in person like we did on the phone and in video chat. We had literally fallen asleep on the phone together, like high school kids.

I actually think one of the greatest compliments someone can give is, "My life is so much better with you in it." And in June of 2021, I could actually say this about all three.

Gatsby and RJ were two sides of pursuit- one had only wanted a committed relationship; one had never wanted a committed relationship. Pursuit. It was a big word debated in singles' groups. Did men still pursue? My experience? Yes.

Looking back to my twenties, I was proposed to four times, twice by men whose friends knew they were interested in me, and arranged a meeting.

Once by a man who told our coworkers I was his wife so much that I confronted him about it, and we ended up on our first date. We married less than a year later.

The last time by a neighbor who went out of his way to be helpful to me so many times I gave him my number. We married less than a year later.

My point? A man pursuing a woman doesn't always lead to marriage. It never did for me. I don't consider any of my four proposals as coming from men who pursued me. They actually engineered me coming to them. Had I not done so, we would not have been together.

So why does this myth persist that there is only one path to marriage- the path of direct pursuit?

Situationships- people complain about how they're the downfall of committed relationships and marriage. That's so short-sighted to me. For every action, there's a cause. The causes for situationships are broken committed relationships, the fast pace of our society, and social media/dating sites and apps. Complaining about stituationships but not changing any of the causes is like:

Complaining about Kap kneeling but not police brutality and white supremacy

Or complaining about the use of payday loans but not stagnant wages, inflation, and higher cost of living

If people hadn't had their hearts broken, if they believed their partners wouldn't cheat, if they didn't see a smaller return from commitment than being casual- situationships wouldn't exist

So everyone not in one can help by doing the things they should already want to do- treat their partner well, be faithful and work through problems. Maybe then committed relationships will become the norm again.

Once upon a time, society pushed every person to marry and have kids. Then society realized everyone wasn't cut out for parenthood and backed off a little on that.

Will there come a day when society admits everyone wasn't cut out for marriage or even committed relationships?

Do you think we've reached that day?

Would it be a horrible thing to admit this?

I believe women and men need each other. That does not mean I believe every woman or man needs a committed partnership. Men, famous and average, throw around, "You'll die alone" like that's a bad thing.

Marriage can be magical and miserable. Singleness can too. But here's what I've noticed over the last several years.

1. Women almost always outlive men.
2. Women are generally healthier than men as they age and are more likely to be financially stable.

3. The older a woman is, the less likely she is to choose to marry.
4. Some women have chosen to be cougars and pursue men they want for casual short term or long term encounters
5. Stats say women want to marry, raise a family, and then after a certain age, when men are hunting for partners, women don't want to be bothered.

To me, this echoes other trends. Some of us grew up in the church, and now church is unimportant.

Some of us grew up wanting marriage, and now it's something that might be nice but is no priority.

I'm speaking really for those 45 and up. I don't expect younger people to feel this way.

I actually think this is the trend of the future. It's where I am now, but never thought I'd be a decade ago. I actually didn't even know how happy I could be single because I poured all my time and energy into relationships. Now I pour that into my life, my family, my friends, any person I may date who becomes important. And it's a blast.

But I have and have had quite a few single friends over the last six years, and I realized something today. Something surprising. People claim online that fwbs are a one-track road to heartbreak.

But everyone I've ever known who had an fwb was way more hurt in and by committed relationships than the fwb experience.

No interaction with other humans is without risk, so is warning people about pain really stemming from the idea that fwbs are "less moral"? So people engaging in them "deserve" or should expect heartbreak?

And why do some people see the arrangement that way when many sleep with people they're dating but not committed to anyway?

*I don't know the first time a bass voice made me weak,*
*Or I craved the feel of his beard on my cheek.*
*Or the smell of his skin,*
*Or the muscles within,*
*Or the walk that enlivened his melanin*
*Creeped through my mind*
*Made my tension unwind.*
*Whether friend, boo or MAN,*
*I just must admit that masculine*
*energy*
*Is a potent high.*

*Lit*
*I be from his gaze,*
*From his touch,*
*From his ways.*

*I love masculine men,*
*Make me feel feminine.*
*Make me soften and bend.*
*My hard edges rescind.*

*Superwoman I be,*
*But his presence by me,*
*A vacay so free,*

*The cape rested,*
*I sleep,*
*Protected, secure,*
*coquettish, demure.*
*Maternal allure*
*All nurture,*
*I purr.*
*Can I fix you a plate?*
*Massage your back?*
*Meditate*
*On the love that we make.*
*On the convos so great..*
*On the possibilities,*
*Latent.*
*My patience awakened.*
*I just let him be man.*
*I just understand.*
*If he is . .*
*Then I am...*
*Just what*
*I am.*

## Dating with a purpose?

I don't think I do anything in life with one purpose, ie, people who date only for marriage.

I don't go to work only for money. I didn't have kids, only for them to grow up. I didn't buy a house just to sign the deed.

And if you asked me what was the purpose for striking up a friendship with the people I call friends, I'd have no answer- Do you?

There is a journey in every major life experience. Looking only at the end goal can blind you to the journey, especially with people.

For the last six years, San Antonio has been my friend. You followed our journey, and we still talk several times a year. I haven't seen him in four years. He now lives in California.

For six years, he's been part of my support system. Had I stuck to dating with a purpose, we'd never have talked beyond the moment I learned he wanted kids, and I was done having them. And he is one of the best dudes I've met in life. He and JJ restored my faith in brothers after my divorce.

Could I have known what his purpose was when we met? Hell no. Did he know? Hell no.

Was this a waste of time because we were never in a relationship? Are you kidding?

And that is my take on dating with purpose. Besides:

1. What do you want from marriage?
2. Does it take marriage to get that?

I wanted-

1. Unconditional love
2. Emotional support and companionship

3. Financial partnership
4. A leader in my household
5. Passion and sexual satisfaction
6. Attention and affection
7. Someone to love on and take care of
8. A family
9. Chemistry, compatibility, great conversation
10. Longevity

I found out from life only 3 and 4 really require me to live with or marry someone. (I don't want more kids.)

What this tells me is 80% of what I ultimately want doesn't require marriage. It just requires intimacy. Knowing that changed my perspective a lot. This list became my goal, not a relationship status. And getting #9 plus anything else on this list from a man I was dating became a win.

So I went from "I thought I'd be remarried by now" to "I have a lot to be grateful for even though I'm still single."

Some days I get the idea from Facebook that single people really want other single people to be in some sort of stasis mode till they meet Mr. Or Ms. Right and then be willing to give up any and everything, including

1. Opposite sex friends
2. Time-consuming hobbies
3. No sex while single
4. Beds any old partners slept in

And on and on

I, on the other hand, would hope each person, single or attached, is living his or her best life, TODAY, sucking the marrow out of every moment, NOW.

It's almost as if people fear other people's happiness. It's as if people don't realize tomorrow is not promised, and all we have is the ever-evolving now.

## July 2021

July started off with a bang. According to reviews, shares, subscriptions, downloads, and growth since inception, my podcast was in the top ten percent globally! I was over the moon. I had gotten my first gift of fan mail from a book club in Colorado who had sent me a package of bath and body items in thanks for the great Zoom workshop I had done for them, and a local business owner had hosted a celebratory catered dinner for my ranking. My knee was feeling almost back to normal. I vended, performed twice, did three podcast episodes, guested on two other podcasts, and organized a sold-out Laughz and Lyrics show.

Listen Score

25

TOP 10%

LISTEN NOTES

Romantically, July 7th, I'd texted Gatzby that I wanted to cut ties, that I was moving away from him, growing, and it was time, past time to move on. He responded with an, "I was about to ask you on an overnight getaway. I really just missed you and needed a hug."

The overnight getaway just flew right over my head. He'd said that so much, but the hug somehow got to me. I'd needed hugs so much sometimes and hadn't felt I could get them. Walking away right then just felt harsh.

It gave me a new perspective on the song lyrics, "I know you wanna leave me, but I refuse to let you go. If I have to beg and plead for your sympathy, I don't mind cuz you mean that much to me. Ain't too proud to beg, please don't leave me girl, don't you go."

That song was always so romantic to me, but I never thought about the girl who wanted to go, why did she want to go, what had he done? How did it really feel to want to leave but have him beg and plead for her to stay?

Now Gatzby never begged, but he definitely played on my heartstrings. He knew he had that power.

But my heart was not the ultimate decision-maker. My head was.

My head wanted something that made sense, something stable, safe. I didn't know if that was possible. I didn't know if it was possible to leave Gatzby, permanently. I could hold him at a distance. Sometimes I felt that was as good as it would get till someone who wanted a relationship, someone who was compatible, showed up.

I spent the first three weeks of this month alone, talking to Gatzby and Breath and RJ, but mostly introspective. When I was a teen, I'd loved mythology, and in the last few years, there were stories and ancient wisdom that made my life make sense.

This month, the female archetypes were front and center. I wrote about them in my March Poem "Sleeping Women Rise." I dreamed about them when I was with The Poet, specifically that I was a priestess of Bast. She was an Egyptian goddess, known as the second eye of Ra, or the Sacred and All-Seeing Eye. To bring up her Greek counterparts that are more commonly known, she was a combination of Artemis, the huntress/warrior, Athena, the goddess of wisdom; Hera, the goddess of family and pregnancy; and Demeter, the goddess of crops and nature. The strangest thing about my dream was that although I knew Greek mythology like the back of my hand, I'd never heard of Bast until I saw the movie Catwoman with Halle Berry.

The movie's description was fascinating, a goddess who represented duality, the sun and the moon, the nurturer, and the fighter. I was still married when I saw that movie, but that promise, "Catwomen are not controlled by the rules of society. You follow your own path; it's both a blessing and a curse," had stuck with me like the famous declaration from Spiderman about power.

To be a catwoman must be amazing.

Emerson had said, "To be great is to be misunderstood."

I surmised that to be a catwoman was to experience a freedom that other women would never know, with every strength of the cat-its independent, aloof nonchalance; its total confidence; its ability to love and nurture and completely withdraw into a space that no one could enter without invitation.

In July, I felt I was absolutely becoming that woman. It was so intoxicating that I didn't even want any man near me. I wanted to embrace, lol, my inner cat.

Chills had run down my arms when the mentor in the movie told Halle she'd spent a lifetime caged, but now she could accept all of who she was; she could be free and powerful. The same opportunity was offered to Jon Snow- freedom- and it was there in front of me. I saw it, heard it, tasted it. It sustained me.

That dream of walking the temple was so real to me in those three weeks, more like a memory than any dream I'd ever experienced. I could smell, touch, taste everything for my dream world, and when I'd awakened and looked around my bedroom at the paintings of tigers and lions on all four walls. When I walked into my living room and viewed the sconces, the Greek pillars, the tapestries of Greek gardens and the prints of African pitchers in my bathrooms, there was this sense that antiquity was always surrounding me. Africa and Greece, mythology, were enshrined in my home. My dream reflected my life. My life reflected my dream.

I thought back over my life. My divorce anniversary had been last month. The **female archetype**s laid out in my memory like tarot cards on a table.

I'd started as a girl, a teen, a young woman- **The Maiden.**

Then **The Mother** took front and center till June 2015.

JJ's hand had reached in my heart and mind, and **The Minx** had taken it, dancing with him through six months of passion. She was **The Lover.**

But when The Muse arrived as my new dance partner, there was no ancient archetype to greet him. He'd awakened my own- T**he Artist**. I could see him as the professor in Catwoman, opening his photography portfolio, showing me his pictures, and turning to me and saying- you are an artist, accept it. And I had. He had held up this mirror that was so clear that it wiped away decades of being told that I couldn't make a living writing, that I needed to be practical, sensible, responsible. He had said to me, "I did it. I traveled the world and met amazing people, and you can do it, too. You're a better writer than I ever was as a photographer. It's what you were born to do. " In ancient Greece, The Muses were women, but mine was a man. But although with The Muse, I was prolific, getting published once a month the whole time we were together, the poetry book I had started writing that day had remained untouched till 2020. Heartbreak had stolen my confidence and made all those words seem like pipe dreams.

The Minx and Gatzby were best friends, but it was Harlee who brought **The Nurturer** onto the dance floor of my life. She was a different form of The Mother, a combination of sensuality and domesticity focused on uplifting the man in my life as well as my sons and grandkids. The love that she poured out was not the totally sacrificial love of The Mother that had left so much damage behind that I had lost myself- twice. Her love was wise, responsive, and measured. It had boundaries and self-respect.

Gatzby brought out an archetype in me, but it was not one any man wanted to inspire. With Gatzby, I was **The Huntress**, fiercely independent, relentlessly goal-driven, pioneering, and autonomous; she was the exact opposite of the docile, submissive, pliantly responsive woman that I was in Mother mode. I needed her to blaze the trails I was forging. Every accolade was a dual effort between her and The Artist sides of me, but as I had told Gatzby hundreds of times, I had no idea how to be her and be with him.

But for the first time in my life and the six years I'd known him, I could now explain why I felt such intense conflict; committing to him meant death to her. She saw herself fade more and more as The Nurturer took over, and she fought that other side of me fiercely to stay alive. I realized The Huntress had never been a part of my life for any length of time before Gatzby. She was the fight or flight impulse that rose up and fought back when my first husband struck me. She was called to action in crisis, a wartime hero, but there was no war now, and she was front and center with The Minx and The Artist, working hand in hand seamlessly. She loved it. And I felt more alive than I ever had in my entire life with this trio guiding me. Together they created a life of exploration, passion, fun: the life of my dreams.

I now also understood why there always seemed to be at least one verbal companion, a member of my intellectual harem on the sidelines; San Antonio and Mo danced around with **The Sage**, the part of me that has loved writing this book, the part that searches for answers and connections, and seeks wisdom and understanding, the philosopher savant.

Although not in the slightest bit romantic, Baba Fana had danced with my psyche also and awakened **The Mystic**. Gone were the religious dogmas replaced by intuition, alignment, connection to nature, groundedness, spiritual peace, and a reverence for divine laws and the mysteries of creation. This was the part of me that had railed at religion, the part that had felt devalued by patriarchy which was now uplifted by a focus on the yin yang balance of male and female energy, the unity of the Ankh- male/female bonding. I had let go of the toxic culture and embraced a holistic one. And nowhere was this more readily seen than in my hair.

This woman with mohawks, braids, afros, and styles I couldn't even name was a very different woman from the one who had worn her hair the same way since high school. She was alluring, unpredictable, mysterious, seductive, and very, very powerful. She was unapologetic and unique, just like every hairstyle. Shout out to Bella of The Hive Salon and Moutin Bazile Photography.

I had said often that I had been five different women in my life, that different men brought out different things in me, but something unprecedented happened this month, or maybe I just realized it had been happening.

As the end of July drew near, there was a new archetype emerging, one that, for the first and only time in my life, symbolized total integration. You probably know who brought that one out-Breath. She was **The Queen**. When I talked or video chatted with Breath, I was The Minx, The Artist, The Nurturer, The Huntress. The Sage and The Mystic. I could be vulnerable and break down, fierce and confident, share poetry with him, flirt with abandon and sensuality, and be utterly spiritual and philosophical. I was not one thing; I was all things, choosing among them. Sometimes he even seemed to bring out one side on purpose and then switch to calling out another side for variety. I'd never felt so understood, accepted, validated by any man as I did with him, except for RJ. I realized now that was what had drawn me to him, what had made me keep talking to him when I refused to date him, what had made me a little afraid to get closer to him. How could I be content, never progressing with a man able to handle the total me?

So the first three weeks of July, I just wanted to distance myself from Gatsby, from RJ.

I had come so far, gained so much. I was so happy, happier than I'd ever been in my life. I understood myself better than I ever had. And I knew what I wanted in a man.

I wanted Breath, but a local version, a man like him in Houston who could speak to all my sides, an RJ who wanted commitment.

July 20th, I got a dm. By the 22nd, he'd made an impression, a really good one. When we talked, I felt excited, like I had literally manifested in days what I had only imagined hours before. He seemed like The King who would court my Queen.

*I haven't even met you, yet you know it's true; I dig more than the sound of your voice; I really like you.*
*Some men answer like a gremlin,*
*Baring teeth under their breath,*
*You answer like a love song,*
*Transparent benevolence.*
*The smile is in your timbre,*
*The warmth is in your lines,*
*I relax just hearing bass,*
*You make my soul unwind.*
*We talk for hours, laughing,*
*a flirt insert a time or two,*
*So effortless, whoever knew,*
*A dm could bring you..*
*Intellect and wittiness,*
*Common sense and eloquence,*
*Great questions sans ignorance.*
*A smile long overdue*

*I am impressed regardless of where this convo leads,*
*Already I feel blessed,*
*Endowed with all I need.*
*You've captured my attention,*
*I lie awake these words to spread,*
*Christmas in July it seems*
*And now I'm off to bed.*

## Date One Hundred and One:

I saw The King twice, a week apart, and then a third time. And then I realized once again age would be a factor. He was 39. I was 50. He had a five-year-old son. I had a five-year-old grandson. And time was also not on our side in other ways. He lived in Sugar Land, over an hour away. He spent half his off time in Port Arthur with his son. And he worked A LOT.

There was no practical way our lifestyles could mesh. None. It was sad but also invigorating. Just meeting him proved a King did exist, and I felt like the universe had sent him days after my epiphany on my need for a King just to give me that message. I felt a security in my future, this feeling that all I needed to do was keep growing, keep learning, keep evolving, and all would fall into place.

## August 2021

The month started normally. I recorded one podcast.

The word of the month seemed to be "Settling." It was all over Facebook.

People wrote that no one wanted to settle anymore. In fact, one guy said that ending marriage was punished in America through alimony and the division of property. After all, people had gotten so used to walking away when they felt the relationship shifted from something they desired to something they just tolerated that society had to act because society has historically depended on marriage to be a foundation of civilization. That originally, marriage was designed as something the courts had no say in. I didn't know if he was historically correct. Still, it did seem that so many other "contracts" were dissolved without the court that it seemed highly probable.

Facebook groups were asking who was to blame for this epidemic of not "settling,": mothers who warned their daughters against marriages or relationships, fathers who disappointed, single friends who gave bad advice. Who had shaped us the most?

The double standard in dating came up a lot. If single women complained about their status, they were pushed to change to attract men- lose weight, downplay their job, education and accomplishments, and lower their standards, i.e., settle.

But if single men complained about their status, they were rarely told to be more romantic, improve their communication skills, or the stability of their lifestyles. The narrative switched to women not wanting "good men" and friend-zoning them

I thought this double standard created animosity and distrust and left each gender with apprehension concerning being accepted.

Then there was a partner word that showed up: entitlement. The theory was some men and women were spoiled; entitled. Therefore a perfectly good relationship seemed utterly flawed and inadequate; good enough was seen as settling.

I thought *it's a beautiful thing to be spoiled; enjoy it, but setting that as your new standard can be at best unrealistic and at worst, yes: entitled.* Just because your last boo saw you were worth that much doesn't mean your new boo will (doesn't even mean you actually were). Trying to recreate the last relationship in the new encounter seems slightly delusional and possibly selfish. Accept that new person, or go back to the ex. Stop comparing apples and oranges

Speaking of apples and oranges, I called RJ to discuss a post that said there were two types of men-

1. I got you.
2. Damn, that's crazy.

I thought this was brilliant. The only thing I thought the post was missing is that sometimes women push a #1 man to act like a #2 guy by

1. Shooting down the guy's help/ideas
2. The woman acting so invincible that the man feels awkward offering to help
3. Making him feel used/taken advantage of/unappreciated
4. Consistently making poor choices, so he feels he will always be saving her

I thought it was natural for masculine men to be #1 and that feminine women often bring that protector/provider side out.

I also seemed to see women "settle" for guy number two because all the number ones were married or taken.

And then there were the hits on women's judgment. How did we know we were "settling"? Intuition? Intuition was being attacked by men left and right. If women knew so much, how did they end up with guy number 2 anyway? Didn't their intuition tell them that he was unreliable or immature?

Well, women's intuition is amazing, but it's not omnipotent or omniscient. Some men and some memes act like it should be. They blame women solely for single motherhood. While there are women who choose poorly, here are a few questions

1. Have you ever seen someone who can finesse their way through an interview and through the 90 day probation period on a job? Yeah, people do that in relationships too.
2. You ever heard the saying, "Everyone has a plan till they get hit?" No one knows for sure how someone else will react to added responsibility or stress. A person you've known your entire life could turn into a deadbeat dad with little or no warning.
3. And then there's the romantics, those guys who always wanted to be a dad, but suddenly the reality is not what they expected, and they bail. Sometimes these guys are the worst because they might even have another kid THAT THEY TAKE CARE OF, and then they abandon the new one. Nostradamus wouldn't even have seen that one coming.

So those guilty of these snap judgments, maybe before assuming all single moms are irresponsible poor judges of the men they slept with, admit you don't know the specifics of every case and stop ragging on women.

Then there were all the comments on "settling" for poor or infrequent communication. It seemed whole relationships were being judged on how "consistently" a person called or texted. This was strange to me. I had to use a planner to remember what I needed to do and what I'd already done. People could actually remember how often someone called or texted, and who liked or commented on their posts? I noticed and was grateful when people interacted or engaged with me online socially, but it never occurred to me to keep track. And I never remembered except for the one guy I mentioned who spectacularly misinterpreted my posts.

I wondered if this keeping score of interactions was an introvert/extrovert thing or an over-scheduled /less scheduled thing.

Bottom line, when it came to "settling," my idea was that women dropped men fast in the dating stages, slowly after being in a relationship. The change was because of the investment. We don't like losing the love, time, energy, etc., investing in a relationship. When there's no investment, it's easy to walk away. What we might settle for dating might not cut it in a relationship because we were planning to invest more and wanted more.

And then there were the tests. I'd seen posts and comments where men and women seem to be testing a person's tolerance for their worst behavior.

Instead of putting their best foot forward or just being themselves, they seem determined to scare off anyone who's not "really committed" to getting to know them.

1. Why would anyone expect someone to be committed to getting to know a jerk?
2. If that suitor does stick around, why is that NOT a sign of low self-esteem or desperation?
3. These people felt justified in weeding out those who "weren't serious" didn't they see their own behavior as

toxic and a horrible foundation to build the relationship on.

They really wanted that person to prove worthiness by getting to the end of this gauntlet, like the test of bravery the Indians would use to determine whether a prisoner would become a slave or be adopted into the tribe as a warrior.

These tests seemed designed to also probe what reactions lay inside. There was this underlying belief that good men/good women can't or won't do________________and that once that person's true nature was revealed, the tester could feel safe, secure, in knowing what that woman or man was capable of doing under emotional stress, what their character was.

It amazed me. I spent the last several pages discussing my different sides. My reactions would vary depending on who was at the helm at the time. I and others could react in myriad ways. Didn't adults know that? And there was this amazing thing called free will. Just because I reacted one way to your test did not mean I would react that same way every time. Good men, good women were capable of doing, saying, thinking whatever these testers unilaterally decreed they couldn't do, think or say and retain their designation of "good." Good is in the eye of the beholder. Settling is in the eye of the beholder.

The week before the return to school was crazy. I'd never dreaded going back as much as I did this year, never feared it as much either. There was Covid, but even more, it was like going back into that proverbial cage that the summer let me escape from. If singleness had been my escape from the cages imposed by marriage and committed relationships, summer was the escape from endless meetings, confusing dictates from bureaucracy, nonsensical educational practices, and mind-deadening drudgery.

Breath was helping me adjust, and we were preparing for his birthday when he disappeared. He had never disappeared, ever. If I called or texted, he answered or called me back immediately. It's crazy when someone is so consistent that if you don't hear from him/her, you know there is only one reason, only one thing that would keep them from you, the one thing none of us can control.

Death.

I knew he was dead before it was confirmed on the 17th. I felt it. My soul reached out for him, and for a week, he wasn't there. The loss was so startling that I couldn't breathe, think, feel anything. It was Covid related. And I was catching my breath and beginning to adjust to this new reality when I got the news that Baba transitioned four days later. I was glad I had interviewed Baba on multiples episodes- #7, #9, #35, #37[14].

There were ten more days in August, and I think I spent all ten crying. I did a tribute podcast "Benediction", did another podcast on 9/4, and celebrated the anniversary of Victor, my son's best friend's passing, on the same day that I celebrated three years of Laughz and Lyrics. I guested on a radio show, recorded two more podcasts, wrote the two poems below ( performed the first at one of Baba's memorials. He was so beloved, there were many), and did not celebrate my birthday at all.

---

14 https://linktr.ee/zenase

# This River

*I've known a river,*

*An ancient, golden river,*

*My soul has grown deep like this river.*

*I remember the first night I saw you.*

*Intent, hands moving, lost in the flow of wordz and rythymz.*

*Intoxicating, mesmerizing,*

*I was awed.*

*The music/words living, breathing healing. Flowing,*

*Like water.*

*My soul will grow deep like this river.*

*I don't remember you playing behind me, but the pictures tell that union.*

*Both our eyes closed*

*Like a trance.*

*Our melody deep like the rivers.*

*And at Capone's, you were.*

*I was.*

*A dozen musicians.*

*Jazz*

*deep like the rivers.*

*You followed me to a second show.*

*And played two more hours.*

*Energy... deep like the rivers.*
*And then you invited me to your class, for months.*
*Patience deep like the rivers.*
*I came, learned, grew, changed,*
*found a new family*
*An old family*
*A soul family*
*A spirit family*
*Bonding deep like the rivers.*
*When one steps in a river, it flows, uncontrolled, untamed,*
*"ancient as the flow of human blood*
*in human veins,"*[15]
*It cleanses, pushes, pulls,*
*Currents moving, never still,*
*Civilizations are built*
*on the banks of mighty rivers.*
*We built shows, 4? 5?, classes.*
*We taught together.*
*Ate together,*
*spoke, cried, laughed together*
*And even when we were silent,*
*The vibe alive like a river.*
*Understanding, wisdom, change, growth*
*Deep like the rivers*
*Memory, history, reverence*

15 Langston Hughes "The Negro Speaks of Rivers"

*Wide like the rivers.*
*Compassion, generosity, help*
*Strong like the rivers*
*Out of our bellies shall flow*
*rivers of living water.*
*I tried to count the years and failed*
*for who can measure a river?*
*Who can honor its magnitude?*
*Its potential?*
*Its impact?*
*It would take a lifetime.*

*My soul will grow deep like this river.*

*I've known a river,*
*An ancient, golden river,*

*I have not cried,*
*My tear ducts produce no rivers.*
*My soul will channel this river*
*And flow.*
*And become the legacy*
*Of*
*This River.*

## Patience

*It's late at night I miss you still,*
*We night owls be, for real, for real.*
*You were my golden man of skills.*
*Jack of all trades was he.*
*Entrepreneur extraordinaire,*
*A heart so big, no one compares.*
*Devotion to his kids unparalleled.*
*I marveled at you, you see.*
*Your wisdom, cut right to the chase.*
*Your potty mouth, no one escapes.*
*Your great advice, I always take.*
*You understood all me.*
*I cannot put in words the vibes.*
*The hours you helped me survive.*
*My spirits you kept so alive*
*When they were dashed, you see.*
*I met you grieving, so alone.*
*A little bitter, monotone.*
*You made me laugh, all cares were gone.*
*You saw the best in me.*
*With your support, I came so far.*
*My best friend, confidant for sure.*

*I miss you more than ever before.*

*It's hard to find relief.*

*Nothing's the same since you've been gone.*

*I'm trying, now to move along.*

*But my heart is broken, all is wrong.*

*I loved you so, you see.*

*I love you still, you see.*

## October 2021

I recorded four podcasts, went to a show, and decided to write this book, for me, for them, for the journey. There was no moving forward till I went back, all the way back to that first day, my divorce, and then came all the way back to this point.

On my mom's birthday, October 3rd, I woke up with an urgency I've only felt one other time over a decade before. I was about to open the door to my car, and an impulse hit me in my chest so hard for a minute I could not breathe. I heard one message. "Send your sons away for the summer. They cannot be here." I listened. That summer three of my sons best friends were involved in a carjacking. Two were incarcerated. One died. Had my sons been here, who knows what might have happened.

The message this time was, "It's been seven years. A cycle is over. This is the final path to completion. Before 12/31/21, you need to write the book, the one San Antonio suggested, the one Breath wanted. You must go back, before you can move forward. Your gift must become part of your path of healing and your own evolution. Write, become. Reveal, rise."

When inspiration had spoken over a decade ago, my sons' lives and futures felt like they hung in the balance. Now, it felt like mine did.

That day, I wrote for five hours. On Halloween, I told my editor I was writing a new book. We hadn't finished editing the old one.

## November 2021

I recorded two podcasts, vended, spent time with family on Thanksgiving, and I went on this journey with you.

Although I cataloged 101 dates here, there were actually 147. I'm still friends with many of those 147, most specifically Gatsby, RJ, and The King, who still exert a huge influence on me.

I belong to that classification of women that men don't think exists, single by choice, and content. This is my road, my story, quirky, surprising, sometimes confusing, at moments tumultuous, but vibrantly alive, enriched, a journey I cherish.

I don't know if I will ever meet a King with a compatible lifestyle.

Whether I do or don't is very irrelevant. I firmly believe in the "iron sharpens iron" mentality, and that has been my life these past seven years, sharpening and being sharpened by the men I've been lucky enough to converse with, meet, and get to know, men who were wise enough to get me to ask the right questions, of myself, of life, of the universe.

One statement got me married. Two questions got me divorced. One question got me performing, and one made me an entrepreneur. One changed the entire direction of my life and led to three books.

The right questions are powerful. They break ruts, provide possibilities, destroy limitations

These men taught me that relationship goals are great, but life goals are better.

And now, I want to talk to you. I wrote this book fast, in 65 days. And I cried some nights, some chapters, and I thought of you. I thought of the battered wife- like me, the person who didn't know how to get to the next day, like me. The person who drank and slept to forget. The person who saw every day as the same, no hope in sight, like me. The one who was told he/she/they were not good enough- too fat, too much, too different.

I thought of you.

I would cry and think, "I'm in pain, but they are too. My life is better, even though I'm grieving again. I'm so broken, again. They suck it up. I can too. They push through. I can too. They heal. I can too.

And so, this book is my love letter to you, my hug, my cry with you, my wipe your tears and say we can - together. It is my effort to be Breath and Fana to you.

I'm editing now, and it's 12/28, and I've cried the last three days- like a baby, uncontrollably sometimes. I miss them so much, more than words could ever express. But as my coworker, Monica Merchant, told me, "Beauty can come from ashes."

I hope you found beauty here.

Sometimes the only thing that gives me comfort is to step back and look at my life as myth, as poetry, as the hero's journey as Joseph Campbell called it- though I don't think of myself as a hero. I find my heroes elsewhere, in Breath, in Baba Fana, in my ancestors.

I took you from my **Ordinary World**, leaving the courthouse, to my **Quest** for love and identity. I've received many **Calls to Adventure**- inboxes, an offer to start my own show, a challenge to write the guided journals, and this book. **Assistance**- pick your favorite sidekick; I got more assistance than most, and not always from men. My sister has been my sidekick more than once. **Trials**- yeah, those are all throughout this book. **Crisis**- which one was that, was there more than one? **Rebirth and Treasure**- I think there was more than one of these also. **Result and Return**- I am here, talking with you, older, wiser, nothing like the girl that left my ordinary world seven years ago.

This book is my love letter to you. My journey is my journey. I've given it to you as raw, as real as I could. Take what helps. Toss what doesn't.

My life has many goals, but if I were to sum it up in a few- transparent transformation, perfect self-expression, to die empty.

In a few minutes, I'll be sleeping. And I'll wake up tomorrow, God willing, with the same mission I had today- to make a difference, to sow a good seed, to use my voice and skills and talent and education to drum out ignorance and uplift self-reflection. To make the world a better place by getting people to enhance their own lives and thus impact their circles positively. To get people to use the tools they have- relationships, their brains, reflection, and more to fill the urge for more peace and fulfillment in life- individually and collectively.

I want to be a microscope and magnifying glass and a camera and a megaphone.

I want to be the whisper of conscience that picks up the chant for justice when other voices get tired - till every child is safe, till every man has equal rights, till America becomes a level playing field, till the words on the Statue of Liberty and the words of the constitution are seen enacted in everyday life.

And to move forward, we have to see where we are, both the shining light of opportunity and the dark abyss of repression.

America is pregnant with change. And pregnancy is uncomfortable, and birth is painful. But delivery is also glorious and miraculous, and life-changing. Together let's breathe through the contractions and push a better future into the light. Zen

**Lesson 26:**

Zennurgy: Your life is your story. Don't let anyone else hold the pen. Take the lessons life gives you and use them to grow into the self-actualized version of yourself. Let your life be an adventure with you as the hero. May you walk in Zennurgy!

# Lessons

| | |
|---|---|
| **LESSON 1** | Attitude: Stop being a rose. Be the whole damn bush. |
| **LESSON 2** | Boldness: Boldness. Be bold enough to want to know, to want to grow, and to slay your own dragons. No more patient, passive damsels in distress. |
| **LESSON 3** | Caution: Beware, the maintenance man may be laying crack pipe. |
| **LESSON 4** | Delve: Discuss what role sex will play in your relationship before you commit. |
| **LESSON 5** | Explore: Define commitment. |
| **LESSON 6** | Focus: Learn your healthy and unhealthy relationship patterns |
| **LESSON 7** | Guidance: Follow Your First Mind |

| | |
|---|---|
| **LESSON 8** | Heartiness: Enjoy the journey. Eat the fruit. Drink the wine. Carpe Diem. |
| **LESSON 9** | Imagine: Turn up your heart's radio. Blast your inner stereo loud. |
| **LESSON 10** | Judge: Find out what's in his toolbox. It may be just the tool you need. |
| **LESSON 11** | Kindred: Some connections are inexplicable. |
| **LESSON 12** | Listen: When words and actions don't match, listen to the actions. |
| **LESSON 13** | Mooring: When you've lost everything, find a place to moor yourself. |
| **LESSON 14** | Nature: Life goes on. |
| **LESSON 15** | Opposition: Sometimes it feels like everything is against you. |
| **LESSON 16** | Power: Healing is a journey, not a destination, and that journey may require the voyager to kill old beliefs, patterns, and dogmas. Take back your power. |
| **LESSON 17** | Qualify: Only certain princes need apply. You define your qualifications of real and fake relationships. |
| **LESSON 18** | Revelation: All revelations aren't pleasant. Some are downright painful. |

| | |
|---|---|
| **LESSON 19** | Standards: You have the right to decide what is acceptable or desirable for you, regardless of whether any man or society at large agrees. |
| **LESSON 20** | Triggers reveal what makes us tense, what freezes us, what represses us and stresses us. |
| **LESSON 21** | Unbind: Question everything. Explore your dreams. Challenge your mindset. Grow. Then Grow again. And again. Ad Infinitum. |
| **LESSON 22** | Vibrancy: Death can make you feel more alive, make you appreciate the moments of conversation, of music, dance, poetry, comedy that make life this unpredictably vibrant experience. |
| **LESSON 23** | Wonder: We may not be able to answer all the questions we wonder about. But we can choose to create wonderful experiences and revel in the wonder of the twists and turns life brings us. |
| **LESSON 24** | X: The unknown can be scary or exhilarating. It's all a matter of perspective. |
| **LESSON 25** | Yearning: Let your longings lift you rather than being weights to the past. |
| **LESSON 26** | Zennurgy: Your life is your story. Don't let anyone else hold the pen. Take the lessons life gives you and use them to grow into the self-actualized version of yourself. |

Made in the USA
Columbia, SC
30 November 2024